Enhance your learning experience with the accompanying interactive e-book, featuring video clips, exercises, quizzes and more!

Visit **www.wileyopenpage.com** to access your interactive e-book.

INCLUDES INTERACTIVE E-BOOK
LOOK FOR THIS ICON AS YOUR GUIDE TO THE EMBEDDED MEDIA

Easily navigate your e-book using the chapter menu, search and bookmark options.

You can save notes or voice annotations as a reminder of key points.

Watch video clips to bring the data and topics to life and expand your understanding of the concepts.

Test your understanding with key term flashcards and quizzes.

WILEY

Operations Management

THIRD EDITION

Operations Management

THIRD EDITION

Andrew Greasley

WILEY

Registered office

John Wiley & Sons Ltd, The Atrium, Southern Gate, Chichester, West Sussex, PO19 8SQ, United Kingdom

For details of our global editorial offices, for customer services and for information about how to apply for permission to reuse the copyright material in this book please see our website at www.wiley.com.

Library of Congress Cataloging-in-Publication Data

Greasley, Andrew
    Operations management / Andrew Greasley — Third edition.
        pages   cm
    Includes bibliographical references and index.
    ISBN 978-1-119-97854-1 (pbk.) — ISBN 978-1-118-60662-9 (ebk) — ISBN 978-1-118-60663-6 (ebk) —
    ISBN 978-1-118-60667-4 (ebk)
        1. Production management.   2. Project management.   3. Business logistics.   4. Production management—
Examinations—Study guides.   5. Project management—Examinations—Study guides.   6. Business logistics—
Examinations—Study guides.   I. Title.
    TS155.G8172   2013
    658.5—dc23
                                                                                            2013005801

A catalogue record for this book is available from the British Library

Set in 10/12 pt Minion Pro by MPS Limited, Chennai, India

Printed in Italy by Printer Trento Srl.

CONTENTS

www.wileyopenpage.com

www.wileyopenpage.com

www.wileyopenpage.com

www.wileyopenpage.com

Andrew Greasley MBA PhD FHEA is a lecturer at the Aston Business School, Aston University, Birmingham, UK. He lectures in Operations Management, Operations Strategy and Simulation Modelling. He is author of the book *Simulation Modelling for Business* published by Ashgate Ltd. and is co-author of the book *Business Information Systems* (4th edition) published by Pearson Education Ltd. His research interest is in the area of simulation modelling. He has over 80 publications, including papers in journals such as the *International Journal of Operations and Production Management, Journal of the Operational Research Society, Simulation, Technovation* and *Business Process Management Journal*. He has undertaken a number of teaching and consultancy projects in the area of simulation in the UK, Europe and Africa.

Operations management deals with the management of the creation of goods and the delivery of services to the customer. It thus plays an essential role in the success of any organization. The aim of this book is to provide a clear and concise treatment of operations management. The text covers the main areas of operations strategy, the design of the operations system and the management of operations over time. The book is intended as an introduction to operations management and as such attempts to cover all relevant areas in the field but in a clear and concise manner in which the students are not overwhelmed by the amount of material presented. The target audience is undergraduates on business studies and joint degrees where no prior knowledge of the subject area is required. The book will also interest postgraduate students on MBA and specialist masters programmes.

ACKNOWLEDGEMENTS

The author would like to thank the team at Wiley & Sons Ltd for their assistance in the compilation of this book. The author would also like to thank the team of reviewers for their constructive comments which have helped develop the book. Special thanks go to Briony Boydell for her helpful comments and Briony Boydell and Chris Milner for the development of additional case study material.

After an introductory chapter the book is structured into three main parts of introduction, design and management. Within this part structure the book consists of eighteen chapters. This design has been used in order to maximize the clarity of the presentation of material.

Chapter 1 provides an introduction to the field of Operations Management, defines the role of operations in the organization and discusses the increasing role and importance of service operations. Chapter 2 covers the area of operations strategy. The vital role of operations in providing the capability to implement an organization's strategy is covered as well as guidance on how to formulate a successful operations strategy.

The role of design in operations is covered in Chapters 3–9. Areas covered include the configuration of processes in manufacturing and services firms, the design and location of operations facilities, technology used in the operations process, product and service design, the design of the processes that deliver services and the design of jobs. An emphasis on service design is provided in this section by covering topics such as Business Process Management and Service Blueprinting.

The management of operations is covered in Chapters 10–18. Areas covered include operations planning and control, capacity management, inventory management, lean operations, Enterprise Resource Planning, Supply Chain Management and Project Management. The impact of e-Commerce on operations is covered using topics such as e-procurement. Also covered are topics such as total quality management, continuous and breakthrough improvement approaches, statistical process control and acceptance sampling.

A GUIDE FOR STUDENTS

The text provides a number of features to help student learning. These include:

- A list of the main learning objectives for the material covered at the beginning of the chapter.
- Case studies with questions to encourage critical reflection on the key issues.
- Examples providing additional real-life detail of operations concepts.
- Worked Examples providing a step-by-step guide to the procedure to solve quantitative problems.
- End-of-Chapter Exercises indicating topics for discussion and providing examples to help develop practical skills.
- References and Further Reading references to enable students to explore topics in greater depth.
- Web links add an extra resource to assist students in locating further additional materials.

ONLINE RESOURCES

You can access your **interactive e-book** at **www.wileyopenpage.com** using your scratch code included on the inside front cover of the printed book. A wealth of additional content is embedded throughout the book to bring operations management to life, including:

- Videos
- Animated worked examples
- Simulations
- Virtual Tours
- Quizzes
- Key term flashcards

LECTURER RESOURCES

Lecturers who adopt this text can obtain the following resources to support their teaching at **www.wiley.com/college/greasley**:

- PowerPoint slides for each chapter
- Case studies suggested solutions
- End-of-Chapter exercise suggested solutions
- Multiple-choice question test bank

NEW FOR THE THIRD EDITION

The structure of the book has been maintained from the second edition, but a number of improvements have been made for the third edition:

- An additional short section at the beginning of each chapter discussing the topic from an operations strategy perspective.
- The number of case studies has been increased from the second edition.
- New content has been included in such areas such as operations strategic alignment, international operations, value stream mapping and agile supply chains.
- Chapter material has been organized for greater clarity.
- An e-Book accompanies the text and features a wealth of embedded media, including: Animated worked examples, Simulations, Virtual tours, Videos, Flashcards and Practice quizzes.

Introduction

Introduction

LEARNING OBJECTIVES

- Define the term operations management
- Understand the role of operations in transforming the organization's inputs into finished goods and services
- Describe the process view of organizations
- Define the main types of service operations
- Understand the distinction between front-office and back-office tasks
- Understand the strategic role of operations
- Explain the relationship between technology and operations

INTRODUCTION

This chapter introduces the concept of operations management and describes some of the decision areas it covers. The operations activity is examined in terms of its components and its role in the organization. It is defined as a transformation process and as such occurs throughout the organization. The operations function itself is defined as being concerned with transformation processes that provide goods and services for customers. Some key themes of operations management are also explored, namely service operations management, the strategic role of operations and the use of technology in operations management.

WHAT IS OPERATIONS MANAGEMENT?

Operations management is about the management of the processes that produce or deliver goods and services. Not every organization will have a functional department called 'operations' but they will all undertake operations activities because every organization produces goods and/or delivers services.

Operations management has made a significant contribution to society by playing a role in areas such as increasing productivity, providing better quality goods and services and improving working conditions. Productivity has been increased through such measures as the use of technology (Chapter 6) and new production methods (Chapter 13). Increased productivity permits the more efficient production of goods and services and so helps raise living standards. Better quality goods and services are available through the use of quality initiatives such as total quality management (TQM) (Chapter 17). The rate of improvement in quality levels is reflected in programmes such as Six Sigma (Chapter 17). Improved working conditions are an outcome of the realization that the contribution of people is vital to an organization's success. Job design (Chapter 9) is used to help reach the full potential of employees.

The operations manager will have responsibility for managing resources involved in this process. Positions involved in operations have a variety of names, and may differ between the manufacturing and service sectors. Examples of job titles involved in manufacturing include logistics manager and industrial engineer. Examples in the service industry include operations control manager (scheduling flights for an airline for example), quality manager, hotel manager and retail manager. An example job description for an operations role is shown in the box 'Job Description for Operations Director'.

JOB DESCRIPTION FOR OPERATIONS DIRECTOR (SALARY CIRCA £65,000)

Operations Director

This company has established itself as a leading manufacturer within an industry sector where growth is encouraging overseas competitors to venture into the UK market. Profitable, yet aware of the need to change, a plan has been put into place that will allow greater cohesiveness between manufacturing and commercial operations. Increased flexibility in production techniques is also on the corporate agenda with cost out and development of new products associated with initiatives in this area. This is a key position within the executive team carrying responsibility for all aspects of company activity with the exception of finance and commercial functions.

 www.wileyopenpage.com

The Role

- Devise and implement a business operations strategy that secures the achievement of p&l objectives that are in line with the overall business plan.
- Management, motivation and development of the workforce (c. 120) through a period of change whilst ensuring continuous improvement in quality and operational efficiency.
- Create a culture of customer awareness that leads to collaborative product development and prompt resolution of issues that might affect perceptions of customer service.
- Influence the future direction of the business by being a fully participative member of the executive board.

The Candidate

- Graduate, operations or general manager of a customer-focused manufacturing business.
- Adept leader of change, able to devise innovative ways of working and ensure employee buy in.
- Has implemented, or at the very least explored the feasibility of, transferring some manufacturing activities to lower cost offshore alternatives.
- Clear communicator, numerate. Committed to achieving objectives and determined in overcoming obstacles.

People involved in operations participate in a wide variety of decision areas in the organization, examples of which are given in Table 1.1. The scale, importance and hopefully the excitement of operations management is indicated by the range of decision areas shown. Like many texts on the subject area of operations management, this book is structured around these decision areas (see chapter references in Table 1.1). The book is divided into sections on introducing operations and strategy (Chapters 1 to 2), design (Chapters 3 to 9) and management (Chapters 10 to 18) to aid clarity.

THE HISTORY OF OPERATIONS MANAGEMENT

Operations management did not emerge as a formal field until the 1950s and 1960s when textbooks specifically dealing with operations management were published. Major developments up to this point affecting the field of operations management start with the Industrial Revolution of the eighteenth century. Before this time products were made individually by skilled craftspeople in their homes and so were relatively expensive to produce. The use of inventions such as the steam engine (by James Watt in England in 1764) and concepts such as the use of interchangeable parts (from Eli Whitney in 1790) and the division of labour (described by Adam Smith, 1776) led to the move to volume production. Here mechanization (provided by steam power) was combined with the use of low-skilled labour (people were given small, simple tasks using the concept of the division of labour) to produce standard parts in high volumes, which could be assembled into products. These ideas were refined and the use

TABLE 1.1

Decision Areas in Operations Management.

Chapter	Decision area	Example decision
2	Operations strategy	What strategy should be followed?
3	Process types	How do we configure the process that will deliver our service to customers?
4	Layout design	How do we organize the physical layout of our facilities and people?
5	Facility design	What is the location of our operations facilities?
6	Process technology	What role should technology have in the transformation of materials in the operations system?
7	Product and service design	What products and services should the organization provide?
8	Process design	How do we design the service delivery process?
9	Job and work design	How do we motivate our employees?
10	Planning and control	How do we deploy our staff day-to-day?
11	Capacity management	How do we ensure that our service is reliably available to our customers?
12	Inventory management	How can we keep track of our inventory?
13	Lean operations	How do we implement lean operations?
14	Enterprise resource planning	How do we organize the movement of goods across the supply chain?
15	Supply chain management	What benefits could e-procurement bring to our operations?
16	Project management	How do we ensure our projects finish on time and within budget?
17	Quality	How can we implement a TQM programme?
18	Improvement	What role could continuous improvement have in our operation?

of scientific management, developed by Frederick W. Taylor and incorporating such elements as time study (Chapter 9), and the invention of the moving assembly line, first used by the car manufacturer Henry Ford in 1913, led to the era of mass production at the start of the twentieth century. This represented a major breakthrough in the ability of production systems to offer goods to a large amount of customers at a price they could afford.

An additional element in the makeup of operations management occurred during the First World War when the need to solve complex problems of logistics and weapons-system design led to the development of operations research. A number of the techniques developed then are still part of the operations management field today. As stated earlier, operations management as a discipline then began to emerge in the 1960s and has continued to develop since.

The 1970s saw the use of computers in materials requirements planning (MRP) software (Chapter 14) for inventory control and scheduling. The 1980s saw the emergence of the just-in-time (JIT) philosophy

(Chapter 13) from Japan, which transformed the way businesses deliver goods and services. In response to the need to improve the quality of goods and service the ideas of total quality management (TQM) (Chapter 17) were widely adopted in the 1980s. The 1990s saw the emergence of such concepts as supply chain management (Chapter 15) and business process re-engineering (BPR) (Chapter 17). Most recently the use of the Internet to conduct transactions or e-Commerce (Chapter 6) has changed the way operations management is performed.

The history of operations shows how the field has adapted and continues to change as it tries to respond to an ever greater range of challenges, from the needs of customers who require high quality, low price goods delivered quickly to managing the impacts of global competition and addressing environmental concerns.

THE ROLE OF OPERATIONS MANAGEMENT

We will start by considering that the role of operations management is to manage the transformation of an organization's inputs into finished goods and services (Figure 1.1).

The input activity involves two categories of resources. Transforming resources are the elements that act on, or carry out, the transformation process on other elements. The two main types of transforming resources are:

- Facilities, such as buildings, equipment and process technology. The management of these operations' resources is covered in Chapters 3 to 8.
- Staff, all the people involved in the operations process. In services the customer may well be involved as a transforming resource. Think of a fast-food restaurant where customers are expected to order the food and take it to their table and clear up afterwards. The management of human resources in operations is covered in Chapter 9.

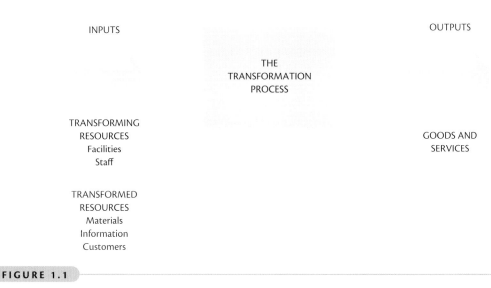

FIGURE 1.1

The Role of Operations Management.

The nature and mix of the transforming resources will differ between operations. The transformed resources, which are the elements acted on by the transforming resources, give the operations system its purpose or goal. The three main types of transformed resource, covered in Chapter 6, are:

- *Materials.* These can be transformed either physically (for example, manufacturing), by location (for example, transportation), by ownership (for example, retail) or by storage (for example, warehousing).
- *Information.* This can be transformed by property (for example, by accountants), by possession (for example, market research), by storage (for example, libraries), or by location (for example, telecommunications).
- *Customers.* They can be transformed either physically (for example, by hairdressers), by storage (for example, hotels), by location (for example, airlines), by physiological state (for example, hospitals), or by psychological state (for example, entertainment).

The transformation process itself will transform the material, information and customer resources in the way described above in order to produce goods and services. See Case Study 1.3 for a student's perspective of the transformation process.

THE PROCESS VIEW OF OPERATIONS

So far we have dealt with providing an overview of operations itself. This section discusses the role of operations in relation to other areas within the organization. Three of the most important functional areas in an organization can be classified as the operations, marketing and finance functions. The marketing function works to find and create demand for the company's goods and services by understanding customer needs and developing new markets. The need for marketing and operations to work closely together is particularly important as the marketing function will provide the forecast of demand from which operations can plan sufficient capacity in order to deliver goods and services on time. The finance function is responsible for obtaining and controlling funds and covering decisions such as investment in equipment and other operations resources such as personnel and materials.

Other functions that play a supporting role in the organization include the human resources (HR) function, which will play a role in regards to recruitment and labour relations; the research and development (R&D) function, which generates and investigates the potential of new ideas, and the information technology (IT) department, which supplies and coordinates the computer-based information needs of the organization.

The relationship between functions can be seen as a number of subsystems within the system called the 'organization'. Thus each function (such as marketing) can be treated using the same input/process/output transformation model as the operations function. In other words each function within the organization can be treated as performing an operations activity, as they are transforming inputs into outputs. This implies that every part of the organization is involved in the operations activity (to an internal or external customer) and indeed the topic of process management (Chapter 8) is an indication of how operations concepts are used across the organization.

The view of the organization as a number of functions has been criticized. Melan (1993) considers the following conditions are usually built into the functional structure.

- Rewards systems that promote values and support the objectives of the functional department rather than the business in its entirety.
- Group behaviour, which encourages a strong loyalty within the department and an 'us-versus-them' attitude toward other departments within the firm.
- A high degree of decentralization, creating 'firms within the firm', each with its own agenda.

These and other deficiencies of the functional organization have led to a move away from considering business as a set of discrete functional areas and towards a view of the organization as consisting of sets of processes that link together in order to meet customer needs. Each process can be treated using the input/process/output transformation model as with the functional perspective, but there is a clear emphasis on breaking down the barriers between departments and ensuring that outputs meet customer requirements. Processes can be carried out by separate individuals (individual processes), contained within a department (functional processes) or can occur in several functional areas (cross-functional processes).

In functional terms the processes would be situated in areas such as operations, marketing and finance but from the customer's view the value they gain is dependent on the performance of the set of linked processes involved in the delivery of the product/service. Figure 1.2 shows four key processes that cross functional boundaries. The supplier relationship management or 'buy' process involves working with suppliers of services, materials and information. The new product development or 'design' process involves designing new products and services. The order fulfilment or 'make' process involves activities that are required to produce and deliver the service or product to the customer. The customer relationship or 'sell' and 'service' processes involves identifying and attracting orders from customers either for products and services or support services for those primary outputs. In addition to these core processes other support processes might include budgeting and recruitment.

FIGURE 1.2

Core Processes across Functional Areas in the Organization.
Source: UNCTADstat, unctadstat.uncstad.org (2012). Reproduced with permission.

The term 'value added' can be used to denote the amount of value a process creates for its internal or external customer. The set of processes used to create value for a customer is often called the **value chain** (Porter and Millar, 1985). The value chain includes primary processes that directly create the value the customer perceives and support processes that assist the primary process in adding value. The key issue is that the configuration of the value chain should be aligned with the particular way the organization provides value to the customer. The design of operations from a process perspective is covered in Chapter 8.

 A link to a video o showing how different processes work together in a clothing manufacturer is available in your interactive e-book at **www.wileyopenpage.com**

SERVICE OPERATIONS MANAGEMENT

Operations management has been historically associated with the manufacturing industry but there has been a shift in its theory and practice to incorporate service systems. This is partly due to the importance of the service industry, which accounts for an increasing proportion of the output of industrialized economies. In European developed countries manufacturing output has generally fallen steadily as a proportion of GDP. This can be seen from Figure 1.3.

Some of the decline in manufacturing in developed economies in Europe can be explained by the increased competition and output from China and the effect of the recession in 2008 as Figure 1.4 shows.

The services GDP figures show the relative strength of the USA and Europe in this sector (Figure 1.5).

Case Study 1.2 at the end of the chapter outlines some of the reasons behind the shift from manufacturing to service output in the UK. The case study provides evidence that some of the decline in

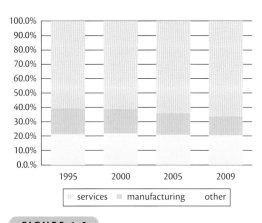

FIGURE 1.3

Sector Percentage Share of GDP in Europe.
Source: UNCTADstat, unctadstat.uncstad.org (2012).
Reproduced with permission.

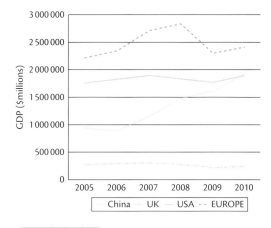

FIGURE 1.4

Manufacturing GDP in Selected Markets 2005–2010.
Source: UNCTADstat, unctadstat.uncstad.org (2012).
Reproduced with permission.

 www.wileyopenpage.com

manufacturing output is not because these manufacturers have gone out of business but because they have reinvented themselves as service providers.

Because of the increased importance of services one of the developments in operations management has been the need to integrate manufacturing and service operations to ensure they are compatible with each other and are strategically aligned with the organization's goals. The concept of **servitization** involves companies moving from being manufacturers with 'add-on' services to service companies whose output includes manufactured products. This service orientation is adopted in order to satisfy customer's needs, achieve competitive advantages and enhance firm performance. The belief is that an integrated service and product offering is more distinctive to the customer and provides a way of competing against competition from manufacturers in lower cost economies.

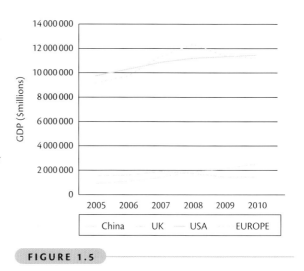

FIGURE 1.5

Services GDP in Selected Markets 2005–2010.
Source: UNCTADstat, unctadstat.uncstad.org (2012). Reproduced with permission.

It is difficult to measure the size of the service sector accurately because there is some disagreement about what constitutes the service sector but in the widest sense it can be seen as organizations that do not fall into what the economists call the primary sector (farming, forestry and fishing) or secondary sector (industries including manufacturing, mining and construction). Thus private-sector activities include retail, restaurants, hotels, transport and business services (this includes accounting, legal and computer services). Public sector service activities include health, defence, education and administration.

One reason for the increasing prominence of the service sector in the economies of developed countries is due to an increase in what are termed consumer services and producer services. **Consumer services** are services aimed at the final consumers and these have risen in line with people's increasing disposable income in developed countries. Once expenditure on essentials such as food and shelter has been accounted for, people will then spend on purchases such as travel, hotels, restaurants and other social and personal services. **Producer services** are used in the production and delivery of goods and services and constitute firms providing services to other businesses such as consultancy advice, legal advice and IT support (classified under business services) and transportation and other facilities. The rise of producer services indicates that although the share of manufacturing is declining, it still plays an important part in a nation's economy. This is because many of the producer services are actually in business to provide services to manufacturers as well as other service providers. Many of the services that are now outsourced were once undertaken by manufacturers themselves and were thus formerly classified as part of the manufacturing sector.

Another reason for the relative increase in services and decline in manufacturing in developed countries is seen to be competition from countries with lower labour costs such as China. Unlike manufacturers, services are often assumed to be required in the location they are consumed so cannot be outsourced overseas in the same way production activities are. However, the provider and user of the service may not be required to move to the location of the consumption of the service as in 'separated services' such as the media channels of television and newspapers, Internet sites for down-loading music and call-centre services. Generally, however, either the producer is required to move to the location of consumption in 'demand-located services' (for example management consultancy) or the user is required to move to the location of consumption in 'provider-located services' (for example hotels and hospitals). Some services, termed **peripatetic services**, require both the provider and user of the service to move their location to consume the service (for example trade shows and antique fairs). Users may be prepared to travel overseas for some services, such as medical treatments, but generally services need to be based near their users to be competitive and to meet local needs.

Types of Service Operation

In order to assess the challenges for operations in managing services it is useful to determine the characteristics of different services. It is useful to distinguish between the design of the service (Chapter 7) and the design of the system that delivers the service (Chapter 8). Services themselves can be classified by their **tangibility**, while the way they are delivered can be classified by their simultaneity.

Classifying Services by Tangibility

This is the most commonly used distinction between goods and services. Goods are tangible – they are physical things that you can touch. A service is intangible and can be seen as a process that is activated on demand. In reality, both goods and services have both tangible and intangible elements and can be placed on a continuum ranging from low to high intangibility. For example, the food in a fast-food restaurant is a major tangible element of the service. The food in a restaurant is still an important element, but other intangible elements such as waiter service and decor are important factors too. In fact most operations systems produce a mixture of goods and services. Most goods have some supporting service element (for example a maintenance contract with a new washing machine), called a facilitating service; many services will have supporting goods (for example a report provided by a management consultant), termed a 'facilitating good'. More information on the design of the service package (the bundle of goods and services) is given in Chapter 7 on product and service design.

The fact that services are intangible implies another important characteristic: **perishability**. A service is not a physical thing that can be stored, but is a process, so it must be consumed when it is produced or it will perish. The service provided by an empty seat in a restaurant or by an empty seat on an aircraft cannot be stored for use later. Thus revenue lost from these unused resources can never be recovered. This would not be a problem if the demand (in terms of volume and timing) for a service could be accurately determined and service capacity provided to match this. However, this is unlikely to be the case and unlike most goods, which can be stored if demand is lower than capacity to be used when demand is greater than capacity, services must always attempt to match supply with the pattern of demand. In fact, although services will need to match overall changes in the demand pattern service supply will need to be more due to fluctuations in that supply or a time lag in changing service capacity. A capacity buffer will be required the size of which will be greater when service quality is high (e.g. for high margin goods), service failure costs are high (e.g. emergency calls) or there is a large time lag in supply (e.g. for workers with technical knowledge in short supply such as IT workers). This topic is considered in more detail in Chapter 11 on capacity management.

 www.wileyopenpage.com

FIGURE 1.6

Front Office and Back Office in Operations Management.

Classifying Service Delivery by Simultaneity

Simultaneity relates to the characteristic that services are produced and consumed simultaneously. This means the service provider and customer will interact during the service delivery process. The amount of interaction is termed the **degree of customer contact**. In fact the customer is unlikely to be a passive receiver of the service but will generally be involved to a greater or lesser extent in the actual delivery of the service itself. For instance a supermarket requires the customer to choose and transport the goods around the store and queue at an appropriate checkout till. However, it should not be assumed that all services are consumed at the point of production (for example, financial services) and that employees in a service operation have to deal directly with a customer. For the supermarket example, the checkout till is an example of high customer contact but the stores' personnel may not have to deal directly with the customer at all.

A distinction in services is denoted by 'back-office' tasks, which add value to the inputs of the service operation, and 'front-office' tasks, which deal with the customer both as an input and output of the operation (Figure 1.6).

Different organizations will have a different balance between front and back-office operations. A front-office-based operation will be focused on the service experience of the customer and this is where most value will be added. Some traditional back-office focused organizations, such as manufacturers, are increasing the role of service experience and thus their front-office operations. This is because they judge that the ability to differentiate on the service aspect of their offering may provide a longer term source of competitive advantage than they can achieve by differentiating with the goods themselves. Some other organizations, however, are moving in the opposite direction and recognizing that customer value is being added by the tangible aspect of the service package delivered by the back-office operations. For example budget airlines have eliminated many front-line service aspects of the flight experience and focused on the transportation of customer process itself.

The fact that services require simultaneity and are produced and consumed simultaneously implies another important characteristic: **heterogeneity**. This refers to the interaction of the customer, service provider and surroundings causing variability in the performance of the service. From the perspective of the service provider, humans, by their nature, are likely to vary their actions and sometimes make mistakes. Individual customers will also perceive the quality of the service differently and the context of the service encounter (for example the existence of queues or weather conditions) may also impact on the service. This variability in performance and perceptions may lead to difficulties in maintaining a consistent level of service quality.

Some services, termed **mass services**, which operate at high volume and low variety of outcome, attempt to reduce variability due to heterogeneity by standardizing the service. This can be achieved by using approaches such as training staff to follow standard procedures and using equipment to support the service delivery process. This approach may not be appropriate for professional services, which operate at low volume and high variety, because here the customer requires high levels of contact with the service provider and a customized service. Service types such as mass service and professional service are covered in more detail in Chapter 3.

THE STRATEGIC ROLE OF OPERATIONS

Despite the term 'operations', operations management is not simply about the day-to-day (operational) running of an organization. Operations management does in fact have an important strategic role in ensuring that the management of the organization's resources and processes move the organization closer to its long-term goals. Operations strategy can be seen from market-based and resource-based perspectives. Using a **market-based operations strategy**, the organization makes a decision regarding the markets and the customers within those markets that it intends to target. This market position is then translated into a list of criteria or objectives, which define what kind of performance is required in order to successfully compete in the markets chosen.

Some examples of criteria for performance are fast delivery, a wide range of services or a low price. A **resource-based** view works from the inside-out of the firm, rather than the outside-in perspective of the market-based approach. Here an assessment of the operation's tangible and intangible resources and processes leads to a view of the operation's capability.

Both of these views of strategy are that it should be developed and implemented depending on the unique circumstances of the organization. However it should be noted that some organizations view operations strategy as the implementation of generic approaches to change such as lean operations or business process management. More detail on operations strategy is provided in Chapter 2.

TECHNOLOGY AND OPERATIONS MANAGEMENT

Technology plays a key role in the transformation process for which operations is responsible. **Process technology** is used to help transform the three main categories of transformed resources which are materials, customers and information. One of the most widely used and useful process technologies is computer-aided design (CAD), which allows testing of product and service designs using computer-based drawings. Customer processing technology such as automated teller machines can reduce or eliminate the need for employee contact in customer-facing operations. Information technologies such as e-Business systems are having a major effect on how firms organize their supply chains and use their capacity (see Case Study 1.1). More details on process technology are provided in Chapter 6.

CASE STUDY 1.1

'First Bank' PLC

'First Bank' has recently begun to offer Internet banking to extend its range of services to the customer and decrease the demand on branch personnel. However, the web site has been experiencing difficulties with a slow response rate to customer inquiries. Demand for the Internet service has also been much lower than expected. As operations manager the company requires your view on the following issues:

Questions

1. What are the competitive consequences of 'pulling out' of Internet banking for the company?

2. What impact will a decision to 'pull out' of Internet banking have on the company in terms of future technology-based initiatives.

3. How can the bank improve customer take-up of its Internet banking initiative?

SUMMARY

- Operations management is about the management of the processes that produce or deliver goods and services.
- The operations system can be seen as a transformation process. It converts inputs known as transformed resources (classified as materials, information and customers) using transforming resources (classified as staff and facilities) into finished goods and services.
- An alternative to the functional perspective of an organization is a process view in which the organization is seen as consisting of a set of processes that link together to meet customer needs.
- Service organizations can be classified by their tangibility (the extent that they incorporate a physical thing that you can touch). The way services are delivered can be classified by their simultaneity (the extent that the service is produced and consumed at the same time).
- Service operations can be denoted by front-office tasks, which deal directly with the customer, and back-office tasks, which add value to the inputs of the service operation.
- Operations management has an important strategic role in ensuring that the management of the organization's resources and processes direct the organization closer to its long-term goals.
- Technology plays a key role in the transformation of materials, customers and information for which operations is responsible.

Manufacturing's Decline Partly Due to Services Shift

Up to a fifth of the decline in manufacturing's share of the UK economy could be attributable to a shift by production companies towards service activities in place of turning out goods, according to UK government statisticians. The phenomenon of manufacturers undergoing a subtle metamorphosis so they become 'hybrid businesses' that combine production with services could explain why many individual companies regarded as manufacturers are performing a lot better than the sector's generally gloomy macroeconomic data. Lord Kumar Bhattacharyya, director of the Warwick Manufacturing Group at the University of Warwick, and a highly regarded observer of manufacturing trends, says: 'The fact that many more manufacturers in the UK have gone into services is one reason many have been able to survive.' Since 1995 the share of manufacturing in the economy has shrunk from 20% to less than 15%. This is a change generally linked to the faster growth of services plus productivity improvements in manufacturing reducing the value of factory output by making goods cheaper. Another factor is the growing share of global manufacturing output accounted for by countries with cheaper labour costs. UK data on the split between manufacturing and services are assembled by the government's Office for National Statistics. It does this by asking companies to classify their output between the two activities. If a manufacturer has abandoned most of its UK-based manufacturing – but continues to function in the UK as a distributor or provider of other services such as repair and maintenance – the company can be recategorized and may officially no longer be considered a manufacturer. According to a senior government statistician, no one has properly accounted for how much service activity is now being done by

companies formerly considered as 100% manufacturers but today are classed either as hybrids or wholly service businesses. The official said it was 'quite plausible' that as much as a fifth of the apparent relative decline in manufacturing in the past 10 years could be explained by this shift.

One of the best examples of companies making such a shift is Pace Micro Technology, a West Yorkshire business, which is a world leader in digital set-top boxes for televisions. In the late 1990s it employed 1500 at its main site in Shipley, most of them in manufacturing. Today the company's UK manufacturing output is non-existent – all its production being done by contractors in low-cost countries – but continues to employ 450 on the site, mainly in design engineering and software. Output from the site is categorized as a distribution activity – sales of set-top boxes to retailers – while the value of the engineering work is captured also in an unclassifiable part of these distribution sales. In a similar way Alstom, a French engineering company that in the 1990s operated large factories in the UK producing power turbines and trains, today employs 5000 in Britain - all but about 350 of whom are involved in services such as designing new power systems or maintaining railway equipment while it is being operated by customers. Indesit, an Italian white goods company formerly known as Merloni and which makes the Hotpoint brand of domestic appliances, has 5500 workers in the UK, only 2000 of them in conventional factory jobs. The rest are in activities such as servicing appliances in people's homes, distribution and logistics, sales and running a call centre in Peterborough for customer problems. Marco Milani, chief executive of Indesit, says: 'Services are an extremely important part of what we do.' UK company Dialight is a world leader in making light-emitting diodes – small electronic devices that can take the place of light bulbs and last a lot longer while providing more light. With most of its manufacturing in Mexico, it runs a plant in Newmarket, Cambridgeshire, employing 120. Most work is not in conventional manufacturing activities but jobs such as logistics and planning for the company's global operations. 'It's important to remember the work of a production company goes a lot further than what people regard as manufacturing,' says Roy Burton, chief executive.

Source: Peter Marsh, *Financial Times,* May 22, 2006. Reproduced with permission.

Question

Discuss the main reasons given for the growth in services in the case study.

CASE STUDY 1.3

A Student's Perspective

From waking to an unwelcome alarm and going through the process of our own early morning rituals and the preparation and consumption of breakfast to enjoying a night out with friends, a student's life is dependent upon, and surrounded by a web of operations.

Let's take breakfast as an example; it can be viewed in the context of step by step process or due to having a defined start and end, and being measured in terms of cost, time and quality, as a project. The ingredients need to be sourced and purchased from a supplier, whether that be a local shop or supermarket, which themselves have a complex web of efficient and effective operations through the supply chain in order to bring the customer 'value' whilst ensuring profitability.

You as a student may take a public or university bus, which you will need to pay for through a ticket or pass, jump on your bike, or into your car, which requires insurance, tax and the expense of petrol, all in order to arrive in time for your lectures on time; all have operational parameters.

The university that you attend, the course that you are enrolled on and the unit/subject for which you are attending a lecture or seminar, are nothing without an interconnected system of back- and front-office operations, including administration, management, academic, timetabling, and the café that you have the option to visit to grab a coffee and sandwich over lunch.

Whether you make the choice to stay on campus or visit further afield for lunch, the restaurant that you choose will offer a mix of a product and service with a specially designed layout to ensure the best use of space and efficient flow to serve customers. The menu is a selection of products designed to suit, attract and satisfy a targeted segment of the market, of which raw materials are transformed inputs bought from a selection of suppliers that chefs (a transforming resource/input) make into your meal which is the operations output, that should meet the customer's (your) expectation.

A student's evening can range from a night out at the union or a visit to the cinema to one working away in the library at a soon due assignment, but whatever it may bring or the choices that you make, you can be certain that the operations management web will be all around you.

www.wileyopenpage.com

Questions

1. Complete a time line of your day from waking up to going to sleep listing the operations that you encounter.

2. Choosing two examples from your timeline complete a model of transformation for each.

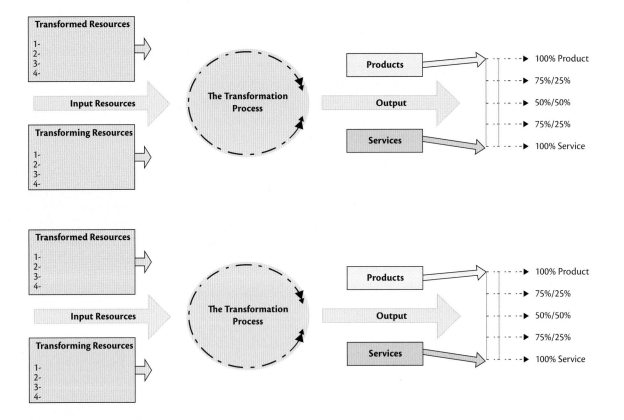

Source: Written by Briony Boydell and Chris Milner. Reproduced with permission.

Quizzes to test yourself further are available in your interactive e-book at **www.wileyopenpage.com**

Flashcards to test yourself further are available in your interactive e-book at **www.wileyopenpage.com**

EXERCISES

1. Look at a recruitment web site or the recruitment section of a newspaper and locate three operations roles in job advertisements in the manufacturing industry and three in the service industry.

2. How would you distinguish between the fields of operations management and operations research?

3. Identify the main transformed and transforming resources for the types of organizations below:

   - fast food restaurant
   - hotel
   - university
   - food retailer
   - car manufacturer.

4. Explain the use of the process view of organizations.

5. What are the implications of moving tasks between the front-office and back-office areas of a service operation?

6. Explain the term heterogeneity as applied to service operations.

WEB EXERCISE

The UNCTAD web site (http://unctad.org) has a number of reports on the world economy. Visit the web site and discover the value of the trade balance for developing and developed economies. Why do you think that many developed economies have such a high negative trade balance (imports are higher than exports)?

FURTHER READING

Baines, T.S., Lightfoot, H.W., Benedettini, O. and Kay, J.M. (2009) The servitization of manufacturing: A review of literature and reflection on future challenges, *Journal of Manufacturing Technology Management*, 20 (5).

Johnston, R. and Clark, G. (2008) *Service Operations Management: Improving Service Delivery*, 3rd edn, Pearson Education Ltd.

Slack, N., Chambers, S. and Johnston, R. (2010) *Operations Management*, 6th edn, Pearson Education Ltd.

Slack, N. and Lewis, M. (2011) *Operations Strategy*, 3rd edn, Pearson Education Ltd.

Van Looy, B., Gemmel, P. and Van Dierdonck, R.V. (eds) (2012) *Services Management: An Integrated Approach*, 3rd edition, Pearson Education Ltd.

WEB LINKS

Selected List of Operations Management Web Sites

www.ame.org (accessed 23 November 2011). The Association for Manufacturing Excellence. Events and publications aimed at improving productivity.

www.apics.org (accessed 23 November 2011). The Association for Operations Management. Resources such as industry news in operations management.

www.eiasm.org (accessed 23 November 2011). European Institute for Advanced Studies in Management (EIASM). International network for management research and teaching.

www.euroma-online.org (accessed 23 November 2011). European Operations Management Association (EUROMA). Leading association for operations managers. Contains information on conferences, workshops and publications.

www.informs.org (accessed 23 November 2011). Institute for Operations Research and Management Science. Resources such as web guides, journals and links to societies in the field of operations research.

www.iomnet.org.uk (accessed 23 November 2011). Institute of Operations Management. A professional body for those involved in operations management in the UK. Contains links to online resources.

www.manufacturinginstitute.co.uk (accessed 23 November 2011). The Manufacturing Institute contains news and events concerning manufacturing in the UK.

www.mas.berr.gov.uk (accessed 23 November 2011). Manufacturing Advisory Service. Department for Business Enterprise and Regulatory Reform (BERR) site for UK manufacturers.

www.poms.org (accessed 23 November 2011). Production and Operations Management Society. International society providing resources such as journals and encyclopedia of operations management terms.

https://sites.google.com/site/tomiportal/home (accessed 23 November 2011). The Technology and Operations Management Index (TOMI) portal.

www.unctad.org (accessed 23 November 2011). United Nations Conference on Trade and Development. Provides links to a number of reports regarding world trade and economic development issues.

Selected List of Operations Management Academic Journals

http://jsr.sagepub.com/ (accessed 23 November 2011). *Journal of Service Research.*

www.emeraldinsight.com/ijopm.htm (accessed 23 November 2011). *International Journal of Operations and Production Management (IJOPM).*

www.poms.org/journal (accessed 23 November 2011). *Production and Operations Management* (POM).

www.sciencedirect.com/science/journal/01664972 (accessed 23 November 2011). *Technovation.*

www.sciencedirect.com/science/journal/02637863 (accessed 23 November 2011). *International Journal of Project Management.*

www.sciencedirect.com/science/journal/02726963 (accessed 23 November 2011). *Journal of Operations Management* (JOM).

www.sciencedirect.com/science/journal/07376782 (accessed 23 November 2011). *Journal of Product Innovation Management.*

www.sciencedirect.com/science/journal/09255273 (accessed 23 November 2011). *International Journal of Production Economics.*

www.sciencedirect.com/science/journal/09697012 (accessed 23 November 2011). *European Journal of Purchasing and Supply Management.*

REFERENCES

Melan, E.H. (1993) *Process Management: Methods for Improving Products and Services*, McGraw-Hill.

Porter, M.E. and Millar, V.E. (1985) How information gives you competitive advantage, *Harvard Business Review*. July–August, 149–60.

UNCTAD (2012), UNCTAD Handbook of Statistics 2011, http://unctad.org (accessed 8 June 2012).

CHAPTER 2

Operations Strategy

- **Introduction**
- **What is strategy?**
- **Judging the contribution of operations to strategy**
- **Measuring the contribution of operations to strategy**
- **Operations strategy approaches**
- **Operations strategy alignment**
- **Operations strategy formulation**
- **Operations strategy implementation**

LEARNING OBJECTIVES

- Explain how strategy can exist at three levels within the organization
- Discuss the five performance objectives
- Contrast the market-based and resource-based approaches to operations strategy
- Discuss the Hill framework for operations strategy formulation
- Discuss approaches to identify the relative importance of the competitive factors
- Explain the concept of trade-offs in operations
- Explain the concept of focus in operations

INTRODUCTION

This chapter describes the role and formulation of operations strategy in the organization and discusses the increasing importance of the role of operations strategy. The purpose of operations in terms of an organization's strategy has often been seen as supportive, whereas functions such as marketing provide a competitive edge. Operations can, however, provide the basis of a firm's competitive strategy. The purpose of an operations strategy is to interpret the overall business strategy, which will be concerned with goals such as growth and profitability, into goals that direct how operations will be managed.

These goals may be defined by the five operations performance objectives of quality, speed, dependability, flexibility and cost. In this chapter an approach to developing a strategy to achieve these goals is considered that is concerned with matching internal operations capability with external competitive market requirements.

WHAT IS STRATEGY?

Strategy can be defined as follows (Johnson, Whittington and Scholes, 2011):

> Strategy is the *direction* and *scope* of an organization over the *long term,* ideally, which matches its *resources* to its changing *environment* and in particular its *markets, customers* or *clients* so as to meet *stakeholder* expectations.

Thus strategic decisions occur as a result of an evaluation of the external and internal environments. The external evaluation may reveal market opportunities or threats from competitors. The evaluation of the internal environment may reveal limitations in capabilities relative to competitors. Strategy is seen as complex in nature due to factors such as the high level of uncertainty in future consequences arriving from decisions, the need for integration of long-term and day-to-day activities across the business and the fact that major change may have to be implemented as a consequence of strategic choices made.

Levels of Strategy

Strategy can be seen to exist at three main levels within the organization – corporate, business and functional (Figure 2.1).

Corporate Level Strategy

Highest or **corporate level strategy** provides long-range guidance for the whole organization, often expressed as a statement of its mission. The mission statement should define the key **stakeholders**

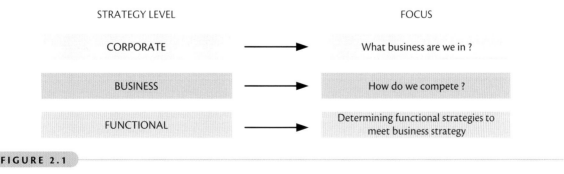

FIGURE 2.1

Levels of Strategy.

whom the corporation will seek to satisfy and describe the overall strategy it will pursue to meet their objectives. Stakeholders can be defined as anyone with an interest in the activities of the organization. They can be divided into three main groups:

- *Internal stakeholders* – include the organization's managers and employees. Employees will be concerned with issues such as job security, rewards, recognition and job satisfaction. In addition to these concerns one of the key roles of management is to try to reconcile the competing interests of stakeholder groups of customers, investors and employees.
- *Connected stakeholders* – are parties with a direct connection with the organization such as customers, investors, shareholders, moneylenders, distributors and suppliers. These will all have a variety of needs from the organization. For example customers will be interested in the price, quality and service level of the goods and services that the organization delivers to the marketplace.
- *External stakeholders* – cover other parties that can impact on the organization, the most important of which is usually the government. Governments are involved in such activities as setting regulations in areas such as health and safety and environmental policies. Government grants may be available in certain geographical areas which may affect the operations location decision. Other external stakeholders include the local community and pressure groups.

Using the stakeholder model the goal of the organization should be to satisfy the needs of stakeholders, which are necessary for the success of the organization in the long term.

Business Level Strategy

The second level of strategy is termed a **business level strategy** and may be for the organization or at the strategic business unit (SBU) level in larger diversified companies. Here the concern is with the products and services that should be offered in the market defined at the corporate level. The SBU must develop a strategy at this level, which defines a competitive advantage for its products or services in the market. Competitive advantage may be achieved by strategies such as low cost, product innovation, or customization of a service to a niche market.

Functional Level Strategy

The third level of strategy is termed the operational or **functional level strategy** where the functions of the business (for example, operations, marketing, finance) make long-range plans that support the competitive advantage being pursued by the business strategy.

The 'levels of strategy' model implies a 'top-down', structured approach to strategy formulation in which corporate goals are communicated down to business and then functional areas. Although there has always been interaction within this hierarchy in both directions the role of functional areas such as operations in setting the framework for how a company can compete from the 'bottom up' is being recognized. For example the theory of emergent strategies (Mintzberg and Waters, 1995) shows how the implementation of strategy, rather than following a structure determined by a long-term plan, emerges from day-to-day experience at an operational level.

The contribution of operations to strategy development and its relationship to the levels in the organization where strategy is developed is the focus of discussion in this chapter.

 www.wileyopenpage.com

Findus

Here is an example of a vision/mission statement from a company web site.

The Findus Vision

We have a common purpose within the Company to make the following 'Visions' a reality and these statements reflect the culture of the organization we are trying to develop. People make success, and so we want everyone to believe in our visions and work to achieve them.

Purpose

Findus will be one of the premier frozen food companies in Europe. Our consumers, employees, shareholders and communities will know us by the improvements we are making to their quality of life, through our superior products and the responsible way we create them.

Visions

- Findus products will be the consumer's first choice due to their superiority in taste, freshness and goodness.

- Findus will constantly lead the growth of the frozen food category at a pace never seen before.

- Findus will be the preferred supplier to all our customers.

- Findus will be a good place to work.

- Findus will set a new standard for corporate responsibility in the food industry.

- Findus will be organized to meet our business needs and will focus on the achievement of perfect customer and consumer service.

- Findus – The One Company.

Source: Findus, reproduced with permission.

Questions

1. Identify how the vision statements in the Findus mission relate to the different stakeholder groups.
2. Why is corporate responsibility so important across the supply chain in the food industry?

JUDGING THE CONTRIBUTION OF OPERATIONS TO STRATEGY

As stated, the role that operations can play in strategy development and implementation is being recognized. Hayes and Wheelwright (1988) assert that the success of organizations depends on their overall operations capability and so provide a model which enables managers to identify operations' current strategic role and the changes needed in order to improve competitiveness. The four-stage model traces the contribution of the operations function from a largely reactive role in stage 1 to a proactive element in competitive success in stage 4 (Figure 2.2).

Stage 1: Internal Neutrality

Here the operations function has very little to contribute to competitive success and is seen as a barrier to better competitive performance by other functions. The operations function is simply

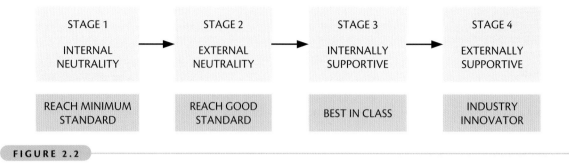

FIGURE 2.2

Four Stages of Judging Operations' Contribution to Strategy.

attempting to reach a minimum acceptable standard required by the rest of the organization whilst avoiding any major mistakes, thus the term internal neutrality. However, a major mistake by operations could still have serious consequences for the rest of the organization (for example, product recall).

Stage 2: External Neutrality

Here the operations function begins to focus on comparing its performance with competitor organizations. Although it may not be innovative enough to be in the 'first division' of companies in its market, by taking the best ideas and attempting to match the performance of competitors it is attempting to be externally neutral.

Stage 3: Internally Supportive

Here the operations function is one of the best in its market area and aspires to be the best in market. The operations function will thus be organizing and developing the operations capabilities to meet the strategic requirements of the organization. Operations is taking a role in the implementation of strategy and being 'internally supportive'.

Stage 4: Externally Supportive

In stage 4 the operations function is becoming central to strategy making and providing the foundation for future competitive success. This may be delivered through the organization of resources in ways that are innovative and capable of adapting as markets change. When operations is in the role of the long-term driver of strategy it is being 'externally' supportive.

Figure 2.2 shows the four stages of judging operations' contribution to strategy and the corresponding role of the operations function in delivering the organization's strategy. As the organization moves from stage 1 to stage 4 its role moves from being reactive in response to strategic objectives passed down to it, to ensuring resources are developed to support the strategy, to (in stage 4) providing the business with its competitive advantage.

The video 'Henry Mintzberg interviewed by Michael Kull' to explain the relationship between strategy and operations is available in your interactive e-book at **www.wileyopenpage.com**

MEASURING THE CONTRIBUTION OF OPERATIONS TO STRATEGY

The Performance Objectives

The five basic **performance objectives** (Slack, Chambers and Johnston, 2010) allow the organization to measure its operations' performance in achieving its strategic goals. The performance objectives are:

- quality
- speed
- dependability
- flexibility
- cost.

Each of these objectives will be discussed in terms of how it is measured and its significance to organizational competitiveness.

Quality

Quality (Chapter 17) covers both the quality of the design of the product or service itself (Chapter 7) and the quality of the process that delivers the product or service (Chapters 3, 6 and 8). From a customer perspective quality characteristics include reliability, performance and aesthetics. From an operations viewpoint quality is related to how closely the product or service meets the specification required by the design, termed the quality of conformance. In terms of measurement quality can be measured by the 'cost of quality' model covered in Chapter 17. Here quality costs are categorized as either the cost of achieving good quality (the cost of quality assurance) or the cost of poor quality products (the costs of not conforming to specifications). The advantages of good quality on competitiveness include:

- *Increased dependability* – fewer problems due to poor quality means a more reliable delivery process.
- *Reduced costs* – if things are done correctly first time, expenditure is saved on scrap and correcting mistakes.
- *Improved customer service* – a consistently high quality product or service will lead to high customer satisfaction.

Speed

Speed is the time delay between a customer request for a product or service and then receiving that product or service. The activities triggered from a customer request for a product or service will be dependent on whether a make-to-stock or customer-to-order delivery system is in place. The concept of P:D ratios

(Chapter 10) compares the demand time D (from customer request to receipt of goods or services) to the total throughput time P of the purchase, make and delivery stages. Thus in a make-to-stock system D is basically the delivery time, but for a customer-to-order system (for example a service system) the customer demand time is equal to the purchase, make and delivery stages (P). In this case the speed of the internal processes of purchase and make will directly affect the delivery time experienced by the customer.

Although the use of a make-to-stock system may reduce the delivery time as seen by the customer, it cannot be used for services and has disadvantages associated with producing for future demand in manufacturing. These include the risk of the products becoming obsolete, inaccurate forecasting of demand leading to stock-out or unwanted stock, the cost of any stock in terms of working capital and the decreased ability to react quickly to changes in customer requirements. Thus the advantage of speed is that it can be used to both reduce costs (by eliminating the costs associated with make-to-stock systems) and reduce delivery time leading to better customer service.

Dependability

Dependability refers to consistently meeting a promised delivery time for a product or service to a customer. Thus an increase in delivery speed may not lead to customer satisfaction if it is not produced in a consistent manner. Dependability can be measured by the percentage of customers that receive a product or service within the delivery time promised. In some instances it may even be important to deliver not too quickly, but only at the time required (for example a consignment of wet concrete for construction!). Dependability leads to better customer service when the customer can trust that the product or service will be delivered when expected. Dependability can also lead to lower cost, in that progress checking and other activities designed to ensure things happen on time can be reduced within the organization. Key activities needed to increase dependability include planning and control mechanisms to ensure problems are uncovered early, and making dependability a key performance measure.

Flexibility

Flexibility is the ability of the organization quickly to change what it does. This can mean the ability to offer a wide variety of products or services to the customer and to be able to change these products or services quickly. The concept of mass customization uses flexibility to offer high variety at a relatively low cost base and is discussed in Chapter 7. The concept of agility uses flexibility to ensure organizations within a supply chain can react quickly to changing customer demands (see Chapter 15). Flexibility is needed so the organization can adapt to changing customer needs in terms of product range and varying demand and to cope with capacity shortfalls due to equipment breakdown or component shortage. The following types of flexibility can be identified:

- *Product or service* – to be able to act quickly in response to changing customer needs with new product or service designs.
- *Mix* – to be able to provide a wide range of products or services.
- *Volume* – to be able to decrease or increase output in response to changes in demand. Volume flexibility may be needed for seasonal changes in demand. Services may have to react to demand changes minute by minute.
- *Delivery* – this is the ability to react to changes in the timing of a delivery. This may involve the ability to change delivery priorities between orders and still deliver on time.

TABLE 2.1

The Range and Response Dimensions for the Four System Flexibility Types.

	Range flexibility	Response flexibility
Product or service flexibility	The range of products and services which the company has the capability to produce	The time necessary to develop or modify the products and services and processes which produce them to the point where regular delivery can start
Mix flexibility	The range of products and services which the company can deliver within a given time period	The time necessary to adjust the mix of products and services being delivered
Volume flexibility	The total output which the company can achieve for a given product and service mix	The time taken to change the total level of output
Delivery flexibility	The extent to which delivery dates can be changed	The time taken to reorganize the delivery system for the new delivery date

Flexibility can be measured in terms of range (the amount of the change) and response (the speed of the change). Table 2.1 outlines the range and response dimensions for the four flexibility types of product or service, mix, volume and delivery.

The range and response dimensions are connected in the sense that the more something is changed (range) the longer it will take (response). The relationship between the two can be observed by constructing range-response curves. In general the benefit of flexibility from the customer's point of view is that it speeds up response by being able to adapt to customer needs. The ability of the internal operation to react to changes will also help maintain the dependability objective.

Cost

Cost is considered to be the finance required to obtain the inputs (transforming and transformed resources) and manage the transformation process that produces finished goods and services. If an organization is competing on price then it is essential that it keeps its cost base lower than the competition. Then it will either make more profit than rivals, if price is equal, or gain market share if price is lower. Cost is also important for a strategy of providing a product or service to a market niche, which competitors cannot provide. Thus cost proximity (to ensure costs are close to the market average) is important to maximize profits and deter competitors from entering the market.

The major categories of cost are staff, facilities (including overheads) and material. The proportion of these costs will differ between operations but averages are staff 15%, facilities 30% and material 55%. Thus it can be seen that the greatest scope for reducing cost lies with a reduction in the cost of materials. A relatively small proportion of costs are usually assigned to direct labour.

The level and mix of these costs will be dependent on the volume and variety of output and the variation in demand. Increased volume means that the cost per unit will decrease as resources can be dedicated to the production or delivery of a particular service. However, diseconomies of scale (Chapter 5)

CASE STUDY 2.2

Gecko

Jeff Sacree turned his small, struggling, surfboard business into one of Europe's leading specialist helmet manufacturers on the basis of a casual conversation. His business was extremely seasonal and so he was looking to find a way of diversifying his products. Speaking to a lifeboat man, he found the Royal National Lifeboat Institute needed a lighter, more suitable helmet for use on the seas. It happened that he had been working on a helmet for surfers and so was well placed to supply the RNLI. After eventually securing the contract with RNLI, the question for Sacree was where to take the business next.

Some potential markets sprang to mind immediately: specialist helmets could be usefully worn by river police, coastguard and customs officers – and a recent model has been designed specifically for helicopter winchmen. But, as the craze for new, extreme sports blossomed throughout the 1990s, a much wider market suddenly presented itself. Skateboarders, snowboarders, mountain bikers and powerboat racers all needed protection.

Prototype headgear was produced, tested and modified for each discipline and users were encouraged to respond with comments and suggested improvements. Gecko soon discovered that producing low-volume, handmade products was a distinct advantage when it comes to satisfying the niche markets of extreme sports. It involved less financial risk and allowed for the continual, minor improvements that customers wanted. 'We decided not to go down the automated production route,' says Sacree 'and it seems to have paid off. Making everything by hand gives us the crucial advantage of flexibility, so we can add altimeters and video cameras, torches and two-way radio systems – pretty well anything a customer asks for.'

Source: The Department of Trade and Industry. Reproduced with permission.

Question

How has Gecko used flexibility to compete?

---

can still occur due to increased organizational complexity, which can lead to poor communication. Increases in volume may be achieved with current resources or require significant investment in equipment and labour. The cost implications of increases in volume must therefore be considered carefully. Variety of output will increase complexity and thus costs. However, this complexity can be reduced by using such techniques as design simplification and standardization, increasing mix flexibility in moving from one product to another.

Finally cost is dependent on the other performance objectives. It was noted earlier that increased flexibility can lead to a decrease in the cost of the product or service design. In fact improvements in all the performance objectives can lead to a reduction in cost.

The Performance Objectives from an Internal and External Perspective

We can categorize the benefits of excelling at the performance objectives from an internal and external perspective (Table 2.2). This is useful because even though a performance objective may have little relevance in achieving performance that external stakeholders (such as customers) value it may

TABLE 2.2

Internal and External Benefits of the Performance Objectives.

Performance objective	Internal (operations) benefits	External (market) benefits
Quality	Error-free processes	Satisfying customer needs
Dependability	Minimizes disruption	Meeting delivery commitments
Speed	Minimizes throughput	Get products and services to customers fast
Flexibility	Able to react to change	Offer frequent new products/services, a wide product/service range and cope with changing volume and delivery requirements
Cost	High productivity from low cost	Market share and/or high margin

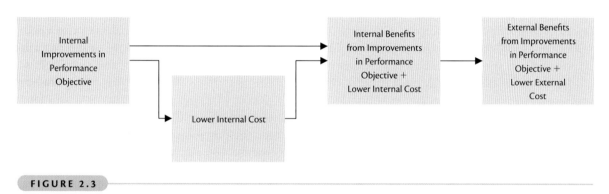

FIGURE 2.3

Internal Improvements in a Performance Objective also Lower Internal Costs.

bring benefits in improving the capability of operations from an internal perspective. When we look at approaches to strategy in the next section we find that competitiveness is not just a matter of simply improving performance along specific external competitive dimensions but incorporates the development of internal capabilities that provide specific operating advantages.

You might have noticed in the descriptions of the performance objectives in the previous section that improvement in the performance objective of cost derives from both lowering costs directly but also by improving the performance of the other performance objectives. Figure 2.3 shows this relationship.

Figure 2.3 shows how the internal improvements in the performance of a performance objective will show benefits for that performance objective but also lower costs. This can then be translated into external benefits from improvements in the performance objective as well as a reduction in costs. This relationship provides an indication of how operations can combine the performance criterion of low cost with criteria such as high quality and flexibility. It also shows that strategies that rely on immediate cost cutting (and thus risk damage to the operations capability) could be replaced by strategies that aim to improve performance on the other performance objectives, which will then lead to a reduction in cost. The issue of how to manage changes in the levels of performance objectives is discussed further in the later section on trade-offs.

CASE STUDY 2.3

Operations Strategy in Action

Almost every company seems to be restructuring itself to face the downturn, be it through financial engineering, or by retrenching to core activities. So they sell off foreign subsidiaries (Aviva), recent diversifications (ABB), or in desperate cases almost anything that's worth something and isn't nailed to the floor (Vivendi and Marconi). Oddly, few firms make a thing about going back to the real basics, which is manufacturing or, more accurately, operations. Odd, because competing operationally – making and selling things better and more cheaply than the opposition – is the simplest and best strategy of all. In tough times like these, most other 'strategies' look like sorry substitutes for failing to get the basics right in the first place.

Schefenacker Vision Systems (formerly part of Britax) is a maker of car wing mirrors. Schefenacker has been improving its mirrors for more than 10 years. It can now satisfy the most demanding customers – for example, from its plant in the south of England it delivers a possible 420 permutations of mirror daily direct to Jaguar's assembly line in the Midlands to match each car that comes down the assembly line.

The ability to do this cost-effectively is an entry ticket to lots of international business. Less obviously, the company's virtuosity allows it to design and build better, more sophisticated parts – for instance, with lighting or electronics built in. That allows it to go upmarket, where margins are wider. At the same time, as with Dell, it also gives it the possibility of expanding up and down the value chain. Thanks to relentless emphasis on doing more with less . . . Schefenacker has freed up space on the factory floor for five new production cells. It uses these to manufacture simple parts which it had previously outsourced to others. Strategic result: Schefenacker no longer pays the other guy's profit margin, spreads overheads across a larger base, and can suck waste out of a larger section of the supply chain. Manufacturing director Mickey Love says: 'Lean production gives you an opportunity to make things that you can sell to customers you didn't have before.'

Of all the advantages of operations excellence as a strategy, its impact on people is the most momentous. In firms that take this route, improvement of every aspect of design, manufacture, distribution, delivery and service is by definition strategic. Better product quality or a day sliced off delivery lead time is a strategic, not tactical, move. That means improvement is part of the day job for every individual; which also means 100 per cent participation, with no choice.

The secret is that operating excellence makes strategy easy. As Richard Schonberger, one of the original proselytizers for lean manufacturing, said: 'What makes a great team is the basics. Then almost anything the coach chooses to do makes the coach look like a shrewd strategist.'

Source: Excerpt from 'Business: The basics that beat the world: Making things better and cheaper is the best strategy of all' by Simon Caulkin, The Observer November 3, 2002. Reproduced with permission.

Questions

1. Read the article and discuss how operations can provide strategic advantage.
2. Discuss the performance of the company in terms of the five performance objectives.

OPERATIONS STRATEGY APPROACHES

The nature of the development of approaches to operations strategy has changed over time. For most of the twentieth century, market conditions were characterized by a mass-production era with an emphasis on high-volume and low-cost production. Operations strategy was characterized by improving efficiency through aspects such as achieving a high utilization of equipment and having a closely supervised workforce undertaking standardized operations. This perspective was challenged by a new approach from Japan – lean operations (Chapter 13). Here the emphasis was not on low cost and high volume but on operations providing capabilities in areas such as reliability, speed and flexibility. This was achieved through such aspects as training staff in problem solving, using general purpose equipment for flexibility and eliminating waste in all its forms. Neither the 'mass' approach nor the 'lean' approach can be seen as a strategy in itself in that, to be successful, an operations strategy should support the competitive advantage being pursued by the business strategy. Nevertheless many organizations will view their operations strategy as the implementation of one or a combination of the 'improvement' approaches covered in this text such as lean operations (Chapter 13), business process re-engineering (Chapter 18), enterprise resource planning (Chapter 14), total quality management (Chapter 17) and agile operations (Chapter 15). Whilst these approaches will undoubtedly improve overall performance strategy they are essentially generic and operations strategy in this text is taken to mean a specific process tailored to an organization's individual circumstance in the marketplace. This means that the aim of the organization's operations strategy will be to seek a fit between the way it competes in the market and how operations is designed and managed. This 'fit' can be achieved in many ways and will in part be dependent on the operations current capabilities. The two perspectives of this fit, from a market-based or resource-based approach will now be discussed.

Market-Based Approach to Operations Strategy

Figure 2.4 shows the main elements of the **market-based approach to operations strategy**.

Using this approach an organization makes a decision regarding the markets and the customers within those markets that it intends to target. Along with meeting customer needs within a market the position the organization takes in that market will in part depend on the actions of its competitors. Thus the organization's market position is one in which its performance enables it to attract customers to its products or services in a more successful manner than its competitors. The next step is to translate the market position into a list of criteria or objectives which define what kind of performance is required in order to successfully compete in the markets chosen. Different authors use different terms for these measures, for example 'competitive criteria' (Hill and Hill, 2012) and 'competitive priorities'

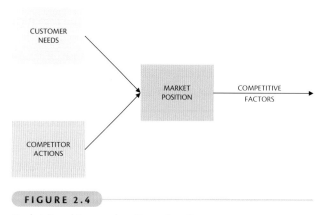

FIGURE 2.4

Market-Based Approach to Operations Strategy.

(Gaither and Frazier, 2002), but the term 'competitive factors' will be used here. Competitive factor is the term used to describe the dimension on which a product or service wins orders in the Hill methodology for operation strategy formulation described later in this chapter. Some examples of competitive factors are terms such as fast delivery, a wide range of services or a low price.

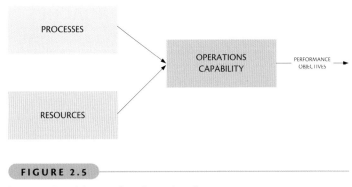

FIGURE 2.5

Resource-Based Approach to Operations Strategy

Resource-Based Approach to Operations Strategy

A **resource-based view of operations strategy** works from the 'inside-out' of the firm, rather than the 'outside-in' perspective of the market-based approach. Here an assessment of the operation's resources and processes leads to a view of the operation's capability (Figure 2.5).

The operations resources are categorized in Chapter 1 into transforming and transformed resources. Transforming resources are the facilities and staff that do the work on the transformed resources that deliver the goods or services to the customer. The transformed resources can be classified into materials, customers and information. However, even more important to the capability of an organization may be its intangible resources such as brand loyalty, supplier relationships, technological skills, design skills and a detailed understanding of customer markets. The important point to consider regarding an organization's intangible resources is that their value may not be recognized (they may not necessarily be included on the firm's balance sheet) and they are most likely to have been developed over time through experience and a process of learning. This second attribute makes them less easy to copy by competitors than tangible assets that can be bought in relatively rapidly. Processes are the way in which the firm operates its resources. Processes may follow formal rules laid down in company documentation, but informal processes are likely to form a large part of the way in which the organization operates. Informal processes are undertaken in a way that is dependent on factors such as the knowledge accumulated by staff, the relationships between staff members and the shared values and understandings of members of the organization. The nature and complexity of formal and informal processes and tangible and intangible resources is central to the resource-based view of strategy that the externally unobservable (within firm) factors are at least as important as observable industry market (between firm) factors in determining competitive advantage. The area of organizational learning (Chapter 18) is relevant to a resource-based view of operations strategy in terms of managing and developing capabilities.

Reconciling the Market-Based and Resource-Based Strategy Approaches

It has been found that not all companies pursue strategy in accordance with a pure market-based approach and it has been found that competitiveness is not just a matter of simply improving performance along specific competitive dimensions, but incorporates the development of capabilities that provide specific operating advantages. Thus the resource-based view of strategy is that operations takes a more active role in providing long-term competitive advantage. Thus resource and process decisions are not only concerned with implementing a chosen competitive strategy but are required to provide the platform for the development of new capabilities that are difficult for competitors to replicate. Thus the idea is that a resource-based view is not a substitute for a market position developed under a market-based view of strategy, but operation capabilities can allow a company to take up an attractive market position and can protect it from competitive threat (Figure 2.6).

What makes the development of operations strategy particularly challenging is that not only should the market-based and resource-based views of strategy be considered at a point in time but the changing characteristics of markets and the need to develop operations capabilities over time means a dynamic as well as a static view of strategy is required. For example, dynamic capabilities (Teece and Pisano, 1994) are built from the firm's resources and processes mediated by external market influences, but also driven by how managers make judgements about the firm and its future. In a market-based

FIGURE 2.6

Reconciling the Market-Based and Resource-Based Approaches to Operations Strategy.

CASE STUDY 2.4

Texon

Sales of Texon jeans label material T484 continue to grow across the globe. Texon T484 cellulose material is available in eight different colour options, offering a distinct advantage over competitors who offer a very limited choice. Our product gauges run from 0.55 mm to 0.80 mm thick, and the material is available in rolls or sheets. Texon T484 was first introduced in 1991 – when over 50 tons were sold. By 2003, the volume had increased to nearly 800 tons. From this quantity of almost 2 million m² of material, labels can be produced for around 460 million pairs of jeans. 2004 is expected to see a significant growth with sales going into 34 countries around the world. According to statistics, the world production of jeans is estimated at around 3 billion pairs, of which approximately

1.5 to 1.7 billion pairs feature a label made from cellulose material. In other words, one third of the world's production of jeans has a Texon jeans label. Texon continues to build on our shoemaking and innovative materials expertise to apply skills beyond footwear to other industries requiring high quality, high performance non-woven and cellulose products in apparel, automotive, furniture, luggage and filtration.

Source: Texon T484 'Jeans label' Success Continues", www.texon.com/news/2004. Reproduced with permisson.

Question

Relate market-based and resource-based strategy approaches to Texon.

approach, in addition to market needs changing over time, different product/service groups will have different performance objectives. For example, First Class air travel will focus on performance objectives of quality in terms of safety and a high specification, flexibility in terms of ticketing options and speed in terms of fast-track processing at airports. Economy class travel will focus on the performance objectives of price and quality in terms of safety. The issue of ensuring the operations strategy matches requirements in a dynamic system is discussed in the next section on alignment.

OPERATIONS STRATEGY ALIGNMENT

'Alignment' in operations strategy is the process of continually reconciling operations capabilities with market requirements so that there is an approximate degree of 'fit' between them. This process is difficult to achieve because it is not always clear what the capabilities of operations are at a particular point in time and also market requirements may not be understood. In addition, different parts of the firm may be pursuing different objectives and so there may not be agreement on the point at which operations capabilities and market requirements are in alignment. Taking the two variables of market requirements and the level of capability of operations there are four ways in which the 'fit' (i.e. alignment) between the two variables can be lost (Figure 2.7).

In practice most operations strategies emphasize a market-based (rather than resource-based) approach to strategy alignment because more tools and techniques are available for classifying and identifying market requirements, most organizations' strategy formulation is driven top-down where operations' role is to support market-driven decisions, all organizations have customers/markets they probably understand better than their operations capabilities and not all organizations have 'distinctive' capabilities they can compete on.

As well as the fit between market requirements and operations capability another aspect to consider is the *level of alignment* between these two variables. This relates how difficult the market requirements

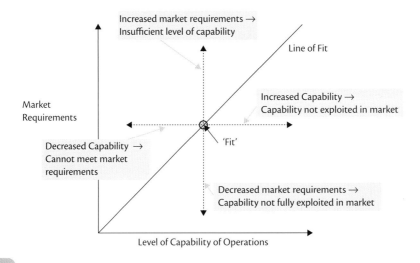

FIGURE 2.7

Fit between the Alignment of Market Requirements and Operations Capability.

 www.wileyopenpage.com

and the corresponding operations capability are to achieve. In a low alignment scenario market needs are relatively undemanding and you don't need particularly well developed capabilities to meet them. In a high alignment scenario demanding levels of market requirements are matched with unique and strategic operations capabilities. It follows that a high alignment strategy could be seen as more desirable as it is generally more difficult for competitors to match (Figure 2.8).

An additional aspect to consider is how close the match between market requirements and operations capability is needed in a particular scenario. The closeness of alignment can be expressed on a scale from loose (implies that a close fit is not required) to tight (implies a close fit is required). The relevance of this aspect is that as market requirements and resource capabilities change over time a tight alignment will mean any change can mean a loss of fit whilst a looser set of capabilities and market requirements can provide some insurance against any unexpected shifts (Figure 2.9).

In summary the concept of fit implies that operation strategy formulation should be repeated over time in order to ensure that alignment is maintained. This will be particularly relevant when there is a tight fit between market requirements and operations capability. In addition an organization can either defend their current market/resource position or increase their level of alignment to achieve sustained alignment.

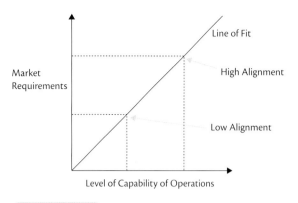

FIGURE 2.8

Low and High Alignment of Market Requirements and Operations Capabilities.

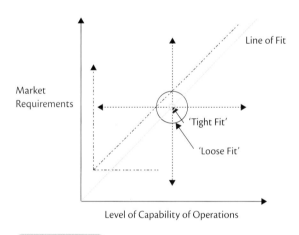

FIGURE 2.9

Tight and Loose Fit between Market Requirements and Operations Capability.

OPERATIONS STRATEGY FORMULATION

There are various approaches to operations strategy formulation including the Platts-Gregory procedure (1992). The following approach to operations strategy provides useful guidance in dealing with the issue of aligning operations to competitive needs. The emphasis within the Hill methodology (Hill and Hill, 2012) is that strategic decisions cannot be made based on information regarding customer and marketing opportunities addressed solely from a marketing-function perspective; the operations capability must also be taken into account. Hill proposes that the issue of the degree of 'fit' between the proposed marketing strategy and the operation's ability to support it is resolved at the business level in terms of meeting corporate (strategic) objectives. Thus Hill provides an iterative framework that links together the corporate objectives (which provide the organizational direction), the marketing strategy (which defines how the organization will compete in its chosen markets) and the operations strategy (which provides capability to compete in those markets). The framework consists of five steps:

1. Define corporate objectives.
2. Determine marketing strategies to meet these objectives.
3. Assess how different products win orders against competitors.
4. Establish the most appropriate mode to deliver these sets of products.
5. Provide the infrastructure required to support operations.

In traditional strategy formulation the outcome of step 3 is 'passed on' to steps 4 and 5 and no further feedback occurs between steps in the process. The Hill methodology requires iteration between all five steps in order to link operations capability into decisions at a corporate level. This model is shown graphically in Table 2.3.

The steps in the Hill methodology are now described in more detail.

TABLE 2.3

Framework for Reflecting Operations Strategy Issues in Corporate Decisions.

			Operations strategy	
1	2	3	4	5
Corporate objectives	**Marketing strategy**	**How do you qualify and win orders in the marketplace?**	**Delivery system choice**	**Infrastructure choice**
Sales revenue growth	Product/service markets and segments	Price	Choice of various delivery systems	Function support
Survival	Range	Quality conformance	Trade-offs embodied in these choices	Operations planning and control systems
Profit	Mix	Delivery: speed, reliability	Make-or-buy decisions	Quality assurance and control
Return on investment	Volumes	Demand increases	Capacity: size, timing, location	Systems engineering
Other financial measures	Standardization versus customization	Colour range	Role of inventory in the delivery system	Clerical procedures
Environmental targets	Level of innovation	Product/service range		Payment systems
	Leader versus follower alternatives	Design leadership		Work structuring
		Techical support supplied		Organizational structure
		Brand name		
		New products and services – time to market		

Source: Terry Hill, Operations Management: Context and Managerial Analysis, 2000, Palgrave Macmillan. Reproduced with permission.

 www.wileyopenpage.com

Step 1: Corporate Objectives

Step 1 involves establishing corporate objectives, which provide a direction for the organization, and performance indicators, which allow progress in achieving those objectives to be measured. The objectives will depend on the needs of external and internal stakeholders and so will include financial measures such as profit and growth rates as well as employee practices such as skills development and appropriate environmental policies.

Step 2: Marketing Strategy

Step 2 involves developing a marketing strategy to meet the corporate objectives defined in step 1. This involves identifying target markets and deciding how to compete in these markets. This will require the use of product/service characteristics such as range, mix and volume that the operations activity will be required to provide. Other issues considered will be the level of innovation and product development and the choice of 'leader' or 'follower' strategies in the chosen markets.

Step 3: How do you Qualify and Win Orders in the Marketplace?

This is the crucial stage in Hill's methodology where any mismatches between the requirements of the organization's strategy and the operations capability are revealed. This step provides the link between corporate marketing proposals and the operations processes and infrastructure necessary to support them. This is achieved by translating the marketing strategy into a range of **competitive factors** (for example, price, quality, delivery speed) on which the product or service wins orders. These external competitive factors provide the most important indicator as to the relative importance of the internal operations performance objectives discussed earlier in this chapter.

At this stage it is necessary to clarify the nature of the markets that operations will serve in order for us to identify the relative importance of the range of competitive factors on which the product or service wins orders. This will in turn enable us to identify the performance objectives that operations will need to focus on. The following three approaches are considered:

1. Customers (Hill)

Customers will value a range of competitive factors for any particular product/service, thus it is necessary to identify the relative importance of a range of factors. Hill distinguishes between the following types of competitive factors which relate to securing customer orders in the marketplace:

- *Order-winning factors.* These are factors that contribute to winning business from customers. They are key reasons for customers purchasing the goods or services and raising the performance of the order-winning factor may secure more business.
- *Qualifying factors.* These are factors that are required in order to be considered for business from customers. Performance of qualifying factors must be at a certain level to gain business from customers but performance above this level will not necessarily gain further competitive advantage.

From the descriptions above it can be seen that it is therefore essential to meet both qualifying and order-winning criteria in order to be considered and then win customer orders.

FIGURE 2.10

The Relationship between Order Winning Competitive Factors and Performance Objectives.

Hill's concept of 'order-winning' and 'qualifying' factors helps distinguish between those factors that directly contribute to winning business and those that are necessary to qualify for the customer's consideration between a range of products/services. The importance of this is that while it may be necessary to raise performance on some (qualifying) factors to a certain level in order to be considered by the customer, a further rise in the level of performance may not achieve an increase in competitiveness. Instead competitiveness may then depend on raising the level of performance of different 'order-winning' factors higher than competitors. Because it is more difficult to raise performance to the best-in-class than it is to be considered in the race it is the order-winning competitive factors that should be translated into the internal performance objectives that the organization must excel at. Figure 2.10 provides examples of how different (external) order-winning competitive factors will require a focus on the corresponding (internal) performance objectives. Figure 2.10 does not imply a one-to-one relationship between order-winning competitive factors and performance objectives. This is because of the interrelationships between the performance objectives, for example, speed will be partly dependent on other performance objectives such as cost and dependability. Thus the figure shows that a particular external order-winning competitive factor will provide an indication of the relative importance of the internal performance objective.

2. Customers and Competitors (Slack)

Competitor actions will also influence the basis on which competition is based and may require a change in priorities of the competitive factors used by the organization. For example, if an organization is competing on price and a competitor enters the market and takes market share by competing on faster delivery, the organization may need to consider that as a new competitive factor. The significance of this influence is that the initiative for change has been provided by a competitor, not the customer.

Slack (1991) uses a combination of customer and competitive factors using two dimensions – importance and performance – to help operations managers prioritize performance objectives. The relative *importance* of a competitive factor is assessed in terms of its importance to internal or external customers using a nine-point scale of degrees of order-winning, qualifying and less important customer viewed competitive factors (Table 2.4).

www.wileyopenpage.com

TABLE 2.4

A Nine-Point Scale of Importance.

Order	Strong	1	Provides a crucial advantage
winner	Medium	2	Provides an important advantage
	Weak	3	Provides a useful advantage
Qualifier	Strong	4	Needs to be up to good industry standard
	Medium	5	Needs to be up to median industry standard
	Weak	6	Needs to be within close range of the rest of industry
Less important	Strong	7	Not usually of importance but could become more so
	Medium	8	Very rarely considered by customers
	Weak	9	Never considered by customers

Source: Slack, Chambers and Johnston (2007), Operations Management, Fig 18.6a, Prentice Hall. Reproduced with permission.

The next step ranks the relative *performance* of a competitive factor against competitor achievement. Benchmarking in this way clarifies the competitive position of the organization and helps identify where performance should be improved. A nine-point performance scale (rating from consistently better than the nearest competitor to consistently worse than most competitors) is used for each performance objective (Table 2.5).

The next step is to plot each importance rating and performance rating in an importance–performance matrix. This indicates what customers find important in achieved performance when compared with competitor performance. The importance–performance matrix is divided into four zones (Figure 2.11). The zones are defined as follows:

- *Appropriate* – performance objectives in this zone are satisfactory in the short to medium term, but there should be a wish to improve performance towards the upper boundary of the zone.
- *Improve* – performance objectives below the lower bound of the appropriate zone will be candidates for improvement.

TABLE 2.5

A Nine-Point Scale of Performance.

Better than competitors	Strong	1	Considerably better than competitors
	Medium	2	Clearly better than competitors
	Weak	3	Marginally better than competitors
Same as competitors	Strong	4	Sometimes marginally better than competitors
	Medium	5	About the same as most competitors
	Weak	6	Slightly lower than the average of most competitors
Worse than competitors	Strong	7	Usually marginally worse than most competitors
	Medium	8	Usually worse than competitors
	Weak	9	Consistently worse than competitors

Source: Slack, Chambers and Johnston (2007), Operations Management, Fig 18.6b, Prentice Hall. Reproduced with permission.

www.wileyopenpage.com

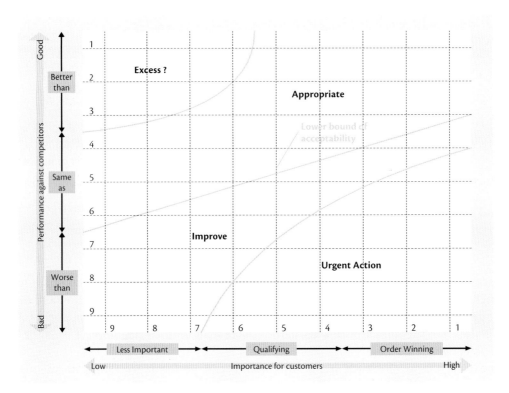

FIGURE 2.11

Priority Zones in the Importance–Performance Matrix.
Source: Slack, Chambers and Johnston (2007), Operations Management, Fig 18.7, Prentice Hall. Reproduced with permission.

- *Urgent action* – here performance objectives are far below what the customer requires and so should be improved to 'same as' or 'better than' competitor performance.
- *Excess* – here too many resources may be being used to achieve this level of performance. There is a possibility that they could be deployed to a less well performing area.

Although the main thrust of the operations function will be to move the performance objectives up the vertical scale and so outperform competitors, horizontal movement (changing customer perceptions of the relative importance of competitive factors) should be considered. The position of the performance objectives on the matrix will change, without any actions from the organization, as customer preferences change and competitor performance improves. Thus improvement strategies should take the dynamic nature of the variables into account.

3. Customers and Competitors (The Product/Service Life Cycle)

The product/service life cycle (PLC) provides one way of generalizing customer and competitor behaviour over time. The PLC is an attempt to describe the change in sales volume for a particular product or service from being introduced into a market until its withdrawal. The model shows sales volume

www.wileyopenpage.com

passing through the four stages: introduction, growth, maturity and decline (Figure 2.12). The model is useful in that each stage in the life cycle requires a different approach from the operations function and thus emphasizes the need for a range of capabilities from the operations function. The drawback of the approach is that it may be difficult to predict when the product/service will enter the next stage of the cycle or even determine what stage of the cycle the product/service is currently in! The main stages of the PLC can be described as follows:

- *Introduction.* On introduction the product/service specification may frequently be changed as feedback is received from customers. Operations will need to maintain flexibility in terms of design changes and response to changes in demand levels. Quality levels need to be maintained, despite frequent design changes, in order to ensure customer acceptance.
- *Growth.* If the introduction of the product/service has been successful then a period of sales growth occurs. Competitors may also enter the market. The main concern of operations will be to meet what may be a rapid increase in demand whilst maintaining quality levels.
- *Maturity.* After a period of growth, customer demand will be largely satisfied and demand will level off. The market may be dominated by a few organizations offering a standard product/service. Competition on price will be important and so the main issues for operations will be minimizing costs and maintaining a dependable supply.
- *Decline.* After a certain time the need for a product/service will be satisfied, or a new product/service will be introduced undertaking the tasks of the original. At this point sales will decline, competitors will drop out of the market and remaining competition will be focused on price, indicating a need for operations to minimize costs.

Step 4: Delivery System Choice (Structural Decisions) and Step 5: Infrastructure Choice (Infrastructural Decisions)

Steps 4 and 5 of Hill's methodology involve putting the processes and resources in place that provide the required performance as defined by the performance objectives. Hill categorizes

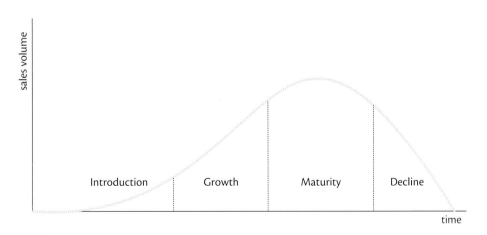

FIGURE 2.12

The Product/Service Life Cycle.

operations decision areas into delivery system choice, which is often referred to as structural decisions, and infrastructure choice, commonly termed infrastructural decisions. These categories are useful because they indicate how the potential of the operation is limited by its structure, but it can only reach that potential if used with the appropriate infrastructure which governs the way it works on a day-to-day basis. It should be noted though that operations decision areas will have both a structural and infrastructural element to them. For example, the implementation of process technology will affect both physical resources and systems and the policies and practices of the operation. The steps are now outlined, with references to the relevant chapters for decision areas within this text.

Delivery system choice, also termed **structural decisions**, concerns aspects of the organization's physical resources such as service delivery systems and capacity provision. These elements may be expensive and difficult to change quickly and so provide the basic capability of the operations system. Structural decisions include the choice of process type implemented in manufacturing (project, jobbing, batch, line or continuous) or services (professional, shop or mass) covered in Chapter 3 and the associated layout types covered in Chapter 4. Capacity issues include the volume, timing and location of capacity provision covered in Chapter 5. The provision of process technology for materials, information and customers is covered in Chapter 6.

Infrastructural decisions describe the systems, policies and practices that determine how the structural elements covered in step 4 are managed. Structural decisions determine the overall capability of the operations system but infrastructure elements determine how much of this capability is realized. Infrastructural decisions include the management of the product and service design process (Chapter 7), the management of organizational processes (Chapter 8), the design of jobs (Chapter 9), the management of capacity (Chapter 10), scheduling of operations (Chapter 11), inventory management (Chapter 12), planning and control systems such as JIT and ERP (Chapter 13 and Chapter 14), supply chain management (Chapter 15) and project management (Chapter 16). In addition, quality systems (Chapter 17) and performance measurement (Chapter 18) systems are also included under this heading.

It is important that structural and infrastructural decisions should be in alignment with one another and with the operations strategy in order to create the required capabilities defined by the performance objectives. This can be difficult as structural and infrastructural decisions are often taken at various points in time by people within different areas of the organization. This implies that the operations strategy needs to be clearly communicated across the organization if implementation of structural and infrastructural changes is to keep pace with changing competitive priorities. It should also be noted that there is no single solution to achieving a certain set of competitive priorities for the organization. For example, one firm may concentrate on structural elements such as process technology and another competing firm may concentrate on infrastructural elements such as a TQM programme. Slack and Lewis (2011) describe operations strategy as the intersection of a company's performance objectives with its decision areas. The process of reconciliation between the market-based and resource-based views of operations strategy takes place between these intersections. A strategy matrix (Slack and Lewis, 2011) can be used to show the intersections between what is required from the operations function (the relative priority given to each performance objective) and how the operation tries to achieve this through the set of choices made (and the capabilities which have been developed) in each decision area.

www.wileyopenpage.com

OPERATIONS STRATEGY IMPLEMENTATION

Earlier in this chapter it was stated that the aim of the organization's operations strategy will be to seek a fit between the way it competes in the market and how operations is designed and managed. This 'fit' can be achieved in many ways and will in part be dependent on the operations' current capabilities. Step 3 of Hill's methodology involves providing a 'fit' between the external competitive factors derived from the market position and the internal performance objectives derived from the operations processes and resources (infrastructure). This section attempts to understand the relationship between the performance objectives and how we can approach changes in their absolute and relative performance through a discussion of the concepts of trade-offs and focus.

Trade-offs

The idea of **trade-offs** (Skinner, 1985) provides a way of understanding the way in which the performance objectives relate to one another. The original idea of trade-offs is that there is a trade-off relationship between competitive objectives, such as cost, quality or delivery, which means that to excel in only one objective usually entails poor performance in some or all of the others. Thus an attempt to be good at everything will lead to being mediocre at everything. The existence of trade-offs means that optimum solutions must be sought within the inherent limits (constraints) of the operation. Any pair of performance measures potentially constitutes a trade-off and it is important to identify operations trade-off relationships. An example of a trade-off between customer service (which can be considered to constitute the four performance objectives of quality, speed, dependability and flexibility) and resource efficiency (which can be considered as determining the remaining performance objective of cost) is shown in Figure 2.13.

In order to analyse this trade-off it is necessary to understand that the resource efficiency of a system determines the cost of producing a product while customer service will influence selling price. Profitability is a function of both total production cost and sales revenue. The trade-off relationship means that to gain an improvement on one side of the profitability model, there will be a consequent penalty to be paid on the other. An example of this relationship is a trade-off

FIGURE 2.13

Trade-off Relationship between Customer Service and Resource Efficiency.

between delivery performance and the cost of holding high stocks of materials. The better delivery performance is in a trade-off with the cost of material stocks. Alternatively, the improvement and penalty may both lie on the same side of the model. An example of this is between overhead and material costs. Machine overheads can be reduced by increasing their utilization and by building stocks of materials; conversely reducing material stocks adversely affects utilization and increases overheads.

In general there are three scenarios for the use of trade-offs.

1. Working within Capabilities

A characteristic of trade-offs is that if the operation is working well within its capability then one aspect of performance may be improved without a decrease in performance in its trade-off relationship. In effect the capabilities of the operation exceed the requirements of the markets and excess capability is being unused.

2. Repositioning Trade-offs

Repositioning trade-offs is to manage the trade-off factors within the constraints of the operations system. This involves ensuring that an operation's relative achievement in each dimension of performance should be driven by the requirements of the market. This is not a straightforward process as there may be costs and risks involved in changing relative performance levels and the complexity of trade-off relationships can mean that other trade-offs are affected. This approach is characterized by an acceptance of the constraints of the operations system but it can in itself lead to an improvement in overall performance.

3. Overcoming Trade-offs

This approach is through improvement and loosening the constraints on the operations system, termed 'overcoming trade-offs'. This involves increasing the capability of operations to enable improvement in both dimensions of performance or improvement in one dimension while preventing or limiting any deterioration in the other. This, again, is not a straightforward process and requires costs and risks in improving performance levels. Chapter 18 covers improvement approaches.

Performance Frontiers

The three approaches to trade-offs outlined above can be described through the use of the concept of the performance frontier (Figure 2.14). The performance frontier shows the overall limit of performance at a particular trade-off between performance objectives. The first approach of working within capabilities shows that performance can be improved without a decrease in the performance of the trade-off relationship (moving from A → B in Figure 2.14). A repositioning approach means moving along current performance frontier (moving from B → C in Figure 2.14). Overcoming trade-offs means extending the current performance natural frontier to an extended performance frontier (moving from B → B1 in Figure 2.14). Note that at the extended performance frontier trade-offs still exist but at a higher level of overall performance.

Showing Approaches to Trade-offs Using the Performance Frontiers.

The Sandcone Theory

The idea of trade-offs is challenged by the belief that performance can be improved simultaneously along multiple dimensions. Indeed, Figure 2.3 shows how improvements in the performance objectives of quality, dependability, speed and flexibility can lead to both benefits from these improvements themselves as well as leading to an improvement in the performance objective of cost. Furthermore, Ferdows and de Meyer (1990) state that operational excellence can be built in a cumulative fashion. Their **sandcone theory** maintains that there is an ideal sequence in which operational capabilities should be developed of quality, dependability, speed, flexibility and finally achieving excellence in cost. A cumulative effort to improve should begin with improvements in quality and when a minimum acceptable level of performance is reached, improvements are pursued in both quality and dependability. The full sequence of improvement is:

1. Quality.
2. Quality + dependability.
3. Quality + dependability + speed.
4. Quality + dependability + speed + flexibility.
5. Quality + dependability + speed + flexibility + cost.

This approach both highlights the need to only target reduction in costs after improvements in the other performance objectives have been secured and implies that certain operational capabilities enhance one another allowing improvements across multiple performance objectives.

Focus

The whole nature of the trade-off relationship can be changed by how resources are deployed and processes organized with the operations system. One such change is the implementation of the idea of focus. The concept of **focus** (Skinner, 1974) is to align particular market demands with individual facilities to reduce the level of complexity generated when attempting to service a number of different market segments from an individual organization. This is because it is difficult and probably inadvisable for operations to try to offer superior performance over competitors across all of the performance objectives. Usually organizations succeed when they organize their resources and compete across one or two performance objectives. Also the capabilities of the organization will usually mean that it can do some things better than others and a strategy that uses inherent strengths will be more likely to offer a competitive advantage. This does not mean that capabilities cannot be changed over time, but it is likely that at any one time there are certain things that an organization can do well and certain things that it cannot do satisfactorily, if at all.

The idea of focus has been used by many firms to break up large and complex organizations into more simple and focused operations. Although many managers argue that the breakup of organizations leads to higher costs in terms of duplication of equipment, floor space and overheads, many companies have found that focusing has led to a decrease in operating and overhead costs. Many of the advantages of focus can be obtained without the subdivision of the organization using methods such as:

- Simplification through elimination of product or services that are seldom requested by customers.
- Operation-within-an-operation. This involves dividing a facility into separated work areas, with the advantage of reducing the considerable expense of setting up independent operations. Just-in-time or lean production facilities often use the idea of the *focused factory* to organize their functions around a relatively narrow range of products or a product family (a group of products that share similar production requirements) in order to ensure simple and consistent operations.
- Cell layout – dedicating a small group of people and equipment to a subset of products or services (Chapter 4).
- Process design – using business process management to provide an integrated design for the processing steps involved in the manufacture of a product or delivery of a service (Chapter 8).

The implementation of a focus strategy requires a decision regarding both the dimension on which the focus is based and the level of focus that is required across this dimension. There are many different dimensions in which focus can be applied, including on a range of products or services (product focus), on market or customer groups (market focus) or on the process needs of products or services (process focus). Focus could also be based on competitive factors (such as low cost). This approach aims to ensure that the conditions are created where operations can excel at the criteria that are necessary for market success. Focus based in this way will need to reflect changes in the relative competitive factors of customer needs and competitor actions.

The level of focus can range from, say, separate cells producing each product or service at one extreme to producing all products and services from one operations facility at the other. The temptation is to add new products and service types to existing facilities over time in order to secure market share, adding complexity and losing focus. At some point a decision should be made on either simplifying the product or service range or subdividing the operation.

Benefits of the focus approach include increased clarity in the day-to-day management of operations resources and the ability to focus processes and resources for a specific subset of operations. Process improvement initiatives can also be more successful within a focused operation. However, the idea of focus, by definition, limits the scope of what the operations system can do and thus makes it vulnerable to shifts in the competitive environment. Focus also risks losing economy of scale advantages when resources that were once shared are now dedicated to separate departments (for example, discounts on high-volume purchasing may be lost).

SUMMARY

- Strategy can be seen to exist at the corporate, business and functional levels of the organization. Operations may provide the organization with the basis for its competitive advantage.
- The five basic operations performance objectives are quality, speed, dependability, flexibility and cost. The performance objectives allow an operation to measure its performance in achieving strategic goals.
- The market-based approach selects a market position and defines a list of objectives in order to successfully compete in that market. A resource-based approach provides an assessment of the operations processes and resources, which leads to a view of a capability of operations.
- The Hill methodology for strategy development provides an iterative framework that links together corporate objectives, the marketing strategy and the operations strategy.
- Systems are used by operations managers to measure the influence of customers (Hill) and the influence of customers and competitors (Slack) on the relative importance of the competitive factors in securing customer orders.
- The idea of trade-offs can be used to help understand the way in which the performance objectives relate to one another.
- The concept of focus aligns particular market demands with individual facilities.

CASE STUDY 2.5

Pure Gym

Tony Harris, Pure Gym Chief Executive Officer, joined the company to continue with the company's ongoing expansion throughout the UK, aiming to further develop its position as the nation's leading low cost gym operator. On his arrival he said: 'Affordable gyms are redefining the market for fitness in the UK. Pure Gym is at the forefront of this revolution with its focus on providing quality and value to a rapidly expanding membership. I am proud to be joining such an energetic and imaginative team.'

In February 2012 Pure Gym's annualised turnover was £23.8 million (up from 10.4 million), with confidence in its operation boosted with pre-tax profits up from just £10,613 to £1.2m in 2011? and funding to push forward its expansion (each club requiring an investment of

£800 000–£1m) with an agreement with Barclays Bank extended their £3.5 million facility to £7.0 million in August 2011 and to £15.0 million in January 2012.

The budget gym group, started in 2009 with just four clubs, Pure Gym has achieved significant growth over the last couple of years, with over 170 000 members (February 2011: 60 000) who look after their health and fitness needs in one of 40 of their clubs, with an additional 22 planned to open soon (October 2012) and a roll out strategy that aims to achieve 65 open and operational sites by the end of 2013.

In what has proved to be a big shake-up of the £2.5bn fitness Industry, Pure Gym has been removing industry stereotypes such as inflexible contracts, limited opening hours and high cost memberships. The network of clubs are open 24/7, offer a full range of state of the art equipment grouped together within some of the most spacious clubs in the country, with showers, changing rooms and locker facilities. The organization offers great value memberships, which are not hard sold, starting from £10 per month, completed on touch screen on-line computers, without all the paperwork or the dreaded 12 month contract.

Competition is rife, David Lloyd, Fitness First, and Roko naming just a few who all offer an impressive range of facilities, but with member ships reaching £60, they come at a cost. Pure Gym's operation strategy strips away club receptions, swimming pools, sky sports, squash and tennis courts, saunas, cafe bars and fluffy towels to keep costs low. And the tradeoff does not stop there, the clubs to not have parking facilities, new equipment is only added when membership number targets are reached, and queues can form at the code rotating doors that form the entrance/exit. Whilst the clubs are kept clean, neither hygiene gels nor paper towels are provided within the gymnasium, the club looks at such as an unnecessary cost, they instead ask members to bring a towel.

The strategy certainly looks to be working in a health conscious market with reduced public disposable income, whether it will prove to be sustainable, many will have eyes open with great interest.

Sources

http://www.telegraph.co.uk/finance/newsbysector/retailandconsumer/leisure/9248121/Pure-Gym-in-good-shape-for-a-sale.html

http://uk.finance.yahoo.com/news/pure-gym-37m-expansion-push-202610632.html

http://www.puregym.com/concept

http://www.puregym.com/downloads/Pure-Gym-new-CEO-appointment-press-release.pdf

Source: Written by Briony Boydell and Chris Milner. Reproduced with permission.

Questions

1. How sustainable do you think the 'Pure Gym' Strategy is?
2. What performance objectives have Pure Gym aimed to achieve?

Quizzes to test yourself further are available in your interactive e-book at **www.wileyopenpage.com**

Flashcards to test yourself further are available in your interactive e-book at **www.wileyopenpage.com**

EXERCISES

1. Evaluate strategy development at the corporate, business and functional levels of an organization.

2. Indicate how a major investment decision could be analysed in terms of its effect on the capability of the operations function.

3. How can the relative significance of the five performance objectives be determined in the formulation of the organization's strategic direction?

4. Discuss the main types of flexibility.

5. Explain the significance for management of linking operations strategy, marketing strategy and corporate objectives.

6. Evaluate the strategic role of the operations function.

7. Evaluate the potential advantages and disadvantages of focused manufacturing.

8. Compare and contrast the concepts of trade-offs and agile operations (Chapter 15).

9. Does an improvement in one performance objective necessarily mean a reduction in the performance of others?

WEB EXERCISE

Visit the web site containing the annual reports for Marks and Spencer PLC at http://annualreport.marksandspencer.com/_assets/downloads/Marks-and-Spencer-Annual-report-and-financial-statements-2012.pdf (accessed 12 June 2012). What role does operations have in supporting the company's strategy?

FURTHER READING

Brown, S., Bessant, J. and Lamming, R. (2013) *Strategic Operations Management*, 3rd edn, Routledge.

Fetzinger, E. and Hau, L.L. (1997) Mass customization at Hewlett Packard: the power of postponement. *Harvard Business Review*, 75 (1), 116–21.

Hayes, R., Pisano, G., Upton, D. and Wheelwright, S. (2005) *Operations, Strategy, and Technology: Pursuing the Competitive Edge*, John Wiley & Sons, Ltd.

WEB LINKS

www.geckoheadgear.co.uk (accessed 12 June 2012). Gecko headgear site.

www.softwareceo.com (accessed 12 June 2012). Many articles available on operations strategy.

REFERENCES

Caulkin, S. (2002) Business: the basics that beat the world: making things better and cheaper is the best strategy of all. *Observer*, 3 November 2002.

Ferdows, K. and de Meyer, A. (1990) Lasting improvements in manufacturing. *Journal of Operations Management*, 9 (2), 168–84.

Gaither, N. and Frazier, G. (2002) *Operations Management*, 9th edn, SouthWestern.

Hayes, R.H. and Wheelwright, S.C. (1988) *Restoring Our Competitive Edge: Competing Through Manufacturing*, John Wiley & Sons, Ltd.

Hill, A. and Hill, T. (2012) *Operations Management*, 3rd edn, Palgrave Macmillan.

Johnson, G., Whittington, R. and Scholes, K. (2011) *Exploring Strategy: Text and Cases*, 9th edn, FT Prentice Hall.

Mintzberg, H. and Waters, J.A. (1995) Of strategies: deliberate and emergent. *Strategic Management Journal,* 6 (3), 257–72.

Platts, K.W. and Gregory, M.J. (1992) A Manufacturing Audit Approach to Strategy Formulation. In: Voss, C.A., *Manufacturing Strategy – Process and Content*. London: Chapman & Hall.

Skinner, W. (1974) The focused factory. *Harvard Business Review,* May–June, 113–21.

Skinner, W. (1985) Manufacturing: *The Formidable Competitive Weapon,* John Wiley & Sons, Ltd.

Slack, N. (1991) *Manufacturing Advantage: Achieving Competitive Manufacturing Operations*, Mercury.

Slack, N., Chambers, S. and Johnston, R. (2010) *Operations Management*, 6th edn, Pearson Education Ltd.

Slack, N. and Lewis, M. (2011) *Operations Strategy*, 3rd edn, Pearson Education Ltd.

Teece, D.J. and Pisano, G. (1994) The dynamic capabilities of firms: an introduction. *Industrial and Corporate Change,* 3 (3), 537–56.

Process Types

- **Introduction**
- **Manufacturing process types**
- **Service process types**
- **Matching process type with volume and variety**
- **Choosing a process type**

LEARNING OBJECTIVES

- Describe the main manufacturing process types
- Describe the main service process types
- Discuss an alternative service process type definition
- Explain the relationship between process type and the operations volume and variety of output
- Discuss the process type decision.

PROCESS TYPES AND OPERATIONS STRATEGY

Process type choice is strategic because it can represent a large amount of capital investment in terms of equipment and workforce and so sets a constraint around which the company can compete, in particular it may limit entry to markets and the products and services that can be delivered. The difficulty of the procedure of process type choice is that process decisions can take a relatively large amount of time and money to implement whereas market needs in a competitive environment can change rapidly. The project and jobbing process types imply a wide variety of output which will require meeting market requirements for design and innovation. The batch process type covers a wide range of volume and variety outputs and so to ensure strategic focus the organization needs to distinguish between batch towards the jobbing end of the continuum and batch towards the mass end of the volume/variety continuum. Mass and continuous process types imply selling a narrow range of standard products in high volumes.

INTRODUCTION

In operations, the design of the process is categorized into manufacturing and services. The choice of process design depends mostly on the volume and variety of the product or service that the organization offers. Manufacturing and services providers generally serve their customers on a continuum between a combination of low-variety and high-volume products and services to a combination of high-variety and low-volume products and services. This chapter provides categories for process designs, called process types, for different volume and variety combinations. The reasons for matching a particular volume and variety combination with a particular process type are then discussed.

MANUFACTURING PROCESS TYPES

In manufacturing, process types can be considered under five categories: project, jobbing, batch, mass and continuous (Figure 3.1). A description of each process type is followed by some examples of where each process type might be used.

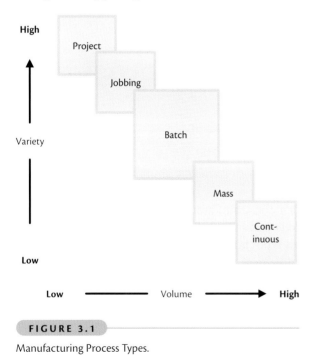

FIGURE 3.1

Manufacturing Process Types.

Project

Processes that produce high-variety and low-volume products are termed projects. **Project processes** are used to make one-off products to a customer specification. A feature of a project process is that the location of the product is stationary. This means that transforming resources such as staff and equipment that make the product must move or be moved to the location of the product. Other characteristics of projects are that they may require the coordination of many individuals and activities, demand a problem-solving approach to ensure they are completed on time and have a comparatively long duration of manufacture. The timescale of the completion of the project is an important performance measure. Because each project is unique it is likely that transforming resources will comprise general-purpose equipment that can be used on a number of projects. Examples of the use of a project process include building construction (Figure 3.2), movie film production and custom-built furniture.

Jobbing

Processes that produce high-variety and low-volume products are termed 'jobbing'. **Jobbing processes** are used to make a one-off (or low volume) product to a customer specification. A feature of a jobbing process is that the product moves to the location of transforming resources such as equipment. Thus resources such as staff and equipment can be shared between many products. Other characteristics of jobbing processes are the use of skilled labour in order to cope with the need for cus-

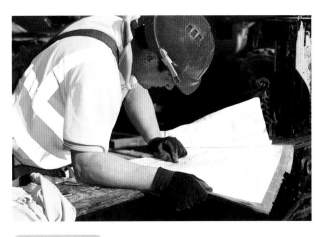

FIGURE 3.2

A Construction Site: An Example of a Project Process.
Source: Image Copyright Joe Gough, 2013. Used under license from Shutterstock.com

tomization (variety) and the use of general purpose equipment which is shared between the products. There tends to be low utilization of equipment in jobbing processes due to the need to undertake frequent setting up of the machinery when moving from processing one product to another. Examples of the use of a jobbing process include bespoke tailors and precision engineers (Figure 3.3).

FIGURE 3.3

Precision Engineering: An Example of a Jobbing Process.
Source: http://gimp-savvy.com//cgi-bin/img.cgi?ailsy0rqhbLXCHU659

www.wileyopenpage.com

Batch

Processes that produce products of medium variety and medium volume are termed 'batch processes'. **Batch processes** cover a relatively wide range of volume and variety combinations. Products are grouped into batches whose batch size can range from two to hundreds. In a batch process the product moves to the location of transforming resources such as equipment and so resources are shared between the batches. Instead of setting up machinery between each product, as in a jobbing process, setups occur between batches, leading to greater utilization of equipment. Because of the relatively high volumes involved in batch, compared to project and jobbing, it can be cost-effective to use specialized labour and equipment dedicated to certain product batches. A feature of batch processes is that, because it is difficult to predict when a batch of work will arrive at a machine, a lack of coordination can lead to many products waiting for that machine at any one time. These queues of work may dramatically increase the time the product takes to progress through the process. Examples of the use of a batch process include vehicle component assembly, clothing manufacture, bakeries (Figure 3.4), magazines and books.

Mass/Line

Processes that produce high-volume and low-variety products are termed mass (or line) processes. Although there may be variants within the product design the production process will essentially be the same for all the products. Because of the high volumes of product it is cost-effective to use specialized labour and equipment. A feature of **mass processes** is that the movement of the product may be automated using a conveyor system and the production process broken down into a number of small, simple tasks. This helps to ensure the process time is as fast as possible in order to meet delivery speed

FIGURE 3.5

Car Manufacturing: An Example of a Mass Process.
Source: Image Copyright Alistair Scott, 2013. Used under license from
Shutterstock.com

FIGURE 3.6

Oil Distribution: An Example of a Continuous Process.
Source: Image Copyright Oleg-F, 2013. Used under license from
Shutterstock.com

requirements. In order to ensure a smooth flow of product the process times per unit must be equalized at each stage of production using a technique called line balancing (Chapter 4). Because of the low product variety, setting up of equipment is minimized and utilization of equipment is high. Examples of the use of a mass process include vehicle manufacturing (Figure 3.5) and assembly of consumer durables such as televisions and computers.

Continuous

Processes that operate continually to produce a very high volume of a standard product are termed 'continuous'. The products produced by a continuous operation are usually a continuous flow such as oil and gas. **Continuous processes** use a large amount of equipment, which is specialized and dedicated to producing a single product (such as an oil refinery for example). To make this large investment in dedicated equipment cost-effective continuous processes are often in constant operation, 24 hours a day. The role of labour in the operation of the processes is mainly one of monitoring and control of the process equipment with little contact with the product itself. Examples of a continuous process include an oil refinery (Figure 3.6), electricity production and steel making.

SERVICE PROCESS TYPES

The classification of service process types is more recent and less standardized than the manufacturing process types outlined above. In this text three service process types – professional service, service shop and mass service – are categorized in terms of their ability to cope with different volume and variety characteristics (Figure 3.7).

FIGURE 3.7

Service Process Types.

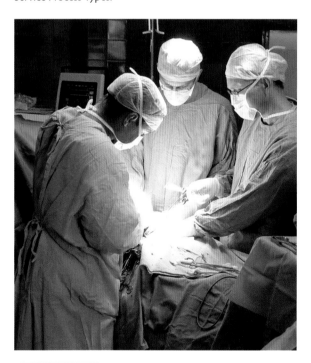

FIGURE 3.8

Surgery: An Example of a Professional Service.
Source: Image Copyright Brasiliao, 2013. Used under license from
Shutterstock.com

www.wileyopenpage.com

Professional Service

Professional service processes operate with high variety and low volume. They are characterized by high levels of customization in that each service delivery will be tailored to meet individual customer needs. This customization requires communication between the service provider and customer and so professional services are characterized by high levels of customer contact and a relatively high proportion of staff supplying the service in relation to customers. The emphasis in a professional service is on delivering a process rather than a tangible product associated with a process. An example of this is a management consultancy where the client is paying for the expertise and problem solving skills of the consultants. The physical report that is generated at the end of the consultancy assignment is a documentation of the process but it is the success of the process itself that is of interest to the client. Examples of a professional service include management consultancy, doctors (Figure 3.8) and health and safety inspectors.

Service Shop

Service shop processes operate with a medium amount of variety and volume. There will be a certain amount of customization of the service but not as extensive as in professional services. There will therefore be a mix of staff and equipment used to deliver the service. There is an emphasis both on the service delivery process itself and any tangible items that are associated with the service. For example, the success of a restaurant is dependent on the level of service attained in terms of achieving an appropriate ambience but also the quality of the food itself. The variety of food offered provides a compromise between a personal chef who can cook meals to order (professional service) and a standard food item such as a hamburger (mass service). Examples of service shops include banks, shops (Figure 3.9), restaurants and travel agencies.

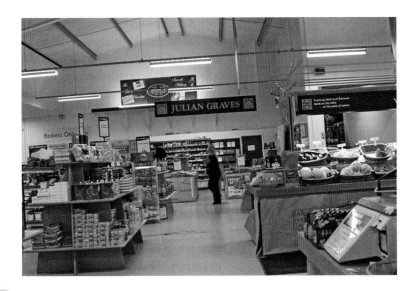

FIGURE 3.9

A Delicatessen: An Example of a Service Shop.
Source: http://morguefile.com/archive/?display=155334.

Mass Service

Mass service processes operate with a low variety and high volume. There will be little customization of the service to individual customer needs and limited contact between the customer and people providing the service. Because the service is standardized it is likely that equipment will be used to improve the efficiency of the service delivery process. The emphasis in a mass service is on the tangible item that is associated with the service delivery. For example supermarkets have certain differences in terms of layout and ambience but the major emphasis is on the provision of food items of the required price and quality. Examples of mass service providers are supermarkets, rail services and airports (Figure 3.10).

Alternative Service Process Type Definitions

As mentioned earlier, the process type definitions for services are not standardized and in particular the definition of service shops may be subdivided into those that lie on the professional service boundary relating to professional services that have grown in volume and standardized their service and organizations that lie on the mass service boundary relating to mass services that have increased their service variety to differentiate them from competitors.

FIGURE 3.10

An Airport: An Example of a Mass Service.
Source: Image Copyright egd, 2013. Used under license from Shutterstock.com

www.wileyopenpage.com

A strategy for manufacturing companies who are successful and wish to grow is to standardize products and enter higher volume markets over time as they acquire more financial backing. This growth may take place gradually, however, so the point at which increased volumes necessitate a change in process type to match the volume/variety characteristics of the market may not be apparent. The choice of process type in these cases may be made using a break-even analysis that calculates profit at different volume levels (Russell and Taylor, 2011). One consequence of process choice is that for increasing volume, the level of investment in equipment required to ensure a cost-efficient operation increases. This requirement for capital investment can be a barrier for new companies entering a market and so many small companies with limited finances provide a customized service to a niche market, in which labour skills are more important than supporting infrastructure.

Many service companies operate in a niche market and the Web has provided a platform for many of them to market their services effectively. However, many service companies wish to grow and so may need to standardize their service. Thus in order to provide a consistent service level at higher volumes it may be necessary to 'package' the service the company provides to enable a lower skill base to deliver the service and to ensure consistent service quality. However, low-volume, professional-type services rely on the capability of the individuals working for them who provide tailored solutions for their clients. Thus a key factor in managing growth is that it may involve both a loss of autonomy of these existing staff and a need for training of additional staff to deliver the 'packaged' service.

At the level of the individual product or service there is a link between the order winning and order qualifying criteria, defined by Hill (2005) and discussed in Chapter 2, with the process type choice. For example, a criterion of high quality design capability as an order winner may imply a jobbing process type whilst an order winner of price may imply a mass or continuous process type. As the order winners and order qualifying factors shift in response to changes to the market requirements, competitor actions and the product/service life cycle this has implications for the process type choice. For example, within the portfolio of products and services that an organization delivers, an individual product or service will progress through a life cycle in terms of sales from introduction to maturity to decline; the process that best suits the needs of the firm will need to change to match the volume and variety of the output (Noori and Radford, 1995).

Two concepts that should be considered when designing an operations process to meet volume and variety characteristics are 'focus' and 'mass customization'. The idea of 'focus' in manufacturing and services is used to help reduce the level of complexity involved when attempting to service a number of market segments and is covered in Chapter 2. The concept of 'mass customization', which attempts to provide the capability to produce both a high volume and high variety of products and services through the use of flexibility, is covered in Chapter 7.

SUMMARY

- The main manufacturing process types are project, jobbing, batch, mass and continuous.
- The main service process types are professional, shop and mass.
- An alternative service process type definition is shop, factory, professional and mass.
- Each process type should be matched to a particular volume and variety of output to minimize cost.

www.wileyopenpage.com

Ashburton Products

Ashburton Products manufactures wooden fireplace mantels. They have a retail showroom in which various models are displayed. A small workshop close to the showroom was taken on a short term lease, and various items of DIY power tools and second hand woodworking machinery were acquired. The firm has also acquired a routing machine to provide flutings and other decorative details for the mantels. The firm prides itself on meeting customer requirements and most mantels are customised. Hence, manufacture is organised on a one-off basis. Variations in output are catered for by working overtime. One of the joiners in particular frequently comes in at weekends to cut timber.

A mantel consists of three sub-assemblies comprising two legs and a shelf. A variety of bought-in decorative motifs are also attached. The production process begins with cutting sheets of MDF and planks of hardwood. It can sometimes be difficult to move in the workshop due to its small size and the amount of cut timber stored. After cutting the timber is put onto the routing machine. Next, at the sub-assembly stage, the legs are brought together, glued and then clamped. The glue takes time to dry, so clamped sub-assemblies are left overnight. The shelf is also glued and clamped. The final assembly stage consists of gluing and clamping the legs to the shelf to make a complete mantel. When dried the assembly is taken into an adjoining 'finishing' area. Here excess glue is scrapped off and sealant is painted on to the exposed grain to seal it. Filler is applied to gaps around the joints or points were the surface is uneven. The whole is then rubbed down with sand paper and taken to the spraying area for painting. MDF mantels are sprayed with up to 5 coats of white paint, with filling and rubbing down between coats. Hardwood mantels are sprayed with 2 coats of varnish. Finally, finished mantels are taken downstairs for packing. Since space is a major problem the stock of finished mantels is extremely small.

Demand for mantels has been rising for some time. Sales which were, in the past, based exclusively on single orders for individual customers have recently been supplemented by multiple orders from two local builders. In view of this trend, Ashburton's management is concerned about how best to meet the increase in demand. Unable to expand the current site because of planning restrictions, and reluctant to spend large sums on new equipment, the management is uncertain what to do.

Questions

1. List the inputs and outputs to the transformation process.

2. Draw a flow diagram to show the current production stages.

3. Identify the current process type employed at Ashburton.

4. Indicate the main constraints on current operations.

5. Indicate any problems with the current production process.

6. How might the company improve its operation on terms of process type, process layout, process technology and job and work design?

CASE STUDY 3.2

Democracy Made with Personalised Products

In contrast to the clutter and noise that characterises most factories, a small plant in Minneapolis feels unnaturally ordered and quiet. It contains little but neat rows of machines resembling large refrigerators.

The plant, run by Stratasys, a US company, is using 3D printing, or high-tech 'additive' manufacturing. Each of the 100 or so machines, which require just a handful of human attendants, contains an internal chamber in which plastic is fused layer upon layer to build complicated shapes. In other kinds of 3D printers, layers of powder are fused using lasers to create components that may end up in anything from boat seats to optical instruments.

The machines are controlled by computer codes defining the shapes of the items to be made that can be sent by the internet.

Probably the biggest cheerleader for the sector is Abe Reichental, a 55-year-old Israeli-American who is chief executive of 3D Systems, another US company which with Stratasys is one of the world's two biggest producers of 3D printing machines.

He says the technology can contribute to the 'democratisation of manufacturing' by lowering the barriers between design and production. '3D printing can provide the garage entrepreneur with the same productive capabilities as the large corporation,' says Mr Reichental. Another key attribute is that the technology makes it possible to produce 'one-off' or highly personalised parts more easily than with other manufacturing methods.

Jeff Immelt, chief executive of General Electric, the US industrial group, is similarly enthusiastic. 'I think it's going to be big, I really do,' Mr Immelt says. The technology's biggest impact, Mr Immelt reckons, will include 'shortening cycle times' between designing products and making them. That could help manufacturers in the rich world compensate for higher wage costs compared with those in emerging economies such as China.

GE is using 3D printing to make prototype components for testing in its divisions that produce domestic appliances and aerospace engines. Other big companies trying out the technology include Mattel, Medtronic and Boeing of the US, the German car group Daimler, and Luxottica, the Italian glasses producer.

One of the leading UK companies in this field is Renishaw, a maker of measurement probes, which is selling its own versions of 3D printing machines, while using them to make its own parts.

Other big users are in the medical equipment sector, where often items such as parts for orthopaedic implants or hearing aids need to be made on a one-off basis to fit the physiological features of individuals.

So far, however, 3D printing has yet to find much application in routine parts production, where items are made in batch runs counted in tens of thousands or even millions, and where the technology is normally too expensive compared with orthodox procedures such as metal cutting or plastics injection moulding.

But Scott Crump, chief executive of Stratasys, sees 3D printing as 'part of a spectrum' of manufacturing technologies that are creating new opportunities. These include novel ways to produce the advanced software required to define shapes of products, together with new versions of more conventional cutting tools.

Viewed in this way, 3D printing is the latest manifestation of a broad range of 'additive' technologies in manufacturing – where materials are fused or bonded – as opposed to the way of making parts by conventional 'subtractive'

machining. Here metal or plastic is cut away from a solid mass using machine tools.

A third broad type of manufacturing technology involves forming processes where the material is shaped through means such as moulding in a so-called static process. In this area of technology, the material's mass and volume stays unaltered while its shape changes.

As well as selling 3D printing machines, Stratasys also operates factories, including the one in Minneapolis, to use the technology to make parts for customers. It recently announced a merger with Objet, an Israeli maker of 3D printing systems, to create a larger group that will this year have comparable sales to 3D Systems – where the figure is expected to be about $340m.

As this number illustrates, 3D printing is still a fairly small sector. According to Terry Wohlers, an independent US consultant, sales of 3D printing equipment last year came to about $500m, less than 1 per cent of the comparable sales of conventional machine tools based on the subtractive method. Mr Wohlers estimates the total revenues of the 3D printing industry, including sales of equipment and materials together with contracting revenues by 3D printing services businesses, added up to just $1.7bn in 2011.

However, he says that these raw numbers fail to provide a true picture of the sector's significance. In the field of prototype parts production, says Mr Wohlers, the value of the technology is worth 'billions of dollars a year' to companies which find the technology helpful to speeding up product development.

Joe Hogan, chief executive of ABB, the Swiss-Swedish engineering group, says: '3D printing means it's possible to go from concept to reality [in making one-off parts] in just a few hours. That's a big help when you are trying to be quicker and more reactive.'

In the medical equipment industry, hearing aid manufacturers such as Starkey of the US, Widex of Denmark and Phonak of Switzerland are big users of 3D printing techniques. In the orthopaedic implant sector, big groups such as Stryker, a leading US maker of artificial joints such as hips, is also using the process, while another leader in this application is Adler Ortho, a much smaller Italian specialist business.

Over the next few years, the biggest optimists in the sector believe applications of the technology will gradually broaden out to make it possible to use the process for making parts in large production runs. That could be especially the case for small complex shapes where the economic advantages of using 3D printing are more established than for big, simple ones.

Hans Langer, chief executive of Eos, a Munich-based company making 3D printers, says the new processes should not be regarded as mere substitutes for current techniques, but as paving the way to make new types of factory items that would be close to impossible to create with current techniques.

'We now have a way to make items that are lighter, use materials more economically and behave differently to products made today. 3D printing could lead to a completely new way to approach manufacturing,' adds Mr Langer.

Source: Financial Times (2012). Reproduced with permission.

Question

What are the implications of technology developments such as 3D printers on the choice of process type selected by organizations?

The link to the video 'Stratasys - Medical device manufacture with FDM technology' is available in your interactive e-book at **www.wileyopenpage.com**

The Mini

Few small cars can inspire such as level of enthusiasm as the Mini. A former British classic that is now owned by BMW is exported to nearly 100 countries around the globe, in a wide variety of colours and specifications. Yet this product is largely manufactured in the 'Mini triangle' of middle England; BMW's 3 factories of Plant Oxford, Plant Swindon and Plant Hams Hall.

The three plants between them provide the full manufacturing operation to produce the Mini, Hams Hall produces the engines, Swindon makes the pressed panels and sub assemblies, and Oxford produces the body shell, paint operation and final assembly. In 2011 just over 191 000 Minis rolled off the production line in Oxford and 80% of those were destined for the overseas market.

Mini produces 5 models; the Hatchback, the Convertible, the Coupe, the Roadster and the recently rediscovered Mini Clubman. In addition to petrol, diesel and turbo options there are 372 different interior trim options, and 319 different exterior options. Such a high level of flexibility means that BMW Mini claim there are a possible 15 000 000 000 000 000 different combinations of Mini!

The consequences of providing such a range of customisation, pose the factories with a significant operational challenge. All minis start life with a barcode, containing all their specific order information. All three facilities need to work in sequence; once the order is started for production, Hams Hall will have 4 days to fulfil the specific engine requirement to Oxford. These engines will range from specification and each is built to order, daily updates ensure each is delivered in sequence.

Swindon provides all the moulded components and many sub assemblies too. The production is 95% automated and works to the demand from Oxford.

The frame, paint and final assembly are separated points of production; the frames are made and painted. Painting itself takes approximately 10 hours and there are over 14km of conveyors in the paint shop containing over 600 frames in process. There are 14 different colour options – plus the option for a contrasting roof panel. The frames are then held for assembly requirement.

Containing over 2,800 components 18 modules including the engine, doors, front module (fitted with headlights), are integrated in the mainline assembly function.

The Mini triangle adopts a just in time system, integrating approximately 350 global suppliers to deliver to order to minimise work in progress and excessive inventory levels. 80% of Minis are built to order, hence there are low levels of finished goods. As the Minis are preordered the level of customisation is achievable. BMW's significant

investment in technology has also meant that each car can be treated as unique within the process.

In addition to this efficient synchronisation of processes, the sophisticated logistics concept also enables a high degree of flexibility even after an order has been made. Customer requests for changes can be taken into account regarding colour, engine type or options up to seven days prior to the start of assembly.

Oxford has produced more than two million Mini models since 2001.

Sources

http://www.bbc.co.uk/news/business-18764730

http://www.mini-production-triangle.com/production.aspx

http://www.bmwgroup.com/e/nav/index.html?

http://www.bmwgroup.com/e/0_0_www_bmw group_com/produktion/produktionsnetzwerk/produktionsstandorte/werk_oxford.html

http://www.guardian.co.uk/business/2012/jul/09/bmw-invests-250-million-uk-mini-factories.

Source: Written by Briony Boydell and Chris Milner. Reproduced with permission.

Questions for Discussion

1. What type of process has Mini followed?
2. How can Mini achieve such a high level of variety in its products, yet still make so many?

Quizzes to test yourself further are available in your interactive e-book at **www.wileyopenpage.com**

Flashcards to test yourself further are available in your interactive e-book at **www.wileyopenpage.com**

EXERCISES

1. Describe the characteristics of project, jobbing, batch, mass and continuous processes in manufacturing, providing real-life examples.

2. Describe the characteristics of professional, shop and mass processes in services, providing real-life examples.

3. Compare alternative service process type definitions using real-life examples.

4. What are the consequences of having too little process flexibility or too much process flexibility when making a product or delivering a service?

5. Describe three factors that can lead to a change in the volume and variety mix for a product or service over time.

6. Explain the concept of batch production.

FURTHER READING

Slack, N., Chambers, S. and Johnston, R. (2010) *Operations Management*, 6th edn, Pearson Education Ltd.

WEB LINKS

www.mas.berr.gov.uk (accessed 1 November 2011), UK Department for Business Enterprise and Regulatory Reform. Numerous case studies of operations concepts.

http://www.youtube.com/watch?v=IvyPV5DOzIg (accessed 31 October 2011), Example of project process type – shipbuilding.

REFERENCES

Gaither, N. and Frazier, G. (2002) *Operations Management*, 9th edn, SouthWestern.
Hayes, R.H. and Wheelwright, S.C. (1984) *Restoring our Competitive Edge*, John Wiley & Sons, Ltd.
Hill, T. (2005) *Operations Management*, 2nd edn, Palgrave Macmillan.
Lovelock, C.H. (1992) *Managing Services: Marketing, Operations and Human Resources*, 2nd edn, Pearson Education Ltd.
Noori, H. and Radford, R. (1995) *Production and Operations Management: Total Quality and Responsiveness*, McGraw-Hill.
Russell, R.S. and Taylor, B.W. (2011) *Operations Management: Creating Value along the Supply Chain*, 7th edn, John Wiley & Sons, Ltd.

CHAPTER 4

Layout Types and Layout Design

- **Introduction**
- **Layout types**
- **Layout design**

LEARNING OBJECTIVES

- Describe the basic layout types
- Evaluate the appropriateness of a layout type for a manufacturing or service process type
- Explain the concept of group technology
- Understand the concept of production flow analysis
- Understand the line-balancing technique

LAYOUT TYPES AND LAYOUT DESIGN AND OPERATIONS STRATEGY

Layout type choice is strategic because it can represent a large amount of capital investment in terms of equipment and workforce and so sets a constraint around which the company can compete. The layout type choice is linked to the process type choice (Chapter 3) and so provides the context around which the operation performs across its performance objectives.

INTRODUCTION

The layout concerns the physical placement of resources such as equipment and storage facilities and is designed to facilitate the efficient flow of customers or materials through the operations system. Layout is important because it can have a significant effect on the cost and efficiency of an operation and can entail substantial investment in time and money. Layout is relevant to administrative activities such as the design of office layouts which can facilitate teamwork amongst groups of people and is also relevant in service processes such as customer retail outlets where the placement of products can affect sales. In many operations the installation of a new layout, or redesign of an existing layout, can be difficult to alter once implemented due to the significant investment required on items such as equipment. This chapter describes the main categories of layout, termed 'layout types', and techniques for configurations of these layout types, termed 'layout design'.

LAYOUT TYPES

Following the selection of the operations process type (see Chapter 3) it is necessary to select the layout (arrangement of facilities) of the operation. As with process types there are categories of layout termed **layout types**. Figure 4.1 shows the relationship between manufacturing and service process types and layout types.

As can be seen from Figure 4.1, there are four basic layout types: fixed position, process, cell and product layout. As stated, the choice of layout type will follow from the process type choice. However, as can be seen from Figure 4.1, there is often a choice of layout type for a particular process type (such as a process layout or cell layout for a batch process type). In this case the choice will depend on the characteristics of the layout type that are particularly relevant for the product or service that is to be delivered. An analysis may also be made using the trade-off between unit cost of production and variety of output that was used to determine process type in Chapter 3. For example, a cell layout is more likely to be relevant for relatively high volume batch systems where the cost of dedicated resources can be met by the lower unit cost of a high volume of product or service flowing through the cell. Case Study 4.2 provides an example of considering layout in a retail environment.

The characteristics of each of the layout types will now be considered.

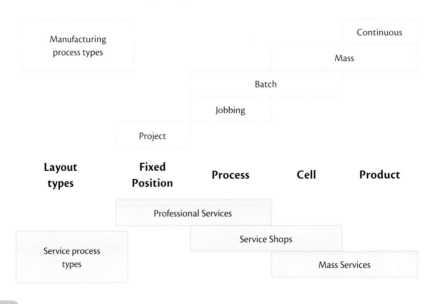

FIGURE 4.1

The Relationship between Process Type and Layout Type.

www.wileyopenpage.com

Fixed-Position Layout

This layout type is used when the product or service cannot be moved and so the transforming process must take place at the location of product creation or service delivery. Figure 4.2 shows an example of a fixed-position layout in a restaurant.

In a fixed-position layout all resources for producing the product, such as equipment and labour, must move to the site of the product or service. The emphasis when using a fixed-position layout is on the scheduling and coordination of resources to ensure that they are available in the required amounts at the required time. For example on a construction site most activities are dependent on the completion of other activities and cannot be undertaken simultaneously. The space available on the site may also constrain the amount of work activity that can take place at any one time. This means detailed scheduling of resources is required to minimize delays. In a restaurant it is important that the order is taken and food delivered to the table at the appropriate time. Chapter 16 examines planning techniques such as network analysis, which are used to assist in the scheduling of resources to a fixed-position layout.

Figure 4.2

Fixed-Position Layout in a Restaurant.

From Figure 4.1, process types associated with a fixed-position layout are the project process type in manufacturing and the professional service type in services. Examples of fixed-position layouts include construction sites such as for buildings or for large ships, aircraft manufacture and full service restaurants (Figure 4.3).

FIGURE 4.3

A Construction Site: An Example of a Fixed Position Layout.

Source: Image Copyright 9comeback 2013. Used under licence from Shutterstock.com

www.wileyopenpage.com

Process Layout

A process layout, also termed a **functional layout,** is one in which resources (such as equipment and people) which have similar processes or functions are grouped together. Figure 4.4 shows a process layout in a manufacturing facility.

Process layouts are used when there is a large variety in the products or services being delivered and it may not be feasible to dedicate facilities to each individual product or service. A process layout allows the products or customers to move to each group of resources in turn, based on their individual requirements. Their flexibility means that process layouts are widely used. One advantage is that in service systems they allow a wide variety of routes that may be chosen by customers depending on their needs. Another advantage is that the product or service range may be extended and, as long as no new resources are required, may be accommodated within the current layout.

An important issue with process layouts is the management of the flow of products or services between the resource groups. One problem is that transportation between process groups can be a significant factor in terms of transportation time and handling costs. Another problem is the number of products or services involved and the fact that each product/service can follow an individual route between the process groups makes it difficult to predict when a particular product will be delivered

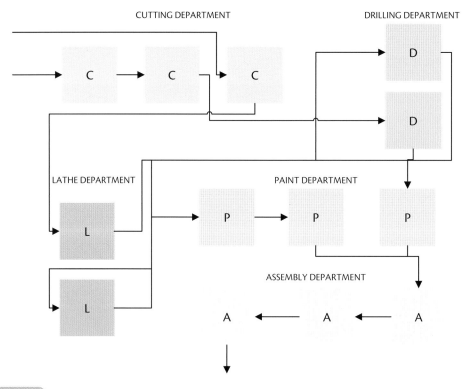

FIGURE 4.4

A Manufacturing Process or Functional Layout.

 www.wileyopenpage.com

or a service completed. This is because at certain times the number of customers or products arriving at a particular process group exceeds its capacity and so a queue forms until resources are available. This queuing time may take up a significant part of the time that the product or customer is in the process. This behaviour can lead to long throughput times (the time taken for a product or customer to progress through the layout). In a manufacturing organization a significant amount of time may be spent 'progress chasing' to give certain products priority to ensure they are delivered to customers on time. In a service system the customers may feel they are queuing in the system longer than they perceive is necessary for

the service they require. However, in services there may be flexibility to add or remove staff to match the current arrival rate of customers to the service delivery point.

From Figure 4.1, process types associated with a process layout are jobbing and batch process types in manufacturing and service shops in services. Examples of process layouts include supermarkets, hospitals (Figure 4.5), department stores and component manufacturers.

Cell Layout

A **cell layout** attempts to combine the efficiency of a product layout with the flexibility of a process layout. Cells are created from placing together resources which service a subset of the total range of products or services. Figure 4.6 shows how a process layout with similar resources in departments has been redesigned as a series of three cells. Note how the routing of products is simplified using the cell layout format. The products are now processed in a single cell and need not be transported between departments.

When grouping products or services together in this way the grouping is termed 'a family'. The process of grouping the products or services to create a family is termed **group technology**.

Group technology has three aspects:

1. Grouping parts into families. Grouping parts or customers into families has the objective of reducing the changeover time between batches, allowing smaller batch sizes and thus improving flexibility. Parts family formation is based on the idea of grouping parts or customers together according to factors such as processing similarity.

2. Grouping physical facilities into cells to reduce transportation time between processes. Physical facilities are grouped into cells with the intention of reducing material or customer movements. Whereas a process layout involves extensive movement of materials or customers between departments with common processes, a cell comprises all the facilities required to manufacture

a family of components or deliver a service. Material and customer movement is therefore restricted to within the cell and throughput times are therefore reduced. Cells can be U-shaped (see Figure 4.9) to allow workers to work at more than one process while minimizing movement.

3. Creating groups of multiskilled workers. Creating groups of multiskilled workers enables increased autonomy and flexibility on the part of operators. This enables easier changeovers from one part to another and increases the job enrichment of members of the group. This in turn can improve motivation and have a beneficial effect on quality.

Creating cells with dedicated resources can significantly reduce the time it takes for products and services to pass through the process by reducing queuing time. It also offers the opportunity for automation due to the close proximity of the process stages. Thus process technology can be used to replace

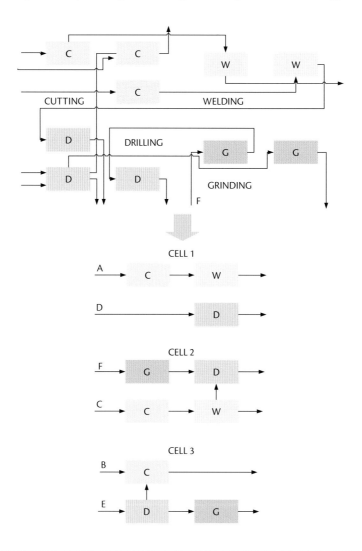

FIGURE 4.6

Moving from a Process to a Cell Layout.

 www.wileyopenpage.com

A Retail Department Store: An Example of a Cell Layout.
Source: http://en.wikipedia.org/wiki/Image:Departmentstoreinterior.jpg

a number of general purpose resources with a single dedicated multifunctional system such as a flexible manufacturing system (see Chapter 6). A disadvantage of cell layouts can be the extra expenditure due to the extra resources required in moving to a cell layout.

From Figure 4.1, process types associated with a cell layout are batch and mass process types in manufacturing and service shops and mass services in services. Examples of cell layouts include custom manufacture (Figure 4.7), a maternity unit in a hospital and a cafeteria with multiple serving areas. In services a cell layout could involve an insurance company organized by type of claim (such as car, home or travel).

Product Layout

Product layouts, also termed 'line layouts', arrange the resources required for a product or service around the needs of that product or service. Figure 4.8 shows a configuration of a product layout. Here the material flows through four stages. The line may be automated or people may be assigned to one or more stages.

In manufacturing applications, such as assembly lines with a high volume of a standard product, the products will move in a flow from one processing station to the next. In contrast to the process layout, in which products move to the resources, here the resources are arranged and dedicated to a particular product

FIGURE 4.8

Product Layout.

or service. The term product layout refers to the arrangement of the resources around the product or service. In services the requirements of a specific group of customers are identified and resources setup sequentially so the customers flow through the system, moving from one stage to another until the service is complete.

A key issue in product layouts is that the stages in the assembly line or flow line must be 'balanced'. This means that the time spent by components or customers should be approximately the same for each stage, otherwise queues will occur at the slowest stage. The topic of line balancing is considered later in this chapter.

The product or line layout is an efficient delivery system in that the use of dedicated equipment in a balanced line will allow a much faster throughput time than in a process layout. The major disadvantage of the approach is that it lacks the flexibility of a process layout and only produces a standard product or service. Another issue is that if any stage of the line fails, then in effect the output from the whole line is lost and so it lacks the robustness to loss of resources (for example equipment failure or staff illness) that the process layout can provide.

FIGURE 4.9

'U-Shape' Product Layout.

An alternative to the straight-line configuration shown in Figure 4.8 is to adopt a 'U-shape' design as in Figure 4.9. Here material flows through eight stages of production or assembly, which are assigned to three people. An advantage of the U shape is that it may allow people (or equipment) to be assigned to multiple stages and thus help balance the line.

From Figure 4.1 process types associated with a product layout are mass and continuous process types in manufacturing and mass services in services. Examples of product layouts include car assembly, self-service cafes, car valeting, golf courses and assembly lines (see Figure 4.10).

FIGURE 4.10

A Golf Course and an Assembly Line: Examples of Product Layouts
Source: Image Copyright Krivosheev Vitaly and Rainer Plendl, 2013. Used under license from Shutterstock.com

 www.wileyopenpage.com

A timelapse tour of a BMW production process is available in your interactive e-book at **www.wileyopenpage.com**

Characteristics of Layout Types

Table 4.1 summarizes the main characteristics of operations systems using each of the four main layout types.

Although the main layout types can be adapted to meet the needs of a particular manufacturing or service system, it may be the case that a mix of layout types is required within a single operation. For example, hospitals are basically a process layout with people with similar needs (for example, intensive care) grouped together. However, the layout also shows characteristics of a fixed position layout in that staff, medicines and equipment are brought to the location of the customer.

TABLE 4.1

Characteristics of Operations for each Layout Type.

Layout type	Characteristics of operations that use layout type
Fixed-position	Very high product and mix flexibility, but very high unit cost.
	Products or customers do not move; the resources are arranged around them.
	There can be a high variety of tasks for staff.
	A major issue for operations is the scheduling and coordination of activities over time.
Process	High product and mix flexibility.
	Complex flow can lead to high levels of work-in-progress and high throughput times.
	Low utilization of resources.
	Flexible in terms of handling additions to the product/service mix.
	Robust in that nonavailability of resources does not stop delivery of product/service if other group resources remain.
Cell	Can provide flexibility of process layout and efficiency of product layout.
	Resources can be matched to product or service demand so work-in-progress and thus throughput times are much lower than for process layout.
	Variety of tasks offers opportunity for automation and more variation in duties for personnel
	Can be costly to move and purchase additional plant – necessary to rearrange existing layout.

(Continued)

www.wileyopenpage.com

TABLE 4.1

Characteristics of Operations for each Layout Type. (*Continued*)

Layout type	Characteristics of operations that use layout type
Product/line	Standard product or service in high volumes at low unit cost.
	Can specialize equipment to product or service needs.
	Allows relatively little variety in product or service.
	Line configuration leads to danger of failure of one process stage effectively stopping output from the whole line.
	Work can be repetitive if personnel are always based at one process stage.

LAYOUT DESIGN

Once the layout type has been chosen, its detailed configuration must be designed to meet the needs of a particular implementation.

In a fixed-position layout there will be a relatively low number of elements and there are no widely used techniques to help locate resources.

The relative positioning of equipment and departments in a process layout can be analysed in terms of minimizing transportation costs or distances using an activity matrix. When a number of factors need to be taken into account, including qualitative aspects, relationship charts may be used. Details of the techniques of block diagramming and relationship diagramming which are based on logic and visual representation of data can be found in Russell and Taylor (2011). Process maps (described in Chapter 8) can also be used to show the flow of materials, customers and staff through the layout. In some instances, such as retail layout design, software is available that takes into consideration both financial aspects of layout design and customer requirements such as aesthetics and lighting (Hope and Muhlemann, 1997).

In this chapter the techniques of production-flow analysis for cell layouts and line balancing for product layouts will be covered.

The video '3 bowls of cereal' is available in your interactive e-book at **www.wileyopenpage.com**

The video 'Spaghetti diagram' is available in your interactive e-book at **www.wileyopenpage.com**

Production Flow Analysis

A cell layout can be created by the use of the concept of group technology to group resources into cells to process families of parts or customers. Group technology is covered earlier in the cell layout section. Production flow analysis (PFA) (Burbidge, 1996) is a group technology technique that can be used to identify families of parts with similar processing requirements. To show how PFA works see the worked example. In practice many parts and machines would be involved in production flow analysis and a 'clean' solution that allocates all parts to a cell such as shown above would be unlikely. To deal with this issue may require a strategy of allocating certain parts to move between cells, investment in additional machinery to add to cells or the use of 'remainder' cells that process the parts that do not 'fit' with any of the other cells.

WORKED EXAMPLE 4.1

PRODUCTION FLOW ANALYSIS

Five parts (A, B, C, D, E) are produced in a process layout consisting of a drill department with three drills (D), a lathe department with two lathes (L), a milling department with one mill (M) and a heat-treatment department with one-heat treatment machine (HT). The process flow is shown in Figure 4.11

FIGURE 4.11

Example of Process Layout.

The routing sequences taken by each part in Figure 4.11 are shown in Table 4.2.

TABLE 4.2

Part Routing Sequences for Machine Shop.

Part	Routing sequence
A	lathe, mill
B	drill, heat treatment
C	drill
D	heat treatment, drill
E	mill, lathe

In order to identify families of parts, the first step in PFA is to draw a grid of parts against machines and mark which parts are processed on which machine (Table 4.3).

TABLE 4.3

PFA Routing Matrix.

	Lathe	Mill	Heat treat	Drill
A	✓	✓		
B			✓	✓
C				✓
D			✓	✓
E	✓	✓		

The next step is to observe which machines have parts in common. In this case it can be seen that lathe and heat treatment could form one cell and drill and mill could form another cell. Redraw the grid, rearranging the rows and columns to place parts using the machines in the adjacent cells. Two or more cells can be formed (Table 4.4).

TABLE 4.4

Rearranged PFA Routing Matrix.

	Lathe	Mill	Heat treat	Drill
A	✓	✓		
E	✓	✓		
C				✓
D			✓	✓
B			✓	✓
	CELL 1		CELL 2	

The cell layout can now be drawn using the cells defined using the PFA analysis and referring back to the routing sequences in Table 4.2

Figure 4.12 shows the cell layout routing. It is immediately apparent that the routing of parts is much clearer and routing distances are smaller than in the process layout (Figure 4.11).

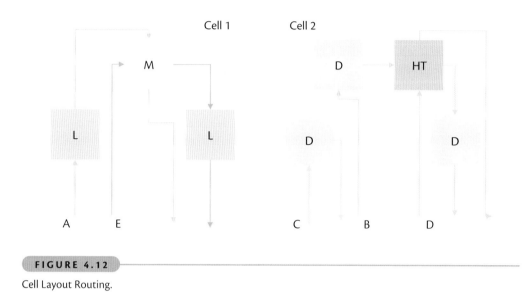

FIGURE 4.12

Cell Layout Routing.

Line Balancing

A product layout consists of a number of processes arranged one after another in a 'line' to produce a standard product or service in a relatively high volume. These systems which have a characteristic flow (product) layout use specialized equipment or staff dedicated to achieving an optimal flow of work through the system. This is important because all items follow virtually the same sequence of operations. A major aim of flow systems is to ensure that each stage of production is able to maintain production at an equal rate. The technique of line balancing is used to ensure that the output of each production stage is equal and maximum efficiency is attained (see Case Study 4.1).

Line balancing involves ensuring that the stages of production are coordinated and bottlenecks are avoided. The line flow configuration means that the tasks in the line must be undertaken in order (precedence) and the output of the whole line will be determined by the slowest or bottleneck process. The actual design of the line is thus guided by the order of the tasks which are involved in producing the product or delivering the service and the required output rate required to meet demand. This provides information that determines the number of stages and the output rate of each stage. It should be noted that the issue of line balancing will be complicated by constraints such as factory layout, material handling between stages and availability of worker skills.

www.wileyopenpage.com

Other factors in line balancing for product layouts include:

- *Variability in task times.* A major factor in achieving a proper line balance is to gather accurate estimates of task times in the line flow process. If timings are just based on an average of observations then there is a danger that the effect of variations on task times will not be considered. This can be limited somewhat by keeping a number of job elements in a task, which reduces variability and increases flexibility. Simulation modelling (Chapter 8) can be used to investigate these variations as well as the effect of random variations such as machine breakdown.
- *Mixed-model lines.* The use of a multimodel line (Chapter 13) to process a range of products, rather than a single product type, also increases the complexity of the line-balancing process.
- *Shape of the line.* Although the sequence of workstations in a product layout is linear, the actual shape of the line need not be straight. It can be an S shape, U shape, O shape or L shape. Factors that are used when deciding on a suitable shape include the ability of people to communicate, the ability of robots and people to reach parts and transportation distances between workstations.
- *Job enlargement.* After taking into consideration the constraints imposed by precedence and cycle time, a decision must be made regarding the level at which a task is broken down and how the elements of the task are allocated to personnel. For instance, motivation can be improved by allocating the whole process to a single person instead of allocating smaller tasks to a number of people in a line.

The steps in line balancing are as follows:

1 Draw a Precedence Diagram

The first step in line balancing is to identify the tasks involved in the process and the order in which these tasks must be undertaken. Once the tasks have been identified it is necessary to define their relationship to one another. There are some tasks that can only begin when other tasks have been completed. This is termed a 'serial relationship' and is shown graphically in Figure 4.13.

The execution of other tasks may be totally independent and thus they have a parallel relationship shown graphically in Figure 4.14.

Precedence diagrams are used to show the tasks undertaken in a line process and the dependencies between these tasks. Thus it is easy to see that task C, for example, can only take place when task A and task B have completed (see Figure 4.15).

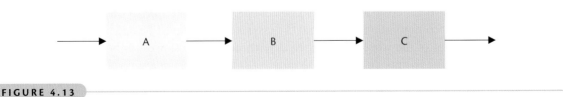

FIGURE 4.13

Serial Relationship of Tasks.

www.wileyopenpage.com

2 Determine the Cycle Time for the Line

For a particular line process we will wish to reach a desired rate of output for the line to meet projected demand. This is usually expressed in work items per time period, for example 30 parts per hour. Another way of expressing this output rate is that 30 parts per hour means that a part must leave the system every 2 minutes (60 minutes/30 parts). This measure, termed the 'cycle time', represents the longest time any part is allowed to spend at each task. To calculate the task time:

$$\text{Cycle time} = 1/r$$

Where

    r = desired output rate in units per hour

Taking into consideration the discussion of bottleneck processes above, the cycle time for the line process is thus determined by the task with the highest cycle time or lowest output level.

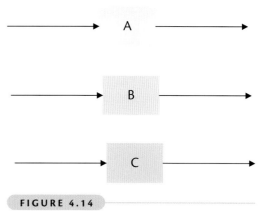

FIGURE 4.14

Parallel Relationship of Tasks.

3 Calculate the theoretical minimum number of workstations

The theoretical minimum (TM) number of workstations is a benchmark for the smallest number of stages possible where the total time required to undertake all the tasks is divided by the cycle time. To calculate the theoretical minimum number of work stations:

$$\text{Theoretical Minimum (TM)} = \Sigma t/c$$

where

    Σt = total time to undertake all tasks
    c = desired cycle time

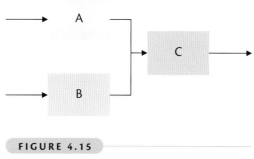

FIGURE 4.15

Precedence Diagram.

Any fractional values for TM are rounded up because fractional stations are not possible.

4 Assign Tasks to Workstations

Once the cycle time for the line has been calculated we have the cycle time for each stage or workstation in the line process. We can now allocate tasks to each workstation based on their task times. As a rule of thumb it is more efficient to allocate eligible tasks to a workstation in the order of longest task times first. When the total task time would exceed the cycle time for a workstation then it is necessary to start a new workstation and repeat the allocation of tasks as before. If a task time is longer than the workstation cycle time then it is necessary either to allocate multiple tasks in parallel in order to meet the target time or to break the task down into smaller elements.

5 Calculate the Efficiency of the Line

When tasks are assigned to workstations it is very unlikely that their total task times at each workstation will match the cycle time exactly. A measure of how close these two values do meet for the whole line is called the 'line efficiency'. To calculate the line efficiency:

$$\text{Efficiency (\%)} = \Sigma t / nc \ (100)$$

where
Σt = total time to undertake all tasks
n = number of work stations
c = desired cycle time

6 Determine if the theoretical minimum of work stations or an acceptable efficiency level have been reached

Line balancing is a trial and error process in which for systems of any size it is not possible to try all combinations. In practice the theoretical minimum number of stations may need to be exceeded due to the constraints placed by the precedence relationships and uneven task times. The line efficiency measure can be used as a guide to the appropriateness of a line balancing configuration.

WORKED EXAMPLE 4.2

LINE BALANCING

A product has 6 tasks with the precedence relationships and task times shown in Table 4.5. A company has a target of producing 4000 products per 40 hour week. Construct a balanced line taking into consideration constraints imposed by uneven task times and the precedence relationships.

TABLE 4.5

Product Precedence Relationships and Task Times.

Work Task	Precedence	Task Time (min)
A	-	0.1
B	A	0.4
C	A	0.5
D	-	0.2
E	C, D	0.6
F	B, E	0.4

 www.wileyopenpage.com

1 Draw a Precedence Diagram

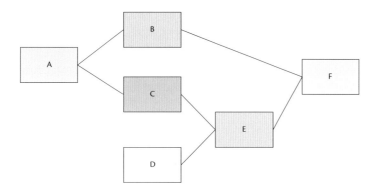

2 Determine the cycle time for the line

Cycle time = 1/r
Desired output rate (hours) = 4000/40 = 100 per hour = 100/60 per minute
Desired Cycle time = 1/(100/60) = 0.6 minutes

3 Calculate the theoretical minimum number of workstations

Theoretical Minimum (TM) = $\sum t/c$
TM = (0.1 + 0.4 + 0.5 + 0.2 + 0.6 + 0.4)/0.6 = 3.67 or 4 work stations

4 Assign Tasks to Workstations

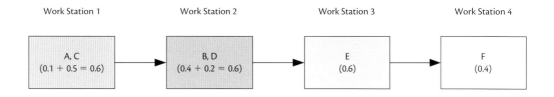

5 Calculate the Efficiency of the Line

Efficiency (%) = $\sum t/nc$ (100)
Efficiency = [(0.6 + 0.6 + 0.6 + 0.4)/(4 × 0.6)] × 100
Efficiency = 91.67%

6 Determine if the theoretical minimum of work stations or an acceptable efficiency level have been reached

The theoretical minimum number of work stations (4) has been met and the line efficiency is over 90% so this could be considered an acceptable solution.

SUMMARY

- There are four basic layout types: fixed position, process, cell and product.
- A fixed-position layout is used when the product or service cannot be moved. A process layout is one in which resources that have similar processes or functions are grouped together. A cell layout is created by placing together resources which serve a subset of the total range of products or services. A product layout arranges the resources required for a product or service around the needs of that product or service.
- Group technology has three aspects of grouping parts into families, grouping physical facilities into cells and creating multi-skilled workers.
- Production flow analysis is a group technology technique that can be used to identify families of parts with similar processing requirements.
- The technique of line balancing is used to ensure that the output of each stage in a product line layout is equal and maximum utilization is attained.

CASE STUDY 4.1

Line Balancing in a Manufacturing Plant

This study concerns a former division of a major UK-based manufacturer of railway rolling stock and equipment. The plant manufactures a range of bogies, which are the supporting frames and wheel sets for rail vehicles. The company has a history of supplying the passenger train market in the UK but over a period of time low demand and increased competition had led it to enter new markets including European inner-city transport and the supply of freight bogies to Far East countries. The need to compete on a global basis led the company to re-evaluate its manufacturing facility with particular emphasis on the need to increase output, reduce lead times and increase flexibility. To meet these demands management had identified areas where substantial investment was required.

The Production Process

The facility layout is on a product-line basis with the manufacturing process consisting of six main stages of fabrication, welding, frame machining, paint, fitting and quality audit. Each stage must be completed in order before the next stage can begin. The stages are now briefly described:

- *Fabrication.* The fabrication stage prepares the bogie frame sections from sheet steel and bought-in castings. A custom template is designed from which the parts required are cut from sheet steel to standard batch sizes. Parts not needed immediately are held in storage. Processed parts and castings are brought together to form a bogie 'kit', which is assembled on a jig and taken to the subsequent welding stage.

- *Welding.* A bogie subassembly is manually welded on a jig at a workstation to form a main bogie frame.
- *Frame machining.* The main bogie frame is then transferred to a CNC [computer numerically controlled machine] centre for the machining of any holes or bores needed for the fixing of subassemblies such as the braking and suspension systems. Bogies are fixed to a slave table and the machine processes the frame according to a preset operation sequence.
- *Paint.* The frame is then manually painted while being suspended from an overhead moving circular track.
- *Fitting.* Manufactured subassemblies and bought-in components such as motors are then assembled on the bogie frame. The frames are placed on supports and are moved along a line at different stages of assembly with overhead cranes.
- *Quality audit.* Final inspection is carried out to ensure all bogies meet the required specification. It is usual that a certain amount of paint touch-up work is required at this stage due to damage caused to the paint finish during the fitting stage.

The Line Balancing Study

The focus of the study was on product layout design with the main objective being to ensure that the performance of the whole manufacturing system would meet required output levels. The output level was converted into a target cycle time (time between manufacture of products or output rate). As stated, the product layout consists of six main stages with the product passing through each stage in turn. This means that the effective cycle time for the whole system

FIGURE 4.16

Cycle Time of Manufacturing Stages.

is determined by the stage with the longest cycle time. The study objective was to obtain a balanced line (all cycle times equal), which would enable a smooth parts flow through the production stages facilitating the introduction of a pull-type just-in-time (JIT) production control system.

A simulation model (Chapter 8) was used to estimate the cycle time at the main manufacturing stages. The graph (Figure 4.16) shows clearly where management effort needed to be directed to achieve the target cycle time.

The quality audit stage was set at a nominal amount by management. Significant problems had occurred at this stage with the spray finish on the bogie frames being damaged during the subassembly fitting stage. This had to be rectified by a manual touch-up process, which could take longer than the original spray time. The paint area would also need to be reconfigured due to new environmental controls. Management had recognized the problems and an investment in an epoxy paint plant producing a hard-wearing finish was planned.

The bogie frame machining centre had previously been recognized by management as a bottleneck process. The bogie frame went through a

FIGURE 4.17

Setup Reduction.

number of preprogrammed steps on the machine and the cycle time was dependent on the capability of the machining centre itself. Consequently a major part of the planned investment was a new machining centre with a quoted cycle time below the target. An investigation of the fabrication processes revealed that although the cycle times were above target, the majority of this time was used for machine setup. Figure 4.17 shows the effect on cycle time of a reduction in setup time of 10% to 90%.

From Figure 4.17 it is clear that a setup reduction of 50% is required to achieve the target cycle time. A team was assembled to achieve this target and it was met by the use of magnetic tables to hold parts ready for processing. The simulation was rerun and the results (Figure 4.18) show the system achieving the required performance. It can be seen that a further reduction in fabrication setup times and a reconfiguration of the welding line would reduce the overall cycle time further,

producing a more balanced line and increasing capacity utilization.

By implementing the changes outlined in the study the simulation was able to predict the following improvements in performance (Table 4.6). In the table cycle efficiency $=100\%-\%$idle time where %idle time $=$ idle time per cycle/total cycle time.

These are substantial improvements in performance and meet the output targets set by management. However, the results in Figure 4.18 show that further reductions in the cycle times for the fabrication and weld stages would lead to

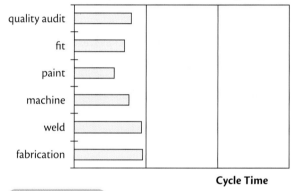

FIGURE 4.18

Cycle Time of Manufacturing Stages.

TABLE 4.6

Line Balancing Study Results.

Performance measure	Change (%)
Cycle time	−65
Lead time	−19
Output per week	+220
Cycle efficiency	+29

a further increase in cycle efficiency, reflecting a more balanced line, and thus a further increase in output.

Source: Excerpt from Greasley, A. (2004) "The case for the organisational use of simulation", Journal of Manufacturing Technology Management, Vol. 15, No. 7, pp. 560–566, Emerald Group Publishing. Reproduced with permission.

Questions

1. What are the reasons given for the need to balance the line?

2. What strategies are used to balance the line?

3. Identify alternative strategies to balance the line.

M&S

Marks & Spencer's current store layout failings are not down to a lack of investment; before Sir Stuart Rose departed in 2010 he had spent £2bn over five years improving the stores I.S. and store infrastructure, facilities, walls, ceiling and lighting. His successor Marc Bolland has with refreshed objectives continued such, leading an annual investment of £900m over the last 4 years, an increase of £300m from its normal rate, two thirds of which targeted the UK store operation, stating that only the basics had been fixed and he had to finish the job.

The organisation needed to rectify past mistakes, build a high level online environment, and delivering greater customer value by modernising the product ranges, designs and layout of the stores; in whole, making them 'shoppable'.

In what has been called the M&S Maze, many customers have complained they can't find what they're looking for in its shops and that they are difficult to shop in. The results of a Guardian Online survey found that 67% of customers suggested that M&S is tricky to get around and Management Consultancy McKinsey concluded in their review that many customers find M&S's stores hard to navigate.

In an attempt to recognize the depth of the problem through the eyes of a customer, Marc Bolland himself asked ten shoppers to go into an M&S branch and collect a list of ten items within an hour, but none of them were successful!

Store layout has been under a major review in order to stop customers wandering round in confusion.

The company is attempting through pilot stores and the redesign on existing outlets to make stores 'more inspiring', to improve store layout, in-store signage and navigation.

Trials of new layouts have been underway for some time, rolled out to 66 stores over the last 12 months, and increasing on a weekly basis, segmenting the stores better, whilst taking into account the product ranges and needs of customers relating to affluence, demographic, competition, region and ethnicity.

In September of 2011 M&S launched its brand new store at Westfield, Stratford City adjacent to the London Olympic Park. With 136,000 sq ft of selling space over four floors, M&S Stratford is one of the company's largest stores packed with the latest 'Only at Your M&S' innovations and customer experiences.

In the 2012 annual report, Bolland brings forth promising results through the 731 (an increase of 28) UK stores, "In a challenging marketplace M&S has performed well, as we continue to make progress against our plans". Clothing & Home revenue is £4.2bn, a reduction of 0.9%, and food revenue at £4.7bn, an increase of 3.9%.

For a company with the tradition and reputation of M&S, the question is should they have responded to customer demand quicker; with a continuation of store layout investment, we will have to wait for the answer.

Sources

http://www.guardian.co.uk/business/2011/may/24/customers-investors-lost-mar. . .

http://www.guardian.co.uk/business/2011/may/24/marks-spencer-tailoring-over. . .

http://www.guardian.co.uk/business/2010/nov/09/marks-and-spencer-foreign-ex. . .

http://corporate.marksandspencer.com/page.aspx?pointerid=85c1c7fb231c49fd9c4befca0f5532ac

http://www.dailymail.co.uk/news/article-1390281/M-S-stores-receive-makeover-customers-complain-difficult-navigate.html

Source: Written by Briony Boydell and Chris Milner. Reproduced with permission.

Questions

1. What is the dominant layout type in M&S stores? Is there evidence of any other layout types within?

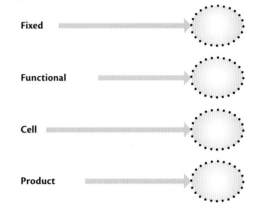

2. From your own personal experience, what retail store layouts frustrate you as a consumer?

3. What changes could be made in order to improve the customer experience?

Quizzes to test yourself further are available in your interactive e-book at **www.wileyopenpage.com**

Flashcards to test yourself further are available in your interactive e-book at **www.wileyopenpage.com**-

EXERCISES

1. What type of layout would you use for the assembly of a television set? What are the reasons for this choice?

2. What are the advantages that a cell layout attempts to achieve compared to the other layout types?

3. What are the benefits of the group technology technique?

4. The following parts are produced in a factory with a process layout comprising separate departments for each of the four operations: lathe, grind, drill and machining.

Part no.	Routing sequence
24	Grind
12	Lathe, drill
67	Grind, machine
45	Lathe, drill
32	Lathe, drill
76	Grind, machine

Use production flow analysis (PFA) to show how the plant could be organized into cells using group technology to identify families of parts.

5. A company is currently organized with machines grouped into departments based on their function. The sequence of operations taken for each component is:

Part no.	Routing sequence
487	Lathe, mill, grind, drill
723	Shear, punch press, grind, deburr
245	Mill, drill, grind
29	Shear, punch press, punch press, deburr

a. Draw a diagram of the plant and trace the routing sequence for each component.

b. Use PFA to analyse the routings and identify similarities between the components.

c. Group the components into families.

d. On the basis of the families identified in (c), specify cells for producing the components and trace the flow of work through the reorganized plant.

e. If the company currently has one of each machine, how many additional machines are required?

www.wileyopenpage.com

6. Use PFA to indicate how the following plant could be reorganized into cells. Currently the process layout consists of a lathe department with two lathes, a grinder department with two grinders, with all other departments having a single machine each

Part no.	Routing sequence
A1	Press, lathe
B2	Drill, mill, deburr
C3	Lathe, grinder, press
D4	Grinder, lathe
E5	Lathe, mill, drill
F6	Drill, grinder, deburr

7. Explain the need for line balancing.

8. What are the main techniques in determining capacity for a product layout and a process layout?

9. A list of tasks has been compiled in an assembly operation.

Task	Precedence	Task Time (mins)
A	-	6
B	A	3
C	B	7
D	B	5
E	C, D	4
F	E	5

a. Calculate the number of work stations required, balance the line and calculate the line efficiency if it is required that the assembly operation is completed within 10 minutes.

b. If there is no constraint on the number of work stations balance the line and calculate the line efficiency in order to maximize output.

c. Compare the number of assemblies that can be made in a four hour period for (a) and (b).

FURTHER READING

Burbidge, J.L. (1996) *Production Flow Analysis for Planning Group Technology*, Oxford University Press, Oxford.

Stephens, M.P. and Meyers, F.E. (2013) *Manufacturing Facilities Design and Material Handling*, 5th edn, Purdue University Press.

WEB LINKS

www.proplanner.com/Product/Details/LineBalancing.aspx (accessed 31 October 2011) ProPlanner software for single- and mixed-model line- balancing applications.

www.protech-ie.com/flb.htm (accessed 31 October 2011). Production Technology software for line balancing applications.

www.sixsigmainstitute.com/training/plb_training.shtml (accessed 31 October 2011). Lean Sigma Institute. Training in line balancing.

REFERENCES

Burbidge, J.L. (1996) *Production Flow Analysis for Planning Group Technology*, Oxford University Press.

Greasley, A. (2004) The case for the organisational use of simulation. *Journal of Manufacturing Technology Management*, 15 (7), 560–6.

Hope, C. and Muhlemann, A. (1997) *Service Operations Management: Strategy, Design and Delivery*, Prentice Hall.

Russell, R.S. and Taylor, B.W. (2011) *Operations Management: Creating Value Along the Supply Chain*, 7th edn, John Wiley and Sons Inc.

CHAPTER 5

Facility Design: Supply, Capacity and Location

- **Introduction**
- **Supply network design**
- **Long-term capacity planning**
- **Facility location**
- **Location selection techniques**

LEARNING OBJECTIVES

- Discuss the issue of supply network design
- Discuss the concept of economies of scale
- Discuss the concept of economies of scope
- Describe the approaches of lead capacity, match capacity and lag capacity
- Consider the facility location decision in terms of supply-side influences and demand-side influences
- Undertake the location selection techniques of weighted scoring, the centre of gravity method and locational cost-volume analysis

FACILITY DESIGN: SUPPLY, CAPACITY AND LOCATION AND OPERATIONS STRATEGY

Facility design covers three main areas of supply; network design, long-term capacity planning and facility location. In terms of a supply network design the supply network is a representation of the organisation's strategic capability. The organisation could attempt to do some activities that others in the supply network do now or could let new supply network partners undertake current work. The supply network shows that the success of an organization will be

www.wileyopenpage.com

dependent not just on their performance but the performance of all the organizations in the supply network. This implies cooperation with customers and suppliers will assist in meeting end customer demands. In terms of long-term capacity planning this decision needs to be made within a long-term plan which provides a fit with the operations strategy of the organization. This means capacity must be available at the time needed and in the current format to ensure that targets are met. Finally, the area of facility location is strategic as it can have a large impact on the investment in the operation's resources and also on the operation's market performance. A wrong location can lead to an inability to configure suitable resources for a resource-based strategy (e.g. lack of IT skills in local workforce). An incorrect location could also mean competitive factors cannot be met (e.g. fast food outlet located in area with insufficient catchment).

INTRODUCTION

In this book facility design is taken in a broad sense to mean the decisions surrounding how capacity will be supplied by the organization to meet market demand. This may be achieved internally by the organization by the construction of facilities or externally by agreement with suppliers. There are three main issues involved in decisions regarding this area:

1. How will the organization's facilities be configured (supply network design)? This includes decisions on the configurations of the organization's relationship with its suppliers and the choice about what activities the organization should undertake internally and what should be subcontracted to other agencies.
2. How much capacity should be supplied (long-term capacity planning)? This covers the question of how much long-term capacity should be supplied by the organization.
3. Where will the capacity be located (facility location)? This covers the question of the geographical location of capacity supplied by the organization.

SUPPLY NETWORK DESIGN

Every operation, as well as supplying capacity to the market in terms of goods and services, will require capacity in the form of inputs to the manufacturing and services process, such as materials, people and equipment. Thus, when designing an operations facility, consideration must be made regarding the relationship of the organization with its suppliers of the capacity required in order to provide the goods and services the facility is producing. Until relatively recently production processes in most organizations were within national or even local boundaries. Now a process of internationalization has led to manufacturing and service operations taking place across national boundaries. The main drivers for this change can be seen as:

- *Political* – the development of global organizations such as the WTO (World Trade Organisation) which negotiates trade agreements between governments, the establishment of trading groups such as the European Union (EU) and the demise of alternative economic systems in the former Soviet

Union and the adoption of a market oriented economy in China since the late 1970s. China joined the WTO in 2001 and is an increasingly important part of the international trading system.

- *Economic* – Until recently the world economy has seen sustained growth in the developed economies which has led to increased international trade of goods and services. Although the growth of Western Europe and the United States has been slow since the 2008 financial crisis, growth is still relatively high in China and other developing nations such as Brazil and India. The growth in these countries offers an opportunity for expansion of organizations that can operate on an international scale.
- *Socio-cultural* – The increase in travel and exposure to world media has led to the establishment of global brands which encourages organisations to expand into international markets.
- *Technological* – The use of Internet technologies such as e-commerce has led to easier communication between workers and suppliers and customers over large distances.

There are many different approaches to configuring facility design and Barnes (2008) provides four generic ways of configuring international operations (Figure 5.1).

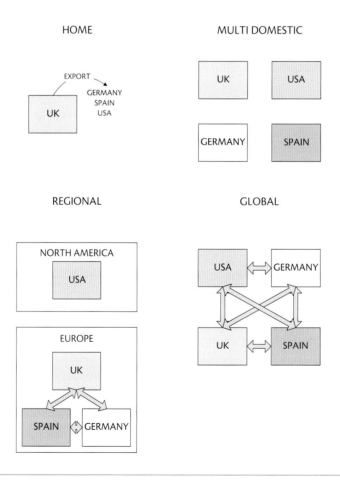

FIGURE 5.1

Four Generic Ways of Configuring International Operations.

 www.wileyopenpage.com

1. Home Operations. In this configuration all supplies of goods and services are made from within the home country and demand from other countries is made by direct export. This strategy enables control of operations in a familiar environment and can provide economies of scale and scope advantages by focusing output in one location. The disadvantages of this approach include the difficulty in meeting variations in customer needs in different overseas markets, the difficulty in providing prompt and reliable delivery over extended distances and the loss of markets where face-to-face services are required.

2. Multi-domestic Operations. This approach configures operations facilities in each country where the organization operates. This provides a relatively straightforward operations control and allows products and services to be tailored to meet local demands. The disadvantages of this approach include the cost of establishing multiple operations and the potential loss of economies of scale and scope in operating in this way.

3. Regional Operations. In this configuration operations is divided into regions (such as Europe, Pacific, Americas) with each region being served by a self-contained operations facility configuration. This is an attempt both to enable a degree of customization of product and service to meet local needs and to obtain economies of scale and scope across the region.

4. Global Operations. The **global organization** is organized into a network, which means that operations at several locations can perform tasks for a given customer group and/or a single facility can perform a task for several customer groups.

Whatever approach is taken when configuring facility design it is clear that in the process of the internationalization of operations the design of the relationship between the operation and its customers and suppliers is key; the way these relationships are configured is termed 'the supply network'. A generic supply network is shown in Figure 5.2 which can be defined as the configuration of the organization's relationship with its suppliers and the choice about what activities the organization should undertake internally and what should be subcontracted to other agencies. Note that although the flow of material is shown from left to right (downstream) there will be a flow of information in the opposite direction (upstream) between organizations in the supply network. Managing this flow of information upstream is a major element of supply network management. The terms supply network and supply chain are often used interchangeably but here the supply chain is taken to mean one of a series of linkages within the supply network (supply chain management is covered in more detail in Chapter 15).

Supply networks can improve delivery and cost performance relative to fixed supply facilities because the network can pool demand and increase volume to reduce cost and choose different facilities to provide products for a given customer under different conditions. The use of a network should lead to a more robust system that avoids capacity bottlenecks through the use of close coordination facilitated by the use of communications technology.

The configuration of the supply network will become more complex as we move from a home operations configuration through to a global operated organization. In global organizations the aim is to create a network of operations that will sell the same products in several countries, increase overall sales thereby reducing the cost per unit of development, coordinate the work of subsidiaries to provide a product/service to the global customer and shift production in response to exchange-rate fluctuations.

One of the main advantages of operating as a multinational company is reported to be the ability to learn and improve operations through knowledge transfer between the organization's units operating in different locations. The main difficulty in operating in this way arises in the need to balance the

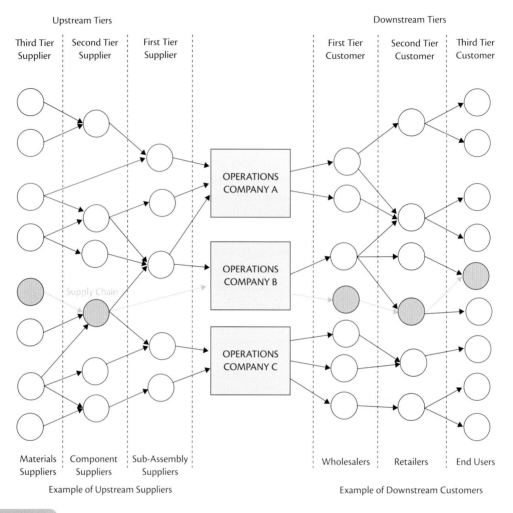

FIGURE 5.2

A Generic Supply Network.

needs of local markets, affected by factors such as different legislative environments and cultural differences, with achieving an efficient coordinated global operations capability.

So how does an organization overcome the basic dilemma for a multinational company of aiming to integrate plants on an international scale to achieve maximum efficiency while at the same time having the flexibility to serve changing customer needs in different markets? Approaches have ranged from having companies manufacturing products close to their customers, tailoring regional operations at scattered plants to meet local needs to centralized manufacturing, offering a selection of standard, lower priced products to all the markets they serve (McGrath and Hoole, 1992). Tom Peters (1994) argues that firms will achieve global reach not through the formal multinational structure but through the use of an informal decentralized network, facilitated by telecommunications technology, providing scale power without vertical integration. Asea Brown Boveri (ABB) is cited as a global manufacturing company attempting to combine the advantages of a global organization with the flexibility and innovation possible from small local units.

www.wileyopenpage.com

IoD Advocates Space Hub to Lift Economy

Building a hub for space tourism could provide a futuristic boost to the British economy, according to a report from the Institute of Directors, which urges the government and private sector to start planning a UK spaceport.

In the first of a planned series of reports on business infrastructure, the IoD argues that Britain's booming space industry needs a UK spaceport for space tourism, research and development to continue the industry's 'Bric-style growth' into the future.

Already an £8bn industry, Britain's space sector employs 25 000 people directly and 60 000 indirectly, with jobs growing by 15 per cent a year, the report estimates.

Requirements for a spaceport include a long runway (at least 5000 metres) and an undisturbed high altitude air corridor. Although that rules out south-east England, several RAF bases in Scotland and Northern Ireland could potentially be converted, the report says; a location in south-west England might be another option.

Although the funding might be mostly private, strong support from local and central government would be essential to establish a spaceport – not just to tackle planning and air traffic control issues, but also to establish a regulatory framework for journeys into space.

'To get the ball rolling, the most important step is to enact a UK regulatory regime that is not too onerous and is as close as possible to the one in the US,' said Dan Lewis, the IoD policy adviser who compiled the report.

'With no safety, environmental or flight regulations in place for trips into space from the UK, it's harder for space pioneers to insure and calculate the cost of setting up – and hopefully clustering – upstream companies that build space hardware and downstream firms that offer space-related services in Britain,' Mr Lewis added.

A spaceport would enable Britain to share in the coming era of suborbital space tourism, pioneered by companies such as Virgin Galactic. Wealthy space tourists who are willing to pay $200 000 for a few minutes of weightlessness and stunning views of the globe would have substantial disposable income to help the local economy, the report observes.

But tourism would just be part of the spaceport's business. It would also be a research and development centre for space-oriented businesses and perhaps a base for launching small unmanned satellites into orbit.

The space sector came about largely as a result of Britain's early adoption of satellite broadcasting, according to the IoD, allowing the country to draw on the skills of overlapping world-class aerospace and defence industries.

By contrast, the government has had very little involvement compared with other industrialised countries. The UK Space Agency received just £313m in public funding – just 0.73 per cent of the combined global space agency budget of $65bn in 2010 – making the space sector one of the least subsidised parts of the UK economy, the report says.

'Now is the time to look at the infrastructure that is needed to take the space industry on to the next stage,' said Simon Walker, IoD director-general of the Institute of Directors. 'It would be fantastic to have commercial space flights operating from a British spaceport, shipping goods and passengers into orbit and boosting the economy.'

Source: Financial Times (2012). Reproduced with permission.

Question

Evaluate the concept of clustering as discussed in the case study.

The issue of the design of the supply network is considered further in Chapter 15 on supply chain management. In particular the issues of supply chain integration and the use of e-Commerce are directly related to supply network decisions.

LONG-TERM CAPACITY PLANNING

The level at which management sets the level of capacity is a key determinant of the competitiveness of the organization. This decision needs to be made within a **long-term capacity plan**, which provides a fit with the operations strategy of the organization. The operations strategy should define the nature of the markets that the organization intends to compete in, in terms of characteristics such as product mix, volume and geographic spread, which will impact on the amount and type of capacity required. Thus it is not simply a matter of attaining a sufficient amount of capacity to meet the expected demand, but the capacity must be available at the time needed and in the current format to ensure that targets are met. For example, if it is required to meet sudden changes of demand in an overseas market, the transportation time for the capacity supplied in a local location may mean it cannot supply the market within the time required. There will also be constraints on overall capacity caused by a scarcity of certain types of capacity (such as employee skills). Thus the availability of different types of capacity must be considered in order to avoid bottlenecks occurring. This section will consider long-term capacity issues in terms of the volume of capacity required and the timing of when that capacity should be acquired. Short and medium-term capacity planning issues in terms of meeting customer demand are covered in Chapter 11.

Capacity Volume

In determining the capacity volume of a facility there will need to be an appreciation of the reduction in unit costs available from increasing the volume of output from the facility, termed economies of scale. There will also be a potential reduction in unit costs available from increasing the variety of output from a facility, termed economies of scope. In addition there needs to be an appreciation that the actual volume of output of a facility will be determined by the process with the smallest capacity, termed the bottleneck. Another important decision is required in terms of deciding if capacity volume is to be obtained within the facility or subcontracted from the supply network.

Economies of Scale

In determining the optimum capacity level for a facility the concept of **economies of scale** is considered. Economies of scale relate to the capital costs of building a new facility and the fixed costs of operating a facility.

The capital costs of building a facility do not increase proportionally as its capacity increases, so, for example, a facility with twice the capacity of another facility will not have capital costs twice as high. This might suggest that the use of a single large facility that supplies all capacity needs is the most appropriate strategy. However, at a certain capacity level for a particular location, **diseconomies of scale** may set in. These may include the transportation costs incurred in supplying a large geographical area from a single location, the speed of delivery from a single location to the customer becoming too slow and the added complexity of a large organization may cause communication and coordination problems.

 www.wileyopenpage.com

The video 'Firm Cost Structure' is available in your interactive e-book at **www.wileyopenpage.com**

 The video 'Long-Run Cost Structure' is available in your interactive e-book at **www.wileyopenpage.com**

 The video 'Long-Run Production' is available in your interactive e-book at **www.wileyopenpage.com**

As a facility is expanded and fixed costs remain the same the average cost of producing each unit will fall until the best operating level of the facility is reached and the lowest average unit cost met. Past a certain point, however, diseconomies of scale occur and average unit costs rise. This is due to the required capacity output of the facility being higher than it has been designed for. Operating at this level can cause loss of efficiency from factors such as poor decision-making due to management layers, congestion of materials and staff, complexity of combining many products and services, extensive use of (relatively expensive) shift working and overtime and reduced morale of staff due to working conditions. The relationship between average unit cost of output and volume for different facility sizes is shown in Figure 5.3.

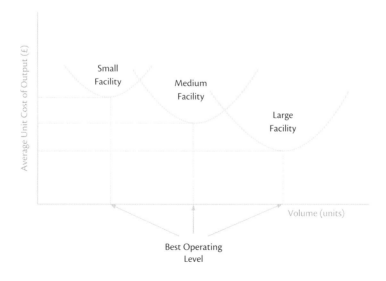

FIGURE 5.3

Best Operating Level for Facility Size.

The decision regarding the volume of capacity is complex because it is unlikely that the amount of capacity required from a facility will be fixed over the long term. Therefore, there is a choice to be made between

- building a facility that provides more capacity than is currently needed but will provide sufficient capacity for planned growth in output; or
- matching the facility design to current capacity requirements, achieving maximum economies of scale, and then incurring the cost of expansion to meet any future increase in capacity requirements.

The expansion route is less risky, particularly when the forecast of future demand is uncertain as it requires less finance to be tied up in the facility infrastructure. However, construction costs can be considerably decreased if the complete facility is built in one phase. The decision will be based on the strategy of the firm and in particular the likely growth rate of the products or services the facility will supply.

When considering economies of scale it is important to understand that the rationalization of a number of facilities into a single large facility will achieve economies of scale only if the multiple facilities are doing the same type of work. Simply putting the work of a number of facilities doing different activities within one building is unlikely to achieve economy-of-scale benefits. There are also likely to be difficulties in achieving economies of scale in front-office service systems where contact with the customer and customization of the service offering may be required by the customer.

Economies of Scope

Traditionally, significant investment in process technology, such as automation, has only been justified for high-volume products where economies of scale provide a lowest average cost per unit. However, modern process technology, such as flexible manufacturing systems (FMS), described in Chapter 6, provide flexibility and allow a range of products to be produced quickly and efficiently. Thus **economies of scope** are created by the ability to produce many products in one highly flexible production facility more cheaply than in separate facilities. In terms of services this means serving many different customer groups from one facility. An example is outsourced call centre operations which use specialist firms to serve many different clients using Internet technology. Nike offers the ability through its Internet site (www.nike.com) for customers to specify custom training shoes which are then produced using flexible operations facilities. Mass customization (see Chapter 7) aims to use economies of scope to use a single process to produce a wide variety of products or services.

Balancing Capacity

In calculating capacity volume another factor to take into account is that the total capacity of any system is dependent on the process with the smallest capacity, called the bottleneck. Thus in order for the system to operate at its most efficient it is necessary to equalize the capacity between processes. The capacity of sequential processes can be visualized as a series of pipes of varying capacity, with the smallest pipe limiting the capacity of the whole system (Figure 5.4).

In Figure 5.4 the total capacity of the system is limited by the capacity at process 3. Thus process 3 is the bottleneck process. See Chapter 4 for details of the line balancing technique for balancing capacity.

IN   OUT

1   2   3   4

FIGURE 5.4

Diagram of the Capacity of Four Sequential Processes.

Subcontracting Networks

An alternative to obtaining capacity volume within the organization is to develop **subcontractor and supplier networks**. Here long-term contractual arrangements are made with suppliers to supply goods and services which means that less capacity is required by the subcontracting organization. An advantage of this approach is that less capital is required for production and delivery facilities. There is also the flexibility to decrease capacity supplied to meet falling market demand without incurring the costs of under-utilization of resources or to increase capacity without the expense of additional resources. A disadvantage is the risk that subcontractors may not be able to meet changing capacity requirements. There is also a risk of the loss of skills inherent in outsourcing activities. **Outsourcing** is the term used when goods and services are obtained outside the organization. **Business process outsourcing** (**BPO**) refers to the outsourcing of processes, such as maintenance processes for example. **Offshoring** is the term used to describe the transfer of activities to another country. This can be achieved by either moving activities to an overseas arm of a multinational firm or by outsourcing activities to a foreign supplier. Different forms of organizational relationships are covered in the supply chain integration section of Chapter 15.

Capacity Timing

As well as determining the correct level of capacity volume it is necessary to decide the timing of capacity additions (or reductions) in order to meet demand. An organization can adopt three main approaches to ensuring the correct amount of capacity is available at the right time to meet future plans. Three approaches of lead capacity, match capacity and lag capacity are outlined.

Lead Capacity

A **lead capacity** policy (Figure 5.5), also called an aggressive expansion approach, aims to obtain extra capacity above forecast demand and so try

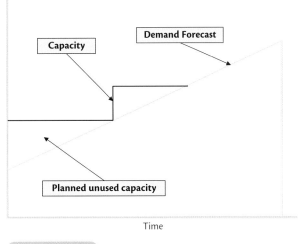

FIGURE 5.5

Lead Capacity Strategy.

The Supply Chains that Could Bind Unsuspecting Managers

Emma Maersk – and I don't think she would mind me saying this – is a very big girl indeed. She's as wide as a motorway. And at almost 400 m in length and 60 m in height she is probably the largest container ship the world has ever seen. When the *Emma Maersk* docked in Felixstowe in the southeast of England this month the sighs of relief from retailers, manufacturers and parents should have been audible all over the planet. Christmas, in the UK at least, had not been cancelled. An amazing 45 000 tonnes of Chinese manufactured goods have now been safely unloaded and despatched to shops and warehouses across the country. This is what it looks like when supply chains work. But the story does not always have such a happy ending. Globalization has led to the development of longer and at times more precarious supply chains. The drive for efficiency has often seen companies rationalize the number of suppliers they use,

leaving them more dependent on a smaller array of partners. As for suppliers, they find themselves under constant price pressure, with less slack or tolerance in the system. The suppliers' relationship with their customers is frequently less 'sticky' than it was in the past. There is the permanent risk of being substituted should problems – delays or quality concerns – arise. Supply chains, in other words, are both leaner and meaner than they used to be. And some observers suggest that this leaves many businesses exposed to much greater risks than perhaps they realize.

Source: Stefan Stern, *Financial Times,* published 28 November 2006, (abridged version). Reproduced with permission.

Question

Discuss the risks of operating in a global supply network.

to ensure capacity is sufficient if demand increases above forecast. This has the advantage of helping to maintain high levels of customer service and responding quickly to increases in customer demand, but has the disadvantage of the cost of maintaining the excess capacity for all the different types of capacity (people, equipment, locations) required over time. An advantage of this approach is that the excess capacity can be allocated to different products and services over time as the nature of demand fluctuates, although this is limited by specialization of resource, for example, only certain trained people can do certain tasks.

The amount of excess capacity, which can be calculated as the percentage of capacity that is not used on average, is termed the **capacity cushion**. A number of factors will impact on deciding the nature of the capacity cushion in a lead capacity strategy. The size of the cushion will be a trade-off between the costs of too much capacity in terms of unused resources against the costs of too little capacity in terms of using options such as overtime and outsourcing to meet customer demands, or losing customer orders through an inability to supply them quickly enough. The capacity cushion decision should also take into consideration the strategic context. For example, a new product or service in its growth phase may require a large capacity cushion to maximize customers, whereas for a product or service in the mature or decline stage of its life cycle a smaller cushion may be more appropriate.

Match Capacity

The second option is to **match capacity** – simply obtain capacity to match forecast demand. The advantage of this option is that it avoids the costs of a capacity cushion and the use of strategies such as outsourcing may be used to quickly fill capacity shortfalls. The disadvantage is the difficulty of forecasting future demand accurately enough in order that capacity can be obtained at the right time (not too early or not too late) to meet that demand. Long project lead times for investments in capacity such as infrastructure projects means demand forecasts have to project further into the future and so are prone to greater error.

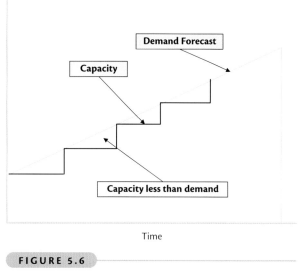

FIGURE 5.6

Lag Capacity Strategy.

Lag Capacity

A **lag capacity** strategy (Figure 5.6), also termed a 'wait and see' approach, is to only add capacity when extra demand is present that would use the additional resources. This has the advantage of delaying investments until it is certain they are needed and ensures a high utilization of capacity acquired. However, this option may mean customers are lost as they move to competitor products and services before the additional capacity has been acquired. There may also be a loss of flexibility as a consequence of the continual high utilization of resources using this strategy.

Timing the Capacity Increments

When undertaking a lead capacity or match capacity approach it is unlikely that the capacity cushion can be adjusted or the capacity matched smoothly, but adjustments will be made in increments (for example, the purchase of new equipment or hiring of new staff). Thus there is a need to determine the timing of capacity increments.

In a lag capacity strategy the acquisition of new capacity is triggered by an increase in demand. One aspect of this strategy is that competitors also following a lag strategy will increase their capacity simultaneously, which may lead to an increase in the cost of capacity. This behaviour may also lead to overcapacity in the market, increasing competitive pressures. Organizations following a lead or match capacity strategy may avoid these problems by adding capacity when demand is low (at the low point of the business cycle). This strategy can reduce costs but carries the obvious risk that the demand planned for may not materialize.

An alternative approach is to build capacity, not simply for relatively short-term fluctuations in demand, but to a strategy of increasing market share over the long term. Again, this approach is risky in the sense that it is not following a forecasted demand pattern. In order to reduce risk some organizations use the fact that their performance in the market is relative to the performance of their competitors. Thus capacity is added in response to the capacity expansion of the market leader. Whether it transpires that the capacity is needed or not, the relative position of the organization in respect to its competitors remains the same. These approaches have the disadvantage of being essentially reactive (either to demand or competitors) and do not take into account how capacity expansion can be used in a proactive manner as part of an operations strategy.

A number of companies have grown rapidly (for example Wal-Mart, easyJet) by continually adding new capacity and lowering costs in an attempt to freeze competitors out of the market. Retailing is an industry where quick expansion into geographical locations can freeze competitors out of these geographical locations that can only support a single retail outlet of a certain type. In some cases it may form part of the business strategy to build overcapacity to secure a locational presence or provide a higher level of performance of an objective such as delivery speed.

FACILITY LOCATION

There are three main reasons why a **facility location** decision is required. The first reason is that a new business has been created and requires facilities in order to manufacture its product or service its customers. The second reason is that there is a decision to relocate an existing business due to factors such as the need for larger premises or to be nearer a customer base. The third reason is to expand into new premises as part of a growth strategy. For each of these scenarios the facility location decision can be considered in terms of its effect on costs and customer service quality. Due to globalization the facility location decision made by an increasing number of manufacturing and service organizations means considering the option of locating their facilities outside their country of origin (see the section on supply network design earlier in this chapter).

A company's competitiveness will be affected by its location, as the choice of location will impact on costs for elements such as transportation and labour. A location decision is costly and time consuming to change. The costs include the purchase of land and construction of buildings. An organization may be located inappropriately due to a previous poor location decision and an unwillingness to face the costs of a subsequent relocation. A change in input costs, such as materials or labour, may also lead to a need to change location.

The cost of establishing a new service facility may be relatively low compared to a manufacturing plant with its associated equipment. Service facilities also generally need to be in close contact with their customers. This has led to multiple service outlets being established in locations which serve a target market. Whereas manufacturing sites will often be located to minimize costs, services will be located to maximize income from customers. However, for services that process information, rather than customers, then telecommunications technology can be used to provide a service from a centralized facility. Services are generally classified as back-office and front-office (see Chapter 1) with back-office services not requiring customer contact and thus providing more flexibility in the location decision. Front-office services, however, require customer contact but when making the location decision it is useful to distinguish them by the nature of the movement of user (customer) and provider of the service. Barnes (2008) provides a customer contact location matrix (Figure 5.7) which contains four types of front-office service considering these movements.

Separated services are providing a service directly to a customer so can be classified as front-office but do not actually require either the user or provider to physically come together to enable the service to take place. Call centres have been established internationally which provide services to customers at a distance.

PROVIDER

	Does not move	Moves
Does not move	SEPERATED SERVICES	DEMANDER-LOCATED SERVICES
Moves	PROVIDER-LOCATED SERVICES	PERIPATETIC SERVICES

USER

FIGURE 5.7

Customer Contact Services Location Matrix.

Demander-located services require movement of the service provider to the location of the customer. An example is management consultancy where it would usually be expected that the service provider would be present at least in part at the premises of the client.

Provider-located services require the movement of the user to the location of the service provider. This may be of necessity in order to access specialist resources and staff such as at a hospital or as a feature of the service itself as in a hotel.

Peripatetic services involve both customer and provider moving to the location of the service encounter. Trade shows and conferences come into this category.

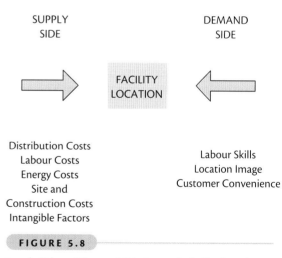

SUPPLY SIDE

DEMAND SIDE

FACILITY LOCATION

Distribution Costs
Labour Costs
Energy Costs
Site and
Construction Costs
Intangible Factors

Labour Skills
Location Image
Customer Convenience

FIGURE 5.8

Supply-Side and Demand-Side Factors in Facility Location.

The Location Decision

The location decision can be considered in terms of factors that vary in such a way as to influence cost as location varies (supply-side factors) and factors that vary in such a way as to influence customer service as location varies (demand-side factors) (see Figure 5.8). The location decision can be seen as

CASE STUDY 5.3

Moving Textile Manufacturing Overseas

Due to global competitive pressures many garment manufacturers have scaled down or closed their operations in the UK and moved overseas. Production has increased in such areas as Asia due to lower labour costs in what is a labour-intensive industry. A textile manufacturer based in Leicester, UK produces a range of cotton and lycra textile mixes, which are used for garments such as t-shirts and women's tights. It has decided to supplement its UK operations and locate a textile production facility in Sri Lanka.

The move will permit the design of a more efficient layout in a purpose-built factory, as opposed to the current facilities, which are placed across a number of locations and buildings within the UK. An important part of the layout planning activity is the estimation of the quantity of work-in-progress inventory within the proposed facility. The estimation of inventory levels is critical because the relative bulk of inventory means the amount of floor-space required could be considerable. The need to sink drainage channels for effluent from the knit and dye machines and the size and weight of the machinery involved mean that it would be expensive and time-consuming to change the factory layout after construction.

Questions

1. Discuss the supply-side and demand-side influences on the facility location decision described in the case study.

2. Describe how the technique of business process simulation (Chapter 8) could help in the design of the new factory layout.

LOCATION SELECTION TECHNIQUES

As a procedure the location selection process consists of identifying a suitable region/country, identifying an appropriate area within that region and finally comparing and selecting a suitable site from that area. A number of techniques for location selection are available and are described in the following section. However, an issue to consider with these techniques is that location decisions are often complex and strategic, involving information which is often qualitative in nature, and so the results of these analyses must be interpreted with this in mind.

Weighted Scoring

In most situations cost will not be the only criterion for a location decision. **Weighted scoring**, also referred to as factor rating or point rating, attempts to provide a rational basis for evaluation of alternative locations by establishing a composite value for each alternative. The ratings include factors based on qualitative as well as quantitative factors. The procedure consists of determining a list of factors that are relevant to the location decision. This may include such factors as convenience to customers, labour skills and transportation facilities. Each factor is then given a weighting that indicates its relative importance compared to the other factors. Each location is then scored on each factor and this score is multiplied by the factor value. The alternative with the highest score is then chosen. The usefulness of the method is dependent on identifying the appropriate location factors and devising a suitable weighting for each. One approach is to use the method to assess the intangible factors (such as quality of life) only and then determine if the difference between the intangible scores is worth the cost of the difference in tangible costs between the locations.

WORKED EXAMPLE 5.1

Weighted Scoring

New Technologies Ltd is an organization that specializes in simulation modelling consultancy. It has identified three sites on the west coast of the USA that have approximately equal initial and operating costs. The sites have been evaluated on a score of 1 to 10 (10 being best) against the following criteria and weighting assigned by management.

	Weight	City		
		Los Angeles	Portland	Seattle
Pool of skilled system modellers	0.5	6	4	5
University research in modelling	0.3	3	5	3
Recreational and cultural activities	0.2	5	3	4

Rank the three cities in order of their total weighted points score.

Solution

$$\text{Los Angeles} = (6 \times 0.5) + (3 \times 0.3) + (5 \times 0.2) = 4.9$$
$$\text{Seattle} = (5 \times 0.5) + (3 \times 0.3) + (4 \times 0.2) = 4.2$$
$$\text{Portland} = (4 \times 0.5) + (5 \times 0.3) + (3 \times 0.2) = 4.1$$

The Centre of Gravity Method

The **centre of gravity method** can be used to determine the location of a distribution centre by minimizing distribution costs. In services when locating a retail outlet the gravity method can be used to maximize profit (Fitzsimmons and Fitzsimmons, 2010). The method assumes distribution costs change in a linear fashion with the distance and the quantity transported. The method also assumes the quantity transported is fixed for the duration of the journey. The relative coordinates of the distribution points are placed on a map and the location of the distribution point should be at the centre of gravity of the coordinates. To find this point the averages of the x coordinates and y coordinates are found using the following equations:

$$\bar{x} = \frac{\Sigma x_i Q_i}{\Sigma Q_i}$$

$$\bar{y} = \frac{\Sigma y_i Q_i}{\Sigma Q_i}$$

where

Q_i = quantity to be transported to destination i
x_i = x coordinate of destination i
y_i = y coordinate of destination i
$\bar{x}$ = x coordinate of centre of gravity
$\bar{y}$ = y coordinate of centre of gravity.

WORKED EXAMPLE 5.2

Centre of Gravity Method

A manufacturing organization wishes to build a centralized warehouse system that will serve a number of production facilities in Germany. The expected demand and relative grid references for the facility are given below.

Location	Demand (units/year)	Relative grid reference
Hamburg	40 000	(3,7)
Cologne	20 000	(1,4)
Stuttgart	35 000	(3,2)
Munich	70 000	(4,1)
Dresden	45 000	(6,5)
Berlin	110 000	(5,6)

At what location, in terms of grid reference, should the warehouse be situated?

Solution

$$\bar{x} = \frac{(3 \times 40\,000) + (1 \times 20\,000) + (3 \times 35\,000) + (4 \times 70\,000) + (6 \times 45\,000) + (5 \times 1\,10\,000)}{40\,000 + 20\,000 + 35\,000 + 70\,000 + 45\,000 + 110\,000}$$

$$\bar{y} = \frac{(7 \times 40\,000) + (4 \times 20\,000) + (2 \times 35\,000) + (1 \times 70\,000) + (5 \times 45\,000) + (6 \times 11\,000)}{40\,000 + 20\,000 + 35\,000 + 70\,000 + 45\,000 + 110\,000}$$

$\bar{x} = 4.2$

$\bar{y} = 4.3$

Locational Cost-Volume Analysis

Locational cost-volume analysis will indicate when a particular location is superior for a particular volume level by analysing the mix of fixed and variable costs. Some costs such as the costs of building the facility will be fixed, while others such as the level of demand will vary with the location. The relationship between both of these factors will vary for each location being considered. The procedure for graphical cost-volume analysis is as follows:

1. Determine the fixed and variable costs for each location.
2. Plot the total cost (fixed plus variable) lines for the location alternatives on the graph (Figure 5.10).
3. Choose the location with the lowest total cost line at the expected volume level.

The equation for expressing costs in terms of location is:

$$TC = VC \times X + FC$$

where
TC = total cost
VC = variable cost per unit
X = number of units produced
FC = fixed costs

FIGURE 5.10

Cost-Volume Graph.

WORKED EXAMPLE 5.3

Locational Cost-Volume Analysis

A manufacturing organization is considering the following locations for its plant.

	Barcelona	Madrid
Variable costs	£1.75/unit	£1.25/unit
Annual fixed costs	£200 000	£180 000
Initial fixed costs	£1 400 000	£1 600 000

(a) Draw a cost-volume graph for both locations over a five-year period at a volume of 200 000 units per year.

(b) Which location has the lowest cost?

(c) At what volume do the locations have equal costs?

Solution

Cost at year 0

Barcelona = 1 400 000

Madrid = 1 600 000

Cost at year 5

Barcelona = $1\,400\,000 + (5 \times 200\,000) + (5 \times 200\,000 \times 1.75) = £4\,150\,000$.

Madrid = $1\,600\,000 + (5 \times 180\,000) + (5 \times 200\,000 \times 1.25) = £3\,750\,000$.

(a) From the graph Madrid has the lowest costs after 5 years.

(b) If X equals the number of years until costs are equal.

Using subscript B for Barcelona and M for Madrid.

$$TC_B = TC_M$$

$$1\,400\,000 + 200\,000X + (200\,000 \times 1.75)X = 1\,600\,000 + 180\,000X$$
$$+ (200\,000 \times 1.25)X$$

$$1\,600\,000 - 1\,400\,000 + 180\,000X - 200\,000X + 250\,000X - 350\,000X = 0$$

$$200\,000 - 120\,000X = 0$$

$$X = 200\,000/120\,000$$

$$= 1.6 \text{ years}$$

 www.wileyopenpage.com

This method has assumed that fixed costs are constant for the volume range when in fact step changes may occur in fixed cost expenditure to meet certain volume levels. Variable costs are also assumed to have a linear (straight-line) relationship with volume, when this may not be so. Some cost-volume models may incorporate a nonlinear (curved) relationship. Another assumption is that output of the facility has also been aggregated into one product that may not reflect the complexity of how a mix of products affects costs over a range of volumes.

If the analysis includes the economics of the logistics activity for a range of volumes then it is possible to review make-or-buy issues and thus the mix between in-house and the subcontracting of components. Again the decision will concern the relationship between fixed and variable costs through the product life cycle. The relationship between fixed and total costs, termed the 'operational gearing', is important in determining whether production should be initiated and when it should cease. The operation with low fixed costs and thus low operational gearing will have more flexibility in responding to changes in market demand over time. In other words, if fixed costs are low the company does not require high volumes to break even and can thus reduce output to match demand more easily. A high-volume producer, however, invests in specialized equipment and thus increases operational gearing in order to reduce unit costs and thus create greater profit potential. An increase in volume for a high-volume producer will thereby only add a small amount of unit variable costs. This approach means the high-volume producer will prefer to operate as close to capacity limits as possible to maximize profit.

SUMMARY

- Facility design can be considered to cover the areas of supply network design, long-term capacity planning and facility location.
- Supply network design concerns the relationship of the organization with its suppliers of capacity.
- Four generic ways of configuring international operations are home, multi-domestic, regional and global.
- Long-term capacity planning is about providing a long-term plan for capacity which provides a fit with the operations strategy of the organization.
- Economies of scale refers to the characteristic that, as a facility is expanded and fixed costs remain the same, the average cost of producing each unit will fall.
- Economies of scope are created by the ability to produce many products in one highly flexible facility more cheaply than in separate facilities.
- A lead capacity strategy maintains a capacity cushion (extra capacity above forecast demand) in order to ensure sufficient capacity if demand increases. A match capacity strategy aims

to obtain capacity to match forecast demand. A lag capacity strategy is to acquire additional capacity when extra demand is present.

- Facility location factors can be considered as influencing cost as location varies (supply-side factors) and influencing customer service as location varies (demand-side factors).
- Location selection techniques include the weighted scoring method, which attempts to take a range of considerations into account when choosing a location. The centre of gravity method determines location by minimizing distribution costs (or maximizing profits for a retail outlet). Locational cost-volume analysis indicates which location is suitable for a particular volume level by analysing the mix of fixed and variable costs.

CASE STUDY 5.4

Mom-and-Pop Companies Face Struggle for Survival

In 1999, Kachio Okuda left his job at a Tokyo printing company to set up his own small printing business. By 2000, he says, he was already regretting the move. 'As soon as a big company bids for a contract, the price plummets and we can't match it,' the 55-year- old entrepreneur says. 'More and more, we're living in a different world from the big firms.' Regrets aside, Mr Okuda has kept his 12-employee operation running for the past eight years. Many other small business owners are not so fortunate. Although bankruptcies declined from 19 000 in 2002 to 13 000 cases in 2006, the number of small firms has continued to fall steadily. 'These are family-run companies. They don't go bankrupt, they just close up shop,' Mr Okuda says.

Seven in 10 working Japanese are employed at small and medium-sized enterprises (SMEs), defined as having fewer than 50–300 workers, depending on the industry. In the US the ratio is five in 10, even though the small-business category there includes bigger companies. Toyota, Sony and other big exporters may carry Japan's flag abroad, but it is the vast pyramid of small suppliers on which they stand that gives the economy its muscle. Mr Okuda's 'different world' lament is supported by earnings data. Small firms' recurring profits grew an average of 2.4 percentage points more slowly in 2005 than those at big companies. In the 1990s the gap was a percentage point smaller.

Pessimism is widespread. Quarterly sentiment surveys by the Bank of Japan show that while business confidence has improved with Japan's five-year economic expansion, as a whole, managers of small businesses remain downbeat. This year they expect to cut capital investment by an average of 10.5 per cent, even as big companies spend almost 9 per cent more. Concerns about the plight of small businesses are tied to broader worries about social and economic inequality, which has increased slightly during the expansion. Promises of more small-business aid helped the opposition Democratic Party of Japan trounce the ruling Liberal Democrats in upper house elections in July.

A core problem for small companies has been their inability to pass on rising costs to their customers. 'The pattern we see is a high break-even point that makes it difficult for small and medium companies to absorb growth in costs such as raw materials and labour,' says Tetsufumi Yamakawa, senior economist at Goldman Sachs. In the auto industry, parts makers have groaned as Toyota and Nissan have pushed through aggressive cost-cutting programmes centred on rationalizing their supply lines and introducing more competition to procurement. Both auto giants are renowned for their ability to keep margins high by squeezing suppliers.

Every small business must contend with an inherent lack of economies of scale. In Japan, that handicap is being felt more keenly amid a general 'sizing up' of the economy, as big companies get bigger due to deregulation and a wave of mergers and acquisitions. In the retail sector, small shops that once dominated distribution of everything from televisions to bananas have been hurt by a relaxation of size restrictions. This has opened the way for large suburban shopping centres and 'big box' stores of the kind pioneered in the US.

'At first, supermarket-sized electronics stores took customers from the Mom-and-Pop dealers,' says a manager at a major electronics chain. 'Then, when the size limits went up again, we took over with huge outlets at the edge of town.'

As a result of this general bloating, sales at retailers with less than 500 m^2 of shop space shrank by a quarter between 1997 and 2004, accounting for the entire drop in Japanese retail sales during the period. Mr Okuda says his printing company could compete with bigger rivals if only banks would lend him enough cash to grow. 'Banks won't tell you "no" straight out, but

the conditions they impose amount to the same thing,' he says. 'They don't understand small business.' Lenders remain cautious after writing off a mountain of bad loans to big and small companies alike over the last decade. Outstanding loans to small businesses fell to a low of Y245 000 billion in 2005 from about Y340 000 billion in 1998, although the total has picked up slightly in the last two years.

The higher margins associated with small-business loans mean big banks such as Tokyo-Mitsubishi UFJ, Mizuho and Sumitomo Mitsui are in fact keen to offer credit, says Naoko Nemoto, analyst at Standard & Poor's. But they 'have no clear strategy for penetrating this market'. Small branch networks relative to their financial clout and a lack of staff trained to assess small companies' books have constrained the banks' ability to lend. Many small business owners want more help from the government, which already offers a range of support programmes. The Ministry of Economy, Trade and Industry's 2007 White Paper on small business includes 15 chapters on aid schemes, from preferential lending and tax breaks to help for ageing small business owners who are trying to recruit successors.

In truth, 'scaling up' the economy has brought gains for Japan as a whole, in the form of greater efficiency and productivity, economists say. That means government intervention is likely to focus on easing the growing pains rather than bringing back old restrictions. Mr Okuda appears resigned. 'It's the destiny of capitalism, I guess. But it doesn't leave you much room to enjoy what you're doing.'

Source: Jonathan Soble, *The Financial Times* (2007). Reproduced with permission.

Question

How can small companies try to overcome competition from large competitors with greater economies of scale?

CASE STUDY 5.5

Coca-Cola

Coca-Cola is arguably the world's most recognised product. The logo itself is identifiable by over 94% of the world's population. It is enjoyed by customers in over 200 countries around the world. There are around 1.7 billion servings of Coca-Cola and coke products sold every day.

Coca-Cola therefore operates in a logistically challenging environment in order to meet this level of fulfilment. A can of coke is around 99% water, the global logistics of shipping this volume around the world would be impossible, let alone finding enough water required for the manufacturing process. However, the recipe for Coca-Cola has been a long guarded secret and production of the formula occurs in a single facility.

This has therefore led Coca-Cola to adopt a mixed facility location policy.

The company therefore adopts a centralised policy for the manufacture and distribution of the syrup. This concentrate is produced in Atlanta Georgia, by The Coca-Cola Company itself. This allows the company to maintain the secrets of production and also control the quality. Hence all Coca-Colas sold around the globe are from the same source and therefore there should be no variation in the product, in whichever country it is consumed.

Known as the 'Coca-Cola System', the actual production and distribution of Coca-Cola follows a franchising model. After production of the concentrate, Coco-Cola then ship the sticky brown syrup to over 300 licensed Coca-Cola bottlers throughout the world. The bottlers, who hold regionally exclusive contracts with the company, produce finished product in cans and bottles from the concentrate in combination with filtered water and sweeteners. The cans and bottles will all use the globally approved packaging, however each one will be set in the local language – all logos, nutritional information and company details are therefore available to the consumer.

The regional spread of these partner organisations depends upon the market volumes required. For example, in South Africa there are four licensed bottlers each one running a number of running bottling plants, to serve the population. However, in South America there are considerably more; the average Mexican, for example, drinks more Coke products than the average American, British, Indian, and Chinese combined.

Once the product is mixed, the bottlers sell, distribute and merchandise Coca-Cola to retail stores, vending machines, restaurants and food service distributors. The distances that the products need to travel, once full of water, are therefore significantly shorter, than if this had been a single facility production.

Coca-Cola maintain strong links with the franchises, and have a financial stake in many of the companies.

Sources

http://www.businessinsider.com/facts-about-coca-cola-2011-6?op=1#ixzz29vIKzk2z

http://www.cocacolasabco.com/territory.aspx/show

http://www.coca-cola.co.uk/

Source: Written by Briony Boydell and Chris Milner. Reproduced with permission.

Questions

1. What benefits are available to Coca-Cola in centralizing their syrup production?
2. What are the operational issues with the de-centralized bottling franchises?

Quizzes to test yourself further are available in your interactive e-book at **www.wileyopenpage.com**

 Flashcards to test yourself further are available in your interactive e-book at **www.wileyopenpage.com**

EXERCISES

1. Outline how a strategy of globalization will impact on a policy of pursuing economies of scale advantages.

2. Evaluate the strategies of lead capacity, match capacity and lag capacity for a retail outlet.

3. Discuss the location decision of an organization with which you are familiar in terms of supply-side influences and demand-side influences.

4. A manufacturing organization is looking at the following two locations:

	Birmingham	Manchester
Variable costs	£14/unit	£16/unit
Annual fixed costs	£12 000 000	£15 000 000
Initial fixed costs	£165 000 000	£145 000 000

   a. Draw a cost-volume graph for both locations over a 10-year period at a volume of 750 000 units per year.

   b. Which location has the lowest cost at the end of the 10-year period?

   c. At what volume do these locations have equal costs?

5. The following table lists the weightings representing the relative importance of factors for the location of a retail site. Four potential sites have been given a score out of 100 for each factor:

		Site			
Factor	Weight	A	B	C	D
Construction cost	0.1	90	60	80	70
Operating cost	0.1	90	80	90	85
Population density	0.4	70	90	80	75
Convenient access	0.2	75	80	90	90
Parking area	0.2	60	70	85	75

Rank the four sites in order of their total weighted points score for suitability for the proposed location.

6. A retail chain has four major stores in the East Midlands area which have the following monthly demand rates.

Store location	Monthly demand (units)
Derby	2000
Nottingham	1000
Leicester	1000
Sheffield	2000

The following map shows the relative coordinates of the four outlets.

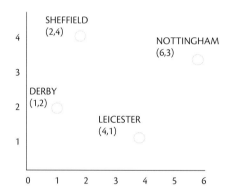

The organization has decided to find a 'central' location in which to build a warehouse. Find the coordinates of the centre that will minimize distribution costs.

7. A company has decided to relocate from three separate facilities: Plant A, Plant B and Plant C to a new facility: Plant D. Using the centre of gravity method determine the best location for Plant D to serve its customers using the facility locations and yearly demand shown below.

Facility	Location coordinates	Demand (per year)
A	(175,280)	6000
B	(50,200)	8200
C	(150,75)	7000

8. The following provides the specification for a line process.

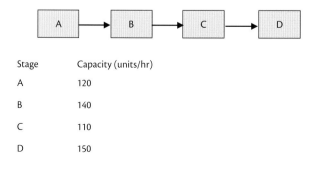

Stage	Capacity (units/hr)
A	120
B	140
C	110
D	150

a. What is the total system capacity?

b. Which stage is the bottleneck?

c. What is the level that system capacity can be increased to by increasing the bottleneck capacity only?

d. Calculate the current cycle efficiency.

e. Calculate the cycle efficiency when the bottleneck capacity is increased as in (c).

WEB EXERCISE

Read the article at www.guardian.co.uk/business/2008/jun/11/tesco.supermarkets (accessed 31 October 2011). How do 'economies of scale' in large organizations such as Tesco help protect it from a business downturn?

FURTHER READING

Dornier, P., Ernst, R., Fender, M. and Kouvelis, P. (2003) *Global Operations and Logistics: Text and Cases*, John Wiley & Sons, Inc.

Flaherty, M.T. (1996) *Global Operations Management*, McGraw-Hill.

Mair, A. (1994) *Honda's Global Local Corporation*, Macmillan.

Opacua, A.E. (2013) *Global Production Networks: Operations Design and Management*, Second Edition, CRC Press.

Schroeder, R.G. and Flynn, B.B. (2001) *High Performance Manufacturing: Global Perspectives*, John Wiley & Sons, Inc.

WEB LINKS

http://news.bbc.co.uk/1/hi/uk/2271914.stm (accessed 31 October 2011) How the BBC found the location of the centre of England using the centre of gravity method!

http://www.ofcom.org.uk/static/archive/oftel/publications/about_oftel/2002/smpg0802.htm (accessed 31 October 2011). Document 'Oftel's market review guidelines: criteria for the assessment of significant market power.' Contains definitions of economies of scope, economies of scale and vertical integration.

REFERENCES

Barnes, D. (2008) *Operations Management: An International Perspective*, Thomson Learning.

Fitzsimmons, J.A. and Fitzsimmons, M.J. (2010) *Service Management: Operations, Strategy and Information Technology*, 7th edn, McGraw-Hill.

Flaherty, M.T. (1996) *Global Operations Management*, McGraw-Hill.

McGrath, M.E. and Hoole, R.W. (1992) Manufacturing's new economies of scale. *Harvard Business Review,* May–June, 102–5.

Meijboom, B. and Houtepen, M. (2002) Structuring international service operations, *International Journal of Operations and Production Management*, 22 (8), 824–42.

Peters, T. (1994) *Liberation Management: Necessary Disorganization for the Nanosecond Nineties*, Pan Books.

CHAPTER 6

Process Technology

- **Introduction**
- **Process technology for materials**
- **Process technology for information**
- **Process technology for customers**
- **Choosing process technology**

LEARNING OBJECTIVES

- Explain the role of process technologies for materials processing
- Explain the role of information technology in the accumulation, organization and distribution of information
- Outline the distinguishing features of operational information systems and management information systems
- Define the terms e-Business and e-Commerce
- Discuss how technology can be used for customer processing in operations systems
- Evaluate process technology investment decisions

PROCESS TECHNOLOGY AND OPERATIONS STRATEGY

Investment in process technology is a strategic decision in that it helps the organization to meet the requirements of the market in which it is competing. Technology can be used to enhance performance along the performance objectives such as improving delivery speed and increasing quality. It is important that the form of the technology investment matches the volume/variety requirements of the market and provides the appropriate trade-off between flexibility and cost. Generally investments in large scale, highly automated and integrated technology are appropriate for a high volume/low variety mix where the emphasis is on low cost rather than flexibility. Investments in small scale, people-based and stand-alone technologies are appropriate for a low volume/high variety mix where the emphasis is on flexibility rather than low cost.

INTRODUCTION

In Chapter 1 we defined the objective of an operations system as being to convert transformed resources from inputs into outputs in the form of goods and services. Transformed resources can be in the form of material, information and customers and this section will show the use of technology in the transformation of these resource categories. Technology is an important aspect of operations as it has led to a large growth in productivity in both manufacturing, where the emphasis is on technology for material and information transformation, and services, where the emphasis is on technology for information and customer transformations. In addition to the technologies described in this chapter, indirect process technologies which are not directly involved in the transformation process but are relevant to operations are discussed throughout this text, including enterprise resource planning (ERP) (Chapter 14) and project-management software (Chapter 16).

PROCESS TECHNOLOGY FOR MATERIALS

There are many technological advances that are specific to a certain industrial sector (for example new material technologies used for construction). This section will describe some of the software systems and hardware technologies that have had a widespread impact on manufacturing firms in many industries.

Software Systems

Computer-aided design (CAD) is one of the most widespread technologies, used in even relatively small firms. A CAD system allows the designer to create drawings on a computer screen to assist in the visual design of a product or service (Figure 6.1). The drawings can be viewed from any angle and drawings can be zoomed to allow inspection of a design in detail. Drawings are held in a database for future use and dissemination between designers and engineers across the company.

Computer-aided process planning (CAPP) extends CAD by transmitting a process plan of how parts will be manufactured to the machine tool. For example, deciding on how individual pieces are to be cut from a sheet of metal. CAPP systems can also sequence parts through a number of process steps.

Computer-aided engineering (CAE) takes the drawings in a CAD system and subjects the designs to simulated tests. For example, the behaviour of an engineering design for elements of a bridge can be observed under various amounts of stress. This allows various design options to be tested quickly and cheaply.

Hardware Technologies

Computer numerically controlled machines (CNC) are machine tools that can be controlled by computer. Machining centres (MC) are more complex technology and incorporate features such as the ability to carry tools that can be automatically changed depending on the requirements of the operation being undertaken.

A **robot** is a programmable machine that can undertake tasks that may be dangerous, dirty or dull for people to carry out. A robot may have an arm and end effector that are used to pick, hold and place items. Robots can generally undertake tasks more quickly and more consistently than humans.

FIGURE 6.1

Computer-Aided Design Image.
Source: Wikipedia.

CASE STUDY 6.1

Spencer Davis Engineering

Thanks to a carefully planned e-Business strategy, Spencer Davies Engineering has dramatically improved the efficiency of its production process and expanded the breadth of its offer.

Spencer Davies has introduced technology across the company, from a web site and customer database to CAD/CAM, an intranet and production control on the shop floor. Its strategy has been to balance bigger, structural investments in core functions – such as in CAD/CAM – with smaller applications that reduce employees' administrative burdens. The result of

this approach is that each successive investment brings specific and cumulative benefits. For example, the original CAD/CAM investment improved the quality, speed and breadth of offer. When combined with email, which now accounts for 60% of client communications, designs can come directly from clients and go immediately to the shop floor, saving up to a week on every job. Handling the processes electronically makes them easier to review and the company can now hold less stock, ordering online from suppliers to secure the best deals.

The company intranet includes a research library, company documentation, job descriptions and a contact database of customers and suppliers. This has been integral in maintaining internal communications, giving staff the tools they need and improving customer service. Offsite engineers, meanwhile, are equipped with laptops, digital cameras and mobile phones so work can be budgeted, completed and approved on the spot. The company is also looking at integrating other aspects of its supply chain: it uses online procurement for office supplies and puts outsourcing enquiries on the Internet via engineering bulletin boards.

Spencer Davies's e-Business strategy has allowed it to expand while continuing to streamline its business. Its ICT investments have also produced greater auditing and management reporting facilities, giving the company the ability to evaluate future investments before committing financial resources. 'We've been able to quantify the benefits thanks to technology', says Owain Davies, Managing Director.

The time taken from design stage to the finished product has been dramatically reduced. Today, if the information is sent electronically by customers, the job can reach the production stage within 30 seconds. The company is now better equipped to tackle more complex engineering projects and consequently appeals to more potential customers. 'Our investment in technology has allowed us to develop the business and look at new markets', explains Owain.

The improvement in communications with suppliers has been due in large part to enthusiasm from Spencer Davies Engineering. 'Most of our suppliers are not eager to work electronically and that's a barrier', admits Owain. 'What I'm trying to do is show the benefits of technology and persuade them to come on board. Once they see the business benefits, we can usually win them over.'

In addition to the direct benefits of the company's investment in ICT, Owain has noticed some equally important but unexpected results. Spencer Davies's positive, forward-thinking attitude is producing a competitive advantage. 'We are getting some valuable customer referrals', explains Owain. 'Our use of technology gives them the confidence to recommend our services. Technology has definitely allowed us to get more for our money. It's now easier for us to sell because of the information that we have.'

Source: The Department of Trade and Industry (www.dti.gov .uk). Reproduced with permission.

Question

What impact does the use of technology have on the competitive performance of Spencer Davies?

Automated material handling systems (AMH) are designed to improve efficiency in the movement, storage and retrieval of materials. Types of systems include automated guided vehicle (AGV) systems that transport material on driverless vehicles to various locations in the plant (Figure 6.2). Automated storage and retrieval systems (AS/RS) handle the storage and retrieval of materials using computers to direct automatic loaders to pick and place items in a storage facility.

Flexible manufacturing cell (FMC) systems integrate individual items of automation described above to form an automated manufacturing system that can consist of two or more CNC machining centres, a robot and a cell computer that coordinates the various operations in the cell. The robot can be used to handle the parts that are being processed and also to perform tool-changing operations. The tool is the element of the CNC machine, for example, the drill bit, which is used to process the part. The robot, under the direction of the cell computer, can sense when a tool needs changing either for processing requirements or if the tool is worn and needs replacing.

Flexible manufacturing systems (FMS) extend the facilities of an FMC by incorporating, in addition to several CNC machining centres and robots, automatic parts loading and unloading facilities and an automated guided vehicle system for parts movement. Flexible manufacturing systems held out the possibility of factories without people, where the robots and computers would perform all the material handling and processing tasks necessary. However, due to the complexities involved in producing a wide product range, fully automated plants have proved to be impractical. Flexibility (the production of a range of products at low cost that can be delivered quickly to customers) is a key strategic aim for operations. In terms of manufacturing this translates into the ability to perform rapid low cost switching from one product line to another. A flexible manufacturing system is designed to provide fast, low cost changes from one part to another, lower direct labour costs due to automation and achieve consistent and better quality due to auto-

FIGURE 6.2

Laser-Guided AGV.
Source: Wikipedia.

mated control. However, the FMS machines may have a limited ability to adapt to changes in the product specification, a substantial amount of pre-planning is necessary before an FMS can be operated and the systems are very expensive in terms of capital investment. Due to these factors flexible manufacturing cells (FMC) are often used as an alternative due to their lower complexity and lower cost. Flexible manufacturing systems are most relevant to the production of items such as small batches of machined goods. Another option to achieve flexibility is to use the JIT philosophy of a flexible workforce and small simple machines.

Computer-Integrated Manufacture (CIM)

When the above technologies are integrated using a computer network and database system the resulting automated system is termed **computer-integrated manufacture (CIM)**. Whereas an FMS system is generally concerned with automation directly related to the transformation process, CIM is an automation of the product and process design, planning and control and manufacture of the product. In a fully integrated system the areas of design, testing, fabrication, assembly, inspection and material handling are automated and integrated using technology. For example, **computer-aided manufacturing (CAM)** extends the use of CAD by transmitting the design held in the CAD system electronically to computer controlled machine tools. Systems that combine these two functions are often referred to as CADCAM. CADCAM systems represent a major tool for operations in linking the design and manufacturing processes.

PROCESS TECHNOLOGY FOR INFORMATION

Most organizations use some form of computer-based technology to accumulate, organize and distribute information. Most computers are now connected together in some form of network. A local area network (LAN) is usually limited to a company occupying a single building or even several buildings across a large company site. A small-scale network such as this allows people to share information, communicate via systems such as email and share facilities such as printing and software applications. A wide area network (WAN) may connect people across a city, country or between different countries. If the WAN enables communication across the whole company, it is referred to as the 'enterprise network' or 'enterprise-wide' network. To minimize the size of investment in wide area communications a company can use a value-added network (VAN) which is a network rented out by a service provider.

In the 1960s the use of **electronic data interchange (EDI)** became established (Chapter 15). This allows the exchange of structured information, such as orders, invoices, delivery advices and payment instructions, over a network. It permits, for example, the automatic reordering and payment for stock from a supplier without human intervention. The automated transfer of money between organizations is referred to as Electronic Funds Transfer (EFT). The most common platform for networked IT is the Internet, which is a global network of millions of connected networks that uses a transmission method called TCP/ IP to communicate with one another. There is no global control over transmissions using this method – these are governed by the requester and sender of the information.

The majority of Internet services are available to any business or consumer who has access to the Internet. However, if information is limited to those within the organization it is termed an **intranet**. If access is extended to some others, but not everyone beyond the organization, this is an **extranet**. The World Wide Web (WWW) provides a standard method for exchanging and publishing information on the Internet. It provides a graphical environment with hyperlinks which allow users to readily move from one document or web site to another by selecting an image or text highlighted by underlining and/or a different colour.

In order to understand how the information technology is applied, it is useful to outline some of the types of information systems that use information technology in manufacturing and service organizations. Operational information systems are generally concerned with process control, transaction processing communications and productivity. Management information systems are concerned with assisting decision-making activities. Other types of information systems considered are e-Business systems, m-business systems and customer relationship management systems.

Operational Information Systems

Operational systems are used for the tasks involved in the daily running of a business. Their performance is often vital to an organization and they are sometimes described as mission-critical or strategic information systems. We consider three types of operational systems:

- *Transaction processing systems (TPS)*. These systems involve recording and processing data that result from an organization's business transactions. Applications include real-time (online) processing of balance enquiries in a cashpoint system and batch processing of customer bills for utilities. Transaction processing systems are generally for frequent and routine transactions at an operational level in the organization. See Case Study 6.3 for an example of the use of transaction processing systems.
- *Office automation systems (OAS)*. These are used to manage the administrative functions in an office environment and are often critical to service-based industries. They include Groupware, which assists teams of people working together through facilities such as email and teleconferencing within or between companies. *Workflow Management Systems* (WFMS) automate a business process by providing a structured framework to support the process. They can assign tasks to people, allow collaboration between people sharing tasks and retrieve information needed to complete a task, such as customer details. They can also provide an overview of the status of each task which can be used in conjunction with *document image processing (DIP)* to provide automated routing of documents across a computer network. Also concerned with the design of business processes, but at a higher level of abstraction, is the technique for business process management (BPM) covered in Chapter 8.
- *Process control systems*. These include systems such as CAD, CAM and FMS which are important in manufacturing industries for controlling the manufacture of goods. These systems have been covered earlier in this chapter.

Management Information Systems

Management information systems can be defined as systems used to support tactical and strategic decision making. Three types of management information systems are:

- *Decision support systems (DSS)*. These provide information and models in a form to facilitate tactical and strategic decision making. Types of DSS include *Expert Systems (ES)* to represent the knowledge and decision-making skills of specialists and *neural networks* which learn problem solving skills by exposure to a wide range of problems.
- *Information reporting systems (IRS)*. These provide prespecified reports for day-to-day decision making. They include periodic reports such as weekly sales summary and exception reports triggered by events such as production levels falling below normal.
- *Executive information systems (EIS)*. These provide senior managers with systems to analyse, compare and highlight trends to help govern the strategic direction of a company. *Data warehouses* are large database systems containing detailed company data on sales transactions, which are analysed to assist in improving the marketing and financial performance of companies. They have to a large

extent displaced EIS in software purchases for strategic and tactical decision making. *Data marts* are small-scale data warehouses that hold departmental information. The term *data mining* of data warehouses is used to refer to an attempt to identify relationships between variables in order to assist decision making.

E-Business

E-Business can be seen as the transformation of business processes through the use of Internet technologies.

In general, e-Business is concerned with making day-to-day business activities more efficient by improving information exchanges within the organization and between the organization and its partners. E-Business opportunities can be classified in terms of whether an organization is using the Internet to transact with consumers, called **business-to-consumer (B2C)** or other businesses, called **business-to-business (B2B)**. Business-to-business transactions predominate over the Internet in terms of value if not frequency. This is explained by the fact that there are many more opportunities for B2B transactions than B2C, both between an organization and its suppliers, together with intermediaries, and through distributors such as agents and wholesalers with customers. Moreover, there is a higher level of access to the Internet among businesses than among consumers and a greater propensity to use it for purchasing.

There are two additional types of transaction: where consumers transact directly with consumers (C2C) and where they initiate trading with business (C2B). Note that the terms C2C and C2B are less widely used but they do highlight significant differences between Internet-based commerce and earlier forms of commerce. Consumer-to-consumer interactions were relatively rare but are now very common in the form of online auctions and communities. As well as the models described it has been suggested that employees should be considered as a separate type of interaction through the use of intranets (internal Internet-based networks) – this is sometimes referred to as employee-to-employee or E2E.

The benefit to business of adopting e-Business is a mix of cost reduction achieved through lower costs of information transfer and processing and the potential for increased revenue arising from increased reach to a larger audience. The benefits of e-Business for operations relate to areas such as supply chain integration using B2B and B2C interactions as well as the increased efficiency and effectiveness of internal business processes using E2E interactions. For an example of an e-Business system see the description of e-procurement in Chapter 15.

E-Commerce

Electronic commerce (e-Commerce) is often thought to simply refer to buying and selling using the Internet: people immediately think of consumer retail purchases from companies such as Amazon. However, e-Commerce involves much more than electronically mediated financial transactions between organizations and customers. Many commentators refer to e-Commerce as *all* electronically mediated transactions between an organization and any third party it deals with. By this definition, non-financial transactions such as customer requests for further information would also be considered to be part of e-Commerce. When evaluating the impact of e-Commerce on an organization, it is instructive to identify opportunities for buy-side and sell-side e-Commerce transactions as depicted in Figure 6.3, since business information systems with different functionality will need to be created to

FIGURE 6.3

Buy-Side and Sell-Side E-Commerce.

accommodate transactions with buyers and suppliers. **Buy-side e-Commerce** refers to transactions to procure resources needed by an organization from its suppliers. **Sell-side e-Commerce** refers to transactions involved with selling products to an organization's customers.

In addition to buy-side and sell-side transactions, Figure 6.3 also shows the internal (or inside) processes that are part of e-Business. They include transactions related to the buy-side such as procurement and sell-side-related transactions such as dealing with customer enquiries as well as basic administrative functions related to employee leave and pay.

M-business

M-business can be defined as the integration of Internet and wireless communications technology. It is a result of mobile communications facilitated by broadband (high bandwidth) Internet connections and wireless technology (for example, mobile phones using radio waves). Mobile computing allows people choice in how they communicate by offering multiple devices, applications and tools from which to select and it permits people to control the time and frequency with which they obtain information. Some of the applications for m-business include:

- *Procurement.* The extension of e-procurement applications to enable orders to be taken using handheld devices (such as barcode readers and radio frequency identification devices).
- *Order fulfilment and delivery management.* Delivery information is input using a tablet and the customer can track their order immediately over the Internet. Asset tracking. The monitoring of materials internally will extend to the monitoring of highly mobile geographically dispersed assets.
- *Service management.* Service requests can be automatically dispatched to field personnel to ensure timely response and efficient scheduling.

Radio frequency identification (RFID) systems consist of a tag that can be attached to an item. The tag contains a microchip, which contains information about the item; its location is transmitted on request using radio signals to an RFID reader. The RFID readers then transmit this information, using a wired or wireless connection, to a computer network. The system uses a short-range radio system for receiving the information from the tag but does not require a direct line of sight that a barcode system requires for example.

CASE STUDY 6.2

Kennedys

With three international offices, seven associate offices and six different locations throughout the UK, supporting the mobility of key staff was an important consideration for Kennedys, a UK litigation firm.

Kennedys wanted to provide its employees with a way to access their work systems, for example, their calendars, contacts and email inboxes, while on the move. The company decided a system whereby staff had remote access to its network would improve efficiency throughout the company and enable flexible working, vital in a business where staff are constantly 'in the field' and not necessarily working to strict office hours. The high-pressure world of litigation means that lawyers need regular access to their work systems to stay on top of their diaries and to manage 'time management' issues while outside the office.

Following a consultation on the company's communications services, Kennedys invested in BlackBerry devices – handheld devices for sending and receiving emails and accessing office features, like contacts and the corporate calendar, on the move. BlackBerry is a more advanced step from traditional personal digital assistants and also allows full access to the Internet. All data sent and received are fully encrypted. The device is made available to any employees who want to use it – to date 70 Kennedys partners have taken up the initiative, while the company claims to be one of the first businesses to take up this new technology.

Kennedys now has plans to roll out the device to a total of up to 200 employees. Kennedys' Carolyn Lees says BlackBerry has provided fast Internet access on the move, the ability to set up 'virtual private networks', which allow out-of-office access, making working practices far more efficient. Lees says: 'We can quantify the improvements only in terms of how much more productivity we see and the great accessibility to our work systems that we all now have.' She adds that the 'immediacy' of electronic communications is a key benefit of the new system, while accessibility to programmes across the Web has been improved greatly.

Key issues at Kennedys have been with educating users about the new systems. The speed of change, says Lees, means that users are often left behind and it is thus vital to train employees and other users such as suppliers effectively so that the new technologies can be exploited effectively. Initial increased complexity presents problems but the new technologies are designed to reduce complexity in terms of working practices. Training, she says, is the key. She says: 'People skills are still the key to success.' Also, Lees says, it is vital to build in contingency plans to cope with problems that may arise, adding that she has used IT publications and online forums on the Web to keep herself updated on the latest ICTs, while Kennedys relies on consultancy help on new technology projects.

While, Kennedys looks to enable more and more of its employees with the new BlackBerry devices, it continues to develop an ICT strategy 'geared towards retaining and acquiring new clients'. Overall, Lees says it intends 'to continue to remain competitive with our ICTs and to improve business efficiencies.'

Source: The Department of Trade and Industry (www.dti.gov.uk). Reproduced with permission.

Question

How does the use of the BlackBerry device help the effectiveness of the service Kennedys provides?

Most RFID tags are 'passive' and do not contain a power source as they are so small (for example see Figure 6.4). Some tags, however, are 'active'; this is when the tag is equipped with a battery that can be used as a partial or complete source of power for the tag's electronic circuitry. The advantage of an active RFID tag is that it can be read at greater distances (up to around 30 m) than a passive tag. The disadvantage of the active tag is that because it cannot function without battery power it has a limited lifetime until the battery requires changing and it is typically more costly to buy.

Radio frequency identification tags have many useful applications including keeping track of hold luggage on flights, tracking containers at sea ports, tracking inventory in the supply chain and tracking employees at work. More controversial applications include the use of RFID embedded in bank notes so that banks can instantly count large amounts of cash and even embedded tags under the skin of a child so they can be tracked if they get lost. The characteristic of RFID tags that causes concern is that they will continue to look for and respond to RFID readers even when their official use has been completed. Moreover RFID readers are freely available. This could mean someone being able to know how much cash you are carrying or tracking your movements by RFID tags embedded in your body or clothes without your knowledge.

FIGURE 6.4

RFID Chip.
Source: Image Copyright Markus Gann, 2013. Used under license from Shutterstock.com

The video 'How RFID Improves Retail Fashion – full episode' is available in your interactive e-book at **www.wileyopenpage.com**

PROCESS TECHNOLOGY FOR CUSTOMERS

One approach to improving service delivery is the use of process technology in the service delivery process itself.

In an **active customer-technology interaction** such as an automated teller machine (ATM) at a bank the technology can enable the customers to avail themselves of the service at a time of their choosing and to make choices regarding that service. From a service provider viewpoint this has the advantage of reducing staffing requirements and empowering customers by giving them a greater sense of control over the type of service they require. However, customers have different preferences and many facilities may well need both customer-driven and traditional people-based service delivery systems such as a call centre or physical outlet. For example, it is common to see a customer using an ATM while another customer prefers to enter the bank and queue to see a clerk for exactly the same service! While ATM technology has allowed banks to significantly reduce their number of branches and staffing requirement there is still a need to provide customer contact for some services and some customers. The ATM is an example of a wider use of technology to provide self-service facilities with Internet services such as travel (for example, www.expedia.co.uk) and books (for example, www.amazon.co.uk) widely used.

Process technology also exists for **passive customer-technology interactions** such as transportation systems, for example, moving walkways for directing people at an airport or an underground tube system in a city. Because of the lack of interaction between the customer and technology customers will need clear instruction in the use of the technology to avoid confusion.

In a **supported customer-technology interaction** there is a human server who acts as an intermediary between the customer and the technology itself. This means that advice and guidance can be given to the customer by the server in making their choices (for example, booking a holiday in a travel agency). There may also be instances when the use of the technology requires skills and experience the customer could not be expected to have (for example, a transportation system). Some organizations encourage their customers to use active rather than supported technology to reduce staffing costs. For example, Ryanair (www.ryanair.com) charges customers extra if they wish to check in at the airport rather than undertaking the task online.

CHOOSING PROCESS TECHNOLOGY

There are a number of factors that should be considered when choosing process technology including a consideration of the fit with current technology and skills, the reliability of the technology (cutting edge technology may represent a greater risk of failure), the project management skills necessary to successfully introduce new technology and a financial analysis of the investment to determine future payback amounts.

In terms of operations management, investment in process technology is a strategic decision in that it helps the organization meet the requirements of the market in which it is competing. In particular, information technology investments can be sees as a bridge between the external business environment and internal business processes. An organization's information systems capability will determine in part how well it can respond to demands placed on it by the external environment and how it can manage and revise its internal business processes to meet those external demands (Bocij et al., 2008). In general, investments in processing technology should be used to enhance performance along the key performance objectives identified in the strategy process (Chapter 2) such as improving delivery speed and increasing quality.

It is also important that the form of the technology investment matches the volume/variety requirements of the task and provides the appropriate trade-off between flexibility and cost (Chapter 3). In order to assist the process technology decision we consider three characteristics of process technology that vary with volume and variety, namely Scale, Automation and Integration (Johnston et al., 2003).

Scale of the Technology

The scale refers to the capacity of individual units of process technology. In general terms we have a choice about whether we make up our capacity with a few high volume units or many low volume units.

 www.wileyopenpage.com

Large-scale units of technology will generally have a high capital cost but a low operating unit cost and thus help achieve economies of scale. Small-scale units of technology can provide more flexibility by enabling capacity to be provided by a number of small units in different configurations rather than by just one large unit. These systems are also more robust against disruption than large-scale units as output is spread over a number of units. The investment required for each additional small-scale unit is also smaller than larger units, with a faster payback period encouraging investment in the latest technology. Large-scale units also have to contend with market fragmentation and the need for customization reducing volume for individual products/services and shortened product/service life cycles also decreasing volumes.

Degree of Automation of the Technology

The degree of automation refers to the extent to which the technology operates without human intervention. There is a continuum from low automation (high degree of human intervention – e.g. driving a car) to high automation (very occasional intervention – e.g. monitoring a chemical plant) depending on the level of complexity and intuition required. The advantages of automation are that it permits the execution of repetitive tasks with precision, speed and power and can lower direct labour costs. The disadvantages of automation include the possible loss of flexibility and creativity due to the lack of human intervention and the potential high support costs such as the labour costs of support engineers.

Degree of Integration of the Technology

The degree of integration of the technology refers to the extent to which individual units of technology are connected together. Process technologies are increasingly connected together, for example, material processing systems such as FMC, FMS and CIM and information processing systems through the use of Internet-based systems. The advantages of integration are that it reduces fragmentation of previously separated processes and can lead to improved synchronization and thus reduced WIP and costs. The disadvantage of integration is high capital costs and the increased exposure to the risk of failure.

In making a choice regarding process technology in general investments in large-scale, highly automated and integrated technology are appropriate for a high volume/low variety mix where the emphasis is on low cost rather than flexibility. Investments in small-scale, low automation (people-based) and stand-alone technologies are appropriate for a low volume/high variety mix where the emphasis is on flexibility rather than low cost (Figure 6.5).

It should be noted that the volume/variety mix is unlikely to be static for long and firms may move along the volume/variety continuum from a low volume/high variety mix towards a higher volume/less variety mix over time and as with process types (Chapter 3) this will require changes in process technology (An example is in Case Study 3.1 where a change in volume/variety has necessitated a change in material processing equipment from

Small Scale	Large Scale
Low Automation	High Automation
Stand-Alone	Integrated
Low Volume/	High Volume/
High Variety	Low Variety

FIGURE 6.5

The Relationship between Process Technology and Volume/Variety.

DIY to professional). In addition, Slack and Lewis (2011) state that information processing technology has been able to partially overcome some of the traditional trade-offs in choosing process technology and because of that, although IT implementation is a challenge (especially in company-wide systems such as ERP), IT strategy should be an integral part of an overall operations strategy.

SUMMARY

- Process technologies for material processing cover a wide range of facilities such as design, engineering and manufacture.
- Information technology such as computer network systems can be used to accumulate, organize and distribute information.
- Operational information systems are used for tasks involved in the daily running of the business. Management information systems are used to support tactical and strategic decision making.
- E-Business can be seen as the transformation of business processes through the use of Internet technologies. E-Commerce can be seen as electronically mediated transactions between an organization and any third party it deals with.
- Technology such as automated teller machines can be used to provide assistance when the customer is present in the service delivery process.
- When choosing processing technology factors to consider include the use of the process technology to enhance performance along the key performance objectives and a form of technology in terms of scale, automation and integration that matches the volume/variety requirements of the task.

CASE STUDY 6.3

Retail Applications of Transaction Processing Systems by Sainsbury's

This case study of UK retailer Sainsbury's considers the different ways in which a retailer may make use of transaction processing systems (TPS).

- Order lead time 24 to 48 hours.
- Distribution centres manage deliveries of 11 million cases to 335 stores.

The Company and its Customer Service Objectives

- Seventeen thousand commodities.
- Aim is for no more than five commodities to be unavailable at any one time.

How is Sainsbury's Helped by TPS Technology?

- Improved customer service through more choice, lower prices, better quality of produce and full shelves.

 www.wileyopenpage.com

- Improved operational efficiency by automatic links to suppliers and better information on product demand and availability.
- Assessment of the effectiveness of product promotions through availability of better information.
- Marketing through customer loyalty schemes.

How does Sainsbury's Use Technologies?

- At the till-EPOS and EFTPOS.
- On shelves – auto-price-changing LCDs.
- On trolleys – 'self-scanning systems'.
- At home – direct wine sales from the Internet BarclaySquare site.
- At warehouses – EDI links between stores, warehouses, suppliers and banks.
- For banking – TPS are vital to providing customer statements and cash withdrawals.

- In the marketing department – the effectiveness of marketing campaigns and loyalty card schemes can be assessed using information on transactions stored in data warehouses. This type of system is covered in more detail later in the chapter.

Source: Bocij, P.; Greasley, A.; Hickie, S. (2008) Business Information Systems, Pearson Education Ltd. Reproduced with permission.

Questions

1. Draw a diagram summarizing the links between all the parties who access Sainsbury's TPS.
2. What benefits will Sainsbury's gain compared to the time before the introduction of TPS?
3. Can you think of any problems with using TPS so extensively? What can be done to counter these problems?

CASE STUDY 6.4

RFID American Apparel

Created in 1989 by a Canadian, with a love of all things US, American Apparel is a, now highly successful global, clothing company. Unusually for a fashion manufacturer, the company is based exclusively in Los Angeles, California. American Apparel describes their operation as a fully integrated organisation; they design, manufacture, distribute and retail all their own products – all of this in LA.

American Apparel have expanded rapidly into the market, in 2003 they had 3 stores in the US yet now have more than 300 worldwide.

With rapid expansion in retail stores and their boutique style approach to retail, with having only one of every item in every size on the shop floor

at once, it is no surprise that, American Apparel have turned to technology to control their inventory.

In conjunction with Avery Dennison tags and Motorola readers, American Apparel piloted an RFID (Radio-frequency identification) scheme to improve their inventory control. The technology uses the RFID tags which can wirelessly transfer data from a simple tag to a reader than can be several metres away.

American Apparel replenish their stores from a back stock room, customers expect the floor to be fully stocked with their size, colour and desired style, so full replenishment occurs before the stores open, and continues periodically throughout the working day. The single item available

www.wileyopenpage.com

policy has allowed American Apparel to maximise their floor space and increase their range.

However, with more than 26,000 items to manage, store staff constantly battled to keep inventory counts accurate and the sales floor stocked. The effort was time-and-labour intensive and expensive. But the cost of inventory errors and stocking delays was even higher – lost sales and disappointed customers.

The company wanted to test the system with clear goals for process improvements:

- Increased stock visibility
- Improved accuracy/reliability of inventory counts
- Decreased labour costs and human errors associated with inventory
- To allow the stock room to be able to replenish the Sales floor stock levels, to be maintained at virtually 100%
- Reduction of internal 'shrink' (loss of products from pilfering or poor management) by over 55%.

The system operated, firstly with all items carrying an RFID tag, and then portable readers and fixed antennas linked this information with in-store inventory tracking software.

The process follows several stages;

Incoming deliveries supply the backroom stores.

As products are sold, demands move through to the system, instructing required goods to be placed in the 'fill station'.

An employee will collect these goods and take them to the shop floor, on the way they pass a 'validation point' reader. This is a key part of the process – if the employee is carrying the wrong goods, the system alerts them to this.

At the point of sale the stock is subtracted and a real time call for a replacement product is sent to the back stock.

In real time the systems update all stock locations as they progress throughout the day. It is therefore not possible to lose stock by simply carrying

it to the incorrect location. Replenishment can be done in under a minute.

Regular stock checks are still carried out – to ensure the full range is available to customers, with the original system, this would take 5–6 members of staff 5–6 hours before the store opened. This can now be done by a couple of employees in just over 2 hours during the working day.

The stores that have implemented the system have experienced an increase in sales of around 14%, this has been attributed to an improvement in product availability.

An additional benefit from the technology has been explained by Stacey Shulman, American Apparel's VP of Technology:

'Like many retailers, internal theft and process issues account for about 60 percent of our shrink. RFID, it turns out, affects internal shrink in a profound way. We measure everything, and have accountability of every item. Every item counts, and when we change that culture, employees start treating product better. Internal theft does go down, and process errors go down.'

Sources

http://www.motorola.com/web/Business/
Products/RFID/_Documents/Case_Studies/_
StaticFiles/American_Apparel_Case%20Study.pdf

Avery Dennison: American Apparel RFID
Case Study http://www.youtube.com/
watch?v=SKqwqLQlXbI

http://www.rfidjournal.com/article/view/9202/2

Source: Written by Briony Boydell and Chris Milner. Reproduced with permission.

Questions

1. How has RFID helped American Apparel?
2. Why does American Apparel only have one of each item on the shelves?
3. What are the limitations of RFID?

Quizzes to test yourself further are available in your interactive e-book at **www.wileyopenpage.com**

Flashcards to test yourself further are available in your interactive e-book at **www.wileyopenpage.com**

EXERCISES

1. What are the advantages of using computer-aided design (CAD) technology?
2. Describe the major elements of FMS and evaluate the concept.
3. Discuss how CIM could provide strategic advantage.
4. What is the relevance of process technology to service organizations?
5. Identify process technology that may be found in a large retail organization.
6. Describe the categories of operational information systems and management information systems and provide business examples of their use for each category.
7. Describe the purpose of workflow management systems throughout the organization.
8. Explain the relationship between the concepts of e-Commerce and e-Business.

WEB EXERCISE

Discuss ethical issues associated with RFID tags. In order to help you think of ideas this web site at www.rfidgazette.org/2007/04/top_15_weirdest.html (accessed 2 November 2011) provides some unusual examples of their use.

FURTHER READING

Bocij, P., Greasley, A. and Hickie, S. (2008) *Business Information Systems: Technology, Development and Management*, 4th edn, Pearson Education Limited.

Cannon, A.R., Reyes, P.M., Frazier, G.V. and Prater, E.L. (2008) RFID in the contemporary supply chain: multiple perspectives on its benefits and risks, *International Journal of Operations and Production Management*, 28 (5), 433–54.

Hayes, R., Pisano, G., Upton, D. and Wheelwright, S. (2005) *Pursuing the Competitive Edge: Operations, Strategy, and Technology*, John Wiley & Sons, Ltd.

WEB LINKS

www.abb.com (accessed 2 November 2011). ABB. Supplier of many automation devices, such as robotic systems.

www.autodesk.co.uk (accessed 2 November 2011). AutoDesk Inc. AutoCAD software for product design.

www.e-consultancy.com (accessed 2 November 2011). Online digest of consultant and analyst reports in e-Business.

www.graphisoft.com (accessed 2 November 2011). Graphisoft Inc. ArchiCAD software for product design.

www.gsmworld.com (accessed 2 November 2011). GSM Association. Global trade association for GSM mobile operators.

www.wfmc.org (accessed 2 November 2011). Workflow Management Coalition. Contains introductory papers on the purpose and components of workflow systems.

www.wired.com (accessed 2 November 2011). Wired Magazine. News and articles on e-Business topics.

REFERENCES

Bocij, P., Greasley, A. and Hickie, S. (2008) *Business Information Systems: Technology, Development and Management*, 4th edn, Pearson Education Ltd.

Johnston, R., Chambers, S., Harland, C. et al. (2003) *Cases in Operations Management*, 3rd edn, Pearson Education Ltd.

Slack, N. and Lewis, M. (2011) *Operations Strategy*, 3rd edn, Pearson Education Ltd.

CHAPTER 7

Product and Service Design

- **Introduction**
- **Developing product and service designs**
- **The relationship between product/service design and process design**
- **The design process**
- **Service design**
- **Improving design**

LEARNING OBJECTIVES

- Evaluate the relationship between product/service design and process design
- Understand issues involved in the design of services
- Explain the main steps in the design process
- Discuss the use of simultaneous development
- Understand the term 'mass customization'
- Describe the role of DFM, QFD and Taguchi methods in improving design

PRODUCT AND SERVICE DESIGN AND OPERATIONS STRATEGY

The ability to develop new products and services quickly can provide a source of competitive advantage in offering something unique to the market that can then lead to increased market share and/or increased profitability. Innovations may come from either a technology-push approach aligned with a resource-based operations strategy or a market-pull approach associated with a market-based operations strategy. The product life cycle model puts the design process into a strategic context by highlighting how different phases within the life of a product or service can impact both the product design and also process design requirements. In general the model predicts an emphasis on innovation and customization in product design in the early introductory phase of a product giving way to standardization and an emphasis on efficient process design at the mature phase of the life cycle. Another concept with a strategic context concerns the approach the organization adopts to product and service innovation. Organizations can compete on the basis of either continuous innovation; modifying existing products for improved performance, radical innovation; generating new products or services that significantly change customer behaviours or disruptive innovation; a new design that cannot in the short term match the performance most customers expect from the current product/service but because technology can progress faster than market requirements will eventually achieve market acceptable performance and then may dominate the market.

INTRODUCTION

Good design of products and services is an essential element in satisfying customer needs and therefore ensuring the long-term success of the organization. In addition, organizations operating in international markets will need to consider the differing requirements of customers in different countries during the design stage. Due to competitive pressures most organizations will need to generate new products and services and make improvements to existing products and services to remain successful. The ability to develop new products and services can provide a source of competitive advantage in offering something unique to the market that can then lead to increased market share and/or increased profitability. The speed at which new products and services can be developed can also provide competitive advantage. For example, the ability to launch new designs quickly in products which are sensitive to changes in consumer tastes and have a complex design such as an automobile.

This chapter will first outline different types of product and service development, the relationship of product/service design with process design, the design process within the organization and the steps involved in the design of a product or service before addressing some of the specific attributes of service design. There is then a discussion of some of the techniques that may be used to improve the results of the design process. Many of the techniques are concerned with ensuring that final quality is high by taking appropriate action at the design stage.

DEVELOPING PRODUCT AND SERVICE DESIGNS

Approaches to developing product and service designs can be classified into three main types. Organizations can compete on the basis of either **continuous innovation**; modifying existing products for improved performance, **radical innovation**; generating new products or services that significantly change customer behaviours or **disruptive innovation**; a new design that cannot in the short term match the performance most customers expect from the current product/service but because technology can progress faster than market requirements will eventually achieve market acceptable

www.wileyopenpage.com

performance and then may dominate the market. Disruptive innovations (see Christensen, 1977) are based on the premise that some customers are less demanding than others and so an innovation can be introduced that is only acceptable to these less demanding customers but because of the potential rapid advances due to technology can be developed to meet the needs of even the most demanding customers. An example of a disruptive product that is often made is that of the electric car. Currently these products do not meet the needs of most customers in terms of driving performance and practicality but for some users they offer a satisfactory solution. Improvements in technology are predicted to mean this product will be acceptable to a much wider customer audience. When considering approaches to developing product and services an organization should consider issues such as whether a continuous innovation approach might lead to competitors gaining market share by introducing new products under a radical approach and whether the organization will be able to respond quickly enough to a competitor introduction of disruptive technology if that technology becomes mainstream.

THE RELATIONSHIP BETWEEN PRODUCT/SERVICE DESIGN AND PROCESS DESIGN

An important issue is the connection between product and service design and the design of the processes that deliver these products and services to customers. For example, the choice of materials used in a product design may have important consequences for process design in terms of the equipment and skills required to make the product. More innovative product designs may be expected to have more impact on the process design but even relatively minor improvements to product and services may necessitate substantial changes in the process design that delivers that product or service.

The product life cycle model puts the design process into a strategic context by highlighting how different phases within the life of a product or service can impact both the product design and also process design requirements. In general this model predicts an emphasis on innovation and customization in product design in the early introductory phase of a product giving way to standardization and an emphasis on efficient process design at the mature phase of the life cycle.

It is for these reasons that process design issues should be considered at the product/service design stage. In service design the service and the process used to deliver it to the customer may be all but indistinguishable and in this case new service development is largely concerned with the process design issues covered in Chapter 8.

THE DESIGN PROCESS

The design process involves the following steps shown in Figure 7.1.

The steps are not necessarily sequential but the order may vary and the development process may cycle back between stages as the design is refined. If a simultaneous development approach is used one stage may begin before the previous stage has completed. A funnel diagram (Figure 7.2) is often used to show how the design process begins with many ideas most of which are eliminated at each step of the design process to leave the 'best design' at the end of the process.

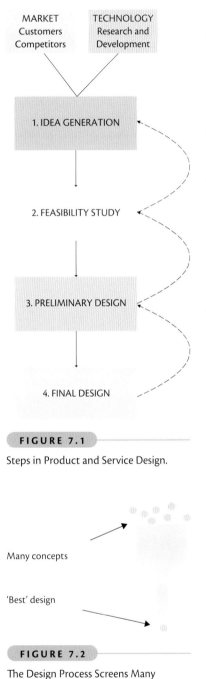

FIGURE 7.1

Steps in Product and Service Design.

FIGURE 7.2

The Design Process Screens Many Concepts to Arrive at a 'Best Design'.

The steps involved in the design process are now described in detail.

1. Idea Generation

Ideas for new products and services can come from a variety of sources and can be classified into either a technology-push approach that seeks to exploit developments in technology primarily through the use of an organization's research and development (R&D) department or a market-pull approach which seeks to fulfil market demand primarily from suggestions from participants in the market such as customers and competitors. A technology-push approach can provide competitive advantage by being the first to offer products and services to the market but runs the risk of misjudging customer requirements. The market-pull approach can provide competitive advantage by meeting customer needs but runs the risk that products may not be distinguishable from competitors who may have access to the same market data. This choice in how the design process is driven will be dependent largely on the organization's strategy with a market-pull strategy associated with a market-based operations strategy and a technology-push approach being aligned with a resource-based operations strategy.

The Research and Development Function

For an organization that has a strategy of being first to the market with a new product or service, ideas will be devised principally from the organization's own R&D department. For an organization with a similar product to their competitors, innovation may be primarily in the design and manufacture stages to attain lower production costs. Successful product innovation comes from understanding the customer and identifying their needs. Various data collection methods such as questionnaires, focus groups and interviews should be used to gain sufficient understanding of customer requirements.

Research and development can take on the following forms:

- *pure research* – knowledge-oriented research to develop new ideas with no specific product in mind
- *applied research* – problem-oriented research to discover new ideas with specific commercial applications
- *development* – product-oriented research concerned with turning research ideas into products.

Pure research is often based in universities and funded by government agencies and so it is necessary for organizations to maintain close contact with the relevant institutions. Applied research will be undertaken by most organizations. The cost of undertaking research and development is high and there will be many failed projects but the payoff from the small number of successes may be vital to the organization's continued profitability.

Customers and Competitors

Customers are an important source of information regarding new ideas in product and service development. Customer views can be collected using research data collection methods such as questionnaires and focus group interviews. An organization that understands its customers' needs better than its competitors can be first to the market with products and services and either increase market share or increase profits.

Competitors can provide a good source of ideas and it is important that the organization analyses any new products or services as they are introduced to the market and makes an appropriate response. **Reverse engineering** is a systematic approach to dismantling and inspecting a competitor's product to look for aspects of design that could be incorporated into the organization's own product. This is especially prevalent when the product is a complex assembly such as a car, where design choices are myriad.

Benchmarking compares a product or service against what is considered the best in that market segment and then makes recommendations on how the product or service can be improved to meet that standard. Although a reactive strategy, benchmarking can be useful to organizations that have lost ground to innovative competitors. More details on benchmarking are given in Chapter 18.

2. Feasibility Study

The marketing function will take the ideas created in the idea generation stage and form a series of alternative concepts on which a feasibility study is undertaken. The concept refers not to the physical product or specification of the service that the person is buying but the overall set of expected benefits that a customer is receiving. For instance, a restaurant meal consists not only of the meal itself but the level of attention and the general surroundings. Thus the concept is referring to the combination of physical product and service, referred to as the package, which delivers a set of expected benefits to the customer. Once a concept has been formulated it must then be submitted to market, economic and technical analysis in order to assess its feasibility.

Market Analysis

A **market analysis** consists of evaluating the design concept with potential customers through interviews, focus groups and other data collection methods. A physical product may be tested by supplying a sample for customer evaluation. The market analysis should identify whether sufficient demand for the proposed product or service exists and its fit with the existing marketing strategy.

At a strategic level the organization can use the product life cycle (PLC) to determine the likely cost and volume characteristics of the product or service. The life cycle describes the volume sales over time in four phases of introduction, growth, maturity and decline (more details on stages in the PLC are given in Chapter 2).

In relating the PLC to the design process in the *introduction* phase production costs are high and design changes may be frequent. However, there may be little or no competition for the new product or service and so it may be possible to charge a premium price to customers. The *growth* phase sees a rapid increase in volume and the possibility of competitors entering the market. At this stage it is important to establish the product or service in the market as firmly as possible in order to secure future sales. Costs should be declining as process improvements and standardization take place. In the *mature* phase competitive pressures will increase and it is important that sales are secured through a brand image to differentiate it from competitors. There should be a continued effort at design improvement to the product or service itself and the process that delivers it. Some products, such as consumer durables, may stay in the mature phase almost indefinitely and techniques such as advertising are used to maintain interest and market share. Many services can be improved by the exploitation of technological developments such as Internet banking. In the *decline* phase, before the product or service is discontinued or modified to meet customer needs, the focus should be on optimizing profits while minimizing new investment.

The PLC is a useful tool in developing a portfolio of products and services to different stages of the life cycle, although it can be difficult to identify when they will enter the next stage of the life cycle or even what stage of the life cycle they are now in.

Economic Analysis

Economic analysis consists of developing estimates of production and delivery costs and comparing them with estimates of demand. In order to perform the analysis an accurate estimate of demand is required, possibly derived from statistical forecasts of industry sales and estimates of market share in the sector the product or service is competing in. These estimates will be based on a predicted price range for the product or service, which is compatible with its position in the market. In order to assess the feasibility of the product or service, estimates of costs in terms of such factors as staffing, materials and equipment must be obtained. Techniques such as cost/benefit analysis, decision theory and accounting measures such as net present value (NPV) and internal rate of return (IRR) may be used to calculate the profitability of a product. Another tool that can be used is the cost-volume-profit model.

The Cost-Volume-Profit Model

The cost-volume-profit (CVP) model, which was used in Chapter 5 for location decisions (see Figure 5.10), can also be used to provide an estimate of the profit level generated by a product at a certain product volume. The model assumes a linear relationship of cost and revenue to volume. If revenue is given by the following formula:

$$TR = SP \times X_S$$

where
    TR = total revenue,
    SP = selling price,
    X_S = units sold

And cost is given by the following formula:

$$TC = FC + VC \times X_P$$

where
    TC = total cost,
    FC = fixed cost,

VC = variable cost per unit,

X_P = number of units produced

then profit can be given by the following formula:

$$P = TR - TC$$

where

P = profit,

TR = total revenue,

TC = total cost

Assuming $X_S = X_P$ (all products made are sold) then the volume for a certain profit can be given by the following formula:

$$X = \frac{(P + FC)}{(SP - VC)}$$

where

X = volume (units),

P = profit,

FC = fixed costs,

SP = selling price,

VC = variable costs

When profit = 0 (selling costs = production costs), the break-even point, volume can be calculated by the following formula:

$$X = \frac{FC}{(SP - VC)}$$

WORKED EXAMPLE 7.1

Cost-Volume-Profit Model

A manufacturer produces a product with the following parameters:

Selling price (SP) = £7/unit

Variable cost (VC) = £4/unit

Fixed costs (FC) = £15 000/week

(a) What is the break-even point?

(b) How many do they need to sell to make £15 000 profit a week?

Solution

(a) At break-even point, P = 0

$$X = \frac{FC}{(SP - VC)}$$

$$= \frac{15\,000}{(7 - 4)} = 5000 \text{ units/week}$$

(b) At P = 15 000

$$X = \frac{(P + FC)}{(SP - VC)}$$

$$= \frac{(15\,000 + 15\,000)}{(7 - 4)}$$

$$= 10\,000 \text{ units/week}$$

Using the CVP Model for Multiple Products

If a firm produces more than one product using the same fixed costs the total profit can be calculated. The weighted contribution (selling price – variable cost) is calculated as follows:

$$WC = \sum_{i=1}^{n} M_i(SP_i - VC_i)$$

where
WC = weighted contribution,
M_i = product mix as a percentage of the total sales for product i
(where i = 1 to n, n = number of products),
SP_i = selling price for product i,
VC_i = variable cost for product i.

The volume for a certain profit level is given by the following formula:

$$X = \frac{(P + FC)}{WC}$$

where
X = volume (units),
P = profit,
FC = fixed costs,
WC = weighted contribution.

WORKED EXAMPLE 7.2

Cost-Volume-Profit Model

CVP Model for Multiple Products
The following product mix is planned.

	Pliers	Saws
Product mix	0.75	0.25
Selling price/unit	£1.50	£3.20
Variable cost	£1.20	£1.80

 www.wileyopenpage.com

Annual fixed cost $=$ £20 000
What is the break-even point?

Solution

$$WC = \sum_{i=1}^{n} M_i(SP_i - VC_i)$$
$$WC = 0.75 \times (1.50 - 1.20) + 0.25 \times (3.2 - 1.8)$$
$$= 0.75 \times 0.3 + 0.25 \times 1.4$$
$$= 0.575$$

At profit $= 0$

$$X = \frac{FC}{WC}$$
$$X = 20\,000/0.575 = 34\,783 \text{ units.}$$

Technical Analysis

Technical analysis involves determining whether the technical capability to manufacture the product or deliver the service exists. This covers such issues as ensuring materials are available to make the product to the specification required, ensuring the appropriate machinery and skills are available to work with these materials and securing staff skills necessary to deliver a service. The technical analysis must take into account the target market and so designers have to consider the costs of reaching the customer with the product or service in order to ensure it can be sold at a competitive price.

3. Preliminary Design

Design concepts that pass the feasibility stage enter preliminary design. The specification of the concept – what the product or service should do to satisfy customer needs – is translated into a technical specification of the components of the package (the product and service components that satisfy the customer needs defined in the concept) and the process by which the package is created. The specification of the components of the package requires a product and service structure which describes the relationship between the components and a bill of materials (BOM) or list of component quantities derived from the product structure (Chapter 14). The process by which the package is created is considered under process design (Chapter 8).

4. Final Design

The final design stage involves refining the preliminary design through the use of a prototype until a viable final design can be made. Computer-aided design (CAD) (Chapter 6) and simulation modelling (Chapter 8) can be used at this stage to build a computer-based prototype and refine the product and process design. The final design will be assessed in three main areas of functional design, form design and production design.

Functional Design

Functional design is ensuring that the design meets the performance characteristics that are specified in the product concept. Two aspects of functional design are reliability and maintainability.

Reliability

Reliability is an important performance characteristic and measures the probability that a product or service will perform its intended function for a specified period of time under normal conditions of use. The reliability of each part of the product or service must be determined by reference to the criteria of 'failure' and 'normal' service. These criteria are determined by reference to customer expectations and cost levels. Reliability can be determined by either the probability of failure during a given test or the probability of failure during a given time. Strategies for improving product or service reliability include simplified design (for example, less parts in a product), improved reliability of individual elements of the product or service and the adoption of backup product or service elements.

The probability of failure during a given test is a function of the reliability of component parts and the relationship of those parts. For a product of two component parts the reliability is the product of the probabilities:

$$R_s = (R_1)(R_2) \ldots (R_n)$$

where

R_s is the system reliability

R_n is the reliability of the nth component.

For Figure 7.3, Reliability $= 0.85 \times 0.8 = 0.68$

Note that the product reliability (0.68) is much less than the component parts and will continue to decline as the number of parts increases.

For a product with backup components the following applies:

$$R_s = 1 - [(1 - R_1)(1 - R_2) \ldots (1 - R_n)]$$

For Figure 7.4, Reliability $= 1 - [(1 - 0.85) \times (1 - 0.90)] = 0.985$

Note that the product reliability (0.985) is higher than the component part but the cost of providing a backup makes its use relevant in only critical components.

FIGURE 7.3

Product Reliability (Serial).

 www.wileyopenpage.com

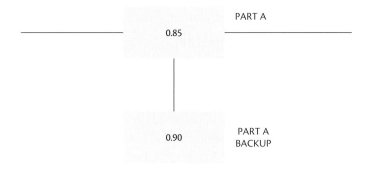

FIGURE 7.4

Product Reliability (Backup).

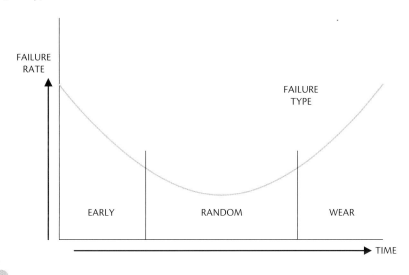

FIGURE 7.5

Failure Pattern over Time.

The probability of failure during a given time is expressed as a distribution pattern of failures over time. Failure rates tend to follow the pattern shown in Figure 7.5 where defective parts fail early and then the failure rate rises again towards the end of a product's life. A small number of random failures occur between these points.

The reciprocal of the actual failure rate, found by product testing, is called the mean time between failures (MTBF) and if it is found to follow a negative exponential distribution the reliability (probability that the product will not fail before time T) can be found as follows:

$$P(\text{no failure before T}) = e^{-T/\text{MTBF}}$$

where

$e = 2.7183$

$T = $ time period

$\text{MTBF} = $ mean time between failures.

Mean Time Between Failures (MTBF)

If the life of a product follows a negative exponential distribution and the average lifespan 10 years, what is the probability that the product will fail after 5 years?

Solution

$$MTBF = 10$$
$$T = 5$$
$$P(\ ) = e^{-5/10} = 0.61$$

Thus there is a 61% chance of lasting five years. Conversely there is a 39% chance of failure during this time period.

Maintainability

Maintainability may include such issues as the ability of the customer to maintain a product or the need for trained personnel to undertake maintenance or repair activities. Maintainability is connected to issues such as the cost of the product (it may be cheaper to throw away rather than to repair the product) and its reliability (very high reliability will reduce the importance of maintainability).

Product maintainability can be expressed as the mean time to repair (MTTR). Thus the availability of a product can be calculated by combining the MTBF measure, along with the time taken to repair these failures (MTTR).

$$Availability = MTBF/(MTBF + MTTR)$$

Maintainability can be improved by modular design to enable whole modules to be replaced rather than the lengthy investigation of faults. Maintenance schedules should also be specified to help prevent problems from occurring. An improved ability to perform under adverse conditions (termed the design robustness) will improve maintainability.

Form Design

Form design refers to the product aesthetics such as look, feel and sound if applicable. This is particularly important for consumer durables but even industrial appliances should at least project an image of quality. In services the design of the supporting facility, such as the room decor, lighting and music in a restaurant, provide an important element of the service design.

Production Design

Production design involves ensuring that the design takes into consideration the ease and cost of manufacture of a product. Good design will take into consideration the present manufacturing capabilities in terms of material supplies, equipment and personnel skills available. The cost of production can be reduced by the following methods:

- *simplification* – reducing the number of components, subassemblies and options in a product thus reducing the amount of manufacturing processes required.
- *standardization* – enabling the use of the same components for different products and modules. Interchangeable parts can lead to lower inventory, lower cost purchasing and easier materials handling.
- *modularization* – combining standardized building blocks in different ways to create a range of products. This can achieve lower production costs from economies of scale and scope.

These methods can be used to assist in the implementation of a mass customization approach detailed later in this chapter.

SERVICE DESIGN

The design process outlined in the previous section of this chapter is relevant both to products and services. This section outlines issues relevant to the design of services in particular. In product design the outcome is a tangible item but in service design the outcome is an overall set of expected benefits that the customer is buying which can be termed the **service concept**. One consequence of this is that service design cannot be protected from being used by competitors, i.e. you can patent a product but not a service, and so new service designs need to be exploited rapidly to preempt competitors.

In addition to the intangible nature of service design the nature of the service can also be impacted by the presence of the customer in the service delivery process and most services are accompanied by some sort of tangible element (a consultancy report presented at the end of a consultancy project for

CASE STUDY 7.1

Product Development at Fracino

By getting designers, engineers and marketers to work closely together, Fracino has been able to establish itself in an incredibly competitive market. Close collaboration means Fracino's coffee machines meet its customers' requirements exactly. The business decided to create project teams of designers, engineers and marketers who could work together at all stages of the process to assure the quality of the final project. Now, a three- or four-strong team sees each project from original concept, through prototyping and testing, to component supply and assembly. This creates real dedication and focus and means that modifications can be made quickly and seamlessly. Fracino also involves key customers in the prototyping phase to make sure the final product meets their needs.

Source: The Department of Trade and Industry (www.dti.gov .uk/bestpractice). Reproduced with permission.

Question

Explain the advantages of the collaborative approach to product development adopted by Fracino.

example). This combination of elements is termed the **service package** (Fitzsimmons and Fitzsimmons, 2011) and is defined as a bundle of goods and services with information that is provided in some environment. The service package consists of the following five features with an example provided of a hotel business and criteria of how each of these features could be evaluated as appropriate for the service package offered.

- Supporting facility – the physical resources that must be in place before a service can be offered (e.g. hotel building). Criteria for evaluation include the location, interior decoration, supporting equipment, architectural appropriateness and facility layout.
- Facilitating goods – the material purchased or consumed by the buyer, or the items provided by the customer (e.g. towels, soap etc.). Criteria for evaluation include consistency, quantity and selection.
- Information – Data that is available from the customer or provider to enable efficient and customized service (e.g. room reservation information). Criteria for evaluation include accuracy, timeliness and usefulness.
- Explicit services – the benefits that are readily observable by the senses and consist of the essential or intrinsic features of the service (e.g. a comfortable bed in a clean room). Criteria for evaluation include training of personnel, comprehensiveness, consistency and availability.
- Implicit services – psychological benefits that the customer may sense only vaguely, or the extrinsic features of the service (e.g. friendly and helpful service at reception). Criteria for evaluation include attitude of service, atmosphere, waiting, status, sense of well being, privacy and security and convenience.

The idea of the service package shows that although service design is often primarily related to the design of the process of the delivery of the service it can be seen that the service package will also require the design of physical aspects such as the supporting facility and facilitating goods. In terms of the design of the service element, the service package emphasizes the point that the providers of the service should not simply focus on the delivery of the explicit service and neglect the other components of the service package. Thus it is important to recognize the effect on the level of service that all the elements of the service package have. The criteria for each feature of the service package should provide a consistent service system design. This can be achieved by relating the service packages features to the service process types of mass service, service shop and professional service covered in Chapter 3.

A service is an experience, not simply the receiving of a good, so the customer will be in contact with the service as it is delivered. This means the service design must take into account how the individual customer will react to the service as it is delivered. This is not easy as all customers are different and have different expectations of what the service will provide. This requires close cooperation between operations and marketing to identify a target customer market and ensure that the service design is meeting their needs.

Another feature of service design is that because the service is intangible it is often difficult to test quality levels before the service is provided. From the customer's point of view quality may only be assessed when the service is provided or perhaps an indication of service quality may be gained by seeking the views of others who have experience of the service required. Quality can be designed into the service by taking the design features and implementing a quality system to maintain conformance to design requirements. The techniques of QFD and Taguchi discussed later in this chapter are relevant in ensuring service design quality.

CASE STUDY 7.2

Benugo

Taking its name from cofounders Ben and Hugo Warner, Benugo cafes opened for business in 1998. They offered customers a new style of cafe with 'pizzazz', in an environment where people could relax and enjoy their food. With 11 cafe shops in and around London, 150 staff employed throughout the business and annual revenues of over £6 million, Benugo has proved to be a big hit with customers. 'At Benugo we know that the customer always has a choice', says Tim Parfitt, Finance Director, 'We want Benugo to be that choice as often as possible.'

But in today's market margins are low and competition is fierce. Business survival depends on sustaining profitability and maintaining customer satisfaction. This is why Tim was intrigued by the proposition from technology solutions provider, Broadscape. The proposal was to provide Benugo's customers with high-speed Internet access over a Wireless LAN with a WiFi access point. This would effectively mean that customers could come into a Benugo cafe, open up their laptop and have instant access to the Internet without having to plug in any cables. Benugo trialled the idea in two of their cafes. They offered wireless Internet connections free of charge as long as customers spent £2 or over on food or coffee for every 30 minutes of use. A short flyer tells customers how to set up the WiFi access on their laptop and within minutes they're online. Broadscape's installation also included Bluetooth which allowed compatible PDAs to connect to the Internet as well. The innovative aspect of the system is that customers are not charged directly for Internet access. Which in turn means that there are no billing issues and nothing complicated to consider with billing updates.

Source: The Department of Trade and Industry (www.dti.gov.uk/bestpractice). Reproduced with permission.

Question

Relate the concept of the service package to the facilities offered by Benugo.

IMPROVING DESIGN

This chapter will now explore a number of techniques that have been developed in an attempt to improve the design process.

The video 'Digitoe: Shoes for the 21st Century' is available in your interactive e-book at **www.wileyopenpage.com**

The video 'The Future of Mass Customization' is available in your interactive e-book at **www.wileyopenpage.com**

Mass customization

Mass customization is based on the assumption that market requirements are becoming increasingly fragmented, while operations resources are allowing a greater degree of flexibility and responsiveness. **Mass customization** (Pine, Bart and Boynton, 1993) attempts to combine high-variety and high-volume output in order to provide the customer with customized products at a relatively low price. Therefore, mass customization aims to 'mass produce' a basic family of products or services which can still be customized to the needs of individual customers. One way of achieving mass customization is to incorporate the ideas related to production design of simplification, standardization and modularization covered earlier in this chapter. Vonderembse and White (2004) describe three levels of customization:

- *Customer-contact customization* – is where the product or service is tailored to individual needs. For example, a haircut or bicycle can be designed and delivered to meet the specification provided by an individual customer.
- *Adaptive customization* – is where a standard product or service can be customized to meet individual needs. For example, a car can be customized by the customer by ordering from a list of options such as metallic paint and air conditioning. Here customization starts at the production rather than design stage.
- *Presentation customization* – is where standard products are presented differently to different customers. This can be achieved through differences in elements such as packaging, delivery channel, terms and conditions of purchase and stated use. Here the level of customization occurs after the product is produced.

The video 'Mass Customization Mistakes' is available in your interactive e-book at **www.wileyopenpage.com**

Simultaneous Development

Simultaneous development, also known as simultaneous (or concurrent) engineering in manufacturing operations, is when contributors to the stages of the design effort provide their expertise together throughout the design process as a team. This contrasts with the traditional sequential design process when work is undertaken within functional departments. The problem with the traditional approach is the cost and time involved in bringing the product to market. In some business sectors (such as consumer electronics) shrinking product life cycles have meant that new products or improvements to existing products are required in an ever shorter time scale. Simultaneous development reduces the time wasted when each stage in the design process waits for the previous stage to finish completely before it can commence. For example, critical equipment, some of which may take an extended time to purchase and install, is identified and procured early in the design process in order to reduce the overall development time.

Another problem of the traditional approach to design is the lack of communication between functional specialists involved in the different stages of design. This can lead to an attitude of 'throwing the design over the wall' without any consideration of problems that may be encountered by later stages. An example of this is decisions made at the preliminary design stage that adversely affect choices at the product build stage. This can cause the design to be repeatedly passed between departments to satisfy everyone's needs, increasing time and costs. Problems of this type can be reduced by facilitating communication through the establishment of a project team.

Design for Manufacture (DFM)

An important aspect of good design is that the product designed can be produced easily and at low cost. **Design for manufacture** is a concept that views product design as the first step in the manufacture of that product. It incorporates guidelines on such aspects as simplification, standardization and modularization but also techniques such as failure mode and effect analysis (FMEA) and value engineering (VE). See the Oxley Woods video for an example of the use of DFM to produce affordable housing.

The video 'Design for Manufacture – Oxley Woods' is available in your interactive e-book at **www.wileyopenpage.com**

Failure Mode and Effect Analysis (FMEA)

Failure mode and effect analysis is a systematic approach to identifying the cause and effect of product failures. The approach involves the following:

- list the functions of the component parts of the product
- define the failure modes (such as leakage or fatigue) for all parts
- rank the failures in order of likelihood and seriousness
- address each failure in rank order, making design changes where necessary.

The idea of FMEA is to anticipate failures and deal with them at the design stage. The ranking of failures is achieved by calculating the product of the following three values on a scale of 1 to 10, termed the risk priority number (RPN).

O (occurrence) = probability of failure occurring (1 = almost never, 10 = often)
S (severity) = the effect the failure has if the failure takes place (1 = hardly noticeable, 10 = serious effect)
D (detectability) = the difficulty of detection (1 = absolutely obvious, 10 = undetectable)

The risk priority number (RPN) is thus = $O \times S \times D$ and can be used as a guide to prioritizing the most serious quality problems.

Value Engineering (VE)

Value engineering aims to eliminate unnecessary features and functions that do not contribute to the value or performance of the product. It is derived from the idea of value analysis (VA) which was developed to improve the design of existing products, particularly taking into account the use of new technology. The technique uses a team approach and follows a formal procedure which has the following core activities:

- *Define function.* This involves defining each function of the product and its cost.
- *Gather alternatives.* A team will brainstorm new ways to accomplish the functions.
- *Evaluate alternatives.* Each idea generated is evaluated for feasibility and cost.

The technique can be used during design or as a continuous improvement tool during production when a flexible design specification is needed to accommodate suggestions at the production stage.

Functional Analysis

Functional analysis is a technique for mapping service processes that starts by defining a high-level description of the service and then successively breaking down that description into a number of functions. Processes are then created by arranging the functions in the sequence in which the activities defined by the functions are performed. In service processes it is useful to have a customer at the start and end of the process in order to evaluate the impact of the quality of the process on the customer. In order to incorporate the interactions between the customer and the service provider during service, processes can be classified into *operational activities,* which are the steps needed to deliver the service to the customer, and *customer service activities,* which are the customer and service-provider interactions.

Quality Functional Deployment (QFD)

Quality functional deployment is a structured process that translates the voice of the customer (what the customer needs) into technical design requirements (how these needs are met). It is particularly relevant to the concept of simultaneous development as it complements the use of teams in attempting to coordinate design objectives. The technique consists of a series of tables that translate requirements at successive design stages as follows:

The House of Quality
Customer Requirements → Product Characteristics

Parts Deployment
Product Characteristics → Part Characteristics

Process Planning
Part Characteristics → Process Characteristics

Operating Requirements
Process Characteristics → Operations

The most used matrix is the House of Quality that converts customer requirements into product characteristics. The House of Quality matrix is shown in Figure 7.6.

 www.wileyopenpage.com

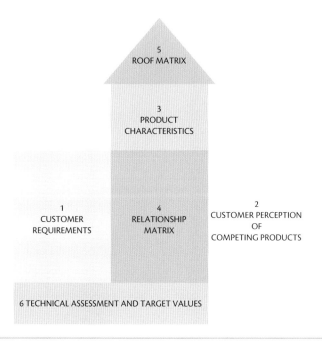

FIGURE 7.6

House of Quality Matrix.

- *Customer requirements.* This element links the attributes of the product that are important to the customer along with their relative importance.
- *Customer perceptions of competitive products.* This compares customer perceptions of the organization and competitors' performance for each of the customer requirements. It provides information on relative performance and also identifies where competitive advantage can be attained by improving relative performance on a highly ranked customer requirement.
- *Product characteristics.* This lists the product characteristics, expressed in engineering terms and grouped where appropriate.
- *Relationship matrix.* The matrix correlates the attributes of customer requirements with product characteristics. The relationship may be a positive or negative one and assists in identifying design changes to product characteristics to meet customer requirements.
- *Roof matrix.* This explores the interaction between product characteristics. This assists identification of an adverse change in product characteristic as a consequence of a change in another characteristic.
- *Technical assessment and target values.* This section includes performance measures to compare the product with competitors. It also contains chosen critical design factors such as cost and importance.

Any change in product characteristic as a result of analysis of customer requirements is then carried forward to the parts deployment matrix and then converted to the process planning and finally operating requirements matrix. In this way QFD enables the full consequences of any design change to be assessed and operationalized. The technology provides a method of communicating the effect of change quickly amongst all the members of the design team.

An example of a House of Quality matrix for a generic product is shown in Figure 7.7.

www.wileyopenpage.com

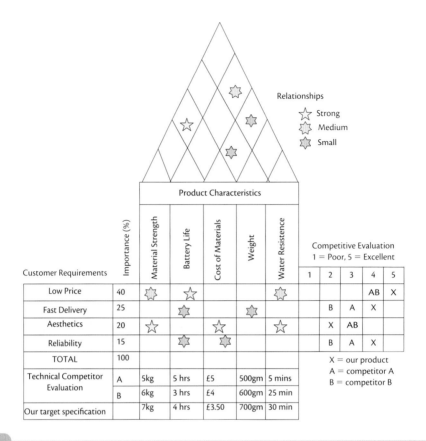

Relationships

☆ Strong
☆ Medium
☆ Small

Customer Requirements	Importance (%)	Material Strength	Battery Life	Cost of Materials	Weight	Water Resistence	Competitive Evaluation 1 = Poor, 5 = Excellent				
							1	2	3	4	5
Low Price	40	☆	☆			☆				AB	X
Fast Delivery	25		☆		☆		B	A	X		
Aesthetics	20	☆		☆		☆	X	AB			
Reliability	15		☆	☆			B	A	X		
TOTAL	100										
Technical Competitor Evaluation A	A	5kg	5 hrs	£5	500gm	5 mins					
	B	6kg	3 hrs	£4	600gm	25 min					
Our target specification		7kg	4 hrs	£3.50	700gm	30 min					

X = our product
A = competitor A
B = competitor B

FIGURE 7.7

House of Quality Example.

Taguchi Methods

Genichi Taguchi suggests that product failure is mainly a function of design. Taguchi argues that quality must be designed into a product and that it cannot be inspected in later if the design is not good. Techniques that Taguchi has provided for improving product and process quality are robust design, the quality loss function (QLF), target-oriented quality and design of experiments (DOE).

The robustness of a product is defined by its ability to withstand variations in environmental and operating conditions. **Robust design** is the process of designing in the ability of the product to perform under a variety of conditions and so reducing the chance of product failure. In order to achieve this Taguchi suggests a focus on consistency of parts rather than just requiring manufacture within a tolerance. The tolerance arbitrarily defines a cut-off point between poor quality and good quality which may not be recognized by the customer. Taguchi has formalized the effect on customer dissatisfaction as the actual value deviates from the target value (i.e. the distance from the tolerance limit) called the **quality loss function (QLF)**. Taguchi argues that consistency is especially important in assembled products where parts at either end of their tolerance limit can result in a poor quality product. Thus the ability to produce a part to a consistent specification through design is important. The QLF is a simple cost estimate which shows how customer preferences are oriented towards consistently meeting quality expectations and that a customer's dissatisfaction (quality loss) increases geometrically as the actual value deviates from the target value (Figure 7.8).

The Quality Loss Function can be expressed mathematically:

$$L = C \times d^2$$

where

L = quality loss
C = cost of the deviation from the specfication limit
d = deviation from target value

The QLF shows the quality loss that occurs when an organization simply aims to achieve quality levels between the upper and lower specification limits, termed conformance-oriented quality. Taguchi's **target-oriented quality** strives through a process of continuous improvement to keep as close as possible to the target specification and so losses are much lower (see Figure 7.8).

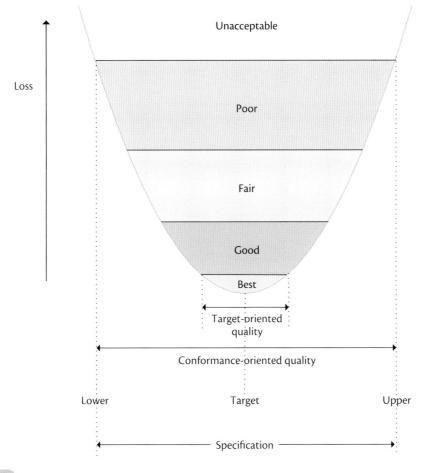

FIGURE 7.8

Quality Loss Function.

Design of experiments (DOE) aims to identify factors that affect a product's performance by providing a way of testing a number of design options under various operating and environmental conditions. In other words DOE provides a method of achieving robust design. The conditions that cause a poor product performance are separated into controllable and uncontrollable factors. In a design situation controllable factors are design parameters such as material type or dimensions. Uncontrollable factors derive from the wear of the product, such as the length of use or settings, or are environmental such as heat and humidity. A good design will have variables that act in a robust fashion to the possible occurrence of uncontrollable factors.

Cause-and-Effect Diagrams

The idea of a **cause-and-effect diagram** (sometimes referred to as a fishbone or Ishikawa diagram) is to work back from the quality problem and identify individual causes on lines radiating from each category branch, associated with the problem in each major category (Figure 7.9). Categories are often referred to as the 4Ms of Manpower, Machines, Materials and Method. Other categories can be used, for example the 4Ps of People, Products, Price and Promotions. Individual causes associated with each category are then tied to separate 'bones' along the category branch. This method often uses group processes such as brainstorming sessions to generate the ideas for causes.

Pareto Analysis

Pareto analysis is used to organize information and quality problems and help focus problem-solving effort on the most important aspects. A Pareto chart is used to display a histogram of the major areas of

FIGURE 7.9

Cause-and-Effect Diagram.

 www.wileyopenpage.com

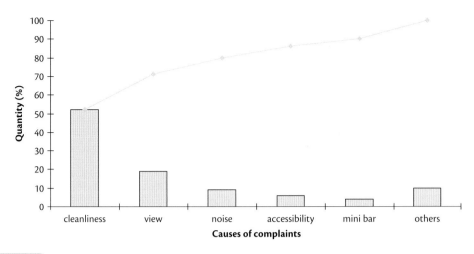

Pareto Analysis of Hotel Room Complaints.

concern and a cumulative line shows the percentage contribution of each category. The data is organized with the highest category to the left and the 'others' category on the right hand side. Figure 7.10 shows a Pareto diagram for data collected using complaint forms in a hotel. The diagram shows a large amount of data visually and allows quick identification of problem areas which when tackled will have the largest effect on quality levels.

SUMMARY

- The steps in the design process are idea generation, feasibility study, preliminary design and final design. Ideas for new products can come from the organization's research and development (R&D) function, customers and competitors. The feasibility study consists of a market, economic and technical analysis. Preliminary design consists of forming a technical specification of the components of the package. The final design will be assessed in the three main areas of functional design, form design and production design.

- Service design relates to the combination of goods and service elements termed the service package.

- Simultaneous development can reduce the time and cost involved in the design process.

- Design for manufacture aims to ensure a product design can be produced easily and at low cost through guidelines on such aspects as simplification, standardization and modularization.

- Quality functional deployment (QFD) is a structured process that translates customer needs into technical design requirements.

- Taguchi methods for improving design quality include robust design, the quality loss function (QLF), target-oriented quality and design of experiments (DOE).

www.wileyopenpage.com

Wine-on-the-go

A wine sold in its own cup has recently won an award at the wine 'Oscars'. James Nash, a packaging expert, came up with the 'cup-a-wine' concept – wine sold in a plastic glass with a tear-off lid or, what could be described as, 'yoghurt pot style' wine glasses.

The 'portable wine' product, called The Tulip, was unanimously dismissed by the TV panel of the BBC's 'Dragons Den' show, having been described as 'tacky'.

Marks & Spencer, however, disagreed – and contacted James, just days after the show aired last August, to place an order trialling his product in 91 stores. James's glasses of wine flew off the shelves and within months they were stocked in all 500 of M&S's food stores.

James' company, Wine Innovations, states:

'The Tulip is a 187ml PET, single serve prefilled wine glass. Perfect for all outdoor events, sporting events and festivals, plus of course for picnics and barbecues or any occasion where the convenience of the Tulip makes it the natural choice.'

The wine is sealed to maintain wine quality and to give a shelf life of over 1 year.

The Tulip is made from a high quality PET that gives the right look, feel and weight of a 'proper' wine glass.

The Tulip is completely shatter proof and in fact near unbreakable.

Each glass contains ¼ of a standard wine bottle. However, convenience of portable wine isn't without its downsides; if the same wine was bought in a full 75cl bottle the price comes to £5.49 versus £9 for the equivalent amount in four of the new packs.

The idea for the design came to James, when he was buying drinks, 'It came to me in a flash – tough plastic goblets with foil lids wouldn't spill and the wine could be served faster. I thought it would increase profits at the bar.' Initially James and his wife self funded the idea – using their garage and living room for development and storage. His first attempt at having the machine made failed when he found leaks in every other goblet.

He invested money borrowed from friends and family of over £500 000 in machinery and technology and patent application. This overcame the product weaknesses and made it ready for volume manufacture.

The product itself is manufactured by using the twin lane ST100R Starwheel machine. This packs 2 400 glasses per hour and is fitted with MAP-F gas flushing to extend the shelf-life of the product for up to one year. The ST100R Starwheel is designed for ease of use and is fitted with quick-release change parts to enable fast product changeovers in under five minutes.

Sales were around £3.5m at the end of 2011, with increased projections for 2012 as it expands across the globe.

Licensing agreements with importers in Australia, America, Brazil and South Africa were in the contractual stage awaiting final sign-off, said Nash, and Marks & Spencer which introduced Tulip glasses of its Le Froglet wine to shelves in April has placed a second order for the concept.

'The number of enquiries from around the world is unbelievable,' said Nash. 'From Hong Kong to India to China we're having two or three enquiries a day from people wanting to become agents.'

Wine Innovations sell a Tulip sealing machine and licence to only one agent in each country and earn royalties from each sale.

As well as Le Froglet in M&S, Wine Innovations supplies its Tulip glass to Booker wholesale and food travel company SSP.

 www.wileyopenpage.com

It is currently in discussions with other multiple retailers with a view to further listings.

Sources

http://money.aol.co.uk/2012/10/12/dragons-den-reject-wins-major-wine-award/

http://www.thisismoney.co.uk/money/article-1695929/Cup-a-wine-success-after-Dragon-rejection.html#ixzz29e4EN600

http://www.thegrocer.co.uk/fmcg/dragons-reject-says-exports-will-double-pre-filled-glass-sales/213757.article

http://www.dailymail.co.uk/property/article-1325191/Dragons-Den-reject-James-Nash-drinking-business-780k-house.html#ixzz29e53bUAm

http://www.cwm-automation.com/742/news/wine-innovations-order-second-starwheel-wine-in-glass-filling-machine/

Source: Written by Briony Boydell and Chris Milner. Reproduced with permission.

Questions

1. How original is this design and what are the considerations from an operational perspective, when a design is more unique?
2. What impact did the delays have upon the design process?
3. What design criteria does this product fulfil?
4. Is the product: useful, usable, desirable, producible, profitable and differentiated?

 Quizzes to test yourself further are available in your interactive e-book at **www.wileyopenpage.com**

 Flashcards to test yourself further are available in your interactive e-book at **www.wileyopenpage.com**

EXERCISES

1. A manufacturer produces a product with the following specification.

    Selling price = £15.00/unit
    Variable cost = £10.00/unit
    Fixed costs = £10 000/week

    a. What is the break-even point?
    b. How many do they need to sell to make £20 000 profit a week?

2. The following product mix is planned.

	Knives	Forks	Spoons
Product mix	0.4	0.4	0.2
Selling price (£/unit)	0.07	0.08	0.05
Variable cost (£/unit)	0.05	0.06	0.03

Annual fixed cost = £1000

a. What is the break-even point?

b. At what volume will profit = £5000, given the current product mix?

c. If the price of a spoon is reduced by £0.01, what volume is required to make a profit of £5000?

3. An assembly is made up of four components arranged as follows:

The components can be purchased from three different suppliers with the following reliability ratings:

	Supplier		
Component	1	2	3
A	0.94	0.95	0.92
B	0.86	0.80	0.90
C	0.90	0.93	0.95
D	0.93	0.95	0.95

a. If only one supplier is chosen to supply all four components, which should be selected?

b. What supplier should be selected for the following configuration?

4. Discuss the objectives of functional design, form design and production design.

5. Explain the role of standardization, simplification and modularization in design.

6. Outline the objectives of FMEA.

7. What is the purpose of QFD?

8. How would you implement a simultaneous development programme?

FURTHER READING

Berman, B. (2002) Should your firm adopt a mass customisation strategy? *Business Horizons,* July–August, 51–60.

Hope, C. and Miihlemann, A. (1997) *Service Operations Management: Strategy, Design and Delivery,* Prentice Hall.

Taguchi, G. and Clausing, D. (1990) Robust quality, *Harvard Business Review,* January–February, 65–75.

WEB LINKS

www.autocad.com (accessed 9 November 2011). AutoCAD. One of the most popular software packages for designing new products.

www.designcouncil.org.uk (accessed 9 November 2011). Design Council. Wide-ranging site including information on all aspects of design.

www.design-iv.com (accessed 9 November 2011). Design IV. Consultancy specializing in design for manufacture and assembly (DFMA). Site has information on conferences, software and training.

REFERENCES

Christensen, C.M. (1997) *The Innovator's Dilemma: When New Technologies Cause Great Firms to Fail,* Harvard Business School Press.

Fitzsimmons, J.A. and Fitzsimmons, M.J. (2011) *Service Management: Operations, Strategy, and Information Technology,* 7th edn, McGraw-Hill.

Pine, B., Bart, V. and Boynton, A. (1993) *Making mass customisation work,* Harvard Business Review, September/October, pp. 108–119.

Vonderembse, M.A. and White, G.P (2004) *Core Concepts of Operations Management,* John Wiley and Sons Ltd.

CHAPTER 8

Process Design

- **Introduction**
- **Steps in process design**
- **Tools for process design**

LEARNING OBJECTIVES

- Describe the steps in process design
- Evaluate the use of process design documentation techniques such as process charts, process mapping and service blueprinting
- Describe the relevance of using business process simulation to study processes

PROCESS DESIGN AND OPERATIONS STRATEGY

A number of functional areas such as marketing, operations and finance are involved in the making of a product or delivery of a service but the value that the customer obtains from that product or service is a result of a set of processes. Thus well designed processes that meet the needs of the customer are essential if an organization is to be competitive. The design of processes may be determined by customer requirements or benchmarking competitors or may be directly related to meeting strategic objectives such as order-winning competitive factors.

INTRODUCTION

The process view of operations is covered in Chapter 1. This describes how operations management is concerned with the design of the flow of people and products through manufacturing and service processes. However, under the process view an organization can be considered to consist of a number of processes and so the term operations, which entails the transformation of processes, can now be seen to cover all aspects of an organization. This means process design will not just be considered at the level of individual activities within manufacturing and service processes but at the level of processes across functional areas such as operations, marketing and finance and at the level of processes across organizations in the supply chain. The design of processes is complex and so the steps in a structured approach to process design are covered as is the use of tools to assist process design activities such as process mapping, service blueprints and business process simulation.

STEPS IN PROCESS DESIGN

The task of designing processes should be undertaken in a structured manner and the steps involved can be described as:

1. Identify opportunities for process improvement
2. Document the process design.
3. Redesign the process.

1. Identify Opportunities for Process Improvement

The main processes within an organization are covered in Chapter 1 and can be described as supplier relationship, new product development, order fulfilment and customer relationship. These represent the core processes involved in providing value added to the organization's customers and thus provide a general guide to where improvement efforts should be focused. These processes will in most organizations be too large and complex to evaluate in a single initiative and thus it is necessary to scope the project to address a particular area of concern. These areas can be derived from customer feedback, employee ideas generated from suggestion schemes (Chapter 18) and benchmarking against competitors (Chapter 18). An alternative approach is to relate the processes to strategic issues. If strategic objectives are expressed in terms of the five performance objectives of operations (Chapter 2) two models that are relevant are Hill and Hill (2012) which expresses strategic objectives in terms of market requirements of 'order winning' and 'qualifying factors' and Slack (1991) which uses a combination of market and competitive factors in an importance/performance matrix. When expressing strategic objectives in a broader perspective the balanced scorecard (Kaplan and Norton, 1996) measures performance across financial, customer, learning and growth and internal business process perspectives. Greasley (2004a) relates critical success factors (CSF) from each of the balanced scorecard perspectives in terms of scoring the impact of the process on the CSF and the extent of process innovation required to meet the CSF. Processes which score highest on both impact and innovation are prioritized for improvement. This method is particularly suited to public sector organizations where the use of market-based measures is less relevant. The methods just described are covered in more detail in Chapter 18 and Case Study 18.4.

2. Document the Process Design

The identification of activities in a current process design is a data-collection exercise using methods such as examination of current documentation, interviews and observation. In order to provide a framework for the design and improvement of service processes the documentation techniques of process mapping and service blueprinting can be used and are described later in this chapter.

3. Redesign the Process

There are many ways in which a process can be redesigned to meet particular objectives and so it is necessary to generate a range of innovative solutions for evaluation. Three approaches that can be used to generate new ideas are:

- *Generating new designs through brainstorming.* This approach offers the greatest scope for radical improvements to the process design but represents a risk in the implementation of a totally new approach. A deep understanding of the process is required in order that the design will be feasible.
- *Modifying existing designs.* This approach is less risky than a blue-skies approach but may mean the opportunity for a radical improvement in process design is missed.
- *Using an established 'benchmark' design.* This approach applies the idea of identifying the best-in-class performer for the particular process in question and adopting that design. Disadvantages with this approach may be that the process design of the best-in-class performer may not be available or the context of the best-in-class performer may not match the context for the new design.

The process map or service blueprint provides an overall view of the current or expected process design and this should be used in order that an overall view is taken when process design options are generated. This helps to ensure that design solutions proposed in a specific area do not have a detrimental effect in other areas of the process and thus affect overall process performance.

The design of service processes in particular is a key factor in meeting the needs of the customer. In services the process incorporates employees, customers and facilitating goods in a dynamic event that may be undertaken in a different manner each time, according to the demands of the individual customer. The interaction between the customer and service provider can be analysed using the service blueprint diagrams described in this chapter.

In designing services Shostack (1987) categorizes services by their complexity – the number and interdependency of process elements – and divergency – how many different ways they can be performed. Once a service has been documented it can be analysed for opportunities either to increase or decrease one or both of these variables.

Peppard and Rowland (1995) provide a number of areas for the potential redesign of processes under the headings of Eliminate, Simplify, Integrate and Automate (ESIA) (Table 8.1).

It will be necessary to reduce the number of design alternatives generated and this can be achieved by a rating scheme that scores each design solution against key performance dimensions such as response time and cost of operation. The outcome of this analysis will be a reduced number of design solutions, which can then be subjected to more detailed analysis.

The valuation of alternative process designs is often undertaken using mathematical models such as queuing theory (Chapter 11) and techniques such as business process simulation (BPS) which is covered later in this chapter. The BPS technique allows the predicted variability in a process design to be incorporated in a computer model and thus the robustness of the design over time can be assessed. It also permits process design performance to be measured along dimensions such as speed, reliability and cost.

 www.wileyopenpage.com

TABLE 8.1

ESIA Areas for Potential Redesign.

Eliminate	Simplify	Integrate	Automate
Over-production	Forms	Jobs	Dirty
Waiting time	Procedures	Teams	Difficult
Transport	Communication	Customers	Dangerous
Processing	Technology	Suppliers	Boring
Inventory	Problem areas		Data capture
Defects/failures	Flows		Data transfer
Duplication	Processes		Data analysis
Reformatting			
Inspection			
Reconciling			

Source: Peppard, J. and Rowland, P. (1995) The Essence of Business Process Re-engineering, Prentice Hall. Reproduced with permission.

TOOLS FOR PROCESS DESIGN

A number of tools are available to assist in the task of redesigning processes. These tools can help in all stages of the design process including documentation of processes and process redesign.

Process Charts

A **process chart** (also called a process activity chart) is often used to analyse the steps of a job or how a set of jobs fit together into the overall flow of a process, for example, the steps involved in processing a customer order received by telephone. There are five main symbols in a process chart, as shown in Figure 8.1. An example process chart for a generic administration process is shown in Figure 8.2.

The process chart performs a number of functions including identifying the task sequence, task relationships, task delays (by including average task times), task movements and worker assignment to tasks. The charts can be used in conjunction with a written job description to form a detailed outline of a job. The charts can also be useful in the first stage of a job improvement scheme. There are, however, a number of limitations to the charts. Processes with decision points and parallel processes cannot be shown on a process chart. Process mapping can be used

OPERATION (AN ACTIVITY DIRECTLY CONTRIBUTING TO THE PRODUCT OR SERVICE)

INSPECTION (EXAMINING THE PRODUCT OR SERVICE FOR QUALITY)

TRANSPORTATION (MOVING THE PRODUCT OR SERVICE FROM ONE LOCATION TO ANOTHER)

DELAY (PROCESS WAIT FOR A TIME PERIOD)

STORAGE (STORAGE OF PRODUCT OR SERVICE)

FIGURE 8.1

Symbols for a Process Activity Chart.

www.wileyopenpage.com

process map shows that following the notification of a road traffic incident to the police by the public, a decision is made to attend the scene of the incident. If it is necessary to attend the RTA scene the officer travels to the location of the incident. After an assessment is made of the incident the officer returns to the station to complete and submit the appropriate paperwork. If a court case is scheduled and a not guilty plea has been entered then the officer will be required to attend the court proceedings in person. Otherwise this is the end of the involvement of the officer.

Process maps are useful in a number of ways. For example, the procedure of building a process map helps people define roles and see who else does what. This can be particularly relevant to public sector organizations in which modelling existing processes can be used to build consensus on what currently happens. The process map can also serve as a first step in using business process simulation as it identifies the processes and decision points required to build the model.

Service Blueprinting

Process maps are widely used in manufacturing to design the flow of a number of linked processes that produce an output. In services, however, process maps may be less relevant when a service consists of a number of subprocesses that are not linked and the service 'output' is a number of customer-employee interactions. In this case the process design may first focus on the design of the customer-employee interactions and then identify external performance measures such as customer satisfaction.

To assist in the analysis of customer-employee interactions process maps can be extended to show how a business interacts with customers. One system is called *service system mapping (SSM)* (Laguna and Marklund, 2005). Shostack (1984) has developed a flow chart (termed a blueprint) which structures the process activities either side of a customer 'line of visibility' (Figure 8.5). The activities above the line are visible to the customer and those below the line are operations that the customer does not see. Activities above the line of visibility are subdivided into two fields separated by the 'line of interaction', this divides activities undertaken by the customer and the service provider. Below the line of visibility a line of internal interaction separates the activities of front-line personnel who carry out setting-up actions prior to service provision (not in view of the customer) and support personnel who contribute materials or services required for the provision of the service. Finally the 'line of

Customer

Front Stage ———————— line of interaction ————————

Service Provider

———————————— line of visibility ————————————

Set-up Functions

———————— line of internal interaction ————————

Back Stage

Support Functions

———————— line of implementation ————————

Management Functions

FIGURE 8.5

Service Blueprint Template.

www.wileyopenpage.com

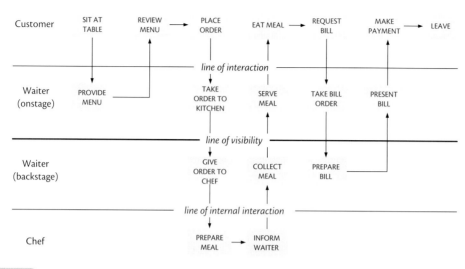

Service Blueprint for Restaurant.

implementation' separates support activities from management activities such as planning, controlling and decision making.

Figure 8.6 shows an example service blueprint for a restaurant.

The objective of the **service blueprint** is that it not only charts the service process flow (from left to right) as does a process map, but also shows the structure of the service organization on the vertical axis, showing relationships between, for example, internal customers, support staff and front-line providers. In particular the diagram aims to highlight the interactions between the customer and process where customer services can be affected. The diagrams can also be used as a design tool to determine staffing levels, job descriptions and selection of equipment and as a control tool to identify gaps in service provision through the analysis of fail points. Fail points are potential service system shortfalls between what the service delivers and what the targeted customers have been led to expect.

Business Process Simulation (BPS)

Simulation is used to mean a number of things from a physical prototype to a video game. As it is used here it refers to the use of a computer model to investigate the behaviour of a business system. This allows the performance of the organization to be observed quickly and under a number of different scenarios. The simulation method usually refers to both the process of building a model and the conducting of experiments on that model. An experiment consists of repeatedly running the simulation for a time period in order to provide data for statistical analysis. An experiment is conducted in order to understand the behaviour of the model and to evaluate the effect of different input levels on specified performance measures. Pidd (2009) characterizes systems best suited to simulation as:

Dynamic their behaviour varies over time
Interactive they consist of a number of components which interact with each other
Complicated the systems consist of many interacting and dynamic objects.

Most organizational systems have these characteristics and thus simulation would seem to be an ideal tool for providing information on the behaviour of an organization.

Computer simulation can be implemented using a wide range of model types from spreadsheet models, system dynamics models and discrete-event simulation. Business process simulation is usually implemented using discrete-event simulation systems that move through time in (discrete) steps. Most discrete-event simulation software is now implemented using graphical user interfaces employing objects or icons that are placed on the screen to produce a model. These are often referred to as visual interactive modelling (VIM) systems. When a discrete-event simulation system using a visual interactive modelling interface is used in the context of a process-based change method it is commonly referred to as a **business process simulation**. Business process simulation is particularly useful when measuring and analysing process performance and providing support in developing future process designs.

Why Use Business Process Simulation?

The ease of use and usefulness of process design techniques such as process mapping has meant that their use is widespread. Business process simulation requires a significant investment in time and skills but it is able to provide a more realistic assessment of the behaviour of manufacturing and service processes than most other process design tools. This is due to its ability to incorporate the dynamic (time-dependent) behaviour of operations systems. There are two aspects of dynamic systems that need to be addressed:

- *Variability*. Most business systems contain variability in both the demand on the system (for example, customer arrivals) and the durations (for instance, customer service times) of activities within the system. The use of fixed (for example, average) values may provide some indication of performance but simulation permits the incorporation of statistical distributions and thus provides an indication of both the range and variability of the performance of the system. This is important in customer-based systems when not only is the average performance relevant but performance should not drop below a certain level (for example, customer service time) or customers will be lost. In service systems, two widely used performance measures are an estimate of the maximum queuing time for customers and the utilization (percentage time occupied) of the staff serving the customer.

- *Interdependence*. Most systems contain a number of decision points that affect the overall performance of the system. The simulation technique can incorporate statistical distributions to model the likely decision options taken. The 'knock-on' effect of many interdependent decisions over time can also be assessed given the simulation's ability to show system behaviour over a time period.

WORKED EXAMPLE 8.1

Variability in Service Systems

A manager of a small shop wishes to predict how long customers wait for service during a typical day. The owner has identified two types of customer, who have different amounts of shopping and so take different amounts of time to serve. Type A customers account for 70% of custom and take on average ten minutes to serve. Type B customers account for 30% of custom and take on average five minutes to serve. The owner has estimated that during an eight hour day, on average the shop will serve 40 customers.

www.wileyopenpage.com

Solution 1

The owner calculates the serve time during a particular day:

Customer A = 0.7 × 40 × 10 minutes = 280 minutes
Customer B = 0.3 × 40 × 5 minutes = 60 minutes
Therefore the total service time = 340 minutes and gives a utilization of the shop till of 340/480 × 100 = 71%.

Thus the owner is confident all customers can be served promptly during a typical day.

A simulation model was constructed of this system to estimate the service time for customers. Using a fixed time between customer arrivals of 480/40 = 12 minutes and with a 70% probability of a ten minutes' service time and a 30% probability of a five minutes' service time, the overall service time for customers has a range of between five to ten minutes and no queues are present in this system.

Service time for customer (minutes)
Average: 8.5
Minimum: 5
Maximum: 10

Solution 2

In reality customers will not arrive equally spaced at 12-minute intervals, but will arrive randomly with an average interval of 12 minutes. A simulation is used to simulate a time between arrivals of customers, which follows an exponential distribution (the exponential distribution is often used to mimic the behaviour of customer arrivals) with a mean of 12 minutes. The owner was surprised by the simulation results:

Service time for customer (minutes)
Average: 17
Minimum: 5
Maximum: 46

The average service time for a customer had doubled to 17 minutes, with a maximum of 46 minutes!

Worked Example 8.1 demonstrates how the performance of even simple systems can be affected by randomness. Variability would also be present in this system in other areas such as customer service times and the mix of customer types over time. The simulation method is able to incorporate all of these sources of variability to provide a more realistic picture of system performance.

Steps in Developing a Business Process Simulation

In order to undertake a successful simulation study a number of steps must be followed. The main steps in developing a simulation model outlined in Greasley (2004b) are:

Define the Study Objectives

A number of specific study objectives should be derived which will provide a guide to the data needs of the model, set the boundaries of the study (scope), the level of modelling detail and define the experimentation analysis required. It is necessary to refine the study objectives until specific scenarios defined by input variables and measures that can be defined by output variables can be specified. General improvement areas for a process design project include aspects such as the following:

- *Changes in process logic* – changes to routing, decision points and layout.
- *Changes in resource availability* – shift patterns, equipment failure.
- *Changes in demand* – forecast pattern of demand on the process.

Many projects will study a combination of the above but it is important to study each area in turn to establish potential subjects for investigation at the project proposal stage.

Data Collection and Process Mapping

Once the simulation project objectives have been defined, and the scope and level of detail set, the modeller should prepare a specification of the data required for the model build. It is useful at this stage to identify the source of the information, its form (for example, documentation, observation, interview) and any personnel responsible for supplying the relevant information. A process map specification should define what processes will be mapped. The process map should provide a medium for obtaining information from a variety of viewpoints regarding the system being organized. In particular, issues of system boundaries (what to include and what to omit from the analysis) can be addressed.

Modelling Input Data

A specification of the type of statistical analysis used for modelling input variables and process durations should be made. A trace-driven model will require no statistical analysis of input data but a forecasting model may require the data to be fitted to a suitable probability distribution. The level of data analysis will depend on the study objectives, time constraints and the amount of raw data available.

Building the Model

A number of vendors offer business process simulation software packages. An example of a BPS is the ARENA™ system shown in Figure 8.7. The simulation is represented by symbols that closely relate to the standard process mapping symbols. The simulation is constructed by dragging the appropriate symbol from the window on the left-hand side of the screen and placing it on the main view window. The symbols are then connected together to represent the process flow. Each symbol is then double clicked with the mouse to reveal a menu that allows entry of parameters such as process times. When all the simulation data are entered, the 'run' button is clicked and the simulation moves through time. Animation features can be added as required and reports provide information on performance measures such as resource utilization and queuing times.

Validation and Verification

Verification or debugging time can be difficult to predict but some estimation of verification time can be made from the estimated complexity and size of the proposed model. Validation will require the analyst to spend time with people who are familiar with the model being studied to ensure model behaviour is appropriate. A number of meetings may be necessary to ensure that the simulation model has sufficient credibility with potential users. Sensitivity analysis may be required to validate a model of a system

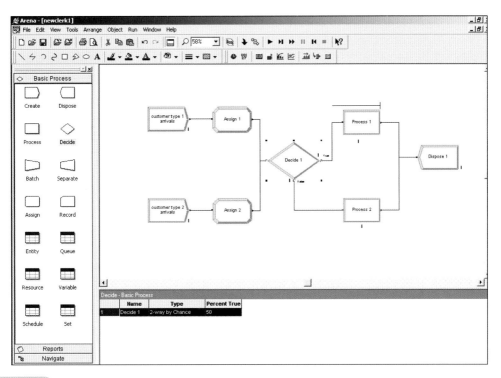

FIGURE 8.7

Screen Display of a Business Process Simulation.

that does not currently exist. The type of sensitivity analysis envisaged should be defined in the project proposal.

Experimentation and Analysis

Experimentation and analysis aims to study the effects which changes in input variables (scenarios defined in the objectives) have on output variables (performance measures defined in the objectives) in the model. The number of experiments should be clearly defined as each experiment may take a substantial amount of analysis time. For each experiment the statistical analysis required should be defined.

Implementation

The results of the simulation study must be presented in report form, which should include full model documentation, study results and recommendations for further studies. An implementation plan may also be specified. The report can be supplemented by a presentation to interested parties. The duration and cost of both of these activities should be estimated. Further allocation of time and money may be required for aspects such as user training, run-time software licence and telephone support from an external consultant.

In terms of the process design steps outlined at the start of this chapter BPS is particularly relevant to the evaluation of process design alternatives. It should also be noted that the process mapping technique, often used to identify and document process activities, represents the basis for the simulation model design. After the use of the process map a decision can be made if the more in-depth analysis provided by the business process simulation is required. Case Study 8.2 provides an example of the use of BPS in a process-centred change project.

SUMMARY

- The steps in process design are to identify opportunities for process improvement, document the process design and redesign the process.
- A process chart can be used to analyse the steps of a job.
- A process map can be used to show the interrelationships between activities in a process.
- A service blueprint is a flow chart that documents the interaction between the customer and the service provider.
- Business process simulation is a technique that can be used to measure the performance of processes over time by taking into consideration variability and interdependence factors.

CASE STUDY 8.1

Why the Bunker Mentality has become a Corporate Liability

Sir Howard Stringer, the Welsh-born boss of Sony, has declared war on them. At Morgan Stanley, new chief executive John Mack has vowed to smash them. The US intelligence system is, infamously, riddled with them. It is a fair bet that your organization is too. The objects of all this executive ire? Silos – divisions or departments that would rather burn in hell than cooperate with anyone on anything at any time.

The phenomenon is not new. Turf wars and internecine rivalries have been around since our ancestors first tried to work in teams. But silos thrive in large, modern organizations. Multinational companies, public sector bureaucracies and universities seem to be especially vulnerable. Before you ask, newspapers are not immune. Most of the time, silos are just another obstacle to be overcome or, more often, to be circumvented. Occasionally, however, silos become so powerful that an organization is rendered dysfunctional.

Thus the bipartisan commission into the terrorist attacks of September 11 2001 concluded that the assault might have been averted if US intelligence agencies had been willing to share information among themselves. Similarly, the initially chaotic, uncoordinated response to Hurricane Katrina was symptomatic of silos at work. In the memorable words of Ray Nagin, the mayor of New Orleans, there were 'too many frickin' cooks'.

The irony is that silos arise from the quest for efficiency. As Adam Smith pointed out, work gets done more quickly when it is divided into chunks and done by specialists. In the modern firm, confident, outgoing types handle sales. Number crunchers look after finance. Engineers are drawn to product development and manufacturing. But, while division of labour is good for productivity it also breeds a complex sociology. One big-company chief executive complained to me this week that her company's design engineers rarely talk to the

www.wileyopenpage.com

frontline sales force. As a result, they rarely visit customers. Getting these reticent silos to communicate – and, ultimately, cooperate – is high on her list of priorities.

Up to a point, this kind of institutional politics is nothing to get steamed up about. But it is worth remembering that organizations achieve their ultimate goals – whether manufacturing pins, countering terrorism or delivering aid to flood victims – only if specialists share information and work together. In the jargon of management, work mostly gets done in functional departments, but value is delivered to customers via 'cross-functional processes' – for example, the flow of a purchase order from sales to manufacturing to fulfilment to finance. Senior executives are getting worried about silos because the costs of noncooperation are rising. In an increasingly competitive global economy, companies across all industries are under pressure to improve efficiency, year after year. The easy cost cuts have already been made. Further progress requires redesigning products and processes from first principles – something that can be achieved only if every department gets with the programme.

Large, multidivisional companies such as Sony and Morgan Stanley face the further challenge of trying to find cross-selling opportunities and synergies between business units. Without these economies of scope, what other reason do they have to exist? The public sector is hardly immune from these pressures. Governments are reluctant to raise taxes. Voters are demanding higher standards from public services. The only answer is more efficient delivery of services, achieved by getting government departments to work together more effectively – what Tony Blair likes to call 'joined-up government'. In public and private sectors alike, meanwhile, the rise of outsourcing and partnering gives a potential competitive edge to organizations that work well with others. Corporate strategy wonks, always quick to coin a buzz phrase, have dubbed this 'relational capital'. Needless to say, organizations characterized by silos and internal

rivalries make for lousy partners. Dismiss it as nonsense if you will. But this line of thinking is being taken very seriously among the managers of corporate America.

If silos are such a liability, why do they persist? Because, like viruses, they occur naturally. Ask any large group of normally defensive, insecure people to work together on a project. Then stand back and watch the silos emerge. Our society of large, complex organizations is a perfect breeding ground. This is not to say that managers are powerless to combat them. The experience of General Electric suggests that a concerted effort to encourage cross-company cooperation can yield results. Jack Welch's 'boundarylessness' initiative of the mid-1990s got the message out in no uncertain terms. GE's subsequent adoption of Six Sigma, the process improvement methodology, is credited with further breaking down barriers by giving managers from across the organization a common language.

Like so much of what goes on within organizations, however, the kind of defensive, political behaviour that encourages silos is a function of corporate culture. A quick flirtation with Six Sigma or any other management technique is unlikely to change the tacit 'way we do things around here'. More important is the steady flow of signals about the types of people who will do well in an organization and the attitudes that are frowned upon. Ultimately, then, the tone is set from the top. Chief executives who demonstrate an uncompromising, all-or-nothing management style can hardly complain when their subordinates are reluctant to cooperate with one another.

Source: Simon London, *Financial Times,* September 14, 2005. Reproduced with permission.

Question

What barriers does the case study identify in moving to a process-oriented approach and what steps can be made to overcome these barriers?

The Simulation 'Custody of Prisoner – Business Process' is available in your interactive e-book at **www.wileyopenpage.com**

Designing a Custody-of-Prisoner Process at a Police Force

The custody process under investigation includes the arrest process, from actual apprehension of a suspect, to processing through a custody suite (which contains booking-in, interview and detention facilities) to a possible court appearance. A number of different police roles are involved in the custody process including arrests by a police constable (PC), taking of personal details by a custody officer and supervision of persons in detention by a jailer. The first objective of the study was to identify staff costs involved in arresting a person for a particular offence under the current design. The second objective of the study was to predict the change in utilization of staff as a result of redesigning the allocation of staff to activities within the custody process. The main stages of the investigation are now outlined:

Identify and Document the Process Activities

A process map (Figure 8.8) was constructed after discussions with police staff involved in the custody process. As this process was legally bound, documentation on the order of processes and certain requirements such as meals, visits and booking-in details was collated. The main activities in the arrest process are shown in the process map. Each decision point (diamond shape) will have a probability for a yes/no option. The first decision point in the arrest process is whether to conduct a search of the location of the arrest. For all decisions during the arrest process an

independent probability distribution is used for each type of arrest (for example, theft, violence, drugs) at each decision point. The staffing rank required for each process is indicated above the process box. Personnel involved in the arrest process include the police constable, custody officer, jailer and inspector. The role of each rank is indicated on the process map for each activity.

To model the variability in process times, a number of estimated times were collected from a number of custody officers. In addition, videotapes of the booking-in and interview procedures were viewed and timings taken.

The demand level of each arrival type is estimated from which a statistical distribution for the 'time between arrivals' is usually determined. In this case data were gathered on the timing of arrests over a period of time from information contained within booking-in sheets. From these data the demand pattern was analysed for a typical police station during a day and for each day in a week. As expected, demand both fluctuated during the day and differed between days in the week. It was decided to use historical data to drive the model due to the nature of the demand, with a number of arrests occasionally occurring simultaneously (as a result of a late-night brawl for example!), which would be difficult to reflect using an arrival distribution. Additionally the use of actual data would assist in model validation as model performance could be compared to actual performance over

 www.wileyopenpage.com

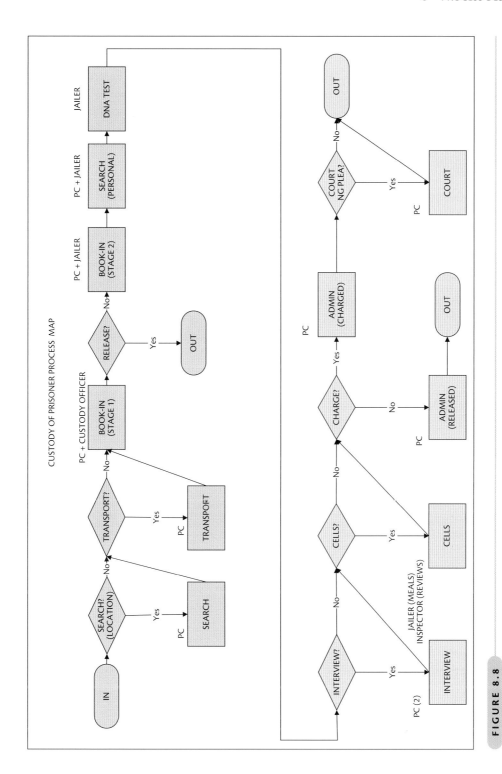

FIGURE 8.8

Process Map of the Custody of Prisoner Process.

the period simulated. This approach was feasible because the focus of the study was on the investigation of the comparative performance between different configurations of custody operation rather than for use as a forecasting tool.

Most processes will consume resource time, which may be of a machine or person, and these resources need to be identified and their availability defined. If the resource is not available at any time, then the process will not commence until the resource becomes available. In this case the main resources are police constable, custody officer and jailer.

Evaluating Process Design Alternatives

In order to measure and analyse process performance, a business process simulation was constructed using the ARENA™ simulation system. This system uses icons (representing processes) that are placed on a screen area. The icons are connected by links to represent the logic of the process. Process duration and resource allocation to processes is made by double-clicking a process icon and entering data in the pop-up menu dialog. An animated display is constructed by using an inbuilt graphics package, which permits the construction of background

(static) elements such as the process layout schematic and animated (dynamic) elements which move across the screen. Figure 8.9 shows the custody display that consists of representations of the main custody area facilities (booking-in desk, interview rooms and cells) and the dynamic elements (arrested persons and police staff) that move between the custody facilities.

Before the model results are recorded model behaviour must be checked to ensure that the model is providing valid results. Verification is analogous to the practice of 'debugging' a computer program. This is accomplished by techniques such as a structured walkthrough of the model code, test runs and checking of the animation display. Validation is about ensuring that model behaviour is close enough to the real-world system for the purposes of the simulation study.

To achieve this the model builder should discuss and obtain information from people familiar with the real-world system including operating personnel, industrial engineers, management, vendors and documentation. Also the technique of sensitivity analysis, to test the behaviour of the model under various scenarios and compare results with real-world behaviour, can be used.

FIGURE 8.9

Custody of Prisoner – Business Process Simulation Display.

 www.wileyopenpage.com

Once the model had been validated, it was run over a set time period and results collected. At this stage the model is simply reproducing the behaviour of the current process. This 'As-Is' model provided a visual representation of the whole process, which was important to provide a consensus that the model provides a convincing representation of the process. Demonstration of the model between interested parties provided a forum for communication of model behaviour and helped identify any anomalies.

In this study the aim of the model was to identify the main sources of cost in the system and thus provide strategies that would enable cost to be reduced. At present a budget-based approach meant that costs were not allocated to activities within the process. Each time a process was activated in the model by an arrested person being processed through the custody system a cost was calculated by multiplying the activity duration by the cost per time unit for the resource allocated to that process. The initial analysis aimed to identify the cost incurred for each type of arrest incorporated in the model. The cost for each arrest type is a function not only of the number of arrests but the likelihood of an arrest leading to interview, detention and court procedures. In this case relatively trivial theft offences (usually involving children shoplifting) are causing a heavy workload and thus a high cost. Thus a driving factor behind the overall cost structure has been identified. A possible way of reducing cost could be to decrease the theft activity through crime prevention activities for example.

In this case the 'to-be' model was used to explore the reduction of staffing cost by reallocating staff roles to processes. By estimating resource costs, in this case staff wages, it was possible to estimate the effects and feasibility of proposals to reallocate and civilianize staffing duties within the custody process.

Once a future process design has been decided, the simulation helps to implement this change in a number of ways. The graphical display provides an excellent tool with which to communicate the process to stakeholders such as management, customers and the workforce. The 'before' and 'after' graphic displays can be used to show how the changes will affect the process in practice. Also the display of the new process design can be used to train staff in the new operation and provide them with an overview of process behaviour, which enables them to see the relationship between a particular process activity and the overall process behaviour.

The graphics are complemented by performance measures to quantify before and after performance and thus demonstrate potential improvement. In the custody of prisoner case, measures of staff utilization were important in demonstrating the feasibility of the reallocation of tasks between staff. The figures also quantify potential savings in the utilization of police staff time, enabling plans to be made for the reallocation of staff time to other duties. In the analysis of workload in terms of arrest types, cost was used as a measure of the aggregated staff resource allocated to each arrest type that is serviced by the police. The simulation analysis could take account, not only of the number of arrests of each type, but the variable number of processes (for example, interview, court appearances by police constables) that each arrest triggered. The modelling of the complexity of interdependencies between arrest processes and the variability of arrest demand allowed an accurate picture of where cost/effort was being spent. These figures provided an impetus to focus expenditure on programmes, such as crime prevention, which could have a substantial effect on cost/effort and could free resources to provide an improved overall performance.

Source: Adapted from Greasley, A. (2003) 'Using Business Process Simulation within a Business Process Reengineering approach', Business Process Management Journal, Vol 9 No 4, pp. 408–420, Emerald Group Publishing. Reproduced with permission.

Questions

1. What benefits does the case study demonstrate can be gained from using business process simulation for process design?
2. Can you identify any disadvantages of using business process simulation?

CASE STUDY 8.3

F1 Pitstop

The F1 Pit Stop can be the difference between being first or second on the podium, the difference of winning and losing a season long title, or in fact completing or being out of a race. The pit crew are responsible for meeting the 3 second target time of a planned pit stop; to prepare, engage, change tires, make adjustments and relaunch, within a pit lane that can prove to be a very dangerous place.

In 2012, Kamui Kobayashi was fined €25 000 by the FIA, for braking late and running over his Sauber team pit crew, injuring three mechanics during a pit-stop in the British Grand Prix, and Williams's celebrations of a first Grand Prix victory in eight years were marred by injuries to 31 people following a pit fire.

Technology allows the cars to be continually reviewed, transmitting key data from the car, to the team's computers in the pit lane, streamed automatically to the team's HQ, where constant analysis is taking place, keeping the team management, pit crews and drivers in touch with every working part of the F1 car.

The pit crew can be made up of up to 20 well trained, fast, highly skilled and disciplined individuals of whom all with a critical job in delivering an efficient, fast and above all dependable pit stop, moving with synergy around each other, in what is a well practiced, finely tuned process that has been continually developed and improved over the last three decades. Any failure is clearly visible to any observer due to the streamlined process, the Pit Stop is truly a process where waste of any form is minimized, continuous improvement is at its core, and the knowledge and movement of people are incremental to its success.

The Process

The driver enters the pit lane, brakes to adhere to speed limitations, and stops the car in the precise spot the pit crew expect, the lollipop man brings down his lollipop in front of the driver, informing the driver to keep his foot on the breaks whilst prevent the engine from stalling.

It is essential that the driver stop at precisely the same place that his crew are awaiting him. Failure to do so means that the crew have to drag their equipment and tires up to the car, costing very valuable time.

Crouching next to the lollipop man is the front jack man. The instant the car stops he levers his jack under the nose of the car and lifts it into the air to an average height of around two inches.

The rear jack man has to wait until the car has passed him before getting into position, he then places his jack beneath the car and raises the rear of the car. The rear jack has a fitting incorporated into it for a starter motor. The starter is there ready to bring the engine back into life if the car stalls.

Each wheel has two crew members. One operates the compressed air-driven gun that removes the single, central retaining nut. The other removes the old wheel and fits the new. The gun man then re-attaches the magnetic nut and tightens it to around 500 lb/ft. To prevent the nuts working loose, the right-hand side of the car uses right-handed threads, the left-hand side of the car left-sided threads. This means that the guns of the right and left sides have to work in opposite ways. Teams usually color code them to denote which is which. Each wheel man has a spare gun with him and usually a couple of spare wheel nuts too, just in case.

The lollipop man, who's been watching the whole operation intently, lifts the lollipop, he does so only when he's satisfied that all anticipated actions have successfully and safely completed.

The driver, while waiting for the crew to finish, will have armed his launch control, this in concert with his pit lane speed limiter, governs his getaway. As he crosses the line denoting the end of the pit lane speed limit he disengages the speed limiter and accelerates hard back up to race speed.

Sources

http://www.formula1.com/default.html

http://www.telegraph.co.uk/sport/motorsport/formulaone/9384927/Kamui-Kobayashi-runs-over-Sauber-pit-crew-at-Silverstone.html

http://www.bbc.co.uk/sport/0/formula1/18051779

http://www.dummies.com/how-to/content/formula-one-racing-what-happens-during-an-F1-pit-s.html

Source: Written by Briony Boydell and Chris Milner. Reproduced with permission.

Questions

1. Why do you think organizations should follow the path of the F1 pit crew in order to improve their process management?

2. What else could be done to improve this process?

Quizzes to test yourself further are available in your interactive e-book at **www.wileyopenpage.com**

Flashcards to test yourself further are available in your interactive e-book at **www.wileyopenpage.com**

EXERCISES

1. Evaluate the technique of business process management.

2. What are the challenges when undertaking process design of service systems?

3. Draw a process chart for the processing of a book order from an Internet site.

4. Draw a process map for a potential property buyer making a telephone enquiry to a residential housing estate agency.

5. Draw a service blueprint for servicing a car. Include in your diagram the customer, the supervisor who takes the bookings and schedules them, the mechanics and the car parts suppliers.

CHAPTER 9

Job and Work Design

- **Introduction**
- **Behavioural aspects of job design**
- **Physical aspects of job design**
- **Work study**

LEARNING OBJECTIVES

- Describe the elements of the job characteristics model
- Discuss the role of empowerment
- Describe the sociotechnical systems approach
- Describe the use of ergonomics in terms of physical and environmental design
- Understand work study techniques

JOB AND WORK DESIGN AND OPERATIONS STRATEGY

New ideas for improved product, service design and the designs of the processes that deliver those products and services come from the ideas generated by people, not from machines or technology. Thus the management of people in the organization will have strategic implications and approaches such as continuous improvement aimed to harness the creativity of people. The management of people is also particularly relevant to a resource-based strategy which may depend on the skills, abilities and learning acquired by human resources.

Teams are an effective way of assigning responsibility and enabling faster communication and decision making between people in the organization. For example, the use of empowerment and team work is important in implementing process improvement activities such as Six Sigma and lean operations. In large organizations it is important that the work of individual teams is aligned with the overall operations strategy. This balancing of individual team autonomy with the need to integrate the work of the teams with the overall strategy may require some central coordination from the operations function.

INTRODUCTION

Operations management deals with the management of personnel who create or deliver an organization's goods and services. Job and work design consists of the formal specifications and informal expectations of an employee's work-related activities and should try to meet the needs of both the jobholder and the organization. The main elements of job and work design are behavioural aspects, which impact on employee motivation and the physical effects of work. Work study represents an attempt to measure the performance of work and thus to create better designed jobs.

BEHAVIOURAL ASPECTS OF JOB DESIGN

In Chapter 1 it was explained that one of the key differences between manufacturing and services was the fact that in services it is likely that the producer of the service will come into contact with the customer. The customer may indeed be to a greater or lesser extent involved in the actual delivery of the service. This means service employees and customers frequently work together and thus the behaviour of employees is likely to have a major effect on the customer's perceived level of service quality. The level of satisfaction of service employees in turn has been found to have an impact on the quality of the service delivered (Schneider and Bowen, 1993).

The implication is that employees that are not motivated (due to factors such as low wages, boring tasks and inadequate training) will be dissatisfied and this will lead to a poor perception of service quality by customers. Technology is often used as a way of 'controlling' employee behaviour in these circumstances, but in services, in particular, it is difficult to replace the element of human interaction completely. The reasons why organizations have dissatisfied employees may be partly due to external factors such as an underinvestment in education and training by government, but also by a short-term focus on minimizing easily quantifiable costs such as for training. The long-term benefits of employee satisfaction leading to customer satisfaction are much harder to quantify and will achieve a payback over a relatively long time period.

Three theories that have had a significant impact on the behavioural aspects of job design are the job characteristics model, empowerment and sociotechnical systems.

The Job Characteristics Model

The Hackman and Oldham (1980) **job characteristics model** is useful in providing suggestions of how to structure jobs to include more motivators. The model links job characteristics with the desired psychological state of the individual and the outcomes in terms of motivation and job performance (Figure 9.1). The model takes into account individual differences and provides a structure for analysing

FIGURE 9.1

The Job Characteristics Model.

motivational problems at work and to predict the effects of change on people's jobs and to help plan new work systems. The model proposes five desirable characteristics for a job:

- *Skill variety (SV)* – the extent to which a job makes use of different skills and abilities.
- *Task identity (TI)* – the extent to which a job involves completing a whole identifiable piece of work rather than simply a part.
- *Task significance (TS)* – the extent to which a job has an impact on other people, both inside and outside the organization.
- *Autonomy (AU)* – the extent to which the job allows the jobholder to exercise choice and discretion in their work.
- *Feedback (FB)* – the extent to which the job itself (as opposed to other people) provides the job-holder with information on their performance.

The model proposes that the presence of these characteristics will lead to desirable mental states in terms of meaningful work (SV, TI, TS), responsibility for outcomes of work (AU) and knowledge of the results of work (FB). These mental states will in turn lead to higher motivation and quality of work performance. The effects predicted by the model are moderated by factors such as the importance an individual attaches to challenge and personal development.

The five core job characteristics can be combined to provide a 'motivating potential score' (MPS) using the following formula:

$$\text{MPS} = \left[\frac{(SV + TI + TS)}{3} \right] \times AU \times FB$$

The formula shows that the addition of skill variety (SV), task identity (TI) and task significance (TS) means that a low score on one of these variables can be compensated by a high score on another. The formula also shows that the combined effect of these three variables (which are divided by 3) is only equal to the other two job characteristics (autonomy and feedback) on their own.

The following are examples of approaches to job design that have been used in an attempt to bring these desirable job characteristics to people's work leading to an improved mental state and thus increased performance.

Job rotation involves a worker changing job roles with another worker on a periodic basis. If successfully implemented this can help increase task identity, skill variety and autonomy through involvement in a wider range of work tasks, with discretion about when these mixes of tasks can be undertaken. However, this method does not actually improve the design of jobs and it can mean that people gravitate to jobs that suit them and are not interested in initiating rotation with colleagues. At worst it can mean rotation between a number of boring jobs with no acquisition of new skills.

Job enlargement involves the horizontal integration of tasks to expand the range of tasks involved in a particular job. If successfully implemented this can increase task identity, task significance and skill variety by involving the worker in the whole work task either individually or within the context of a group.

Job enrichment involves the vertical integration of tasks and the integration of responsibility and decision making. If successfully implemented this can increase all five of the desirable job characteristics by involving the worker in a wider range of tasks and providing responsibility for the successful execution of these tasks. This technique does require feedback so that the success of the work can be judged. The managerial and staff responsibilities potentially given to an employee through enrichment can be seen as a form of empowerment. This should in turn lead to improved productivity and product quality.

There are a number of factors that account for the fact that job rotation, job enlargement and job enrichment are not more widely implemented.

Firstly, the scope for using different forms of work organization will be dependent to a large extent on the type of operation in which the work is organized. Job shop manufacturing will require skilled workers who will be involved in a variety of tasks and will have some discretion in how they undertake these tasks. Sales personnel may also have a high level of discretion in how they undertake their job duties. The amount of variety in a batch manufacturing environment will to a large extent depend on the length of the production runs used. Firms producing large batches of a single item will obviously have less scope for job enrichment than firms producing small batches on a make-to-order basis. One method for providing job enlargement is to use a cellular manufacturing system, which can permit a worker to undertake a range of tasks on a part. When combined with responsibility for cell performance this can lead to job enrichment. Jobs in mass production industries may be more difficult to enlarge. Car plants must work at a certain rate in order to meet production targets and on a moving line it is only viable for each worker to spend a few minutes on a task before the next worker on the line must take over. A way of overcoming this problem is to use teams. Here tasks are exchanged between team members and performance measurements are supplied for the team as a whole. This provides workers with greater variety and feedback, but also some autonomy and participation in the decisions of the team.

Secondly, financial factors may be a constraint on further use. These may include the performance of individuals who actually prefer simple jobs, higher wage rates paid for the higher skills of employees increasing average wage costs and the capital costs of introducing the approaches. The problem is that many of the benefits associated with the technique, such as an increase in creativity, may be difficult to measure financially.

Finally, the political aspects of job design changes have little effect on organizational structures and the role of management. Although job enrichment may affect supervisory levels of management, by replacement of a supervisor with a team leader for example, the power structure which is used to justify management decisions for personal objectives remains intact.

Empowerment

The ideas of job enrichment have led to the concept of **empowerment**. Empowerment is characterized by an organization in which employees are given more autonomy, discretion and responsibility in decision making. Autonomy can be defined as the degree to which people can and do make decisions on their own within their working context (Van Looy, Gemmel and Van Dierdonck, 2003).

Empowerment is especially relevant to service operations as customers and employees interact in the service delivery process. Because the customer is involved in the service delivery process and may require a response to individual requests the process may differ each time it is performed. This implies that the employee will require a certain level of autonomy in order to satisfy customer needs. This level of autonomy, however, will differ between operations. Bowen and Lawler (1992) describe a continuum of service operations from a 'production-line' approach characterized by the simplification of tasks, use of equipment and little discretion in decision making to an 'empowered' approach characterized by more discretion and autonomy and less emphasis on the systems surrounding service employees. The reason for this continuum is that the benefits of empowerment in terms of employee and customer satisfaction need to be weighed against the costs of selection and training and potential poor decisions made by empowered workers. However, it could be argued that all workers need empowerment to some extent, even in 'production-line' type environments as it is easy to underestimate the autonomy that can be exercised even in what may seem simple tasks.

In terms of implementing empowerment at the level of an individual employee, the approach is that providing more autonomy to employees will increase their motivation and thus satisfy customer needs. However, individual motivation will depend on a combination of autonomy and other dimensions which relate to the individual and task in hand. These dimensions are as follows (Van Looy, Gemmel and Van Dierdonck, 2003):

- *Meaning* – which can be seen as the value of a work goal, as perceived by the individual in relation to his or her own ideals and standards.
- *Competence* – the individual's belief that he or she is able to perform the required activities adequately.
- *Self-determination* – the individual's sense of having a say in initiatives and regulating work actions.
- *Strategic autonomy* – which refers to the extent to which people can influence the content of the job.
- *Impact* – the degree to which employees can influence outcomes of their direct work environment.

 www.wileyopenpage.com

Figure 9.2 outlines the relationship between the five dimensions described above. The Figure shows that the meaning and competence dimensions seem to be necessary for the dimensions of self-determination, impact and strategic autonomy. The implication of this is that when attempting to implement empowerment, in addition to examining the degree of autonomy present, a degree of meaningfulness and competence should be present. Empowerment can be seen as a process that starts with the creation of meaning and feelings of competence and evolves towards levels of self-determination, impact and even strategic autonomy.

One way of achieving empowerment is through the use of **self-directed work teams**, which may have responsibility for decision making including areas such as process design. Improvements in performance will usually be awarded at a team level to encourage team working. Self-directed teams can encourage a high level of motivation within team members but their performance can be affected by inadequate training of individual team members and conflict between team members when taking on extra responsibilities.

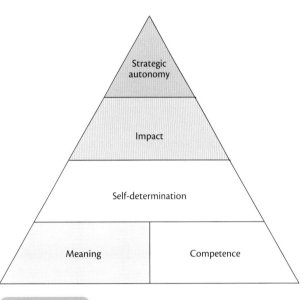

FIGURE 9.2

Empowerment as a Pyramid.
Source: Van Looy, B.; Gemmel, P. Van Dierdonck, R. (eds) (2003) Services Management: An Integrated Approach, Second Edition, Pearson Education, Harlow. Reproduced with permission.

CASE STUDY 9.1

The video 'Richard Reed: Creating an Awesome Culture at Work' is available in your interactive e-book at **www.wileyopenpage.com**

Innocent

Set up in 1998, fruit smoothies company Innocent (www.innocentdrinks.co.uk) sells its drinks in 3000 outlets throughout the UK, Ireland and Paris. The company attributes its success to allowing each member of staff to work in the way that suits them best. Because the company believes that individuals work optimally in different ways, it allows them to design their own work-life balance. In practice, this means that people who like getting up at the crack of dawn get in early and leave early, whereas others choose to come in a bit later and stay later, without any need for a formal flexitime system.

Staff are encouraged to work from home on days when they need some peace and quiet. And they are also able to pursue other interests, which means that Innocent retains skilled people rather than losing them. For example, the company's youngest employee works four days a week to allow him to do a college design course on

Fridays. Another employee wanted to go travelling, so Innocent gave him six weeks off in order to fulfill his ambition. People are also given time off for hobbies and the company offers a hobby fund, workplace yoga and free fruit in the office. The company has won several awards including the Shell Live Wire Award for Best London Entrepreneurs and the National Business Award for Best Investor in People from SMEs 2002, and is the fastest growing food and drinks company in the UK. 'The success of Innocent is down to the performance of each individual within the company.' Richard Reed, Managing Director.

Source: The Department of Trade and Industry (www.dti.gov.uk/bestpractice).

Question

Relate the policies at Innocent to the concept of empowerment.

Sociotechnical Systems

The **sociotechnical systems** approach originated in the UK during the 1950s and distinguishes between the social and technical subsystems within the organization. The idea is that these two aspects should be designed in parallel to achieve an overall optimum system. The approach is focused on group or team work and proposes the use of **autonomous work groups**, which would be able to decide on their own methods of working and should be responsible for handling problems as they arise. This focus on the redesign of work at the group level is the major way in which autonomous work groups can be distinguished from job enrichment. Typically an autonomous work group will be responsible for the whole delivery of a product or service and they are often associated with the use of cell layouts (Chapter 5). An early high-profile adopter of the autonomous work group approach, based on sociotechnical systems theory, is the car manufacturer Volvo.

CASE STUDY 9.2

Keep up Motivation Levels through Long Summer Days

It's August, the sun is shining – in London, anyway – and I cannot help wondering: what the hell am I doing still at work?

Perhaps, secretly, you have been asking yourself the same question. And think how your direct reports are feeling. They may not all share the same sense of responsibility that you do. They, too, are wondering why they are still at work. Their bodies are in the office, but their minds are elsewhere.

Motivation levels are low. What a relief, then, that this summer's bumper edition of the Harvard Business Review contains an article promising to reveal "a powerful new model" for employee motivation. Drawing on the latest research into how the brain works, the article's authors (Nitin Nohria, Boris Groysberg and Linda-Eling Lee) argue that employee motivation depends on four key elements, or 'drivers': the drive to acquire (rewards and experiences), the drive to bond (building a sense of belonging), the drive to comprehend (work must be meaningful) and the drive to defend (fair play for all).

Managers cannot afford to slip up on any one of these four drivers, the article says. The authors' research into different organisations showed 'if employees detected that a manager was substantially worse than her peers in fulfilling even just one drive, they rated that manager poorly'.

 www.wileyopenpage.com

It's a big ask, keeping the needy workforce happy and ready to perform. But without motivated employees, businesses will struggle to compete. And the evidence suggests many managers continue to stumble over this fundamental task.

Recent research by the Hay Group revealed the extent of managers' problems. A survey of more than 3100 organisations found that 41 per cent of employees felt demotivated by their managers. Half of those surveyed said they did not have the authority they needed to take important decisions. Not one of the famous four drivers will be found in a situation like that.

This data would not surprise EL Kersten, co-founder of the subversive US company Despair, Inc. In his slippery and ironic book, *The Art of Demotivation*, Kersten argues that all corporate attempts to boost employee motivation are not merely doomed to fail, but are in fact counter-productive.

Since all that expenditure – on consultants, culture-change programmes, away days and longer off-site trips – seems to produce no positive effects, indeed serves mainly to further demotivate staff, Kersten says, why not save your money and set out deliberately to demotivate your employees in the first place? Make them feel small, but at a fraction of the cost.

The cynicism is justified. And it is hard to suppress a similar kind of response to this latest rather over-engineered 'powerful new model' as featured in the new issue of HBR. The authors' four drivers seem plausible enough at first sight. But how much do they add to what we already knew about motivation? How much do they differ, for example, from the motivational needs theory of David McClelland – not mentioned in the article – which date back to his 1961 book *The Achieving Society*?

McClelland, a psychologist, argued that people at work experience three basic needs in varying degrees: the need for achievement, the need for authority and power, and the need for affiliation. If you want to have motivated staff, take the trouble to find out what is important to them and, crucially, don't put them in jobs that do not suit them.

Achievement-oriented colleagues need regular feedback, and a sense that progress is being made. But those who seek affiliation are the vital team players who can help bind groups of people together.

In fact, there was probably no need for HBR to publish the new article on motivation at all, considering that they could simply have reproduced what is still one of the most widely read HBR articles ever – 'One more time: how do you motivate employees?', by another American psychologist, Frederick Herzberg, which was first published in 1968.

Herzberg argued that motivation really has to come from within. It cannot be willed by managers – although thoughtless acts can certainly help destroy people's motivation.

There are the so-called 'hygiene factors' at work – the office environment, or pay levels – but these do not truly motivate.

What really motivates people are their sense of achievement, recognition for their work, the work itself, responsibility, advancement and personal growth. Herzberg called for 'job enrichment': trying to make sure that people had interesting work to do.

'Kick in the ass' (KITA) management produces only movement, not motivation, he said. So here, one more time, is the single Herzbergian paragraph which tells you all you need to remember about employee motivation:

'If I kick my dog (from the front or the back), he will move. And when I want him to move again what must I do? I must kick him again. Similarly, I can change a person's battery, and then recharge it, and recharge it again. But it is only when one has a generator of one's own that we can talk about motivation. One then needs no outside stimulation. One *wants* to do it.'

Source: Financial Times (2008). Reproduced with permission.

Question

Relate the discussion in the case study to the theories related to the behavioural aspects of job design covered in this chapter.

PHYSICAL ASPECTS OF JOB DESIGN

In addition to behavioural factors, job design should consider the physical effects of work. The term **ergonomics** is used to describe the collection of information about human characteristics and behaviour to understand the effect of design, methods and environment. Two areas of major concern are the interaction with physical devices, such as computer terminals, and with the environment, such as the office.

Physical Design

When required to operate a physical device a worker must be able to reach the controls and apply the necessary force to them. Although the average person is capable of a variety of tasks, the speed and accuracy of any actions can be affected by the location of a device. Because the human part of this system cannot be designed, considerable thought must be placed into the location of the device taking into account human capabilities.

Anthropometric Data

Anthropometric data are information concerning factors related to the physical attributes of a human being, such as the size, weight and strength of various parts of the human body. From this information it is possible to gather data on the range of motion, sitting height, strength, working height and other variables. The data can then be used to ensure that the vast majority, say 95% of the population, has the capability to use the device efficiently. For instance, the reach required to operate equipment should be no greater than the shortest reach of all the persons required to operate it. In some cases equipment may need adjustment devices built in to cater for different needs. The adjustable car seat is an example of this. Other designs are more subtle. For instance, the arrangement of a number of dials so they all point in the same direction during normal operation enables much speedier checking by an operative.

Environmental Design

This involves the immediate environment in which the job takes place. Some environmental variables to consider include the following.

Noise

Excessive noise levels can not only be distracting but can lead to damage to the workers' hearing. Noise is measured in decibels (dB) on a logarithmic scale that means that a 10 dB increase in noise equates to an increase of ten times in noise intensity. Extended periods of exposure above 90 dB have been judged to be permanently damaging to hearing. Higher sound intensities may be permitted for short exposures but no sound as high as 130 dB should be experienced.

Illumination

The level of illumination depends on the level of work being performed. Jobs requiring precise movements will generally require a higher level of illumination. Other lighting factors such as contrast, glare and shadows are also important.

Design space: A more ergonomic earphone

Bowers & Wilkins C5 in-ear headphones

British loudspeaker company Bowers & Wilkins wanted to enter the burgeoning in-ear headphone market and Apple's success with its iPod inspired B&W to develop a product for that category. Rather than competing on style and fashion, the company aimed for premium earphones with superior ergonomics and sound quality.

Native's designers tried out 50 different in-ear headphone sets, taking them cycling and running. Not only did many fall out of their ears but they were uncomfortable. When the designers took them apart, they discovered that they generally comprised the same mass-produced components, encased in a variety of plastic mouldings.

For the C5, Native went back to the drawing board and designed every part of the product from scratch. To improve their functionality, the agency came up with two patented innovations: the Micro Porous Filter on the back improves the quality of the sound, stopping it bouncing around inside the headset; and the adjustable Secure Loop is a cushioned device that sits in the inner ridge of the ear, helping to hold the C5 in place.

What is more, to keep the headphones in position, the C5's inner casing is weighted with a small piece of the very heavy metal tungsten.

In testing, the earphones stayed put comfortably during activities including mountain-biking, running and even break dancing.

Source: Financial Times (2012). Reproduced with permission.

Question

Discuss the design approach taken by the company in the case study in relation to operations performance objectives.

Temperature and Humidity

Although humans can perform under various combinations of temperature, humidity and air movement, performance will suffer outside of an individual 'comfort zone'. Obviously the nature of the task will affect the temperature range under which work can be undertaken.

WORK STUDY

Work study, which has been developed to measure the performance of jobs, consists of two elements, method study and work measurement. To use this approach work should be sufficiently routine and repetitive to make it feasible to derive an average time from a sample of operators and operations. It must also be possible for the worker to vary their rate of work voluntarily in a measurable way. Therefore, it can be applied quite readily to routine manual or clerical work but lends itself less well to indirect work such as maintenance or non-repetitive work such as professional and managerial duties.

Method Study

Dividing and analysing a job is called **method study** and was pioneered by Gilbreth (1911). The method takes a systematic approach to reducing waste, time and effort.

The approach can be analysed in a six-step procedure:

1. *Select*. The tasks that are most suitable will probably be repetitive, require extensive labour input and be critical to overall performance.
2. *Record*. This involves observation and documentation of the correct method of performing the selected tasks. Process charts are often used to represent a sequence of events graphically. They are intended to highlight unnecessary material movements and unnecessary delay periods.
3. *Examine*. This involves examination of the current method, looking for ways in which tasks can be eliminated, combined, rearranged and simplified. This can be achieved by looking at the process chart and redesigning the sequence of tasks necessary to perform the activity.
4. *Develop*. Developing the best method and obtaining approval for this method. This means choosing the best alternative considered taking into account the constraints of the system such as the performance of the firm's equipment. The new method will require adequate documentation in order that procedures can be followed. Specifications may include tooling, operator skill level and working conditions.
5. *Install*. Implement the new method. Changes such as installation of new equipment and operator training will need to be undertaken.
6. *Maintain*. Routinely verify that the new method is being followed correctly.

New methods may not be followed due to inadequate training or support. On the other hand people may find ways to gradually improve the method over time. Learning curves can be used to analyse these effects.

Motion study is the study of the individual human motions that are used in a job task. The purpose of motion study is to try to ensure that the job does not include any unnecessary motion or movement by the worker and to select the sequence of motions that ensure that the job is being carried out in the most efficient manner possible. The technique was originated by Gilbreth who studied many workers at their jobs and from among them picked the best way to perform each activity. He then combined these elements to form the best way to perform a task.

For even more detail, videotapes can be used to study individual work motions in slow motion and analyse them to find improvement – a technique termed micromotion analysis. Gilbreth's motion study research and analysis has evolved into a set of widely adopted principles of motion study, which are used by organizations as general guidelines for the efficient design of work. The principles are generally categorized according to the efficient use of the human body, efficient arrangement of the workplace and the efficient use of equipment and machinery. Table 9.1 summarizes these principles into general guidelines.

Motion study is seen as one of the fundamental aspects of scientific management and indeed it was effective in the design of repetitive, simplified jobs with the task specialization that was a feature of the mass production system. The use of motion study has declined as there has been a movement towards

TABLE 9.1

Summary of Guidelines of Motion Study.

- **Efficient use of the human body**
  Work should be rhythmic, symmetrical and simplified
  The full capabilities of the human body should be employed
  Energy should be conserved by letting machines perform tasks when possible

- **Efficient arrangement of the workplace**
  Tools, materials and controls should have a defined place and be located to minimize the motions needed to get to them
  The workplace should be comfortable and healthy

- **Efficient use of equipment**
  Equipment and mechanized tools enhance worker abilities
  Controls and foot-operated devices that can relieve the hand/arms of work should be maximized
  Equipment should be constructed and arranged to fit worker use

greater job responsibility and a wider range of tasks within a job. However, the technique is still a useful analysis tool and, particularly in the service industries, can help improve process performance.

Work Measurement

The second element of work study is **work measurement**, which determines the length of time it will take to undertake a particular task. This is important not only to determine pay rates but also to ensure that each stage in a production line system is of an equal duration (i.e. 'balanced', see Chapter 4) thus ensuring maximum output. Usually the method study and work measurement activities are undertaken together to develop time as well as method standards. Setting time standards in a structured manner permits the use of benchmarks against which to measure a range of variables such as cost of the product and share of work between team members. However, the work measurement technique has been criticized for being misused by management in determining worker compensation. The time needed to perform each work element can be determined by the use of historical data, work sampling or most usually time study.

Time Study

The purpose of **time study** is to use statistical techniques to determine a standard time for performing one cycle of a repetitive job. This is arrived at by observing a task a number of times. The standard time refers to the time allowed for the job under specific circumstances, taking into account allowances for rest and relaxation. The basic steps in a time study are indicated below:

1. Establish the standard job method. It is essential that the best method of undertaking the job is determined using method study before a time study is undertaken. If a better method for the job is found then the time study analysis will need to be repeated.

2. Break down the job into elements. The job should be broken down into a number of easily measurable tasks. This will permit a more accurate calculation of standard time as varying proficiencies at different parts of the whole job can be taken into account.

3. Study the job. This has traditionally been undertaken by observation of the task with a stop-watch, or electronic timer. Each time element is recorded on an observation sheet. A video camera can be used for observation, which permits study away from the workplace, and in slow motion, which permits a higher degree of accuracy of measurement.

4. Rate the worker's performance. As the time study is being conducted a rating of the worker's performance is also taken in order to achieve a true time rating for the task. Rating factors are usually between 80% and 120% of normal. This is an important but subjective element in the procedure and is best done if the observer is familiar with the job itself.

5. Compute the average time. Once a sufficient sample of job cycles has been undertaken an average is taken of the observed times called the cycle time. The sample size can be determined statistically, but is often around five to 15 due to cost restrictions.

6. Compute the normal time. Adjust the cycle time for the efficiency and speed of the worker who was observed. The normal time is calculated by multiplying the cycle time by the performance rating factors.

$$\text{normal time (NT)} = \text{cycle time (CT)} \times \text{rating factor (RF)}$$

7. Compute the standard time. The standard time is computed by adjusting the normal time by an allowance factor to take account of unavoidable delays such as machine breakdown and rest periods. The standard time is calculated as follows:

$$\text{standard time (ST)} = \text{normal time (NT)} \times \text{allowance}$$

WORKED EXAMPLE 9.1

Time Study

PCB Limited wants to determine the standard time for a manual solder operation on one of their new circuit boards. From the following task times observed during a time study exercise calculate the standard time for the job. Assume the worker who has been observed is 10% slower than average at this task. Assume an allowance factor of 20%.

Sample No.	1	2	3	4	5	6	7	8	9	10
Time (sec.)	6.7	7.1	7.3	7.0	7.1	6.8	6.9	6.8	7.1	7.0

Solution

$$\text{Cycle time (CT)} = \text{average of samples} = \frac{69.8}{10} = 6.9$$
$$\text{Normal time (NT)} = \text{CT} \times \text{RF} = 6.98 \times 0.9 = 6.282$$
$$\text{Standard time (ST)} = \text{NT} \times \text{allowance} = 6.282 \times 1.2 = 7.54 \text{ seconds}$$

Predetermined Motion Times

One problem with time studies is that workers will not always cooperate with their use, especially if they know the results will be used to set wage rates. Combined with the costs of undertaking a time study, a company may use historical data in the form of time files to construct a new standard job time from a previous job element.

Another method for calculating standard times without a time study is to use the **predetermined motion time system (PMTS)**, which provides generic times for standard micromotions such as reach, move and release, which are common to many jobs. The standard item for the job is then constructed by breaking down the job into a series of micromotions that can then be assigned a time from the motion time database. The standard time for the job is the sum of these micromotion times. Factors such as load weight for move operations are included in the time motion database.

The advantages of this approach are that standard times can be developed for jobs before they are introduced to the workplace without causing disruption and needing worker compliance. Also performance ratings are factored into the motion times and so the subjective part of the study is eliminated. The timings should also be much more consistent than historical data for instance. Disadvantages include the fact that these times ignore the context of the job in which they are undertaken – the timings are provided for the micromotion in isolation and are not part of a range of movements. The sample is from a broad range of workers in different industries with different skill levels, which may lead to an unrepresentative time. The timings are also only available for simple repetitious work which is becoming less common in industry.

Work Sampling

Work sampling is useful for analysing the increasing proportion of nonrepetitive tasks that are performed in most jobs. It is a method for determining the proportion of time a worker or machine spends on various activities and as such can be very useful in job redesign and estimating levels of worker output. The basic steps in work sampling are indicated below:

1. *Define the job activities.* All possible activities must be categorized for a particular job, for example 'worker idle' and 'worker busy' states could be used to define all possible activities.
2. *Determine the number of observations in the work sample.* The accuracy of the proportion of time the worker is in a particular state is determined by the observation sample size. Assuming the sample is approximately normally distributed the sample size can be estimated using the following formula:

$$n = \left(\frac{z}{e}\right)^2 \times p(1 - p)$$

where
    n = sample size
    z = number of standard deviations from the mean for the desired level of confidence
    e = the degree of allowable error in the sample estimate
    p = the estimated proportion of time spent on a work activity.

The accuracy of the estimated proportion p is usually expressed in terms of an allowable degree of error e (for example, for a 2% degree of error, $e = 0.02$). The degree of confidence would normally be 95% (giving a z value of 1.96) or 99% (giving a z value of 2.58).

The Creative Space

There are many creative organizations willing to listen to their teams in order to bring forth operational improvement, how to make the organization a happier place to work, and their job designs to become more enriched and effective, Dell, for example, uses Ideastorm.com where last year, from 10 000 submitted ideas, 200 implemented. Pret a Manger have an in-house 'ideas department where online idea submissions and prizes are reviewed each month to find bright ideas that could 'help Pret be a better, kinder, easier place to work and shop.'

The work space where the opportunity to think, communicate and collaborate creatively is an important area that is not well considered within many organizations, but some organizational work environments are increasingly strategically designed to support creativity and communication in an attempt to increase autonomy and staff empowerment. Such can in fact bring together and heighten the respect of role significance and understanding between individuals, teams and departments, which in time can increase satisfaction and therefore have an impact on role and performance.

A number of organizations have physical environments that are engineered to be cognitively and perceptually stimulating and can be inspirational, motivational, and therefore enhance creativity, intrinsic motivation and a place where one can share their knowledge, and feels that their thoughts and opinions are listened to and considered.

Some established organizations are implementing innovation laborite, serving as dedicated facilities for encouraging creative behaviors and supporting innovative projects and, examples of such include Arvetica, Starbucks and Google. Arvetica find that space is very important and is the reason why they have brainstorming rooms with whiteboards and flipcharts, but also a 'living room' area to get inspired. Located in Starbucks Coffee Company's headquarters in Seattle, a once drab conference room, filled with corporate-stock chairs and boardroom style table, is now a 336 square foot haven for brainstorming, problem solving and thinking, the room can hold up to 15 people comfortably – and all the ideas anyone can think of. 'They report that the room is constantly booked, from 10 am onwards . . . it's booked specifically as space for creative and inspired meetings . . . It's not meant to just be another space for a typical meeting.'

Sources

http://www.pret.com/about/our_team.htm

www.dell.com

http://www.idea-sandbox.com/blog/creativity/blog/

http://business-model-design.blogspot.com/2007/03/space-as-instrument-for-business-model.html

Kristensen, T. (2004) The Physical Context of Creativity, *Creativity and Innovation Management*. 13 (2), 89–96.

Haner, U.E. and Bakke, J.W. (2004) 'On How Work Environments Influence Innovation – A Case Study for a Large ICT Firm'. ISPIM

Source: Written by Briony Boydell and Chris Milner. Reproduced with permission.

Question

Why is creativity important from an operational perspective?

Quizzes to test yourself further are available in your interactive e-book at **www.wileyopenpage.com**

Flashcards to test yourself further are available in your interactive e-book at **www.wileyopenpage.com**

EXERCISES

1. Evaluate the job design approaches of job rotation, job enlargement and job enrichment.

2. Discuss the major approaches to job design as they relate to the operations function.

3. Compare the job characteristics model with the concept of empowerment.

4. What is the difference between empowerment and autonomy?

5. Discuss the relevance of empowerment to successful operations management.

REFERENCES

Bowen, D. and Lawler, E. (1992) The empowerment of service workers: What, why, how and when, *Sloan Management Review,* Spring, 31–9.

Gilbreth, F. (1911) *Motion Study*, D. Van Nostrand Co.

Hackman, J.R. and Oldham, G.R. (1980) *Work Redesign*, Prentice Hall.

Porter, M. (1987) From competitive advantage to corporate strategy, *Harvard Business Review*, May/June, 43–59.

Schneider, B. and Bowen, D.E. (1993) The service organization: Human resources management is crucial. *Organizational Dynamics,* 21 (4), 39–52.

Van Looy, B., Gemmel, P. and Van Dierdonck, R. (eds) (2003) *Services Management: An Integrated Approach*, 2nd edn, Pearson Education Ltd.

Management

CHAPTER 10

Operations Planning and Control

- **Introduction**
- **Operations planning**
- **Operations control**
- **Optimized production technology (OPT)**

LEARNING OBJECTIVES

- Evaluate resource-to-order, make-to-order and make-to-stock planning policies
- Describe the principal approaches to the operations control task of loading
- Describe the use of priority rules for the operations control task of sequencing
- Discuss the operations control task of scheduling
- Identify techniques for scheduling in manufacturing and service operations
- Describe the operations control system of OPT

OPERATIONS PLANNING AND CONTROL AND OPERATIONS STRATEGY

Operations planning and control is about matching the capacity of the organization with customer demand and so is crucial in enabling achievement of strategic objectives such as speed and dependability. These can be related to operations control in the area of sequencing where different priority rules can be used to meet performance objectives such as dependability, speed and cost. In terms of operations control systems the theory behind the use of OPT, the theory of constraints

(TOC), claims to have strategic implications. The crucial insight of the theory of constraints is that only a few elements (constraints) in a business control the results of the entire organization and so it is possible to simplify the improvement and management of complex organizations by focusing on these few physical and logical constraining 'leverage' points. The approach then provides a tool set to build and implement the 'levers' that synchronize the parts to achieve an order of magnitude improvement in the performance of the system as a whole.

INTRODUCTION

Operations planning and control is about matching customer demand to the operations capacity. In the long term this can be considered as a design issue and is covered in Chapter 5. In the medium term it can be considered as choosing approaches to reconciling capacity and demand and is covered in Chapter 11. This chapter is concerned with short-term planning and control in order to meet estimated demand. This task is made challenging because of the unstable nature of market demand, which works against the execution of an efficient and effective operations system. In organizations with international operations there is a further difficulty in coordinating planning and control activities across different locations.

One way of dealing with unstable demand is to produce the product or service (or elements of the product or service) in advance. The first part of this chapter evaluates the use of make-to-stock, make-to-order and resource-to-order planning policies.

The second part of this chapter examines the activities that form operations control tasks. These generally consist of loading (determining capacity and volumes), sequencing (deciding on the order of execution of work) and scheduling (allocating a start and finish time to a customer order). A number of techniques for operations control are then described and the OPT operations control system is described. Further operations control systems that are discussed in this text include JIT and lean operations (Chapter 13), ERP (Chapter 14), supply chain management (Chapter 15) and project management (Chapter 16).

OPERATIONS PLANNING

Operations planning is concerned with taking actions, such as ensuring resources are in place, in anticipation of future events. The nature of the planning task is determined by how accurately future events can be predicted. The predictability of demand for goods and services can range from a situation of what is essentially dependent demand (demand can be predicted) to a high level of unpredictability (independent demand). Planning policies to meet this continuum are shown in Table 10.1.

In a dependent demand situation it is not necessary to activate a planning system and acquire resources until a delivery date for an order is received. Both transforming resources (for example, staff, machinery) and transformed resources (for example, bricks for a house) may be acquired at the appropriate time for delivery. This is termed a **resource-to-order** planning policy and is associated with construction and project-based operations.

 www.wileyopenpage.com

TABLE 10.1

Planning Policies for Demand Types.

Demand Type	Planning Policy	Resources Required in Stock
Dependent	Resource-to-order	None
Independent (low variability)	Make-to-order	Transforming
Independent (high variability)	Make-to-stock	Transforming Transformed

In an independent demand situation when demand is relatively predictable the transforming resources such as staff and machinery may be in place on a permanent basis. However, the transformed resources – the raw material that is used to construct the product – may be acquired on the receipt of a customer order. This is termed a **make-to-order** planning policy. Despite the risk of stock-outs many manufacturers and retailers use this strategy as it decreases the amount of inventory through the supply chain. Postponement (Chapter 13) is a way of producing components and modules to make-to-stock but then delaying their use in the final product until a customer order has been received. For example, Dell Computers stock computer parts which are configured in response to a customer order.

Finally, if demand is unpredictable, the organization will use a **make-to-stock** planning policy which produces to a forecast of demand for the product. This approach may be used by retailers who need the products on show for people to buy.

Two implications arise from the planning policy used by the organization. In a make-to-stock system each order must be small compared to total capacity or the risk of making to stock, and not finding a customer for the order, will be too high. Also a resource-to-order system implies each order is large compared to total system capacity to make the organization of resources worthwhile. The other implication is that of customer delivery time performance. Whilst the customer will only 'see' the delivery time from stock in a make-to-stock system, in a make-to-order system the delivery cycle will include the purchase, make and delivery stages. This effect is examined using P:D ratios.

P:D Ratios

The **P:D ratio** is a concept derived by Shingo (1989) and compares the demand time D (from customer request to receipt of goods/services) to the total throughput time P of the purchase, make and delivery stages. The purchase stage involves acquiring necessary resources from internal and external suppliers, the make stage includes the processing of resources through the operations system and the deliver stage involves packing and distribution of the finished good to the customer. The relationship between the planning and control systems and the P:D ratio is shown in Figure 10.1.

Thus in a resource-to-order system the demand time and throughput time are essentially the same. The purchase-make-deliver cycle is not triggered until a customer order is received. In a make-to-stock system the demand time is essentially the time of delivery from stock to the customer.

The P:D ratio makes the implications for the delivery time to the customer explicit. In a resource-to-order system the purchase, make and deliver stages all affect delivery performance. In a make-to-stock system, however, the customer only 'sees' the delivery time. Although delivery performance is improved in a make-to-stock system, the item is being produced to a forecast demand, which is subject to error. The risk of producing to this forecast increases with the ratio of P:D, as an increase in

	PURCHASE	MAKE	DELIVER
RESOURCE-TO-ORDER		D	
		P	
MAKE-TO-ORDER		D	
		P	
MAKE-TO-STOCK			D
		P	

D = time taken from customer ordering to customer receiving goods and services
P = throughput time of purchase, make and deliver stages

FIGURE 10.1

Planning Policies for Demand Types.

throughput times means that the item must be produced to a demand further into the future. Thus reducing the P:D ratio will reduce the risk inherent in the planning policy.

OPERATIONS CONTROL

Although operations planning will attempt to anticipate events, there may be a mismatch between current actions and what actually is required due to unforeseen events or behaviours. An example would be an unforeseen change in customer demand in terms of total output or in the mix of goods and services. **Operations control** is concerned with ensuring that the current behaviour of the operations system conforms with the required behaviour. This section examines the activities that form operations control tasks. These generally consist of loading (determining the current capacity and volumes), sequencing (deciding on the order of execution of work) and scheduling (allocating start and finish times to a customer order).

Loading

Loading involves determining the available capacity for each stage in a process and allocating a work task to that stage. The calculation of available capacity must take account of both planned factors such as machine maintenance and unplanned factors such as machine breakdowns and worker absenteeism. These issues are dealt with in more detail in Chapter 11. There are two principal approaches to loading.

Finite Loading

Finite loading allocates work up to an agreed fixed (finite) upper limit. This may be because:

- The upper limit of capacity is fixed, for example seats on a aircraft (although this does not rule out the policy of overbooking to ensure that all capacity is actually utilized!).

www.wileyopenpage.com

- The upper limit can be fixed through a policy such as using an appointment system.
- There is a policy of limiting availability to the market (a limited edition of an expensive watch may enhance demand).

Infinite Loading

Infinite loading does not place a limit on the work loaded onto a stage. This may be because:

- It is not possible to limit demand. For example emergency hospital treatment should not be refused.
- It is acceptable to have a drop in performance. In manufacturing or services if demand exceeds capacity a queue will form. This may be acceptable in some instances, for example shopping outlets, when the customer understands the cost of always providing instant service is too high.

Sequencing

Sequencing (also known as dispatching) is the sequential assignment of tasks or jobs to individual processes. In order to attempt to control the progress of a job through a process a job priority system is used. The priority of jobs queuing at a process determines the order in which they are processed. The difficulty lies in determining an appropriate priority rule to obtain the best performance. Priority rules include:

- *DDS (customer due date)* – job with nearest customer due date to the current date.
- *FCFS (first come, first served)* – job arriving first at a process (in order of arrival).
- *SPT/SOT* – (shortest process time/shortest operating time) job with shortest process/operating time among waiting jobs.
- *LPT (longest process time)* – job with longest process time among waiting jobs.

All the rules have different advantages and disadvantages. The DDS rule tends to minimize the lateness of jobs, but may lead to more jobs being late than the SPT rule for example. The FCFS rule is easy to apply and is used for ease when no particular sequencing activities are necessary when the workload on the system is low. The SPT rule ensures that jobs with the shortest process time progress rapidly, thus the number of jobs processed should be high. This rule will generally give the best performance in a congested system. However, a disadvantage of the SPT rule is that when the demand on the process is high this may mean a job with a relatively long process time may have an unacceptably long wait and is always at the end of the queue. The LPT rule may be used when larger jobs can be completed in-house and smaller jobs can be subcontracted when their due date is near.

Rules can also use a combination of factors to determine the sequence, such as the critical ratio (CR) which is the ratio of the time left until the job's due date to the expected elapsed time for the job to be processed through the remaining processes to its completion. If the ratio is less than 1 the job is behind schedule and should receive priority.

$$\text{Critical Ratio (CR)} = (\text{due date} - \text{current date})/\text{days required to complete job}$$

Gantt charts (Chapter 16) can be employed to show the effect of different job sequencing strategies on the performance of the process.

WORKED EXAMPLE 10.1

Sequencing

A copyshop offers a photocopying service to customers. Currently it uses an FCFS system because this seems the fairest way of working for the customers. However, the manager of the shop suspects that an alternative sequencing rule may improve performance. Using the data collected below try the FCFS, DDS and SPT sequences and state which rule provides the best performance using the measure of average lateness.

Job arrival sequence	Processing time (days)	Customer due date (days)
A	5	7
B	4	6
C	2	5
D	2	6
E	1	3

Solution

Trying the FCFS rule:

Job arrival sequence	Processing time (days)	Customer due date (days)	Process time (FCFS) (days)	Lateness (days)
A	5	7	0 + 5 = 5	0
B	4	6	5 + 4 = 9	3
C	2	5	9 + 2 = 11	6
D	2	6	11 + 2 = 13	7
E	1	3	13 + 1 = 14	11

$$\text{Average lateness} = \frac{(0 + 3 + 6 + 7 + 11)}{5} = \frac{27}{5} = 5.4 \text{ days}$$

Trying the DDS rule:

Job arrival sequence	Processing time (days)	Customer due date (days)	Process time (DDS) (days)	Lateness (days)
A	5	7	9 + 5 = 14	7
B	4	6	3 + 4 = 7	1
C	2	5	1 + 2 = 3	0
D	2	6	7 + 2 = 9	3
E	1	3	0 + 1 = 1	0

$$\text{Average lateness} = \frac{(7 + 1 + 0 + 3 + 0)}{5} = \frac{11}{5} = 2.2 \text{ days}$$

 www.wileyopenpage.com

Trying the SPT rule:

Job arrival sequence	Processing time (days)	Customer due date (days)	Process time (SPT) (days)	Lateness (days)
A	5	7	9 + 5 = 14	7
B	4	6	5 + 4 = 9	3
C	2	5	3 + 2 = 5	0
D	2	6	1 + 2 = 3	0
E	1	3	0 + 1 = 1	0

$$\text{Average lateness} = \frac{(7 + 3 + 0 + 0 + 0)}{5} = \frac{10}{5} = 2.0 \text{ days}$$

Of the three rules the SPT rule provides the best performance with an average job lateness of two days.

Johnson's Rule

An optimal solution to the job-sequencing problem has been found for the special case in which all jobs flow through two work centres or processes in the same order. Johnson's rule (Johnson, 1954) minimizes the overall lead time (start of first job to end of last job) in this case, assuming other costs (such as machine setup costs moving from one product to another) are not dependent on the job sequence chosen. Setup times are included in job process times.

The following steps should be followed:

1. List the processing time for all jobs for both stages of production.
2. For unscheduled jobs select the job with the shortest time in either stage.
3. If the shortest time is for the first processing stage, put the job as early as possible in the job sequence. If the shortest time is for the second processing stage, put the job as late as possible in the job sequence. If the time on the first stage for one job equals the time on the second stage for some other job then fill the earliest slot with the job having this amount of time for the first stage and fill the latest slot with the job having this amount of time for the second stage. If both jobs have the same time for both stages they can be placed at either end of the sequence.
4. Delete the job selected and repeat the steps until all jobs have been sequenced.

EXAMPLE

WORKED EXAMPLE 10.2

Johnson's Rule

A manufacturing department has five jobs, which must be processed on the sand process and then on the varnish process. Determine the sequence that will allow the set of five jobs to be completed in the minimum time.

	Process time (minutes)	
Job	Sand	Varnish
A	6	3
B	4	5
C	2	3
D	6	6
E	3	7

Solution

1. Shortest time is 2 for C in sand stage, therefore put as early as possible in job sequence.

2. Next shortest time is 3 for A in varnish stage and 3 for E in sand stage. Therefore put E as early as possible in job sequence and A as late as possible in job sequence.

3. Next shortest is 4 for B in sand stage 1. Thus put B as early as possible in job sequence.

4. The only job remaining is job D, therefore final sequence is as follows.

To find the completion time a Gantt chart is used to total the job completion time.

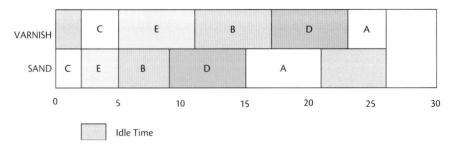

Thus the total completion time is 26 minutes.

It should be emphasized that the rule is only applicable to a flow through two work centres in the same order and does not consider individual job due dates in constructing the schedule.

Scheduling

Scheduling is the allocation of a start and finish time to each order while taking into account the loading and sequencing policies employed. The scheduling process is usually driven by the need to manage a number of jobs or customers in the system and ensure they are completed or receive their order by a target due date. This often necessitates the rescheduling of orders, termed **expediting**, in order to ensure targets are actually met. In theory expediting should not be necessary if planning and control activities have been undertaken correctly. However, in reality due to the complexity of the task and unexpected events (for example poor quality material in the process leading to rework or machine breakdown events) expediting on a day-to-day basis may be needed.

Scheduling issues in services and manufacturing are now discussed before a number of scheduling techniques are described.

Scheduling in Services

What makes scheduling particularly challenging in service systems is that services are generally produced and delivered by people, whose performance may be less predictable and more variable than manufacturing processes. A major factor in scheduling in services is varying the size of the workforce to meet variations in demand. This area is covered in the workforce scheduling technique section later in this chapter. Another issue in service scheduling is the fact that services are not only delivered by people but are also consumed by people. In fact that the customer may be part of the service itself or require the service on request. The combination of the difficulty in predicting when demand will occur (when people will arrive at a bank for example) and the short lead time between requesting the service and requiring its delivery (a few minutes for bank service for example) brings a challenge to scheduling in services. In practice a trade-off is made between providing enough capacity (staff) to provide customer satisfaction (no wait for service) and the cost of providing that capacity when it is not needed.

Scheduling in Manufacturing

In manufacturing systems the issue of scheduling is about ensuring that the capacity available is directed towards activities that will ensure that performance targets for delivery and lead times are met. The approach to scheduling in manufacturing is largely dependent on the volume and variety mix of the manufacturing system itself and so scheduling approaches will be considered under the headings of line, batch and jobbing process types (see Chapter 3 for an explanation of these process types).

Mass Process-Type Scheduling

Mass process-type systems produce a standard product in a relatively high volume. These systems which have a characteristic flow (product) layout use specialized equipment dedicated to achieving an optimal flow of work through the system. This is important because all items follow virtually the same sequence of operations. A major aim of flow systems is to ensure that each stage of production is able to maintain production at an equal rate. The technique of line balancing is used to ensure that the output of each production stage is equal and maximum utilization is attained.

Batch Process-Type Scheduling

Batch systems process a range of product types in batches (groups) thus combining some of the economics of repetitive production with the variety of a job shop. Scheduling in these configurations is a matter of ensuring that the batch of work introduced to the process will be completed to meet customer due dates. Two issues that affect the job completion time and thus the ability to meet due dates are the transfer batch size and the job sequence. The transfer batch size refers to the size of the batch of parts that is processed at a work station before progressing to the next work station. The actual order size may be greater than this, but is divided into a number of transfer batches to decrease the time the jobs take to pass through the production process. The job sequence is the order in which jobs are entered in to the production process. This will not, however, be the order in which they are completed as different jobs will pass through different work stations and will have different process times.

The material requirements planning (MRP) approach (Chapter 14) is often used to determine the batch size and timing (job sequence) of jobs to meet a projected demand expressed in the form of a master production schedule (MPS) that is developed from customer orders and demand forecasts. A closed-loop MRP system will check the feasibility of any schedule against the capacity available over the planning period. An OPT system (see under scheduling techniques) will focus on ensuring that the bottleneck processes are kept busy as they determine the output of the whole process.

A problem with batch production control is the tendency for managers to try to keep all work stations busy at all times, which leads to work-in-progress (WIP) queues at heavily loaded work stations. Excessive WIP can seriously impede the ability to schedule batch systems successfully by creating long lead times and by making it difficult to determine the correct job priority for new work entering the system. An aim of the JIT system (Chapter 13) is to eliminate this inventory and make the production control process more transparent. Material requirements planning systems use a technique called production activity control to try to ensure that the production system is working to plan. The technique consists of two main components – Input/Output Control and Priority Control – which are covered later in this chapter.

Jobbing Process-Type Scheduling

A jobbing system deals with a number of low-volume, high-variety products. Each product is customized to a customer order and so the production planning and control system must deal with a changing mix of jobs. The job may not have been produced before so it might be difficult to estimate the elements of lead time for each job. Because each product has a unique routing and component structure it is also difficult to use systems such as MRP for production planning and control. The pattern of flow through a job shop consists of a number of work stations with queues of work in front of them and what approaches a random flow path connecting the work stations. The technique of job sequencing is used to schedule in jobbing type systems.

Workforce Scheduling

Workforce scheduling aims to ensure that available staff are deployed to maximize the quality of service delivery to the customer. The amount of staff available will have been determined by long-term and more strategic decisions taken on the amount of staff required, often termed manpower planning policies. For day-to-day operations, however, the problem is how to deploy the staff available to best effect.

This may be done with the use of a **workforce schedule**, which determines the daily workload for each member of staff. This daily workload may cover a normal eight-hour day or two- or three-shift working for certain service providers such as hospitals and police. The allocation of staff available must take into consideration a number of factors such as the number of staff available (taking into account absentees), the skills the individual staff possess, the demand over time for the services the staff supply and the working preferences of the staff themselves.

As mentioned earlier, the need to provide a service for immediate consumption by the customer and the inability to store a service delivery as inventory means that the capacity provided in the schedule needs to meet customer demand closely. If sufficient capacity is not provided, this can lead to overworked staff and delays in service provision, both leading to a fall in the quality of service. The flexibility to undertake a number of tasks can be used to provide a strategy for responding to short-term fluctuation in demand. For example, you have probably witnessed the reallocation of staff from replenishing goods in a supermarket to working on a till in response to a sudden increase in customers checking out.

Workforce scheduling can be undertaken by estimating the demand for the operation and then scheduling staff to meet this demand. The use of Gantt charts (Chapter 16) or specialized computer software (for example, project management software such as Microsoft Project™) can be used to facilitate this process.

Workforce Scheduling at a Police Communications Centre

The communications centre of a Police Force undertakes a vital role in receiving and processing emergency and non-emergency telephone calls from the public and other agencies. Calls for service are processed by 'call handlers' who take the relevant information from the caller and grade the call for an appropriate response. 999 (emergency) calls are sent directly to call handlers with non-emergency calls sent via a switchboard. If attendance to an incident is necessary call handlers pass the call onto a team of controllers who manage the deployment of officers on the ground.

The UK Police Force is required to operate its control room under increased funding constraints. The main issue for the efficient deployment of staff, in this case call handler staff, is to try to ensure sufficient staff are available to make a timely response to customer calls when the timing of individual calls is difficult to predict. The force aims to answer all emergency calls within 10 seconds and all non-emergency calls within 30 seconds. The communications centre can be considered a specialised case of a call centre but an important issue for Police Force management is the particularly stressful nature of the work staff are involved with when responding to emergency calls.

Figure 10.2 shows the main processes involved in the communication centre. 999 (emergency) calls are sent directly to call handlers with non-emergency calls sent via a switchboard. Calls for service are processed by call handlers who take the relevant information from the caller and grade the call for an appropriate response. If

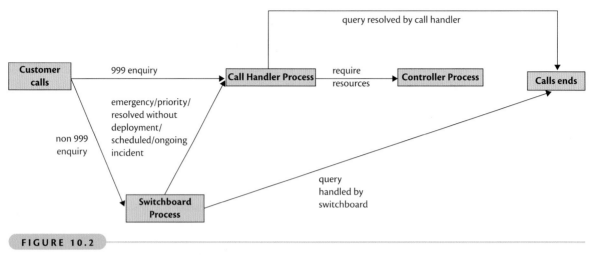

FIGURE 10.2

Process Map of Police Communications Centre.

attendance to an incident is necessary call handlers pass the call on to a team of controllers who manage the deployment of officers on the ground.

Ensuring staff wellbeing is particularly important as the nature of operating a 24/7 contact centre means staff have to work a shift pattern covering 24 hours of the day 365 days of the year. If staff do not have enough recovery time built into the shift pattern they may suffer from low morale and increased absence through sickness. Increased sickness levels reduce the available resources further decreasing performance or increasing costs through overtime.

The communications centre requires appropriate staffing to meet hourly, weekly and monthly changes in demand for the service. In order to cover these needs the Police are considering a move from an eight hour pattern – where three shifts are used to cover each 24 hours – to a nine hour pattern – where three shifts are used to cover each 24 hours, with three hours of overlap. The 8 hour pattern requires 4 shifts in total 3 working and 1 on rest days. The 9 hour pattern requires 5 shifts in total.

Currently the eight hour pattern is standard operation across the UK police force for all operational staff due to its perceived economy. However,

a problem that the Police have identified with the eight hour shift pattern is that staff routinely work seven successive days followed by only two days off, before starting the tour of seven working days again. Officers usually finish on nights, normally at seven am, meaning they only have 48 hours to reset their body clocks for days, rest and recover, before returning to work at seven am. This has led to a call from staff working these shifts for a change in the pattern. The 8 hour pattern also presents problems during shift change over times while briefings take place. It is proposed to move to a 9 hour, five shift pattern due to the following advantages:

- The overlap allows greater flexibility so it's easier to adapt the shifts to better match demand.
- Overlaps allow staff to have effective briefings without impacting on performance.
- The pattern incorporates 5 training days per year.
- 60% of the workforce (before abstractions (absences)) are on duty most days.
- Nine hour shifts can easily be extended at times of peak demand.
- It's popular with employees, enabling a healthy balance between work and home life.

Changing to the five shift model is not as straightforward as it may initially seem. No additional resources are being provided for the 5th shift meaning the number of staff on each shift will need to be lower than the current model. Additional supervision is required to manage the fifth shift, and management structures that are fit for purpose in a four shift system do not always translate neatly to the five shift system. Management therefore need to be confident that by moving to the new model they are not under resourcing the communications centre.

Question

What are the major issues in moving successfully to a new shift pattern for the workforce?

Car Mechanics Ltd

Car Mechanics Ltd currently offer an express service for car exhaust repair and replacement. It is envisaged to widen the range of services offered to the customer by also performing a tyre change service. Many of the current customers tend to wait until the exhaust has failed and thus arrive at the premises requiring a new exhaust immediately! They also usually wait at the premises while the repair takes place and don't in general like to have to wait for more than 30 minutes for the service to be completed.

Question

What steps could you take to ensure customer satisfaction of the exhaust service is not affected by adding the new tyre change service?

Line Balancing

The issue of **line balancing** is important in a line-flow process in a service or manufacturing operation that is broken down into a number of stages. Line balancing involves ensuring that the stages of the process are coordinated and bottlenecks are avoided. Because of the line-flow configuration the output of the whole line is determined by the slowest or bottleneck stage. This means a reduction in process time at a nonbottleneck will have no effect on the overall output rate. The actual design of the line is guided by the tasks that are involved in producing the product or delivering the service and the required output rate required to meet demand. This provides information that determines the number of stages and the output rate of each stage. The output rate is usually expressed in terms of the **cycle time**, which is the time taken to produce or deliver one unit of output.

$$\text{cycle time} = \frac{1}{\text{output rate}}$$

Thus an output rate of 30 units/hour gives a cycle time of 1/30/60 = 2 minutes. Thus a unit of output is delivered every 2 minutes. This means that each stage of the line process must be able to undertake its process within 2 minutes. If the process time is greater than 2 minutes, then it must be reduced by either splitting the stage into multiple stages or assigning more resources (for example, assigning two people or running two machines in parallel) to reach the desired output rate. Note that the stage will be idle if its process time is less than the target cycle time of 2 minutes. Thus in order to achieve maximum efficiency each stage must match the target cycle time as closely as possible.

Once the target cycle is calculated, derived from the output rate, it is necessary to decide on the number of workstations and allocate tasks to them. This can be achieved by using computer software, but heuristic or rule-of-thumb methods can usually give good results. The heuristic methods involve allocating tasks, in process order, to each process stage until the stage process time reaches the target cycle time. Remaining tasks are allocated to further stages. In general if there is a choice of tasks to allocate to a stage then the task with the longest process time is allocated first to provide more flexibility in providing a balanced line.

A major factor in achieving a proper line balance is to gather accurate estimates of task times in the line-flow process. If timings are just based on an average of observations then there is a danger that the effect of variations on task times will not be considered. This can be limited somewhat by keeping a number of job elements in a task which reduces variability and increases flexibility. Simulation modelling (Chapter 8) can be used to investigate these variations as well as the effect of random variations such as machine breakdown. It should also be noted that the issue of line balancing will be complicated by constraints such as layout design, material handling between stages and availability of people skills. The use of a line to produce a range of products or services, rather than a single product or service type, also increases the complexity of the line balancing process. Further details of line balancing are given in Chapter 4.

Input/Output Control

Input/output control helps to control the length of queues in front of processes and thus the process lead time (process time + queue time). The queue time is the most variable and usually the largest factor in determining process lead time. Typical values for the breakdown of process lead times in small batch manufacturing are:

Transportation Time:	20%
Setup Time:	10%
Process Time:	15%
Queue Time:	55%

Queue time can in fact be as high as 80% to 95% of the total lead time in some instances. Each of the above factors can be reduced. Setup time can be reduced by a setup reduction programme, which involves separating internal and external operations (Chapter 13). Process time can be reduced through the use of process technology (Chapter 16) or learning curve effects (Chapter 9). Transportation time can be reduced by improved layout (Chapter 4) or increased use of material-handling equipment such as conveyors (Chapter 6). However, lead time is most affected by queue time. It is not just the length of the queuing time but the variability which affects the ability to successfully undertake planning and control activities. If the queue time is not known then the lead time cannot be estimated and so it is not known whether the item will meet its scheduled completion.

Input/output control attempts to control the size of the queues at processes in order that queue times are more consistent and predictable. The method measures the actual flow of work into a work centre and the actual flow of work from that work station. The difference is the amount of work-in-progress (WIP) at that process. By monitoring these figures using input/output reports, capacity is adjusted in order to ensure queues do not become too large and average actual lead time equals planned lead time as closely as possible. It is particularly important to provide control at each process in manufacturing assembly operations as a delay of a component at one process may affect the progress of a whole assembly at a subsequent process.

Priority Control

Priority control also takes an overall view of the production process so that if an assembly is waiting for one delayed part this part will get priority over jobs arriving earlier at that work station. The priority rule is implemented at each work station by issuing a dispatch list (schedule) for that work station, listing jobs for that operation in order of completion date. Thus jobs further over completion date will get priority. Each time a component leaves a work station it will be added to the dispatch list for the next work station.

OPTIMIZED PRODUCTION TECHNOLOGY (OPT)

Optimized production technology is an operations control system that is based on the identification of bottlenecks within the production process. Goldratt and Cox (2004) define these bottlenecks as 'any resource whose capacity is less than or equal to the demand placed on it'. This approach attempts to avoid much of the complexity of scheduling by focusing on bottlenecks. The idea is that system output is determined by bottlenecks so it is essential to schedule nonbottleneck resources to ensure maximum use of the bottleneck resources themselves.

The simulation 'OPT layout' is available in your interactive e-book at **www.wileyopenpage.com**

In identifying bottlenecks, OPT views the production process as a whole with respect to the market and the business within which it operates. It assumes that all manufacturers aim to make money as their overriding objective. This 'goal' is defined in terms of three performance measures (Goldratt and Cox, 2004):

- throughput
- inventory
- operational expense.

Throughput is the rate at which the production system generates money through sales. Throughput, however, does not equal manufacturing output as any output not sold is seen as waste in the long run. Optimized production technology therefore does not consider 'finished goods' stocks as assets. Inventory is defined as all the money that the system has invested in goods that it intends to sell. OPT excludes labour costs and indirect expenses from inventory valuation. Operational expense is that which the system spends in order to turn inventory into throughput. This includes all expenses, both direct and indirect. Goldratt and Cox (2004) use these performance criteria to restate the goal of a manufacturing organization as: 'To reduce operational expense and reduce inventory whilst simultaneously increasing throughput.'

To understand why OPT focuses on bottlenecks it is necessary to understand how OPT differs from traditional approaches to production planning. The traditional approach is to balance (make equal) capacity at all the work stations in response to anticipated demand from the master production schedule. However, there are two reasons why a production facility cannot be balanced to the demands of production. These are nondeterminance and interdependence and they relate to the issues of variability and interdependence covered in Chapter 8.

Nondeterminance simply refers to the fact that the information used to derive the production schedule may not be of a fixed nature. For example, the process time for an activity will vary each time it is performed. The rate usually quoted will be the average of these times. However, it can be shown that statistical fluctuations around the average can have a significant bearing on plant performance. Interdependence refers to the fact that most stages in production are connected in some way to other stages. For example, stage A cannot start until stage B has finished, which cannot start until stages C and D have finished etc. The effect of interdependence is to accumulate the fluctuations caused by nondeterminance from stage to stage downstream of the production process. This is because the ability to go faster than average depends on the ability of all others in front of the process while there is no limit to go slower. Therefore fluctuations don't average out but accumulate and the end of the line has to make up for the accumulation of all the slowness. This behaviour has led Goldratt (1981) to suggest the following recommendations for dealing with an unbalanced plant:

- Bottlenecks must be identified and since they determine the rate of throughput for the whole plant, must be carefully protected from disturbances and potential delays to assure full utilization.
- The resources must be organized so the bottleneck resource is used primarily at one of the earliest stages of production.
- Instead of trying to eliminate overcapacity of nonbottlenecks at random, we must strive to arrange some resources such that one has sufficient overcapacity to support the bottleneck fully. Ideally this would involve a gradual increase of overcapacity as we go downstream.

These recommendations move away from trying to match capacity with demand to managing the whole system to the pace set by the bottlenecks. The principles underlying this approach are as follows:

1. Balance the flow, not capacity. Trying to maintain flow in a balanced capacity plant means that all stages are expected to work to full capacity. In a nonbalanced system (all systems) inventory will accumulate at bottleneck resources. Thus capacity should be used only when necessary, as in JIT control systems (Chapter 13).
2. Constraints determine nonbottleneck utilization. Bottlenecks should pace production and determine the level of utilization for nonbottleneck resources. The only machine to be working at 100% capacity is the bottleneck.
3. Activation is not always equal to utilization. To activate a resource not needed at the bottleneck is a waste.

4. An hour lost at a bottleneck is an hour lost for the entire system. In effect an hour lost at the bottleneck is an hour lost of factory output, as it can never be made up.

5. An hour saved at a nonbottleneck is a mirage. An hour saved at a nonbottleneck will not actually increase output of the whole system.

6. Bottlenecks govern throughput and inventory. Inventory will accumulate at the bottleneck. There is no point in inventory after this stage because throughput is determined by the rate of production at the bottleneck.

7. The transfer batch size should not always equal a process batch size at nonbottlenecks, transfer batches can be small to speed the flow of WIP as an increase in total setup time is not critical. At bottleneck resources these transfer batches then accumulate into larger process batches to save setups and maximize output.

8. Process batches should be variable, not fixed. The process batch should not be determined by some fixed lot-sizing rule for instance but should be varied to balance the flow of the manufacturing cycle.

9. Set the schedule by examining all the constraints simultaneously.

MRP II systems predetermine batch size, lead times and set schedules accordingly. Optimized production technology suggests that all the constraints of a complex network are considered simultaneously using the simulation capabilities of the OPT software. The OPT planning and control approach uses the terminology of the drum, buffer and rope.

The Drum

The drum determines the rate of production. In MRP and JIT control systems the rate of production is determined primarily from market demand but with OPT the bottleneck resources are used to develop the schedule ensuring that bottleneck capacity is not exceeded. Other nonbottleneck resources are scheduled to serve the bottlenecks by varying process batch and transfer batch sizes. Thus the bottleneck resource sets the drumbeat for the entire process.

The Buffer

Buffers are placed at certain locations to prevent unforeseen events disrupting output of finished goods. There are two types of inventory buffer. Time buffers are determined by the amount of output the system could produce during the period of time it takes to correct a disruption. They are generally placed before bottleneck resources. Stock buffers are inventories of finished goods determined by forecasts of possible demand fluctuations.

The Rope

The rate of the operation of processes that come after the bottleneck is determined by the rate of output from the bottleneck machine. To control the rate of processes before the bottleneck there is a linkage between the bottleneck and the processes that feed it, termed the 'rope'. The rope can take the form of a planned production schedule or an informal discussion between employees at the bottleneck and employees at other work stations.

Figure 10.3 shows the use of the drum, buffer and rope control system. There is a flow of material from process A to process E, with a bottleneck resource being process C. Normally, without any control

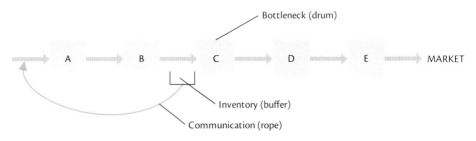

Drum, Buffer and Rope in an OPT Control System.

mechanism excess inventory will build up in front of the bottleneck process C. What is required is an inventory buffer in front of C, so that as the bottleneck resource it is always busy (despite variations in supply) but does not experience the build up of too much inventory. This is achieved by the use of a communication link (the rope) between process C and the upstream process A. This communication could be in the form of a schedule or an informal discussion between personnel. The buffer in front of process C is called a time buffer and ensures work is always present for process C, no matter what the schedule.

Although OPT can be relatively quickly implemented it needs expertise for correct implementation, which may not be available for small organizations. The OPT software may also be expensive for some organizations. OPT could also be criticized for not containing continuous improvement activities of JIT although these could be incorporated and the two approaches could be used in combination to form a continuous improvement effort.

SUMMARY

- In a make-to-stock system each order must be small compared to total capacity or the risk of making to stock and not finding a customer for the order will be too high. A resource-to-order system means that each order is large compared to total system capacity to make the organization of resources worthwhile. Whilst the customer will only 'see' the delivery time from stock in a make-to-stock system, in a make-to-order system the delivery cycle will include the purchase, make and delivery stages.
- Loading involves determining the available capacity for each stage in a process and allocating a task to that stage. The two principal approaches to loading are 'finite loading', which allocates works up to a fixed limit, and 'infinite loading', which does not place a limit on the work loaded onto a stage.
- Sequencing is the sequential assignment of tasks or jobs to individual processes. Sequencing can be undertaken using priority rules such as DDS (customer due date), FCFS (first-come first-served) and SPT (shortest processing time).

www.wileyopenpage.com

- For services, scheduling involves varying the size of the workforce to meet variations in demand. The approach to scheduling in manufacturing is largely dependent on the volume and variety mix of the manufacturing system.
- Techniques for scheduling include workforce scheduling, line balancing, input/output control and priority control.
- Optimized production technology (OPT) is based on the identification of bottlenecks within the production process. The OPT planning and control approach uses the terminology of drum, buffer and rope.

CASE STUDY 10.3

Using Workforce Scheduling to Lower Labour Costs

As a consequence of the credit crunch and the downturn in many economies, companies are finding it increasingly difficult to increase prices to consumers. This is a problem as many firms are experiencing increased costs in resources such as raw materials and energy. However, in the USA businesses have been able to demand that fewer employees do more work for less pay. Industrial output has continued to increase, even as employers have laid off workers. Companies, including retail giant Wal-Mart, are using new flexible scheduling technology to ensure fewer employees work at times when store customer traffic is low. Accordingly, labour costs, which account for about 70% of US corporate costs, have so far remained in check, in stark contrast to escalating wage inflation in countries such as Vietnam and China.

Sources

http://www.reuters.com/article/2012/11/01/us-economy-productivity-idUSBRE8A00PC20121101

http://newstandardnews.net/content/index.cfm/items/2203

Question

Why is workforce scheduling technology particularly suitable to large organizations such as Wal-Mart?

CASE STUDY 10.4

Ocado

Founded in 2000, Ocado has developed a unique approach to online grocery shopping. Their centralised facility bypasses the supermarket store and takes produce from warehouse direct to the customer in a fleet of custom built Mercedes vans.

The company runs a pure warehouse distribution process, with no stores. It operates a 'hub and spoke' system, where the 'hub' is the Customer Fulfilment Centre (CFC) in Hatfield and the 'spokes' are located in regional groups;

www.wileyopenpage.com

Weybridge, Dartford, Coventry, Manchester, Leeds, Southampton, White City London and Bristol. This allows Ocado to reach over 70% of UK households.

The typical model for online grocery shopping, and that favoured by the likes of Tesco and Asda, is to use the supermarket aisles to fulfil the customer order, where an employee will effectively shop on behalf of the customer and then this is delivered.

The Customer Fulfilment Centre currently offers around 22 000 products available at any one time. This range is however, a complex mix of frozen, chilled, fresh and heavy goods (such as liquids). The centre receives constant deliveries of product from suppliers including Waitrose, to the receiving depot, which are then dispatched to be contained in suitable holding zones in plastic crates called 'totes'. A team of personal shoppers then process each customer order; into bags contained in separate totes, these are then passed onto the drivers to be delivered in one hour slots to the customer.

Once a customer has placed an order, Ocado may have only 17 hours in which to process this.

Damaged goods and storage times are key concerns for Ocado, fresh goods need to delivered rapidly – timeliness of delivery of goods in and orders out is a key balance.

Ocado aims to provide superior service, which, it could be said, sets it apart from other online grocery delivery services. However, in 2011, this service level slipped.

Ocado reported that the items delivered exactly as ordered fell from 99.1 per cent to 98 per cent. Deliveries on time or early fell from 94.9 per cent to 92.7 per cent. The fall in targets came from accelerating demand, pushing Ocado close to its operational limits.

This issue led Ocado to significantly expand its Hatfield facility and start a programme of investment into additional hubs and a new Fulfilments Centre in Warwick. The objective is for capacity at the Hatfield CFC to increase to 180 000 orders a week, enabling sales of approximately £1bn a year.

Ocado invested £210m in a second distribution centre in Warwickshire; which opened at the end of 2012, which has the capacity to support another £1bn of sales, and allow Ocado access to 85% of the UK market.

Ocado had underlined its ambition to branch into non food areas by the acquisition of a new facility in Welwyn Garden City; the depot is now fully operational, and is driving forward the efficiency of the storage and distribution of non-food stock with an innovative robotic sorting device.

Demand for Ocado's goods is increasing and the adaption of technology such as 'customer favourites' linking to suggested products have seen significant increase in sales.

Ocado are set to hold a product range of 31 000 items by the end on 2012.

Sources

http://www.telegraph.co.uk/finance/newsbysector/retailandconsumer/8934300/Ocados-delivery-punctuality-slips.html

http://www.ft.com/cms/s/0/96368152-a0e6-11e0-adae-00144feabdc0.html#axzz2AhYw5LFI

http://www.guardian.co.uk/business/2010/oct/12/ocado-to-create-2000-jobs?INTCMP=ILCNETTXT3487

http://www.retail-week.com/city-and-finance/ocado-close-to-covenants-breach-analysts-fear/5042258.article

http://www.whtimes.co.uk/news/online_retail_giant_says_it_plans_to_bring_more_than_200_jobs_to_welwyn_garden_city_1_1670714

www.ocadogroup.com

Source: Written by Briony Boydell and Chris Milner. Reproduced with permission.

Questions

1. What risks do Ocado take with their planning?
2. How is this system better or worse than Asda and Tesco?

Quizzes to test yourself further are available in your interactive e-book at **www.wileyopenpage.com**

Flashcards to test yourself further are available in your interactive e-book at **www.wileyopenpage.com**

EXERCISES

1. What are the implications of the P:D ratio for a manufacturing organization?

2. A job shop has five jobs which must be processed on machine 1 and then on machine 2 (times in minutes). Determine the sequence that will allow the set of five jobs to be completed in the minimum time. State the total job completion time.

Job	Machine 1	Machine 2
A	8	3
B	4	5
C	7	6
D	5	10
E	9	3

3. The following six jobs are to be scheduled on a piece of equipment.

Job	1	2	3	4	5	6
Duration (days)	6	4	2	8	1	5
Due date	6	20	22	24	2	10

a. Prepare a Gantt chart that will provide a schedule showing when jobs are to be undertaken on the machine. Use the FCFS rule.

b. Using FCFS how long will it take to complete all the jobs?

c. Given the due dates shown, calculate the average job lateness when FCFS is used.

d. Given the due dates shown, calculate the average job lateness when SPT is used.

e. What disadvantage is SPT likely to exhibit in a heavily loaded jobs shop?

4. Evaluate the use of the SPT/SOT in a retail and a manufacturing environment.

5. A small manufacturer produces custom parts that first require a shearing operation and then a punch operation. There are five jobs to be processed and the processing times (minutes) are estimated as the following.

Job	Shear	Punch
1	4	5
2	4	1
3	10	4
4	6	10
5	2	3

Use Johnson's algorithm to identify the processing sequence that will give the lowest overall throughput time. Use a Gantt chart to illustrate the sequence and state the total job completion time.

6. What are the main issues in the scheduling of jobbing, batch and line systems?

7. Discuss the advantages and disadvantages of the OPT approach to production planning.

8. Define the terms 'drum', 'buffer' and 'rope' as used in OPT terminology.

WEB EXERCISE

Reading the White Paper at http://www.goldratt.com/pdfs/toctpwp.pdf (accessed 1 December 2011) why does the OPT approach claim to be so widely applicable?

FURTHER READING

Cox, J.F. and Schleier, J. (2010) *Theory of Constraints Handbook*, McGraw-Hill.
Goldratt, E.M. (2002) *It's Not Luck*, Gower.
Jacobs, F.R. and Chase, R.B. (2012) *Operations and Supply Chain Management: The Core*, 3rd edn, McGraw-Hill.

WEB LINKS

www.goldratt.com (accessed 1 December 2011). The Goldratt Institute home page.

www.production-scheduling.com (accessed 1 December 2011). Advice on scheduling using spreadsheets.

www.toyota.co.uk (accessed 1 December 2011). Web site containing detailed information on world car production.

www.wileyopenpage.com

REFERENCES

Goldratt, E.M. (1981) The unbalanced plant, APICS1981 International Conference Proceedings, pp. 195–9.

Goldratt, E.M. and Cox, J. (2004) *The Goal: A Process of Ongoing Improvement*, 3rd edn, Gower.

Johnson, S.M. (1954) Optimal two- and three-stage production with setup times included, *Naval Research Quarterly*, 1, 61–8.

Shingo, S. (1989) *A Study of Toyota Production System*, Productivity Press.

Capacity Management

LEARNING OBJECTIVES

- Describe the elements in medium-term capacity planning
- Understand the effects of product mix on capacity
- Evaluate the three pure strategies for reconciling capacity and demand
- Understand approaches to demand management in services
- Understand the use of cumulative representatives to evaluate a level capacity planning approach
- Discuss the use of queuing theory to explore the trade-off between the amount of capacity and level of demand
- Discuss the relevance of propositions about the psychology of customer waiting time
- Understand qualitative and quantitative techniques for forecasting

CAPACITY MANAGEMENT AND OPERATIONS STRATEGY

Long-term capacity management is covered in Chapter 5 as a design issue and is related to strategy in that it leads to major long-term investments in operations capabilities. This chapter covers medium-term capacity management issues and the ability to deal with demand fluctuations in the medium term. Although individual capacity decisions may be an operational response to a need to meet demand a capacity strategy will provide the context about how these series of capacity decision are made over time. For instance, the choice between approaches to reconciling capacity and demand can be made in a strategic context by reference to the key performance objectives that have been derived for the operation. For example, a level capacity planning strategy is particularly relevant to meet the performance objective of cost whilst the chase capacity planning strategy is particularly relevant to meet the performance objective of quality. Whatever capacity planning strategy is chosen, organizations that have an operations strategy that has a focus on the performance objective of flexibility need to be able to adjust capacity to meet fluctuations in demand.

INTRODUCTION

In operations management a definition of capacity should take into account both the volume and the time over which capacity is available. Thus capacity management is not just about providing customers with services or goods in the amount requested, but involves providing them at the time they are requested too.

Capacity issues can be considered as long term and form part of the operations strategy. For example, a strategy of capacity expansion may be used to provide a presence in geographical locations before competitors can gain access to a market. These long-term capacity issues are considered in Chapter 5. In this chapter, short- to medium-term capacity issues are considered. These are mainly concerned with ensuring sufficient capacity of the right type is available at the right time to meet demand for the planning period.

Setting capacity to meet the demands of the organization is termed 'capacity planning and control'. The capacity planning and control activity should be taken using a systematic approach using the following steps:

- measuring demand
- measuring capacity
- reconciling capacity and demand
- evaluating alternatives and making a choice.

The 'measuring demand' step requires that future demand be estimated; the 'measuring' step requires the measurement of present capacity; 'reconciling capacity and demand' requires analysis of capacity planning approaches and the final step requires a method of choosing a suitable capacity planning approach. This chapter is structured around these steps in capacity planning and control.

MEASURING DEMAND

What makes demand particularly difficult to measure is the fact that it fluctuates in response to a number of infuences. These influences include:

- Competitors introducing product or services into the marketplace that perform better on performance objectives such as higher quality, lower priced or shorter delivery times will affect future demand.

- Competitors introducing substitute products or services may reduce demand.

- Changes in consumer tastes can affect demand.

- Changes in the economy, such as a recession can affect demand as can changes in government policy regarding issues such as sales taxes.

- Fluctuations which can be classified due to trend, cyclical, seasonal and irregular components (see time series analysis later in this chapter).

Demand also needs to be considered across different time horizons. For a long-term estimate of demand the strategic planning process will define the markets in which the organization will compete and such factors as the range and volume of products and services in these market segments. The marketing strategy will be evaluated in terms of corporate objectives. Corporate objectives are usually expressed in terms of financial measures such as growth or profitability. The role of marketing strategy and operations strategy in meeting corporate objectives is discussed in Chapter 2. Based on the marketing strategy and forecasts of demand (see the appendix to this chapter) the organization can formulate a long-range business plan that will include capital budgets for expanding facilities and major equipment investment. Because of the relatively long lead time of acquiring these facilities they are considered in the short- to medium-term planning horizon to represent the effective capacity limit of the organization. Thus long-range demand factors are covered in the design section of this book in Chapter 5 under the heading of long-term capacity planning.

In the medium term (approximately 2–18 months) planning is undertaken by various functions (manufacturing, marketing, finance and so forth) in order to coordinate efforts to achieve the business plan within the constraints of the long-term decisions made in that plan. The planning process can be described as working in cycles, with each cycle confirming detailed plans for the next time period and sketching more tentative plans for the following period. At the next planning meeting these tentative plans are now considered in more detail and the cycle repeats. This process means that the organization can build on previous plans instead of attempting to devise new plans at each planning cycle. This reduces planning time and leads to more continuity in decision making. The aggregate planning process will evaluate the production plan in order to ensure sufficient capacity is available to undertake the output targets.

The production plan (or operations plan in a service organization) states the amount of output which will be delivered from the operations function over the medium-term business plan. The output can be expressed in terms of volume, currency or units. For example, a retail outlet may commit to sales of clothes in terms of sales value or units sold during the next 12-month period. The production plan provides an overall guide to the level of output from the manufacturing/operations department, which will be coordinated with other functions such as marketing and finance.

It is necessary to break the production plan down into a level of detail required for procurement and operational purposes. This means that the demand for each individual product and thus the materials, components and work tasks required to produce it, must be specified. The master production schedule (MPS) states the volume and timing of all products that have a significant demand on manufacturing resources. Further details of the MPS in relation to a materials requirements planning system are provided in Chapter 14.

MEASURING CAPACITY

Measuring capacity may at first seem straightforward, especially when compared to the uncertainty inherent in estimating demand. However, capacity is not fixed but is a variable that depends on a number of factors including the following:

- Capacity takes many different forms such as storage space, availability of employee skills, equipment numbers and transportation facilities.
- Any of these types of capacity may be the limiting factor or bottleneck on the capacity of a process. The actual bottleneck, and thus capacity, may also change over time.
- Working practices such as hours worked and holiday entitlement can also affect capacity calculations and may change over time. For example, a change in company policy may decrease the hours a week of employees and thus reduce capacity.
- The amount of capacity required to deliver a particular process at a particular level may change over time due to the experience gained and improvements made to process design.
- Capacity available in multiple locations may not be simply summed as transportation time and costs may make available capacity in a particular location unsuitable.
- Capacity is time-based and so capacity underutilized due to a drop in demand cannot be used later when demand increases. Thus the actual capacity available will be less the more demand fluctuates. Process time fluctuations will also affect capacity. Queuing theory (later in this chapter) and simulation modelling (Chapter 8) can be used to analyse this time-based behaviour.

Measuring capacity in services is a particular challenge. Generally services need to be more custom-designed and involve more personal contact in order to meet specific customer needs. Thus customer contact has a number of impacts on the way the service can be run. Customer involvement tends to provide an opportunity for special requests and instructions to be issued by the customer that tends to disrupt routine procedures and thus efficiency. Capacity may be lost in providing conversation to the customer in addition to delivering the actual service. Quality is closely related to the customer's perception of satisfactory service. Operations employees employed where high levels of customer contact occur must be skilled in interpreting what the customer really wants. Thus the level of customer/client contact can have a direct effect on the efficiency and thus capacity availability that an operation can achieve.

There are a variety of methods to achieve efficiency and still provide the customer with good service. One way to limit the disruption from unusual requests is to standardize the service – for example, in a fast-food restaurant. A common strategy to improve the overall efficiency of the operation is to keep separate those parts of the operation that do not require direct customer contact. Operations are divided into front office, where interaction with the customer takes place, and back office, where directions are primarily taken from managers, not customers (see Chapter 1).

Two further issues to consider when measuring capacity are product mix and the definitions of design and effective capacity.

Product Mix

Only when a narrow product (or service) range is involved can capacity be measured reasonably accurately and in this case be quoted in terms of output volume. The effect of product mix on capacity is shown in the Worked Example 11.1.

www.wileyopenpage.com

The Effect of Product Mix on Capacity

The following assembly times are given for three models of a washing machine.

	Assembly time (minutes)
Washer (basic)	50
Washer (deluxe)	150
Washer (dryer)	250

The target weekly output is given as 100 units. Calculate the total output for a product ratio of 4:2:1 for washer (basic), washer (deluxe) and washer (dryer) and total output for a product ratio of 3:2:2.

Solution

For a product mix ratio of 4:2:1 the total output is as follows:

$$\text{Ratio} = 4:2:1$$

$$\text{Assembly time for 7 units} = (4 \times 50) + (2 \times 150) + (1 \times 250) = 750 \text{ minutes}$$

$$\text{Assembly minutes available} = 9000$$

$$\text{Therefore weekly output} = \frac{9000}{750} \times 7 = 84 \text{ units}$$

For a product mix ratio of 3:2:2 the output is as follows:

$$\text{Ratio} = 3:2:2$$

$$\text{Assembly time for 7 units} = (3 \times 50) + (2 \times 150) + (2 \times 250) = 950 \text{ minutes}$$

$$\text{Assembly minutes available} = 9000$$

$$\text{Therefore weekly output} = \frac{9000}{950} \times 7 = 66 \text{ units}$$

Thus a change in product mix from 4:2:1 to 3:2:2 alters the weekly capacity output from 84 to 66 units.

With a changing product mix therefore it may be more useful to measure capacity in terms of input measures, which provide some indication of the potential output. Also for planning purposes, when demand is stated in output terms it is necessary to convert input measures to an estimated output measure. For example, in hospitals that undertake a range of activities, capacity is often measured in terms of beds available, an input measure. An output measure such as number of patients treated per week will be highly dependent on the mix of activities the hospital performs. Estimates of capacity based

TABLE 11.1

Examples of Input and Output Measures of Capacity.

Operation	Input Measure	Output Measure
Hospital	Beds available	Patients treated
Airline	Seats available	Passengers flown
Manufacturer	Equipment available	Goods delivered
Retail outlet	Floor space available	Goods sold
Restaurant	Seating available	Meals served

on output can also be misleading as part of this output may be accounted for by either inventory (for example, patients) part way through the process or the use of additional resources (for example, overtime, equipment rental, contracting out) that could not normally be treated as part of the organization's capacity. Examples of input and output measures of capacity are given in Table 11.1.

Design, Effective and Actual Capacity

The **design capacity** of an operation represents the theoretical output of a process as it was designed. However, this level of capacity is rarely met due to occurrences that prevent the operation producing its full output. These occurrences are termed 'planned and unplanned factors' (Figure 11.1).

Planned factors are activities whose timing can be determined in advance. They include such items as maintenance, training and machine setup time. During these activities the output from the operation is lost. One of the ways to reduce this loss of output for manufacturing processes is to use the technique of setup reduction (Chapter 13), which attempts to undertake as much of the setup process as possible while the operation is still in use. In services training of personnel may take place during the year when seasonal demand is low.

The capacity remaining after loss of output due to planned factors is termed the **effective capacity** of the process. However, this will also be above the level of capacity which is available due to unplanned occurrences such as machine breakdowns and worker absenteeism. These are more difficult to deal with than

FIGURE 11.1

Design, Effective and Actual Capacity.

planned factors, because by definition their timing cannot be predicted. In order to minimize these disturbances action such as preventative maintenance should be taken (Chapter 13). This involves undertaking planned maintenance activities, if possible when demand is low. These activities can include replacing equipment parts before they fail, in order to reduce unplanned breakdowns. Worker absenteeism could be reduced by improving motivation. This could be achieved by changing the job design using the ideas of the job characteristics model described in Chapter 9.

After taking both planned and unplanned factors into account there remains the capacity available for processing, termed the **actual capacity** of the operation.

Two measures that you often see used in relation to these capacity measures are utilization and efficiency. **Utilization** gives the proportion of time a process is in actual use compared to its design capacity and **efficiency** gives the proportion of time that a process is in use compared to its effective capacity. Thus:

$$\text{utilization} = \frac{\text{actual ouput}}{\text{design capacity}}$$

$$\text{efficiency} = \frac{\text{actual ouput}}{\text{effective capacity}}$$

Both measures are usually given in terms of percentages. A utilization of 60% means that a process was producing output for 60% of a time period. An efficiency rating of 60% denotes that a process was producing output for 60% of a time period in which it was available to produce output (it was not being used for maintenance or other planned activities).

RECONCILING CAPACITY AND DEMAND

Methods for reconciling capacity and demand can be classified into three 'pure' strategies: level capacity, chase demand and demand management. Due to the complexity of capacity management and the need to optimize a range of performance objectives it is usually necessary to combine the three pure strategies described and form a mixed capacity planning strategy. The three strategies are now described.

Level Capacity

The **level capacity** strategy sets the processing capacity at a uniform level throughout the planning period regardless of fluctuations in forecast demand. This means output is set at a fixed rate, usually to meet average demand. Inventory is used to absorb variations in demand. During periods of low demand any overproduction can be transferred to finished goods inventory in anticipation of sales at a later time period (Figure 11.2). The disadvantage of this strategy is the cost of holding inventory and the cost of perishable items that may have to be discarded. To avoid producing obsolete items firms will try to create inventory for products which are relatively certain to be sold. This strategy is also of limited value for perishable goods.

For a service organization output cannot be stored as inventory so a level capacity plan involves running at a uniformly high level of capacity (Figure 11.3). The drawback of the approach is the cost of maintaining this high level of capacity, although it could be useful when the cost of lost sales is

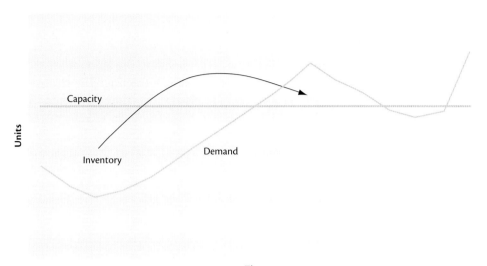

FIGURE 11.2

Level Capacity Plan.

FIGURE 11.3

Level Capacity Plan at a High Level.

particularly high. In order to overcome this problem the concept of 'partitioning demand' is used, which involves keeping capacity in the customer contact area consistently high, so customers are not kept waiting, and keeping capacity in the noncontact areas at a more uniform level. Another strategy is for services to 'store' their output by performing part of their work in anticipation of demand. An example is purchasing and displaying goods before actual customer demand occurs.

Chase Demand

The **chase demand** strategy seeks to match output to the demand pattern over time. Capacity is altered by such policies as changing the amount of part-time staff, changing the amount of staff availability through overtime working, changing equipment levels and subcontracting. The strategy is costly in terms of the costs of activities such as changing staffing levels and overtime payments. The costs may be particularly high in industries in which skills are scarce. Disadvantages of subcontracting include reduced profit margin lost to the subcontractor, loss of control, potentially longer lead times and the risk that the subcontractor may decide to enter the same market. For these reasons a pure chase demand strategy is more usually adopted by service operations which cannot store their output and so make a level capacity plan less attractive. A graphical representation of a chase demand plan is shown in Figure 11.4.

In services, when the operation cannot usually match the demand rate with its capacity level, its objective becomes one of developing a capacity profile that matches its demand profile to the extent that this is feasible and economically viable. Strategies for achieving this include:

- *Staggered workshift schedules.* Scheduling the availability of capacity to cover demand involves constructing work shifts so that the number of operators available at any one time matches the demand profile – for example, in a fast-food restaurant.
- *Part-time staff.* More flexibility to schedule and smooth the work demand is often available for those parts of a service where the customer is not present and the service is provided by working with some surrogate for the customer. A strategy of using part-time staff needs to trade off the cost of not doing some work against the extra cost of employing the staff.
- *Subcontractors.* If there is not enough capacity, additional capacity can be obtained from outside sources. For example, surgeries employing contract doctor services to cover weekends.

FIGURE 11.4

Chase Demand Plan.

- *Multiskilled floating staff.* Having multiskilled staff increases flexibility in capacity decisions. For example, in the case of a hospital it might be desirable to have some floating capacity that can be shifted from one department to another if the number of patients or the amount of nursing attention required in each department varies.
- *Customer self-service.* With this option, the service capacity arrives when the demand does. Customers at supermarkets and many department stores select most of their own merchandise.

Demand Management

While the level capacity and chase demand strategies aim to adjust capacity to match demand, the **demand management** strategy attempts to adjust demand to meet available capacity. There are many ways this can be done but most will involve altering the marketing mix (for example, price or promotion) and will require coordination with the marketing function. A graphical representation of a demand management plan is shown in Figure 11.5.

Demand management strategies include:

- *Varying the price.* During periods of low demand price discounts can be used to stimulate the demand level. Conversely when demand is higher than the capacity limit, price could be increased.
- *Advertising.* Advertising and other marketing activities can be used to increase sales during low demand periods.
- *Alternative products.* This is the use of existing processes to make or sell alternative products during low demand periods. An example is the way many garden centres use their premises to sell Christmas decorations during the winter months when gardening activity is low.

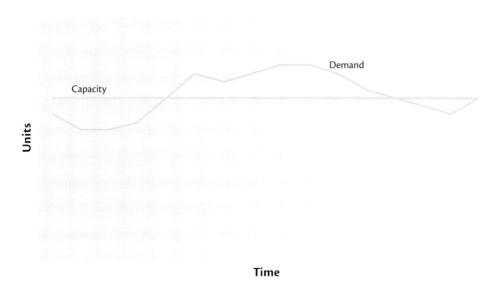

FIGURE 11.5

Demand Management Plan.

- *Maintenance of a fixed schedule.* Some services can schedule the times at which the service is available, for example, airlines and rail services. Demand occurs as people purchase tickets to use some of the previously scheduled transportation capacity.
- *Use of an appointment system.* The pattern of demand variations over the longer term can also have a significant influence on the planning of efficient service operations. The ideal would be to achieve uniform utilization of service capacity but this is unlikely unless an appointment-only policy is operated. Some services are provided by appointment, for example, a dentist or veterinary surgery. Use of an appointment system permits demand to be moved into available time. The delay between a request for an appointment and the time of the appointment may depend on the backlog or queue of waiting work.
- *Delayed delivery.* Delaying jobs until capacity is available serves to make the workload more uniform, for example, a bank teller. In addition routine work may be set aside to make capacity available for rush jobs.
- *Providing economic incentives for off-peak demand.* Some operations have a high capital investment in the capacity they have to provide their services. The unit cost of capacity that is used only occasionally for peak demand is very high. These operations try to keep demand as uniform as possible by the use of economic inducements, for example, off-peak electricity and off-peak telephone calls.

Yield Management

The use of demand management strategies is often particularly developed in service industries where capacity cannot be stored (output cannot be held as stock and used later) and demand is stochastic (there is variability in when customers request the service and how long it takes to service them). **Yield management** aims to maximize customer revenue in these service organizations and is particularly appropriate when the organization is operating with relatively fixed capacity and it is possible to segment the market into different types of customers.

The airline industry provides an example of the use of yield management. It has well-developed policies for ensuring as many seats as possible are occupied on its flights. Once a flight route has been scheduled and an aircraft has been allocated to that route, the costs of operating the aircraft, including staffing, maintenance and fuel costs, are fixed and the variable cost in accommodating each additional passenger on a flight is very low. Moreover, capacity is lost once the flight takes place and cannot be stored for later use. The airline thus will want to fill as many seats as possible whilst maximizing the overall price the customers pay. One business model that airlines use to do this is to charge relatively high prices in advance to customers when the guarantee of a flight is more important than the price (for example, business customers) and then discount fares close to the flight time to maximize revenue (through such outlets as e-Commerce sites, for example, www.lastminute.com). An alternative strategy is to start prices low to ensure a proportion of capacity is sold and then increase the price as capacity becomes scarce as the flight fills. If the flight is not reaching its target for booked seats, discounts may be offered to customers to increase sales (budget airlines such as easyJet (www.easyjet.com) and Bmibaby (www.bmibaby.com) use this model).

As well as price-discounting other yield-management strategies include overbooking service provision, for example, taking bookings from more people for a flight than there are seats on the plane. This strategy is based on the assumption that not all passengers will turn up for the flight and thus maximizes revenue. The obvious downside is that if everyone does arrive then passengers will need to be accommodated in some way (for example, an upgrade to business class, financial compensation or a seat on a later plane or a combination of these), increasing costs. A further yield-management strategy is to vary the service type, for example, different classes of ticket for a train journey. This allows a discounting strategy for price-sensitive customers but travel-time flexibility and higher service levels for higher paying business customers, maximizing overall revenue. Case Study 11.2 provides further information on the sophistication of organizations' yield-management policies.

EVALUATING ALTERNATIVES AND MAKING A CHOICE

Capacity planning involves evaluating the capacity requirements and determining the best way to meet these using a feasible and low-cost capacity-planning approach. The term 'aggregate planning' is sometimes used to describe the process of aggregating (grouping) capacity requirements over a medium-term planning horizon to provide the best way to meet these requirements. In order to choose a capacity plan which meets the above criteria it is necessary to try to predict the consequences of that plan. This can be done with varying levels of accuracy and cost using the following methods:

- cumulative representations
- queuing theory
- the psychology of queuing.

Cumulative Representations

One method of evaluating a level capacity planning approach is to simply plot the cumulative demand and cumulative capacity for a product over the planning time period. As discussed earlier, capacity is required in the right volume, at the right time. When pursuing a level capacity plan, even though over time inventory levels may be sufficient to meet demand, this does not mean that inventory levels will be sufficient to meet demand at a particular point in time. Thus a running total or cumulative count of inventory, which should always meet or exceed cumulative demand, is used to ensure no stock-outs occur. An example of the use of cumulative representations is shown in Figure 11.6.

Figure 11.6 shows the relationship between capacity and demand over time and thus enables an assessment of the capacity plan. When the cumulative demand line is below the cumulative capacity, the distance between the lines is the level of inventory at that time. If the demand line lies above the capacity line then this represents a shortage of capacity at that time. The graph shows the cumulative capacity and demand, so it takes into account the usage of any surplus inventory in periods when demand exceeds supply (when the graphs meet, inventory is zero). The cumulative representation graph can show if the capacity plan is meeting demand. This occurs when the capacity line is always along or above the demand line over the planning period.

Assessing the effect of capacity planning approaches on the capacity plan involves adjusting the gradient of the capacity (for chase demand approach) or demand (for demand management approach) line at the appropriate point at which the change is to take place. The ideal situation would be when the capacity and demand lines follow each other as closely as possible on the graph. However, the cost of changing the capacity or demand pattern must be taken into consideration. It should also be noted

Units

Unable to meet orders

Inventory at zero

Cumulative Production   Inventory

Cumulative Demand

Time

FIGURE 11.6

Cumulative Representations.

that it may be cost effective to only change capacity in certain blocks and the cost of the change may be dependent on the direction of that change. For example, it may be cheaper to decrease capacity rather than increase capacity for a certain process.

Queuing Theory

Cumulative representations rely on the fact that when supply exceeds demand inventory can be stored for use when demand exceeds supply. In service situations, however, the output of the operation cannot be stored. Waiting time can only be eliminated when customers are asked to arrive at fixed intervals (an appointment system) and service times are fixed. Thus waiting time in queues is caused by fluctuations in arrival rates and variability in service times. **Queuing theory** can be used to explore the trade-off between the amount of capacity and the level of demand. Too much capacity and costs will be excessive, but too little capacity will cause long waiting for the customer and loss of service quality leading to loss of business. In a service context queuing theory can provide a useful guide in determining expected waiting time for an arriving customer and the average number of customers who will be waiting for service. This permits an estimate of the amount of capacity that will be needed to keep waiting time to a reasonable level taking into account the expected rate and variability of demand. Examples of queuing situations include customers at a bank, aeroplanes circling waiting to land, patients waiting to see a doctor and parts waiting for processing at a machining centre.

Uncertainty in arrival and service times means that, even although on average there may be adequate capacity to meet demand, queuing may still occur when a number of successive arrivals or long service times occur. Conversely, idle time will occur when arrival rates or service time decreases. Although this behaviour means that full utilization will not be feasible for this type of system, queuing theory does allow analysis of how much capacity is needed to keep average or maximum queue length or waiting times to an acceptable level. This acceptable level or service-quality level will depend on the type of operation involved.

www.wileyopenpage.com

FIGURE 11.7

Single- and Multiple-Channel Queuing Systems.

Figure 11.7 shows how queue systems can be classified into a single-channel queuing system consisting of a single queue of customers who wait until a service facility is available and a multiple-channel queuing system that have parallel server facilities. Although a single queue system is increasingly popular and may be seen by customers as fairer in that it enforces the first-come, first-served (FCFS) rule, its operation may not always be practical; imagine a single line of customers with trolleys in a supermarket! Other disadvantages of a single queue system are that the length of the single queue may seem to imply a longer wait for customers than many short queues and a single-channel queue system assumes that all the servers can meet the needs of all the customers.

Arrivals, representing demand for the use of the facility, enter the system at a particular demand rate. If the service facility is already in use the arrival waits in a queue until capacity becomes available. Several factors determine the performance of a queuing system. The timing of customer arrivals into the system is usually assumed to occur randomly according to a probability distribution such as the Poisson distribution for arrival times and the exponential distribution for service times (Chase, Jacobs and Aquilano, 2005). A priority system may be used to select the next customer to receive service. In most systems the FCFS rule will apply. In some circumstances arrivals may not join the queue if it is too long when they arrive (**balking**), or they may wait for a time, become impatient and leave (**reneging**).

Queuing Theory Equations

There are several equations for different queuing structures but this text will consider the single server and multiple server models only (see Figure 11.7). The following assumptions are made when using the following queuing equations:

- Poisson distribution for arrival rate
- exponential distribution for service times
- first-come, first-served queue discipline
- no limit on queue length (no reneging)
- infinite population (arrival rate is not dependent on outside factors).

The main equations for a single server queue system are as follows:

The average number of customers waiting in the queue, $L_q = \lambda^2/(\mu(\mu - \lambda))$

The average time (in hours) that a customer spends in the queue, $W_q = \lambda/(\mu(\mu - \lambda))$

The probability that the server is busy (server utilization), $\rho = \lambda/\mu$

where

λ = average arrival rate of customers per hour

μ = average service rate of customers per hour,

WORKED EXAMPLE 11.2

Server Queue

A local shop has a single counter/till at which customers are served. Customers arrive at an average rate of 24 per hour according to a Poisson distribution and service times are exponentially distributed with an average rate of 20 customers per hour.

(a) What is the average number of customers waiting in the queue?

(b) What is the average time a customer spends in the queue?

(c) What is the probability that the till is busy?

Solution

$$\lambda = 20$$
$$\mu = 24$$

(a) $L_q = 20^2/(24 \times (24 - 20)) = 400/96 = 4.17$ customers

(b) $W_q = 20/(24 \times (24 - 20)) = 20/96 = 0.2$ hours

(c) $\rho = 20/24 = 0.83$

The main equations for a multiple server queue system are as follows:

The average number of customers waiting in the queue,

$$L_q = \frac{\lambda\mu(\lambda/\mu)^s}{(s - 1)!(s\mu - \lambda)^2} \times P_0$$

$$P_0 = 1\left/\left(\sum_{n=0}^{s-1} \frac{(\lambda/\mu)^n}{n!} + \frac{(\lambda/\mu)^s}{s!(1 - \lambda/s\mu)}\right)\right.$$

where

The average time (in hours) that a customer spends in the queue, $W_q = L_q/\lambda$

The probability that the server is busy (i.e. server utilization), $\rho = \lambda/s\mu$

where

λ = average arrival rate of customers per hour

μ = average service rate of customers per hour

s = number of servers.

P_0 is most easily found by using a lookup table of values of λ/μ and s (see for example Stevenson, 2011).

 www.wileyopenpage.com

Multiple Server Queue

Customers queue in a single line in a department store and are served at one of three tills on an FCFS basis. Customers arrive at a rate of 24 an hour (according to a Poisson distribution) and have a service time that is exponentially distributed with a mean rate of 10 customers served per hour.

    (a) What is the mean number of customers waiting in the queue?
    (b) What is the mean time a customer spends in the queue?
    (c) What is the probability that a till is busy?

Solution

$$\lambda = 24$$
$$\mu = 10$$
$$s = 3$$

P_0 has been given as 0.056

(a) $\dfrac{L_q = 24 \times 10 \times (24/10)^3}{(3-1)! \times (3 \times 10 - 24)^2} \times 0.056 = \left(\dfrac{3317.76}{72}\right) \times 0.056 = 2.58$ customers

(b) $W_q = \dfrac{L_q}{\lambda} = \dfrac{2.58}{24} = 0.1075$ hours

(c) $\rho = \dfrac{24}{(3 \times 10)} = 0.8$

The mathematical equations used in queuing theory make a number of assumptions about the system. They assume steady-state conditions have been reached – that the effects of an empty system start-up phase have been overcome and the system has reached a steady state. This may never happen if the mean arrival rate is greater than the service rate. Also the system may shut down for breaks during the day or may not run long enough to reach equilibrium. The equations can also only be used to describe very simple systems. Business process simulation (Chapter 8) is often used to analyse situations that do not fit adequately the assumed conditions of queuing theory.

The video 'Customer Queuing Systems' is available in your interactive e-book at **www.wileyopenpage.com**

The Psychology of Queues

Maister (1985) suggests that although queuing theory has been used successfully to analyse waiting times it does not take into account customer perception of the waiting time itself. Thus depending on the situation a customer may or may not feel that a wait time of 10 minutes is acceptable for instance.

CASE STUDY 11.1

Lloyds Cameras Cut Time in Queues

Lloyds TSB has been using special video cameras to cut the amount of time its customers are spending queuing in branches. The UK's fifth-largest bank has installed special video cameras in 30 of its branches to monitor customer behaviour and track how long people spend queuing. As a result, the amount of time customers wait to be served in these branches has fallen from 1.86 minutes in November 2004 to 1.46 minutes in March as the bank redeploys key staff at busy times of the day. The number of customers who are served within two minutes of walking into these branches has risen from 72.4% last November to about 82.6% in March. The average time each customer spends in front of a cashier has remained stable at just over 2.2 minutes. Lloyds TSB has identified queuing time as a major gripe amongst customers.

Graham Lindsay, director of the branch network at Lloyds TSB, said: 'We have done customer research and two minutes is generally the gratification threshold. Customers resent waiting five minutes or more. Levels of customer satisfaction in branches are closely connected to waiting times and efficiency of service.' The technology has been developed by Brickstream, the US technology company. There are no comparable figures available from rival banks on how long customers spend queuing. However, at Barclays' annual meeting last month, Roger Davis, head of retail banking, said queuing times had fallen to three minutes at Barclays branches.

Source: Financial Times (2005). Reproduced with permission.

Question

How has the use of video cameras enabled Lloyds to cut queue times in its bank branches?

Using the concepts of expectation and perception of service levels, Maister has developed a series of propositions about the **psychology of queues**, which can be used by service organizations to influence customer satisfaction with waiting times. The propositions are as follows:

- *Unoccupied time feels longer than occupied time.* The important point here is to try to ensure that unoccupied time is taken up with an activity that is seen as useful by the customer and is related in some way to the forthcoming service.
- *Pre-process waits feel longer than in-process waits.* It is important that human contact is made as soon as possible to convey that the service has started and reduce anxiety in the customer. For example, handing out the menu in a restaurant immediately customers arrive ensures that they do not feel they have been overlooked.
- *Anxiety makes waits seem longer.* A particular form of this is when parallel queues are used for a service. What usually happens is that the queue you choose to enter suddenly stops moving while the other queues progress rapidly! Many service organizations (such as post offices) have a single queue system, which seems fairer to customers and reduces anxiety by operating a strict FCFS policy.
- *Uncertain waits are longer than known, finite waits.* It is important to inform the customer how long the wait will be. A particular problem with appointment systems is that they create a specific

 www.wileyopenpage.com

expectation about when a service should begin and if appointments begin to run behind, anxiety increases as the expectation is not met.

- *Unexplained waits are longer than explained waits.* If the customer understands the reason for a wait they will be more satisfied than if no explanation or an explanation which does not provide sufficient justification is given.
- *Unfair waits are longer than equitable waits.* One of the most irritating occurrences for a customer is when someone who has arrived at a later time is served first. This can be eliminated by a single queue system that operates on an FCFS basis.
- *The more valuable the service, the longer the customer will wait.* If the service is seen to be of little value, the tolerance for waiting will diminish greatly. In particular post-process waits, when the required service is over, feel longer than in-process or even pre-process waits.
- *Solo waits feel longer than group waits.* When there is group interaction in a waiting line, perhaps initiated by an announcement of a delay, then waiting becomes more tolerable.

Although the FCFS queue discipline has been mentioned as a possible solution to some of the above problems, it cannot always be applied due to factors such as the implications for available space (for instance, for a supermarket customer using a trolley). The single queue also eliminates the possibility of providing custom service points for different customer types (such as a customer with few items in a supermarket or first-class customers for an airline). Overall the propositions show that in addition to the actual wait or queue time the context of the waiting line will have a significant effect on the level of customer satisfaction.

APPENDIX: FORECASTING

Introduction

Accurate forecasts are an important factor in enabling organizations to deliver goods and services to the customer when required and thus achieve a quality service. Forecasting is important in relation to anticipating changing customer requirements and meeting them with new product and service designs (Chapter 7). The ability to measure demand is also a key part of the facility design (Chapter 5) capacity management process (Chapter 11) and supply chain management (Chapter 15).

In order to produce accurate forecasts an organization must collect up-to-date data on relevant information such as prices and sales volumes and choose an appropriate forecasting technique. The accuracy of a forecast is also dependent on the time horizon over which the forecast is derived. Forecasts for short time horizons tend to be more accurate than for longer term forecasts, so one way of improving accuracy is shortening the lead time necessary for the organization to respond to a forecast. This might mean improving operations in terms of the flexibility performance objective.

Forecasting Techniques

Organizations must develop forecasts of the level of demand they should be prepared to meet. The forecast provides a basis for coordination of plans for activities in various parts of the organization, for example, personnel employ the right amount of people, purchasing order the right amount of material

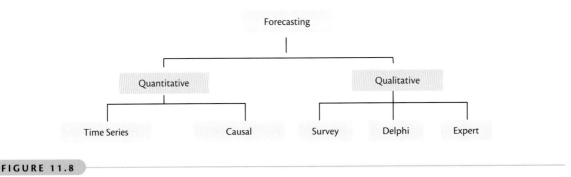

FIGURE 11.8

Forecasting Techniques.

and finance can estimate the capital required for the business. Forecasts can be developed either through a qualitative approach or a quantitative approach (Figure 11.8).

Qualitative Forecasting Methods

Qualitative forecasting methods take a subjective approach and are based on estimates and opinions. The following qualitative techniques will be described: market surveys, the Delphi method and expert judgement.

Market Surveys

A market survey collects data from a sample of customers, analyses the responses and makes inferences about the population from which the sample is drawn. They are particularly useful before the launch of a new product when there is limited information on potential customer demand. For the survey to be statistically valid it is necessary to ensure that a correct sampling methodology is used and that questions are pertinent and unbiased. Care must also be taken with the analysis of responses. Achieving useful results can be an expensive and time-consuming activity.

Delphi Study

This is a formal procedure that aims to bring together the opinions of a group of experts. A questionnaire is completed by a panel of experts. It is then analysed and summaries are passed back to the experts. Each expert in the group can then compare their forecast with the summarized reply of the others. This process is repeated, maybe up to six times, until a consensus has emerged within the group on which decision to take. The accuracy of the Delphi method can be good, but the cost and effort of its use may be relatively high.

Expert Judgement

This can take the form of an individual or group judgement. An individual judgement relies entirely on a single person's opinion of the situation – which includes both the knowledge and ignorance of the problem. The technique is unreliable and although it may give a good forecast, it can also give a very bad one.

A group judgement relies on a consensus being found among a group of people. If the difficulty of finding consensus can be overcome this is a more reliable method than an individual judgement. However, it is still relatively unreliable compared to more formal methods and is subject to group processes such as domination of the group by one person and the taking of risky decisions, which an individual would not take.

Quantitative Forecasting Methods

Quantitative forecasting methods use a mathematical expression or model to show the relationship between demand and some independent variable or variables. The model that is appropriate for forecasting depends on the demand pattern to be projected and the forecaster's objectives for the model.

Time Series Analysis

A time series is a set of observations measured at successive points in time. Time series analysis attempts to discover a pattern and extrapolate this pattern into the future. There are four components of a time series: trend, cyclical, seasonal and irregular.

- *Trend* – a gradual movement to relatively higher or lower values over time (not random fluctuations).
- *Cyclical* – any recurring sequence of points above and below the trend line lasting for more than one year.
- *Seasonal* – any regularly repeating pattern that is less than one year in duration.
- *Irregular* – deviations from the time series values from those expected by the trend, cyclical and seasonal components. We cannot attempt to predict its impact on the time series.

To analyse a time series smoothing methods can be used. Smoothing methods 'smooth out' the random fluctuations caused by the irregular component of the time series. They are only appropriate for a stable time series – one that does not exhibit trend, cyclical or seasonal effects. The moving averages and exponential smoothing methods are described.

Moving Averages

A moving average is a procedure in which, as each new observation becomes available, a new average can be computed by dropping the oldest observation and including the new one. This moving average will then be the forecast for the next period. For example, we might compute a three-week moving average at the end of each week to smooth out random fluctuations and obtain an estimate of the average sales per week. To compute a three-week moving average, at the end of each week we add sales for the latest three weeks and divide by 3. An example of a spreadsheet of a moving average forecast is given in Figure 11.9. An alternative approach is to use the Excel Analysis ToolPak, which has a moving average function.

Averaging multiple periods helps smooth out random fluctuations so that the forecast or average has more stability or does not fluctuate erratically. A moving average will gain stability if a greater number of periods are used in the average. If the number of periods in the average is too great, however, the average will be so stable that it will be slow to respond to nonrandom changes in the demand data. Responsiveness is the ability of a forecast to adjust quickly to true changes in the base level of demand. Both responsiveness and stability are difficult to achieve with a forecasting method that looks only at the series of past demands without considering factors that may have caused a change in that pattern without taking into consideration external causative factors.

FIGURE 11.9

Spreadsheet of a Moving Average Forecast.

Exponential Smoothing

In practice the technique of moving averages as a forecasting technique is not used often because the method of exponential smoothing is generally superior. The most recent observations will usually provide the best guide to the future, so the exponential smoothing procedure uses exponentially decreasing weights as the observations get older. This method keeps a running average of demand and adjusts it for each period in proportion to the difference between the latest actual demand figure and the latest value of the average. The equation is:

$$SF_{t+1} = SF_t + \alpha(A_t - SF_t)$$

where

SF_{t+1} = smoothed forecast for time period following t

SF_t = smoothed forecast for period t

α = smoothing constant that determines weight given to previous data

A_t = actual demand in period t.

The smoothing constant is a decimal between 0 and 1 where 0 is most stable and 1 is most responsive. Values between 0.1 and 0.3 are often used in practice. A large value of α gives very little smoothing,

	A	B	C	D	E	F	G	H	I
1	Sales Exponential Smoothing Calculation								
2									
3	Week	Sales	Exponential Smoothing Forecast (a=0.2)	Forecast Error	Squared Forecast Error				
4	1	51							
5	2	63	51.00	12.00	144.00		Cell	Formula	Copied to
6	3	57	53.40	3.60	12.96		c5	b4	
7	4	69	54.12	14.88	221.41		c6	E18*B5+(1-E18)*C5	c7:c16
8	5	54	57.10	-3.10	9.59		d5	b5-c5	d6:d15
9	6	48	56.48	-8.48	71.86		e5	d5*d5	e6:e15
10	7	60	54.78	5.22	27.23		d17	sum(d5:d15)	
11	8	54	55.83	-1.83	3.33		e17	sum(e5:e15)	
12	9	66	55.46	10.54	111.09		c18	e17/11	
13	10	60	57.57	2.43	5.91				
14	11	45	58.05	-13.05	170.42				
15	12	66	55.44	10.56	111.44				
16	13		57.55						
17			Totals	32.77	889.24				
18	Mean Squared Error =		80.84 alpha		0.2				

FIGURE 11.10

Spreadsheet of an Exponential Smoothing Forecast.

while a small value gives considerable smoothing/damping. For a time series with little random variability, larger values of α are better as they react quicker to changes. For a time series with large random variability, lower values of α are best so they do not overreact and adjust the forecasts too quickly. Figure 11.10 provides an example of a spreadsheet of an exponential smoothing forecast. An alternative approach is to use the Excel Analysis ToolPak, which has an exponential smoothing function.

The major advantages of the widely used smoothing methods described are their simplicity and low cost. More accuracy may be obtained with more sophisticated or decomposition methods. Smoothing methods are particularly appropriate for forecasts of thousands of items in inventory systems.

Time Series Decomposition

Often a pattern cannot be recognized in the raw data and so it must be decomposed into the four components of the time series (trend, seasonal, cyclical and random) that show a pattern that is helpful in projecting the data. Time series decomposition is appropriate if seasonal variation is evident in the demand pattern and the effect of seasonality is to be included in the forecast. The technique consists of smoothing past values to eliminate randomness so that the pattern can be projected into the future and used as a forecast. In many instances the patterns can be broken down (decomposed) into subpatterns that identify each component (for example, trend and seasonal) separately. Two common forms of the time series that can be used for decomposition are as follows:

$$\text{additive form } Y_t = T_t + S_t + I_t$$

$$\text{multiplicative form } Y_t = T_t \times S_t \times I_t$$

An additive model is appropriate if the magnitude of the seasonal fluctuation does not vary with the level of the series. Multiplicative decomposition is more prevalent with economic series because more seasonal economic series do have seasonal variation, which increases with the level of the series. Visual inspection of a plotted series is often used to determine the type of model that most appropriately represents the data. The steps involved in decomposing a series are to compute the seasonal indexes to deseasonalize the data and if a trend is apparent in the deseasonalized data then use regression analysis to estimate the trend.

To calculate the seasonal indexes a number of smoothing methods are available, the simplest being the moving average. To smooth a quarterly seasonal pattern we can use a four-period moving average. Assuming a multiplicative model, the moving average requires an odd number of observations to ensure the average is centred at the middle of the data values being averaged. For a four-period average the average for period 3 could be an average of periods 1–4 or 2–5 giving answers of 21.4 or 22.4. Thus we add another column, which is the average of the two successive values of the four-period average – the average of 21.4 and 22.4 = 21.9. The moving average graph smoothes out both the seasonal and irregular fluctuations in the time series. Divide the observation by the centred moving average to identify the seasonal-irregular effect in the time series.

The fluctuations over the three years can be assigned to the irregular influence, so we take an average value to compute the seasonal influence as below:

$$\text{Q1 S-I values} = 0.971, 0.918, 0.908 \text{ therefore,}$$

$$\text{seasonal index} = \frac{(0.971 + 0.918 + 0.908)}{3} = 0.93$$

$$\text{Q2 seasonal index} = 0.84$$

$$\text{Q3 seasonal index} = 1.09$$

$$\text{Q4 seasonal index} = 1.14$$

Thus the best sales are in Q4, 14% above average; the worst sales are in Q2, 16% below average.

For the multiplicative model, average seasonal indexes must equal 1.0 (average out over the year): $(0.93 + 0.84 + 1.09 + 1.14)/4 = 1.0$. In this case they do, otherwise adjust by multiplying each seasonal index by the number of seasons divided by the sum of the unadjusted seasonal indexes. In a multiplicative model we now divide each time series observation by the corresponding seasonal index. Thus in this case sales are divided by the seasonal index to get the deseasonalized sales figures (Figure 11.11).

To forecast sales a regression analysis can be undertaken using the Excel 'add trendline' function (see next section 'Causal Models'). There are many decomposition methods such as Census II and X-12-ARIMA but these work on the same principles as shown. In practice a straight-line trend model is rarely adequate. Decomposition is a useful tool for understanding the behaviour of a time series, before selection and application of a forecasting method.

FIGURE 11.11

Spreadsheet of Deseasonalized Sales.

Causal Models

Sometimes demand does not exhibit a consistent pattern over time because the level of one or more variables that have an effect on demand had changed during the period when the demand series was collected. Causal models are used to identify variables, or a combination of variables, which affect demand and are then used to predict future levels of demand. Models that may be used in this way include linear regression, curvilinear regression and multiple regression.

Regression methods are used when it is desirable to find an indicator that moves before the company's sales level changes (a leading indicator) and that has a significantly stable relationship with sales to be useful as a prediction tool. Linear regression is a means of finding and expressing a relationship. Regression analysis is the development of a mathematical equation that predicts the value of a dependent variable from single (simple regression) or multiple (multiple regression) independent variables. For example, sales (dependent) is related to advertising spend (independent). Note that, unlike using regression analysis for trend, project causal forecasting relates the forecasted variable to variables that are supposed to influence or explain that variable. It should be noted that causal forecasts are not necessarily time dependent. A model that relates inputs to outputs facilitates a better understanding of the situation and allows experimentation with different combinations of inputs to study their effects on the forecast (output). Thus the effect of decisions made today can be forecast in the future.

3. Interpret the results.

The results of the regression analysis are shown in Figure 11.13.

- The coefficient of determination (R^2) shows the proportion of the variation in Y that is explained by X. In this example $R^2 = 0.64$ which means 64% of total variation can be accounted for by the regression line.

- The coefficients of the regression equation are given as intercept (b_0) as 48 and the X variable 1 (b_1) as 8. Thus the relationship between the variables could be shown by the formula $Y = 8X + 48$. For example, for an advertising spend of 4.5, sales $= 8 \times 4.5 + 48 = 84$.

- The analysis does not provide evidence that one variable *causes* the other. For example, the advertising budget could be based on last year's sales.

Simple regression is a special case of multiple regression, which has two or more independent variables. The general form of multiple regression is:

$$Y = b_0 + b_1X_1 + b_2X_2 + \cdots + b_kX_k$$

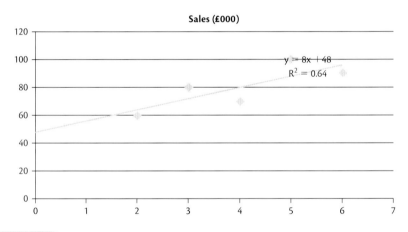

FIGURE 11.13

Regression Analysis.

Thus if sales were the variable to be forecast, several factors such as advertising, prices, competition, R&D budget and time could be tested for their influence on sales. The coefficients in multiple regression can be calculated using the least squares method as for simple regression.

Causal analysis allows the impact of decisions now to be forecast in the future. Correlation is not causation. For example, the number of cola cans sold and the number of deaths by drowning could be correlated, but the number of drowning events that occur does not cause the sales of cola to increase. A pair of variables may be correlated because they are both caused by a third 'lurking' variable – for example, in summer both drowning events and cola sales increase, thus temperature is a lurking variable.

www.wileyopenpage.com

SUMMARY

- The main elements in capacity planning decisions are the measurement of capacity and demand and the reconciling of the two to form a feasible plan.
- The product mix will affect the amount of capacity available as each product or service requires different amounts and different types of capacity at different times.
- A level capacity plan sets capacity at a uniform level throughout the planning period. A chase demand plan seeks to match production to demand over time. A demand management plan attempts to adjust demand to meet available capacity.
- Yield management is a collection of demand management approaches used to optimize the use of capacity in service operations where capacity is relatively fixed and the service cannot be stored in any way.
- Cumulative representations can be used to evaluate a level capacity planning approach by keeping a running total of inventory levels to ensure no stock-outs occur.
- Queuing theory can provide a useful guide in determining expected waiting time for an arriving customer by using statistical distributions of customer arrivals and service times.
- Propositions about the psychology of queues can be used by service organizations to influence customer satisfaction with waiting times.
- Qualitative forecasting techniques include market surveys, Delphi studies and expert judgement. Quantitative methods include time series and causal models.

CASE STUDY 11.2

Queuing Theory

The debacle over the availability of tickets for the football World Cup in France in 1998 could have put lives in danger. English football fans, left hanging on the telephone while happy Frenchmen rejoiced over their tickets, felt the same sense of angry injustice that can lead to violent 'road rage' attacks, says the world's leading expert on queuing theory. Richard Larson of the Massachusetts Institute of Technology told a conference in Montreal that road rage and related phenomena are an urgent new area for research. An electrical engineer by training, Larson is the leading exponent of a branch of science known as operations research. Operations research keeps the world moving and happy by employing science, maths and computer modelling to overcome the logistical and technical challenges associated with efficiently shifting people, commodities and information around the world.

Larson, who is known in his field as Dr Queue, acts as a consultant to major multinational companies and government agencies – satisfied customers include Coca-Cola, American Airlines, United Artists Cinemas and the US Department of Justice. Badly managed queues, he says, can tap into a reservoir of anger, hostility and frustration. He cites a new phenomenon: store rage. A fortnight ago, a woman had half her nose cut off by the woman behind her at the express checkout queue of a Milwaukee supermarket – her basket contained more than the permitted 12 items and she had refused to change queues.

Operations researchers manage queues in areas as diverse as air traffic control systems, passenger reservations and parcel delivery. 'There are billions of possibilities for this type of operation', says Larson. 'These things are too complex for any human mind – you need to employ mathematical modelling, observation, data analysis and computer science.' But, he admits, the most useful tool is still common sense: 'You need to formulate the problem correctly – if you get that wrong it doesn't matter how sophisticated the maths is.' His skill in combining common sense and computer modelling techniques was responsible for saving lives well before the advent of road rage. In the 1970s he pioneered a computer program for finding the most efficient distribution of fire and ambulance crews throughout a city. It has been widely employed throughout the US and Europe. The latest development – the Trauma Resource Allocation Model for Ambulances and Hospitals (Tramah) – was presented at the conference this week and showed how the right distribution of available resources can give a near-perfect emergency response. Using the 27 000 emergency cases in the state of Maryland between 1992 and 1994 as a model, researchers simulated various combinations of positions for trauma centres and helicopters. During this period, 95% of severely injured residents had received access to trauma system resources within 30 minutes and 70% had access within 15 minutes. Using the same amount of resources, but changing their locations, the Tramah program simulated access within 30 minutes for 99.97% of cases. They also found that taxpayers' money could be saved by cutting some helicopter depots and strategically placing the others – without losing any emergency response capability.

But Tramah's developers are aware that scientific advice doesn't always get acted on – local history and political expediency are often much more persuasive in the allocation of emergency resources. 'There will be some rural communities that spent 10 years selling brownies so they could buy a helicopter – there's no changing the location of that facility', says Charles Branas, who presented the report. Healthcare managers may not listen to the voice of reason, but in the airline industry the sound of ringing cash tills always catches the ear. United Airlines revealed at the conference that a computer program developed by their operations research office had saved the company $60 million in the past year. One hour before United's planes take off, the program analyses the latest weather reports and composes a flight plan that uses current wind conditions to the plane's advantage. 'There are millions of possible flight paths for flying from A to B – we came up with an algorithm that searches all those options and gives us the best one', says Bob Bongiorno, the head of United Airlines' operations research department. 'It has saved us a huge amount in fuel costs and pilot time and shaved minutes off our flight times.'

According to Larson, queue management is easiest to implement in Britain and northern Europe, where there is an acknowledgement of the role of courtesy and 'first come, first served'. He told delegates to the conference that the best advice for avoiding road rage was to be found in a British driving manual. 'Wherever there's merging traffic, follow the rule: 'let one in and go' – this is the behaviour of fair standing queues and it seems to be the rule of the road in the UK', he said. Larson has not been to the UK since the 1970s – delegates with more recent experience of British driving no doubt took his observations with a pinch of salt.

Question

Discuss the contribution of queuing theory and the psychology of queuing to queue management.

Glastonbury

Glastonbury Festival is the largest outdoor, arts and music festival in the world. It is located on the farm of the Eavis family having grown from a small concert to a major event, which has now been running for over 40 years. The Festival takes place in a, normally rather, tranquil location, more suited to milking parlours than a rock festival. Using the existing farm and renting additional fields, the festival site covers more than a mile and a half across, with a perimeter of about eight and a half miles.

The concert goers descend on the area most years for Wednesday lunch time until Monday evening around the last weekend in June. There have been a number of 'rest' years in the concert's history, 2012 was a notable break – the London Olympics placed too heavy a constraint on every resource from policing to port-a-loos.

Festival attendees travel to the site in a variety of forms; many drive their cars and park in local facilities offered, some use the park and ride option and other use public transport. The local council and police force have a number of constraints set upon the organisers; an increase of 22 500 additional tickets were only to be sold on the condition they are sold in conjunction with coach travel to and from the event.

The festival site itself is quite diverse; appealing to a wide range of ages and tastes, there are areas set aside for families as well as the more party focussed guest. Most festival goers will camp onsite, there is local bed and breakfast accommodation, but most of this is not within walking distance of the festival. Varieties in accommodation styles have been introduced in recent years; the addition of pre-pitched and furnished yurts,

it is now possible to go 'glamping' at Glastonbury. Therefore with such an expanding range of potential customers, demand for festival tickets has grown over the years.

In an attempt to scupper ticket touts, all those wanting to buy tickets have to pre-register their interest online, pay a deposit and upload their photograph, before the time of ticket release, almost half a million people pre-registered for tickets.

Despite an increase the number of tickets available from 150 000 to 177 500, Glastonbury festival 2013 sold out in a record 100 minutes from going on sale.

Sources

http://www.channel5.com/shows/ok-tv-2/clips/glamping-at-glastonbury

http://www.bbc.co.uk/news/entertainment-arts-19861686

http://www.tntmagazine.com/news/world/glastonbury-festival-tickets-sale-date-and-price-revealed-start-saving-pennies

http://www.glastonburyfestivals.co.uk/

Source: Written by Briony Boydell and Chris Milner. Reproduced with permission.

Questions

1. What are Glastonbury Festival's capacity constrains?
2. How does pre-registering help?
3. What external factors may affect demand for the festival?

CHAPTER 12

Inventory Management

- **Introduction**
- **Types of inventory**
- **Managing inventory**
- **The ABC inventory classification system**
- **Inventory models**
- **Implementing inventory systems**

LEARNING OBJECTIVES

- Describe the different types of inventory.
- Discuss the purpose of the ABC inventory classification system.
- Discuss the role of the reorder point inventory model.
- Discuss the purpose of the EOQ model.
- Discuss the purpose of the FOI model.
- Understand the issues involved in implementing inventory systems.

INVENTORY MANAGEMENT AND OPERATIONS STRATEGY

Although inventory management is often seen as an operational issue it is important at a strategic level in that it may account for a far larger proportion of expenditure than may be allocated to other areas such as labour costs. This situation has occurred in part because of the view that in accounting terms expenditure tied up in inventory is treated as an asset. However, Japanese manufacturers demonstrated that it is in fact a liability in that it represents capital that could be used for other investments. Thus in strategic terms inventory is now seen as a tool in meeting operations performance objectives such as cost in addition to its role in lean operations in meeting speed and flexibility objectives.

In terms of inventory management policies it is now recognized that the Economic Order Quantity (EOQ) approach does not provide a mechanism to achieve a strategic advantage in terms of responsiveness to customer demands. EOQ simply provides a tactical approach to acquiring inventory to minimize ordering and holding costs without taking into account the complexity and changing nature of inventory requirements. More sophisticated and strategic approaches have been the implementation of ERP systems (Chapter 14) for medium to long-term materials management and lean operations (Chapter 13) for short-term management of inventory and relationships with suppliers.

INTRODUCTION

Inventory is present in all service and manufacturing processes. In manufacturing inventory consists of the components that go to make up the product being manufactured. In services inventory may be used as part of the service delivery system (for example disposable implements for a hospital operation) or it may be part of the tangible component of the service itself (for example, the brochure for a car insurance policy). Inventory is important because although it is necessary for customer service it can also be a major cost to the organization. It has been estimated that a typical firm has about 30% of its current assets and perhaps as much as 90% of its working capital invested in inventory (Stevenson, 2009). Apart from the cost of inventory the use of excessive inventory can lead to other issues such as the disruption of workflow and hiding problems related to product quality and equipment breakdown. Addressing these issues is the focus of the concept of JIT and lean operations covered in Chapter 13.

Inventory management can be considered part of materials management in a service or manufacturing organization. Materials management includes the acquiring of inventory (see procurement section in Chapter 15), the organization of the movement of inventory (see physical distribution management section in Chapter 15) and the assessment of when inventory should be ordered and the amount of inventory that should be ordered, covered in this chapter. Inventory management systems calculate the volume and timing of independent demand items. Independent demand is when demand is not directly related to the demand for any other inventory item. Usually this demand comes from customers outside the company and so is not as predictable as dependent demand (the management of dependent demand items is covered in Chapter 14).

TYPES OF INVENTORY

All organizations will carry some inventory or stock of goods at any one time. This can range from items such as stationery to machinery parts or raw materials. Generally inventory is classified by its location or type.

FIGURE 12.1
Inventory Classified by Location.

Inventory Classified by Location

Inventory can be classified by location as raw materials (goods received from suppliers), work-in-progress (at some point within the operations process) or finished goods (goods ready for dispatch to the customer) (Figure 12.1).

The proportions between these inventory types will vary but it is estimated that generally 30% are raw materials, 40% are work-in-progress and 30% finished goods. Waters (2002) indicates the arbitrary nature of these classifications as someone's finished goods are someone else's raw materials.

Raw materials inventory may be supplied in batches to secure quantity discounts and reduce material handling. However, smaller and more frequent order quantities translate into less inventory and may be achieved by negotiating smaller batches from suppliers. Variability in supplier lead times may be reduced by specifying longer but more reliable lead times from suppliers.

Work-in-progress inventory may help uncouple production stages and provide greater flexibility in production scheduling. It can be minimized by eliminating obsolete stock, improving the operation's processes and reducing the number of products or services.

Finished goods inventory may be used to ensure that important inventory items are always available to the customer or to avoid disruption caused by changing production output levels. It can be minimized by improving forecasts of customer demand and reducing fluctuations in demand caused by factors such as meeting end-of-period sales targets.

Inventory Classified by Type

The type of inventory can also be used to provide a method of identifying why inventory is being held and so suggest policies for reducing its level. Inventory types include:

- *Buffer/safety.* This is used to compensate for the uncertainties inherent in the timing or rate of supply and demand between two operational stages. Safety stock is often used to compensate for uncertainties in the timing of supplies from suppliers. It is also used to compensate for uncertainties in supply between operational stages in a process due to factors such as equipment breakdowns. Safety stock can be minimized by reducing the time delay between ordering and receiving goods. This in turn can be achieved by minimizing supply mismatches by increasing visibility of demand to suppliers, improving demand forecasts and cutting the lead time of bought-in items by using local suppliers for example.

- *Cycle*. If it is required to produce multiple products from one operation in batches, there is a need to produce enough to keep a supply while the other batches are being produced. This is an example of how differences between the timing of supply and demand can lead to high levels of work-in-progress inventory. Cycle inventory can be reduced by reducing the batch size which in turn will depend on reducing setup/changeover times between batches.
- *Decoupling*. This permits stages in the manufacturing process to be managed and their performance measured independently, to run at their own speed and not match the rate of processing of departments at different points in the process. Decoupling inventory can be reduced by balancing the processing rates of the different departments.
- *Anticipation*. This includes producing to stock to anticipate an increase in demand due to seasonal factors. Also speculative policies such as buying in bulk to take advantage of price discounts may also increase inventory levels. Accurate forecasting can help reduce anticipation inventory by matching supply with demand. Bulk buying policies will need to take into account the full cost of storing inventory.
- *Pipeline/movement*. This is the inventory needed to compensate for the lack of stock while material is being transported between stages. For example, the distribution time from the warehouse to a retail outlet. Thus pipeline inventory may be the result of delays in the supply chain between customer and supplier. Pipeline inventory is the result of the demand during the lead time so the main way to reduce pipeline inventory is to reduce the lead time delay itself. This may be done by finding a more responsive alternative supplier for example.

Most organizations have a large amount of different types of inventory under their control and operations managers need to assess how they ensure that materials are available when needed, but inventory costs are not too high. Holding inventory reduces the risk of having no stock and can also reduce ordering costs by ordering larger, but fewer batches of materials, reducing stock-out costs by ensuring disruption to the manufacturing or service delivery system is avoided and reducing acquisition costs by securing quantity discounts. However, these costs need to be set against the costs of holding high levels of inventory. These include the cost of storing and handling inventory items, the lack of responsiveness to customer demands because of the large work-in-progress inventories, the increase in lead times due to inventory queuing, the use of inventory to provide a safety net to unreliable processes that need improving and the capital investment in inventory that will not be used for some time. These issues are explored further in Chapter 13.

The risk of having no stock is particularly important in service systems where the customer expects the immediate consumption of the service and its associated good. For example, in a restaurant, customers will be dissatisfied if certain options are not available on the menu due to lack of produce. More importantly, hospitals need to ensure that inventory such as drugs are always available for patients.

 The video 'How to Make Your Inventory Safe and Smart' is available in your interactive e-book at **www.wileyopenpage.com**

CASE STUDY 12.1

Pandora: Box is wide open

Inflate a balloon, attach a lead weight, observe result. Investors in Pandora may feel they are part of just that experiment after the 65 per cent free-fall in the Danish jewellery company's share price on Tuesday. Having trumpeted revenue growth predictions of 30 per cent at last October's initial public offering, its market value, which once topped €8bn, has now suffered an 86% fall. Tuesday's second-quarter results deflated all optimism. Adjusted for one-offs, profits fell 18 per cent and revenue growth forecasts were slashed to zero. The chief executive had no option but to resign.

Pandora's problems appear to lie in executing its business model. It essentially copies the approach championed by Gillette – which sells razors cheaply and then charges a fat margin for blades which only fit that razor. Pandora sells its bracelets (relatively) cheaply and then makes its money – 70 per cent of revenues – from the customised charms.

The trouble is price. Some of the charms cost more than $800 each. Pandora assumed it could keep raising its prices above the already cantering costs of precious metals and still retain customers.

That proved wildly arrogant. Add poor inventory management – stock levels as a proportion of sales have risen by one-third in the past year – and Pandora's box is wide open.

There are no easy solutions. Although sales of charms grew 4 per cent in the second quarter, the more important forward metric is sales of bracelets, which fell 15 per cent. Although the bracelets only generate 10 per cent of the company's sales, fewer bracelets sales now means fewer charm sales in the future.

Pandora's private equity promoter Axcel, which cashed out part of its share in the IPO, has questions to answer about how it went so wrong so suddenly. So do the 12 research analysts who cover the company; 10 buys, 2 holds, all wrong.

Source: Financial Times (2012). Reproduced with permission.

Question

Suggest reasons for the poor inventory management performance indicated in the case study and discuss how it could be improved.

MANAGING INVENTORY

One of the major issues in inventory management is the level of decentralization required in inventory distribution. Decentralized facilities offer a service closer to the customer and thus should provide a better service level in terms of knowledge of customer needs and speed of service. Centralization, however, offers the potential for less handling of goods between service points, less control costs and less overall inventory levels due to lower overall buffer levels required. The square-root law (Maister, 1975) states that a firm currently operating out of five warehouses, which centralizes to one warehouse, can theoretically reduce inventory carried in stock by 55%. The overall demand pattern for a centralized facility will be an average of the variable demand patterns from a number of customers. This will decrease demand variability and thus require lower buffer stocks. Thus there is a trade-off between the customer service levels or effectiveness offered by a decentralized system and the lower costs or efficiency offered by a centralized system. One way of combining the advantages of a centralized facility with a high level of customer service is to reduce the delivery lead time between the centralized distribution centre and the customer outlet. This issue is discussed in more detail in the warehousing section of Chapter 15.

CASE STUDY 12.2

Retail: Knowing your stock is the key to a busy shop

What do shoppers hate? A long search for the item they came in for followed by a lengthy queue at the till.

Mobile technologies mean that retailers can tackle these problems, in the hope of increasing sales and making the shopper more likely to return.

Handheld devices have long been used to ensure that warehouses and distribution centres can handle large volumes of incoming and outgoing stock.

More recently, they have made inroads into inventory management in shops themselves. The arrival of the iPad and other tablet devices has given a boost to their use by store staff to communicate directly with customers.

'The customer wants to navigate the store and complete the transaction quickly, while the retailer needs to take unnecessary cost out of the process,' explains Ian Snadden, European vice-president at Intermec, which supplies wired and wireless data collection systems.

While other sectors have cut spending in the recession, retailers have continued to invest in customer-facing technology, he notes.

'The biggest single problem facing retailers is the accuracy of their stock file,' says Alan Braithwaite, chairman of LCP Consulting and a visiting professor at Cranfield School of Management.

'You might think you have got something, but in fact someone has stolen it or it is not in the right place. It is all about giving the customer accurate feedback.' For every extra percentage point of product availability, a store will increase sales by 0.2 to 0.6 per cent, he says.

The range of products in many stores and rapid staff turnover, which means assistants often lack detailed product knowledge, puts a premium on mobile devices that can be used to see what is in stock.

What customers should increasingly notice when they enter a shop, is a sales assistant with a handheld device who intercepts them before they reach the counter to take and process their order. Retailers such as Apple and the Starbucks coffee chain have roaming sales staff who act as 'queue busters.'

To help it cope with the pre-Christmas rush, Hamleys, the UK toy shop, issued staff in its main London store with an iPad, a handheld Bluetooth scanner, a wireless Pin entry device and a wireless printer.

Worn in a belt round the assistant's waist, these devices allowed staff to move through the store, handling transactions at the display where the customer had seen what they wanted.

As well as helping the sales assistant locate what the customer is looking for, handheld devices allow them to show similar items, possibly prompting a more expensive or multiple purchase in additional styles or colours.

Retailers and distribution centres have long used rugged handheld devices made by manufacturers such as Psion and Motorola, but the launch of the iPad and other tablets has created a device that is both fashionable and familiar to many shoppers.

Unfortunately, these tablets do not connect with the Windows operating system used in back office enterprise resource planning (ERP) systems.

'All kinds of devices that work with Windows integrate with the back office,' says Peter Chadha, chief executive of DrPete, a technology consultancy. 'But iPads have been an issue. They don't run on Windows, so how do they integrate? This has held us back from using these devices, although that will change.'

Windows 8, the next version of Microsoft's operating system, will support the ARM low-energy microprocessors used in many mobile devices, as well as Intel. Windows 8 is also expected to have such features as a touch screen facility.

Enabling tablets to talk to in-store inventory systems is expected to give a big boost to their use. 'People love Apple,' says Mr Chadha. 'The iPad is very attractive to use in retail. It is sexy, has a long battery life and is reasonably robust. The customer and the sales person can work on it together.'

Tablets are expected to prove popular in upmarket retailing, including clothes and footwear, says Mim Burt, research director in the retail team at Gartner, the IT consultancy. But they are expensive and not rugged enough for all settings. 'In a high-volume grocery environment, you would have bog-standard, simple stock management hand-helds,' she says.

But whether retailers opt for a basic handheld device or an upmarket tablet, they should not allow themselves to be mesmerised by technology.

Offered a choice of dealing with a sales assistant, using their own mobile or an in-store screen to answer a query, even young people preferred to deal with a 'real person', found a recent Gartner survey.

'It is a fallacy to say young people want to do everything on their mobile,' says Ms Burt.

Source: Financial Times (2012). Reproduced with permission.

Question

Discuss how technology can help manage inventory in retail outlets.

THE ABC INVENTORY CLASSIFICATION SYSTEM

One way of deciding the importance of inventory items and thus an appropriate inventory management method for them is to use the **ABC classification system**. Depending on the classification of the inventory a fixed order quantity or fixed order period inventory system can be chosen for managing that system.

The ABC classification system sorts inventory items into groups depending on the amount of annual expenditure they incur which will depend on the estimated number of items used annually multiplied by the unit cost. To instigate an ABC system a table is produced listing the items in expenditure order (with largest expenditure at the top), and showing the percentage of total expenditure and cumulative percentage of the total expenditure for each item (Table 12.1).

By reading the cumulative percentage figure it is usually found, following Pareto's law, that 10 to 20% of the items account for 60 to 80% of annual expenditure. These items are called A items and need to be controlled closely to reduce overall expenditure. Forecasting techniques may be used to improve the accuracy of demand forecasts for these items. It may also require a more strategic approach to management of these items, which may translate into closer buyer-supplier relationships. A items may be

TABLE 12.1

Example of an ABC Classification Table.

Item	Annual expenditure (cost × usage) £000s	Percentage expenditure (%)	Cumulative expenditure (%)
D-76	800	24.1	24.1
A-25	650	19.6	43.7
C-40	475	14.3	58.1
C-22	450	13.6	71.6
B-18	300	9.0	80.7
G-44	200	8.0	86.7
A-42	150	5.4	91.3
D-21	100	3.0	94.3
H-67	75	2.3	96.5
E-88	65	2.0	98.5
F-23	50	1.5	100.0
TOTAL	3315		

managed using a fixed order quantity system with perpetual inventory checks or a fixed order interval system employing a small time interval between review periods.

The B items account for the next 20 to 30% of items and usually account for a similar percentage of total expenditure. These items require fewer inventory level reviews than A items. A fixed order interval system with a minimum order level or a fixed order quantity system may be appropriate.

Finally C items represent the remaining 50 to 70% of items but only account for less than 25% of total expenditure. Here a fixed order quantity system may be appropriate or less rigorous inventory control methods can be used, as the cost of inventory tracking will outweigh the cost of holding additional stock. It is important to recognize that overall expenditure may not be the only appropriate basis on which to classify items. Other factors include the importance of a component part on the overall product, the variability in delivery time, the loss of value through deterioration and the disruption caused to the production process if a stock-out occurs. The fixed order quantity and fixed order interval systems for inventory management are now described.

INVENTORY MODELS

Inventory models are used to assess when inventory requires ordering and what quantity should be ordered at that point in time. In a fixed order quantity inventory system, inventory is ordered in response to some event, such as inventory falling to a particular level. The timing of the inventory order can be calculated using a reorder point (ROP) model. The quantity to order at this point in time may be calculated using the economic order quantity (EOQ) model. In a fixed order period inventory system, inventory is ordered at a fixed point in time (say once a month). A fixed order inventory (FOI) model can be used to determine the quantity to order at this point in time. Although these models are used in organizations they are essentially tactical (for example, the use of EOQ to minimize ordering and holding costs) and so do not always fit well with a strategic approach to operations as has been outlined in Chapter 2.

Fixed Order Quantity Inventory Systems

In **fixed order quantity inventory systems** the order quantity is the same each time the order is placed, but the time between orders varies according to the rate of use of the inventory item. When the inventory level has reduced to a certain amount, termed the reorder point, an order for further inventory is made. The reorder point can be calculated by the use of a computer system that can also automate the ordering process. An alternative is the two-bin system. Here inventory is held in two containers, termed 'bins'. When one bin is empty a replenishment order is made and inventory is taken from the other bin until the order arrives. These systems are termed 'perpetual systems' to indicate that the inventory record of the amount of inventory is updated as inventory is used and replenished.

Some systems for less important items only check inventory levels at certain intervals (say once a week or once a month). When using a fixed order quantity system the point in time when an order should be placed can be determined using the reorder point or ROP model and the quantity to order at this time can be determined by the economic order quantity (EOQ) model. These inventory models are now described.

The Reorder Point (ROP) Model

The **reorder point model** identifies the time to order when the stock level drops to a predetermined amount. This amount will usually include a quantity of stock to cover for the delay between order and delivery (the delivery lead time) and an element of stock to reduce the risk of running out of stock when levels are low (the safety stock).

Safety stock is used in order to prevent a stock-out occurring. It provides an extra level of inventory above that needed to meet predicted demand, to cope with variations in demand over a time period. The level of safety stock used, if any, will vary for each inventory cycle but an average stock level above that needed to meet demand will be calculated. To calculate the safety stock level a number of factors should be taken into account including:

- cost due to stock-out
- cost of holding safety stock
- variability in rate of demand
- variability in delivery lead time.

It is important to note that there is no stock-out risk between the maximum inventory level and the reorder level. The risk occurs due to variability in the rate of demand and due to variability in the delivery lead time between the reorder point and zero stock level.

The reorder level can, of course, be estimated by a rule of thumb, such as when stocks are at twice the expected level of demand during the delivery lead time. However, to consider the probability of stock-out, cost of inventory and cost of stock-out the idea of a service level is used.

The service level is a measure of the level of service, or how sure the organization is that it can supply inventory from stock. This can be expressed as the probability that the inventory on hand during the lead time is sufficient to meet expected demand (for example, a service level of 90% means that there is a 0.90 probability that demand will be met during the lead time period and the probability that a stock-out will occur is 10%). The service level set is dependent on a number of factors such as stockholding costs for the extra safety stock and the loss of sales if demand cannot be met.

The reorder problem is one of determining the level of safety stock that balances the expected holding costs with the costs of stock-out. Equations will be derived for the following four scenarios of constant demand and constant lead time, variable demand and constant lead time, constant demand and variable lead time and variable demand and variable lead time.

1. Constant Demand and Constant Lead Time

Assuming that the delivery lead time and demand rate are constant there is no risk of stock-out, so no safety stock is required.

$$\text{reorder point (units)} = d \times LT$$

where
  d = daily demand
  LT = lead time

WORKED EXAMPLE 12.1

Constant Demand and Constant Lead Time ROP Model

A company has a demand for an item at a constant of 50 per week. The order delivery lead time is also constant at three weeks. What should the reorder point be?

Solution

  $d = 50, LT = 3$
  reorder point = $d \times LT = 3 \times 50 = 150$ units.

2. Variable Demand and Constant Lead Time

This model assumes that demand during the delivery lead time consists of a series of independent daily demands and thus can be described by a normal distribution. The average daily demand rate and its standard deviation (measure of variability) are used to determine the expected demand and standard deviation of demand for the lead time period. Thus the reorder point is:

$$\text{reorder point (ROP)} = \text{expected demand during lead time} + \text{safety stock}$$
$$= \bar{d} \times LT + z \times \sqrt{LT} \times \sigma_d$$

where
  $\bar{d}$ = average demand rate
  LT = delivery lead time
  σ_d = standard deviation of demand rate
  z = number of standard deviations from the mean.

Variable Demand and Constant Lead Time ROP Model

An office supply company sells paper with a variable demand, which can be assumed to be normally distributed with an average of 800 boxes per week and a standard deviation of 250 boxes per week. The delivery lead time has been very consistent at three weeks. Determine the recommended reorder level if there is to be no more than a 1% chance that a stock-out will occur in any one replenishment period.

Solution

$$\bar{d} = 800/\text{week}$$
$$\sigma_d = 250/\text{week}.$$
$$LT = 3$$

At 1% service level, $z = 2.33$ (from normal distribution table)

$$
\begin{aligned}
ROP &= \bar{d} \times LT + z \times \sqrt{LT} \times \sigma_d \\
&= 800 \times 3 + 2.33 \times \sqrt{3} \times 250 \\
&= 2400 + 2.33 \times 433 \\
&= 3409 \text{ units}
\end{aligned}
$$

3. Constant Demand and Variable Lead Time

Here the lead time variation is described by a normal distribution and thus the expected lead time is normally distributed. Thus the reorder point is:

$$\text{reorder point (ROP)} = \text{expected demand during lead time} + \text{safety stock}$$
$$= d \times \overline{LT} + z \times d \times \sigma_{LT}$$

where

$$d = \text{constant demand rate}$$
$$\overline{LT} = \text{average lead time}$$
$$\sigma_{LT} = \text{standard deviation of lead time}$$
$$z = \text{number of standard deviations from the mean.}$$

4. Variable Demand Rate and Variable Lead Time

When both demand rate and lead time are variable, the expected demand during lead time is the average daily demand multiplied by average lead time. Both daily demand and lead time are assumed to be normally distributed.

$$\text{reorder point (ROP)} = \text{expected demand during lead time} + \text{safety stock}$$
$$= \bar{d} \times \overline{LT} + z \times \sqrt{\overline{LT} \times \sigma_d^2 + \bar{d}^2 \times \sigma_{LT}^2}$$

www.wileyopenpage.com

The Economic Order Quantity (EOQ) Model

The **economic order quantity (EOQ) model** calculates the fixed inventory order volume required while seeking to minimize the sum of the annual costs of holding inventory and the annual costs of ordering inventory. The model makes a number of assumptions including:

- Stable or constant demand.
- Fixed and identifiable ordering cost.
- The relationship between the cost of holding inventory and number of items held is linear.
- The item cost does not vary with the order size.
- Delivery lead time does not vary.
- No quantity discounts are available.
- Annual demand exists.

Brown, Lamming, Bessant and Jones (2005) are critical of the EOQ method because an approach of ordering a fixed quantity per order item is not seen as relevant in a complex and dynamic market. The assumption of one delivery per order, and then the use of that stock over time increases inventory levels and does not fit with the JIT approach. Annual demand will also not exist for products with a life cycle of less than a year. Another assumption made is that ordering costs are constant with no account taken of the method of ordering (for example email, fax, phone), the time spent placing the order, or the staffing costs of the person placing the order. However, the EOQ and other approaches in this chapter still have a role in inventory management in the right circumstances if their limitations are recognized.

Before the EOQ model is introduced it is useful to know that texts use a number of words to describe the cost of holding inventory and the cost of replacing that inventory. These include:

Inventory held	Inventory replaced
Holding cost	Order cost
Carrying cost	Replenishment cost
Storage cost	Delivery cost

Each order is assumed to be of Q units and is withdrawn at a constant rate over time until the quantity in stock is just sufficient to satisfy the demand during the order lead time (the time between placing an order and receiving the delivery). At this time an order for Q units is placed with the supplier. Assuming that the usage rate and lead time are constant the order will arrive when the stock level is at zero, thus eliminating excess stock or stock-outs. The order quantity must be set at a level which is not too small, leading to many orders and thus high order costs, but not too large leading to high average levels of inventory and thus high holding costs.

The annual holding cost is the average number of items in stock multiplied by the cost to hold an item for a year. If the amount in stock decreases at a constant rate from Q to 0 then the average in stock is Q/2 (Figure 12.2).

Thus if C_H is the average annual holding cost per unit, the total annual holding cost is:

$$\text{Annual Holding Cost} = \frac{Q}{2} \times C_H$$

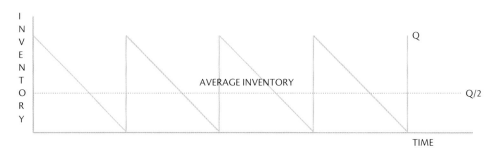

FIGURE 12.2

Inventory Level versus Time for the EOQ Model.

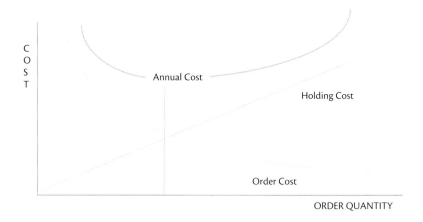

FIGURE 12.3

Inventory Cost versus Order Quantity for the EOQ Model.

The annual ordering cost is a function of the number of orders per year and the ordering cost per order. If D is the annual demand, then the number of orders per year is given by D/Q. Thus if CO is the ordering cost per order then the total annual ordering cost is:

$$\text{Annual Ordering Cost} = \frac{D}{Q} \times C_O$$

Thus the total annual inventory cost is the sum of the total annual holding cost and the total annual ordering cost.

$$\text{Total Annual Cost} = \frac{Q}{2} \times C_H + \frac{D}{Q} \times C_O$$

where

Q = order quantity
C_H = holding cost per unit
d = annual demand
C_O = ordering cost per order.

The total cost and its components of ordering and holding cost are shown graphically in Figure 12.3.

 www.wileyopenpage.com

From the graph it can be seen that the minimum total cost point is when the holding cost is equal to the ordering cost. Note, however, that in practice the actual order size may differ considerably from the calculated EOQ without major effects on total costs.

Mathematically, when holding costs = ordering costs:

$$\frac{Q}{2} \times C_H = \frac{D}{Q} \times C_O$$

Solving for Q gives

$$EOQ = \sqrt{\frac{2 \times D \times C_O}{C_H}}$$

The EOQ formula can also be used to calculate the optimum size of a batch to be manufactured.

$$EBS = \sqrt{\frac{2 \times S \times C_O}{C_H}}$$

where

EBS = economic batch size,
C_H = holding cost per unit,
S = cost per batch,
C_O = ordering cost per order.

In addition to the criticisms of the EOQ calculation, the calculation of the 'economic' batch size does not conform to the JIT aim of minimizing setup times in order to increase flexibility.

WORKED EXAMPLE 12.3

Economic Order Quantity Model

The annual demand for a company's single item of stock is 1000 units. It costs the company £6 to hold one unit of stock for one year. Each time that a replenishment order is made the company incurs a fixed cost of £75.

1. Determine the economic order quantity.

   Suppose that the company's supplier of stock introduces a condition that normally there shall be no more than five orders for replenishment per annum.

2. How much would the company be prepared to pay in order to avoid having to meet this condition?

Solution

1. D = 1000, C_H = 6, C_O = 75

$$EOQ = \sqrt{\frac{2 \times D \times C_O}{C_H}} = \sqrt{\frac{2 \times 1000 \times 75}{6}} = \sqrt{25\,000} = 158 \text{ units.}$$

2. Total cost at five orders per annum

Therefore 1000/5 = 200 units delivered at one time.

$$\text{Total Annual Cost} = \frac{Q}{2} \times C_H + \frac{D}{Q} \times C_O$$

Total Annual Cost = 200/2 × 6 + 1000/200 × 75 = 600 + 375 = £975

Total Annual Cost at EOQ = 158/2 × 6 + 1000/158 × 75 = 474 + 474 = £948

Therefore company would be prepared to pay the difference £975 − £948 = £27.

The Economic Order Quantity (EOQ) with Quantity Discounts

Many firms provide discounts for large quantity orders for a number of reasons. These include economies of scale due to less setup times and other production efficiencies. Then the customer must balance the potential benefits of a reduced price against the holding costs incurred by the higher order quantity. The total annual cost with discounts is thus the sum of holding costs + ordering costs + purchasing costs. This can be expressed as the following equation:

$$TC = \frac{Q}{2} \times C_H + \frac{D}{Q} \times C_O + D \times C_p$$

where
  Q = quantity ordered
  D = annual demand
  C_O = order cost per order
  C_H = holding cost per unit for Q being considered
  C_P = unit price per unit for Q being considered.

Both the unit price and thus holding cost vary with an order quantity that is at a different price point. Thus it may be necessary to calculate the total cost at each price point to find the lowest value. In addition, we need to take into account the fact that we may not be permitted to order the quantity specified at the price discount set. It may also be more economical to purchase just a few more units and achieve a more generous price discount at the next price point.

There are two main scenarios that need to be considered. One is where holding costs are considered constant per unit. In this case there will be a single EOQ for all the cost curves at the different price point. In the second case holding costs are expressed as a percentage of purchase price and so each cost curve will increase the EOQ for each price point.

The procedure for finding the best order quantity is:

1. Begin with the lowest price and solve for the EOQ at this price.
2. If the EOQ is not within the quantity range for this price, go to step 3. Otherwise go to step 4.
3. Solve for the EOQ at the next highest price. Go to step 2.
4. Calculate the total cost for the EOQ that falls within the quantity range and for all the lower price points. Select the quantity with the lowest total cost.

The Economic Order Quantity Model with Discounts

A company is able to obtain quantity discounts on its order of material as follows:

Price per kg	Kg bought
6.00	less than 250
5.90	250 and less than 800
5.80	800 and less than 2000
5.70	2000 and less than 4000
5.60	4000 and over

The annual demand for the material is 4000 kilograms. Holding costs are 20% per year of material cost. The order cost per order is £6. Calculate the best quantity to order.

Solution

Solving the EOQ at the lowest price (Q = 4000 and over)

$$C_O = 6, C_H = 20/100 \times 5.6 = 1.12, C_P = 5.6, D = 4000$$

$$EOQ = SQRT(2 \times 4000 \times 6)/1.12 = 207.$$

The EOQ is not in the quantity range (4000 and above). It is obvious that the EOQ is lower than the price ranges so skip to the highest price.

Solving the EOQ at the highest price. (Q = 250 and under)

$$C_O = 6, C_H = 20/100 \times 6 = 1.2, C_P = 6, D = 4000$$

$$EOQ = SQRT(2 \times 4000 \times 6)/1.2 = 200.$$

EOQ is in the quantity range so calculate the total cost at the EOQ and all lower price points.

Q	Order cost	Holding cost	Cost of goods	Total cost
200	120	120	24 000	24 240
250	96	147.5	23 600	23 843.5
800	30	464	23 200	23 694
2000	12	1140	22 800	23 952
4000	6	2240	22 400	24 646

Therefore the lowest cost and therefore best order quantity is 800.

Fixed Order Period Inventory Systems

For the fixed order quantity inventory systems, *fixed* quantities of items are ordered at varying time intervals. In a **fixed order period inventory system** *varying* quantities are ordered at fixed time intervals.

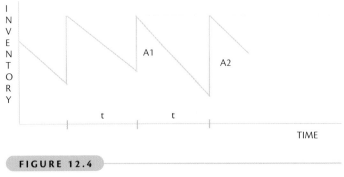

FIGURE 12.4

Inventory Level versus Time for the FOP Inventory System.

This means that a higher than normal demand will mean a larger order size rather than a shorter time between orders as in a fixed quantity model. The main attribute of the fixed interval model is that it only requires a periodic review of inventory levels to determine the order quantity required. A graph of inventory level over time for a fixed order interval system is shown in Figure 12.4.

It can be seen that the amount ordered at the fixed interval time period t is determined by the rate of demand during that period. Thus the order amount, A2, is much greater than the order amount A1 due to the relatively high demand during the period leading up to A2. The main advantage of using this system is that it enables a group of related components to be ordered at any one time, saving the cost of repeat deliveries and simplifying stock control. In addition, the need to continuously monitor stock, as in a fixed quantity system, is replaced by a periodic review and so saves monitoring duties.

Fixed Order Inventory (FOI) Model

The **fixed order inventory model** can be used to calculate the amount to order given a fixed interval between ordering. The calculation for the FOI model is dependent on whether demand and delivery lead time are treated as fixed or variable. If it is assumed that deliveries are relatively constant and demand levels are variable, the equation for the amount to order is given as follows:

amount to order = expected demand during protection interval + safety stock
− amount on hand at reorder time

$$= \overline{d} \times (OI + LT) + z \times \sigma_d \times \sqrt{OI + LT} - A$$

where
$\overline{d}$ = average demand rate
OI = order interval (time between orders)
LT = delivery lead time
z = number of standard deviations from the mean
σ_d = standard deviation of demand rate
A = amount of units on hand at reorder time

A variation on the fixed order interval system is when minimum and maximum levels are set for inventory. Thus at a periodic interval review point inventory is replenished up to the maximum level only if the inventory level is below a minimum level. A graph of inventory level over time is shown in Figure 12.5.

This system is suitable for low-cost items where the additional holding cost incurred when holding higher levels of inventory is offset by reductions in the need to order small amounts more frequently.

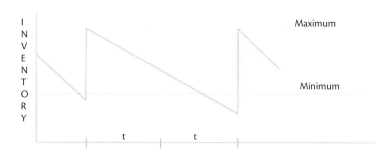

FIGURE 12.5

Inventory Level versus Time for the FOI Model with Minimum/Maximum Inventory Levels.

IMPLEMENTING INVENTORY SYSTEMS

In Chapter 15 the use of e-Business is discussed in its role of facilitating the outsourcing of supply chain activities to third parties. Inventory management can also be outsourced in this way and thus is sometimes referred to as **vendor managed inventory (VMI)**. An example of this is when wholesalers hold stocks for a number of retailers. This allows the retailers to focus on selling activities and order stock from the wholesaler as needed. Several e-Business solutions are available in the area of inventory management and are usually provided as a module within a supply chain management or material management e-Business system.

SUMMARY

- Inventory management is important because it affects both customer service (inventory is needed to ensure goods and services are available) and costs (the purchase and holding costs of inventory items).
- Inventory can be classified into buffer/safety, cycle, decoupling, anticipation and pipeline/movement.
- The ABC classification system can be used in order to identify appropriate inventory control policies for stock items.
- The reorder point (ROP) model indicates the level of inventory at which point further inventory should be ordered to avoid a stock-out. The ROP model can take into consideration variable delivery lead time and variable demand characteristics for an item.
- The economic order quantity (EOQ) model may be used to calculate a fixed order volume that minimizes total inventory costs. Inventory costs are assumed to consist of holding and ordering costs.
- The fixed order inventory (FOI) model may be used to calculate inventory order volumes when orders are placed at fixed time intervals.
- Inventory management systems can be implemented using an e-Business platform and are usually supplied as part of an integrated supply chain management system.

CASE STUDY 12.3

Vauxhall

A drop in demand plus the Euro crisis has left a number of car manufacturers with excess inventory in finished cars. The general demand for new cars in Western Europe peaked in 2007 at 16.8m vehicles; however, predictions from the Alix Partners consultancy expect car deliveries be more in line with 13.6m. This drop in demand has left a number of European car manufacturers such as Fiat and Peugeot and Vauxhall, with significant over capacity in production facilities.

Automotive industry analysts have stated that car and auto manufacturing is out of step with demand. The stockpile of motor vehicles is not only an expensive drain on investment, but also creates difficulties for storage; the cars need to stay pristine and avoid damage by the elements, and also face the risk of obsolescence with new models being expected by the market.

In September 2012, General Motors, Vauxhall's owners, took the decision to shut both their UK factories, of Ellesmere Port in Liverpool and their van producer in Luton, for an entire week. This was an attempt to reduce the buildup of stock and balance the excess with customer orders. In 2011, Vauxhall produced 137 971 cars, the demand for 2012 is expected to be significantly lower, and hence the decision was taken.

The UK plants were not the only ones affected; Opel, Vauxhall's sister company in Germany, halted production for nearly 20 days at the Russelsheim plant. The factories of Kaiserslautern and Eisenach also closed for ten days. Additional weekly closures have also been planned.

Other Western European car manufacturers took a similar approach, the Renault plant at Douai in France closed for four days, while the Fiat factory near Naples was shut for two weeks and Ford's Cologne factory adopted similar measures with a closure of three days.

The car industry has a strong union presence and Vauxhall were also keen to maintain a good public profile therefore employees in the plants were paid in full; however, the hours lost have been 'banked' by the organisation to be available for future requirements.

Vauxhall did not allow the downtime to be fruitless; essential maintenance was carried out and new robots were installed in the Luton plant in readiness for the next generation Vivaro Van due for production in 2014.

There is also a positive outlook for the Ellesmere Port factory; they have been awarded the production of the new Astra, due to start production in 2015. The estimated production is predicted to be 160 000 vehicles per year, which will create several hundred new jobs. Production of the new Astra is expected to run until at least 2020. After the investment, Ellesmere Port will have the capacity to produce up to 220 000 cars annually.

Sources

http://www.guardian.co.uk/business/2012/oct/10/vuaxhall-four-day-week-ellesmere-port

http://www.bbc.co.uk/news/business-18098657

http://www.itv.com/news/anglia/update/2012-09-24/vauxhall-plant-starts-five-day-shut-down/

http://uk.autoblog.com/2012/09/03/vauxhall-forces-factories-to-take-a-break/

http://www.guardian.co.uk/business/2012/aug/31/general-motors-vauxhall-plants-close-week

 www.wileyopenpage.com

http://www.just-auto.com/news/vauxhall-to-balance-inventory-in-week-shutdown_id126489.aspx

Source: Written by Briony Boydell and Chris Milner. Reproduced with permission.

Questions

1. What are the holding costs of inventory for Vauxhall?

2. Why have Vauxhall decided to keep manufacturing product up until now, knowing that the demand is falling?

 Quizzes to test yourself further are available in your interactive e-book at **www.wileyopenpage.com**

 Flashcards to test yourself further are available in your interactive e-book at **www.wileyopenpage.com**

EXERCISES

1. Distinguish between the different types of inventory.

2. Evaluate the EOQ model for inventory control.

3. A typing pool requires 1000 boxes of typing paper each year. Each box is worth £20 and storage costs are 13.5% of stock value a year. The cost of placing an order is £15.

   a. For the order quantities 50, 100, 150, 200 and 250 calculate the storage cost, replenishment cost and total cost.

   b. Plot the costs in (a) on a graph.

   c. Show algebraically that delivery costs and storage costs are equal when 105 boxes are ordered at a time.

4. A company has a demand of 2000 items per annum. Stock ordering costs are fixed at £100 irrespective of the scale of replenishment. It costs £2.50 to hold one item in stock for one year. Calculate the economic order quantity.

5. A company experiences annual demand for 2500 units of the single product that it stocks. The replenishment cost for inventory is fixed at £400 regardless of the size of replenishment. Annual holding costs are £8 per unit. What is the optimum number of replenishments per annum?

CHAPTER 13

Lean Operations

- **Introduction**
- **The philosophy of lean operations**
- **Lean techniques**
- **Lean in service systems**
- **Implementing lean operations**

LEARNING OBJECTIVES

- Describe the two levels of lean operations
- Explain the main elements of the lean philosophy
- Explain the need for lean techniques
- Understand the relevance of the *kanban* production control system to JIT
- Discuss the concept of Heijunka
- Evaluate the use of lean in service and administration systems
- Discuss the use of lean operations in service and administrative systems
- Evaluate when a lean implementation is appropriate

LEAN OPERATIONS AND OPERATIONS STRATEGY

Lean operations is defined in this chapter at one level as a philosophy and at another level as a collection of techniques and its strategic significance can be considered at both of these levels. Implementation of lean techniques such as pull production, total preventative maintenance, setup reduction and Heijunka can lead to improvements in the performance objectives of cost and quality through the reduction of variability and waste. Organizations will need to select techniques that they judge are relevant to their strategic performance. If lean is adopted as a philosophy then it could provide a sustained competitive advantage and be considered as part of a resource-based operations strategy. This is because adoption of lean as a philosophy that permeates the organization, through the engagement of the workforce in continuous improvement techniques, for example, represents a much more difficult aim to achieve and so in turn creates a capability that is difficult to copy.

INTRODUCTION

Lean operations is a concept that involves eliminating non value-added activities from the entire supply chain. The term was first used by John Krafcik in his article 'Triumph of the Lean Production System' that appeared in 1988. The paper found that productivity and quality levels in car assembly plants were not determined by an assembly plant's location but those plants that operated with a 'lean' production policy were able to manufacture a wide range of models, yet maintain high levels of quality and productivity. This message was further disseminated by the book *The Machine That Changed the World* published in 1991 (reissued in 2007 by Womack, Jones and Roos).

The term lean is often used interchangeably with the concept of just-in-time (JIT). However, JIT traditionally only applies to the organization and its immediate suppliers, whereas lean encompasses the entire supply chain (supply chain management is covered in Chapter 15). The term 'lean' is meant to emphasize the concept of elimination of waste in all its forms. The concept continues to develop and Bicheno (2004) uses the term 'new lean' to describe an amalgam of traditional lean, theory of constraints (Chapter 11), Six Sigma (Chapter 17) and 'a range of relatively new concepts for measurements, analysis, and transformation'. In this chapter, **lean operations** is considered as an integration of a philosophy and techniques designed to improve performance.

THE PHILOSOPHY OF LEAN OPERATIONS

Two key issues at the core of the lean philosophy are to eliminate waste and to implement a continuous improvement programme.

Eliminate Waste

Waste is considered in the widest sense as any activity which does not add value to the operation. Bicheno (2004) states that although waste is strongly linked to lean, waste elimination is a means to achieving the lean ideal, it is not an end in itself and waste prevention is at least as important as waste elimination.

Customer service wastes generally can be categorized as follows (Bicheno, 2004):

- *Delay* on the part of customers waiting for service, for delivery, in queues, for response, not arriving as promised.

- *Duplication.* Having to re-enter data, repeat details on forms and answering queries from several sources within the same organization.
- *Unnecessary movements.* Queuing several times, poor ergonomics in the service encounter.
- *Unclear communication* and the wastes of seeking clarification.
- *Incorrect inventory.* Out-of-stock, unable to get exactly what is required, substitute products or services.
- *Opportunity lost* to retain or win customers, failure to establish rapport, ignoring customers, unfriendliness and rudeness.
- *Errors* in the service transaction, product defects in the product-service bundle, lost or damaged goods.

Office wastes are probably the most pervasive of all types of service waste. Some examples are provided below.

- Looking for documents/computer files that have been misplaced.
- Imposing additional work (forms, procedures, measures) on people who are already busy and making a difference to the customer.
- Tendency to do the urgent but not important, rather than the important but not immediately urgent.
- Interference from emails, excessive socializing, noise.
- Office staff waiting for decisions from others.
- Attending meetings with no productive purpose.

In a manufacturing context the seven types of waste identified by Ohno (1988) are as follows:

- *Over-production.* This is classified as the greatest source of waste and is an outcome of producing more than is needed by the next process.
- *Waiting time.* This is the time spent by labour or equipment waiting to add value to a product. This may be disguised by undertaking unnecessary operations – for example, generating work in progress (WIP) on a machine – which are not immediately needed (the waste is converted from time to WIP).
- *Transport.* Unnecessary transportation of WIP is another source of waste. Layout changes can substantially reduce transportation time.
- *Process.* Some operations do not add value to the product but are simply there because of poor design or machine maintenance. Improved design or preventative maintenance should eliminate these processes.
- *Inventory.* Inventory of all types (such as pipeline or cycle – see Chapter 12) is considered as waste and should be eliminated.
- *Motion.* Simplification of work movement will reduce waste caused by unnecessary motion of labour and equipment.
- *Defective goods.* The total costs of poor quality can be very high and will include scrap material, wasted labour time and time expediting orders and loss of goodwill through missed delivery dates.

The root cause of much waste is variability and too high utilization which is expressed in Toyota's 3 'Ms' of mura (variability), muri (utilization) and muda (waste) (Figure 13.1).

What the 3Ms' relationship shows is that mura (variability) leads to muri (higher utilization) which leads to muda (waste) which leads to mura and the cycle is repeated. This implies that mura or variability is the root problem of waste in systems. For example, variability in demand causes stress in staff at peak times, leading to a lack of maintenance of equipment which leads to higher utilization and deadlines being missed. However, muda can result in mura due to lead times being long and quality being uncertain. Techniques to smooth flow and thus decrease variability include levelled and mixed model scheduling and pull production systems covered later in this chapter.

The effect of variability in business systems has been discussed in the section on business process simulation in Chapter 8 and it is shown in Figure 13.2 in terms of the impact of variability and utilization on queue size.

If there is no variability there will be no queues as long as the arrival rate is less than or equal to the service time. However, Figure 13.2 shows that the higher the variability, the higher the average queue length for a given utilization. It is difficult to eliminate variability entirely so it is recommended to try to keep utilization (of staff and equipment) below 80%.

If variability is at the source of much waste then it is important to identify its source. Variability can be classified into customer-introduced variability and internal process variability. Frei (2006) describes 5 types of customer introduced variability:

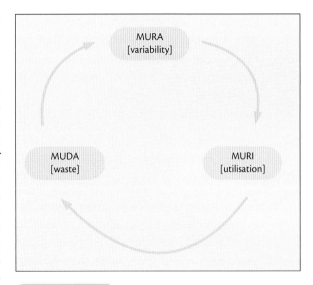

FIGURE 13.1

Mura, Muri and Muda.

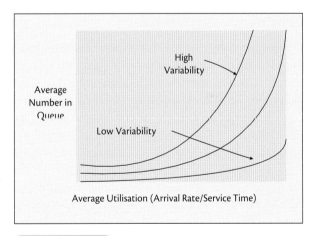

FIGURE 13.2

The Effect of Utilization on Queue Size at Different Variability Levels.

1. Arrival – unfortunately customers don't arrive uniformly. Difficult to influence in the short term, but in the longer term more easily predicted (e.g. seasonal factors). Bookings and price incentives can be used to smooth variations.
2. Request – customers will require different services with different service times. Methods to overcome this include fast track queues and limiting choice.

3. Capability – not all customers have the same skill level! Older customers may require more time. Can be improved by clear signage, reduced choice, clear guidance to customers.

4. Effort – not all customers put the same effort into the transaction, e.g. a customer may not dispose of their rubbish at Burger King. To improve effort, make it easy and obvious and thank customers.

5. Subjective preference – not all customers appreciate the same thing in a service; some like self-service some do not.

As well as variability from customers variability can arise from internal processes including the following:

1. People – within the organization variability can be caused by staff (this includes both variability between different people and variability in the execution of processes by one person over time). Variability can be reduced by the use of training and standard procedures to clarify tasks.

2. Machines – variability can be reduced using total productive maintenance (TPM) to keep the machine in good working order.

3. Materials – variability can be decreased through a purchasing policy.

4. Measures – variability caused by inappropriate performance measures which drive inappropriate behaviour.

Continuous Improvement

Continuous improvement or *Kaizen*, the Japanese term, is a philosophy stating that it is possible to get to the ideals of lean by a continuous stream of improvements over time. Lean aims to create a new culture in which all employees are encouraged to contribute to continuous improvement efforts through generating ideas for improvements and perform a range of functions.

Chapter 18 deals with the continuous improvement approach in more detail.

The video 'Kinaxis: Supply Chain Risk Management Strategy' is available in your interactive e-book at **www.wileyopenpage.com**

CASE STUDY 13.1

Quake Upsets Lean Supply Model

The latest natural disaster in north-western Japan has once again raised questions about the weaknesses of the vaunted lean production system pioneered by Toyota and practised to varying degrees by other automakers. The entire Japanese vehicle industry ground to a halt following an earthquake that stopped production of piston rings for engines provided by Riken, the industry leader in the domestic market. Toyota, in particular, was forced to stop operations at all 12 of its domestic plants. The situation has highlighted problems not only with lean manufacturing, which aims to reduce all waste, including inventories, to the minimum, but also with the Japanese industry's dependence on one manufacturer for a key product.

The earthquake had a larger than expected impact on Japanese auto manufacturers because they have aimed to reduce the inventory level of components, to reduce working capital, noted Tatsuya Miyamoto, analyst at Fitch in Tokyo. However, doing so 'enhances the risk of stalling the production in the event of a disruption of supply', he wrote in a report. Moreover, the latest setback has revealed that automakers were heavily dependent on one supplier for a key part. This was despite their stated policy of signing on multiple vendors to avoid disruptions to production in unexpected situations, like a natural disaster. Riken, with a 50% share of the domestic piston ring market, single-handedly disrupted the production of the entire Japanese auto industry.

Katsuaki Watanabe, president of Toyota, underlined the difficulty of diversifying procurement in an age when the quality of the parts is critical to the competitiveness of the finished product. 'Basically, we adhere to the principle of multiple procurement but for products where we work very closely with a supplier from an early stage in the development [of a vehicle] there is tremendous difficulty in transferring that technology itself or asking [another manufacturer] to make that product', he said. Riken has specialized technology that other suppliers have had difficulty emulating, making it difficult for carmakers to diversify their supplies, said Hirofumi Yokoi, industry analyst at CSM Worldwide. Mr Watanabe conceded that 'we must deepen our

understanding of how to manage risk at suppliers that we rely on for specialized products.' With the increasingly important role parts makers play in determining the competitiveness of carmakers, Mr Mizuno at Fitch expected carmakers to 'put more emphasis on establishing closer relationships with key component suppliers and enclosing them within their group.'

However, analysts and industry officials believe that the advantages of the lean production system far outweigh any weaknesses it may have exposed in emergencies, such as the latest earthquake. Mr Yokoi said if you compared the long-term advantages of lower costs and efficiency that were the fruits of the lean production system with what was lost in a natural disaster, there was no question that the former was of greater value. Indeed, Toyota officials said that having a low level of inventory helped them to assess quickly where the problems lay and address those problems promptly. Because lean producers kept inventory levels to a minimum, it was possible to grasp quickly the level of inventory at every stage of the supply chain. This made it possible to determine speedily where the missing parts were needed and in what quantities, the Toyota officials said. If inventory levels were high – as in the old days – it would be impossible to sort things out quickly and resume production as quickly as Toyota had been able to, they said. There was no going back on lean production, said Mr Yokoi. 'The key is how to recover quickly when an emergency strikes', he said. The rebound by Japanese vehicle makers a few days after the earthquake shows that they had been quick to master that task, he added.

Source: Financial Times (2007). Reproduced with permission.

Question

Use the case study to discuss the advantages and disadvantages of lean production.

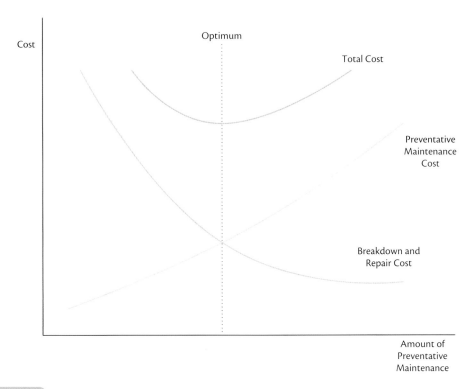

FIGURE 13.3

Cost versus Amount of Preventative Maintenance.

Value Stream Mapping (VSM)

Value stream mapping (VSM) is a flowcharting technique that is used to improve process flows by visually identifying and mapping each step in the process in order to identify non-value added or wasteful activities. The tool is similar to the technique of process mapping covered in Chapter 8. However, whilst process mapping is mainly used for business processes such as order fulfilment, value stream mapping is used for production and service creation processes and depicts how value is added. VSM also highlights both the current state and guidelines for arriving at a future desired state that is to be achieved using lean techniques. Figures 13.4 and 13.5 show before and after value stream maps created using the template available in Microsoft Visio™.

Setup Reduction (SUR)

In order to operate with the small batch sizes required by JIT it is necessary to reduce setup time (the time taken to adjust equipment to work on a different component) drastically because of the increased number of setups needed with small batches – this is known as **setup reduction**. Originally some operations such as stamping car door panels with a press die were done in very large batch sizes, and the output stored in inventory, because the setup time for the press could be measured in hours or even days. Shigeo Shingo was hired by Toyota to study how press die setup could be reduced and he achieved impressive results. For example, he reduced the setup time on one 1000 ton press from six hours to only

FIGURE 13.4

Value Stream Map of Current Process.

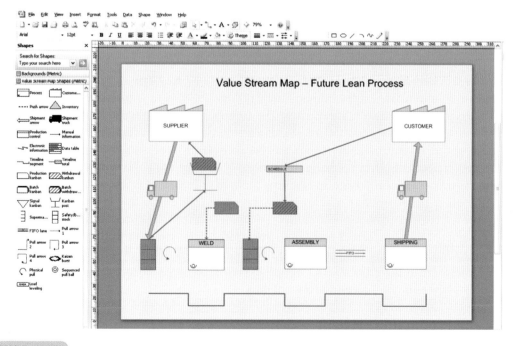

FIGURE 13.5

Value Stream Map of Future Lean Process.

three minutes. The system he developed became known as the single minute exchange of dies (SMED) (Shingo, 1996) and is based on the following principles:

1. Separate internal setup from external setup. Setup tasks are classified as internal – they must be performed while the machine is stopped – and external – they can be performed in advance while the machine is running. Performing external setup tasks during operation and then delaying only for the internal setup tasks can reduce setup times by 30 to 50%.

2. Convert internal setup to external setup. This means ensuring any tasks normally undertaken during the internal setup phase (for example, gathering tools or preheating an injection mould) are undertaken during the external phase.

3. Streamline all aspects of setup. This can be achieved by organizing tools near to the point of use and simplifying or eliminating operations.

4. Perform setup activities in parallel or eliminate them entirely. Deploying extra people to a setup can reduce setup time by a considerable amount, maybe by more than double. Standardization of parts and raw materials can reduce or even eliminate setup requirements.

Visual Control

Visual control is used to facilitate continuous improvement work. Visibility is about maintaining an orderly workplace in which tools are easily available and unusual occurrences are easily noticeable. This is achieved through what are called the five Ss (*seiri, seiton, seiso, seiketsu, shitsuke*), which roughly translate as organization, tidiness, cleanliness, maintenance and discipline. To achieve these factors visibility measures include Andon signs (coloured lights), control systems such as the *kanban* and performance charts such as statistical process control (SPC) charts. Chapter 17 covers the SPC method.

Autonomation

Autonomation or 'automation with a human touch' (Ohno, 1988) is an approach that enables a worker to stop a process if an abnormal situation arises. The approach aims to prevent the production of defective products, eliminate overproduction and focus attention on understanding the problem and ensuring that it never recurs. Autonomation separates workers from processes through mechanisms that detect process abnormalities thus relieving the worker of the need to continuously judge whether the operation of the process is normal and so enabling them to only engage effort when there is a problem alerted by the machine. As well as making the work more interesting this is a necessary step if the worker is to be asked later to supervise multiple processes. Once the process is stopped a supervisor or person designated to help correct problems gives immediate attention to the problem the worker has discovered. One solution to the problem can be to insert a 'mistake-proofing' device, known as a **pokayoke**, somewhere in the process. An example pokayoke is an Excel spreadsheet cell that has been defined to only allow entry of a certain format of data.

Push and Pull Production Systems

In a push production system a schedule pushes work on to machines which is then passed through to the next work centre (Figure 13.6).

www.wileyopenpage.com

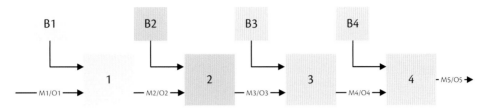

FIGURE 13.6

Push Production System.

FIGURE 13.7

'Pull' Production System.

In Figure 13.6 materials (M_i) and orders for production (O_i) are 'pushed' onto production stage 1. Production stage 1 then produces material for production stage 2 and the cycle repeats through the production stages. At each production stage a buffer stock (B1, B2 etc.) is kept to ensure that if any production stage fails then the subsequent production stage will not be starved of material. For example, if there is a breakdown at stage 2 of the production line, stage 3 will be fed from a buffer stock (B3) until the problem is fixed. The higher the buffer stocks kept at each stage of the line, the more disruption can occur without the production line being halted by lack of material.

The pull system developed by Ohno (1988) comes from the idea of a supermarket in which items are purchased by a customer only when needed and are replenished as they are removed. Thus inventory coordination is controlled by a customer pulling items from the system, which are then replaced as needed. Pull systems are sometimes called 'lean synchronization' meaning the customer only gets what they want when they want it with minimum waste.

In a pull system (Figure 13.7) the process is triggered by an order for the finished product (for example, car) at the end of the production line (O1). This then triggers an order for components of that item (O2), which in turn triggers an order for further subcomponents (O3). The process repeats until the initial stage of production and the material flows through the system as in the 'push' approach. Using the pull system the production system produces output at each stage only in response to demand and eliminates the need for buffer stock.

The aim of the elimination of buffers between production stages is to ensure a responsive system. However, the pull system does not overcome the basic characteristic of a line layout that if one stage fails, all subsequent stages will be starved of work and, in effect, output from the whole production line is lost. This would seem to be a powerful argument for the retention of buffers, but the JIT approach actually argues that the disruption that occurs due to the lack of buffer stock will motivate people to find the root cause of problems. This over time will lead to a more reliable and efficient system. Motivation will be generated by the highly visible nature of any problem occurring (it will bring the whole factory to a halt) and the fact that the problem is now everyone's problem and not just a local difficulty of which no one else is

Goodwin Steel Castings

Goodwin Steel Castings' use of JIT systems has increased profits, reduced timescales and helped develop more competitive products. Faced with an extremely competitive market, steel manufacturer Goodwin Steel Castings decided to introduce JIT working as part of an investment in technology aimed at improving the efficiency of their systems. Now, from taking orders and production through to process control and customer service, the company has integrated its systems. Since JIT is a demand-led process, Goodwin has worked with clients to ensure it can gauge their needs with maximum accuracy. Many of the company's clients now make their delivery schedules and requirements available on their web sites for Goodwin to retrieve. This information is then translated automatically into project updates which are available online for all customers. As orders are fed through to the foundry, electronic monitors place orders with the business's suppliers. Says General Manager Steven Birks, 'The latest stage of our investment in JIT telemetry technology enables us to access information on their web sites so we can get valuable management information like trends and historic usage.' The main business benefit of integrating JIT technology into Goodwin's supply chain has been faster response times, which has led to winning more orders and the business being able to quote more accurately. The company has also managed to improve efficiency through closer monitoring of manufacturing.

Source: The Department of Trade and Industry (www.dti.gov.uk/bestpractice).

Question

Why are faster response times important in a JIT system?

---

aware. In moving from a push to a pull system it is common practice to gradually reduce the buffer levels as the production system reliability is increased. An attempt to move directly to eliminate buffers is likely to cause severe disruption to a system formerly reliant on this safety net.

The pull approach is applied not just to internal production systems but to the relationship between customers and suppliers in the supply chain. Thus suppliers in a lean supply chain are required to only supply customers in response to demand and the customer will not keep buffer stocks 'just-in-case' the supplier fails to deliver on time. This reduces inventory and increases responsiveness in the supply chain but does require close cooperation between customer and supplier and reliability in the supplier operations (see Chapter 15).

Kanban Production System

There are a number of ways of implementing a pull production system including the drum buffer rope approach of OPT covered in Chapter 10. One system for implementing a pull system is called a **kanban production system** (*kanban* is Japanese for 'card' or 'sign'). Each *kanban* provides information on the part identification, quantity per container that the part is transported in and the preceding and next work station. *Kanbans*, in themselves, do not provide the schedule for production but without them production

www.wileyopenpage.com

cannot take place as they authorize the production and movement of material through the pull system. *Kanbans* need not be a card, but should be something that can be used as a signal for production such as a marker, or coloured square area. There are two types of *kanban* system: the single-card and two-card.

The single-card system uses only one type of *kanban* card called the conveyance *kanban*, which authorizes the movement of parts. The number of containers at a work centre is limited by the number of *kanbans*. A signal to replace inventory at the work centre can only be sent when the container is emptied. Toyota use a dual card system which, in addition to the conveyance *kanban*, uses a production *kanban* to authorize the production of parts. This system permits greater control over production as well as inventory. If the processes are tightly linked (one always follows the other) then a single *kanban* can be used.

In order for a *kanban* system to be implemented it is important that the seven operational rules that govern the system are followed. These rules can be summarized as follows:

- Move a *kanban* only when the lot it represents is consumed. This means the whole of the batch of parts must be processed before the *kanban* is sent to the preceding process to ask for more parts.
- No withdrawal of parts without a *kanban* is allowed. No process can move parts without the authorization of a *kanban* request.
- The number of parts issued to the subsequent process must be the exact number specified by the *kanban*. This means a *kanban* must wait until sufficient parts are made before the lot of parts is moved.
- A *kanban* should always be attached to the physical product. The *kanban* should travel with the parts themselves and be visible.
- The preceding process should always produce its parts in the quantities withdrawn by the subsequent process. Processes should never overproduce parts in any quantity.
- Defective parts should never be conveyed to the subsequent process. A high level of quality must be maintained because of the lack of buffer inventory. A feedback mechanism, which reports quality problems quickly to the preceding process, must be implemented.
- Process the *kanbans* in every work centre strictly in the order in which they arrive at the work centre. If several *kanbans* are waiting for production they must be served in the order that they have arrived. If the rule is not followed there will be a gap in the production rate of one or more of the subsequent processes.

The operation for a dual card *kanban* system is outlined in Figure 13.8:

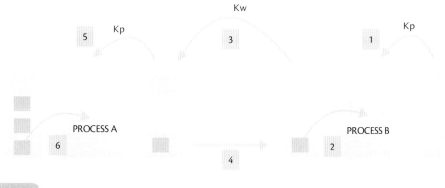

FIGURE 13.8

Dual-card *Kanban* System.

One possible assembly sequence could be ACACBACA. One unit of product A will be produced every 12 minutes on average throughout the day to a level assembly schedule. This means that components must be supplied to product A to match this cycle time. The system must also be coordinated to produce either A, B or C once every 6 minutes. To achieve these results requires that sufficient equipment and labour are configured and setup times minimized.

LEAN IN SERVICE SYSTEMS

Lean and JIT are usually associated with manufacturing applications because this is the setting in which it was developed and has been applied most frequently. However, many of the ideas behind lean can be employed in service settings (Bicheno, 2008). For example, Schniederjans (1993) presents introductory JIT implementation strategies that can be applied to almost all administration organizations.

- Everybody in an administration department should serve as a customer-service agent. Service quality is everybody's responsibility in a JIT administration. When poor quality is observed in the delivery of an administration service that can be corrected the individual worker or department that is responsible should be made to implement the correction.
- Management should be willing to sacrifice production for improved quality and allow workers extra time for JIT activities such as quality control.
- All employees should be multifunctional to increase worker flexibility and help workers understand more of the operation.
- Walls and departmental barriers cause greater routing, filing, walking and proofing and should be restructured into various groups of workers or group technology (GT) cell work stations with multifunctional skills. Multiple cells allow more than one channel through which work can flow, increasing flexibility to better balance workload with variable capacity. In a departmental system if one department is backlogged other offices will become idle and inefficiencies can occur. Elimination of departments also decreases much duplication and can substantially reduce the amount of commonly used equipment, filing cabinets and storage areas.
- Standardizing work procedures can save time in training and improve operational efficiency by removing job complexity. Standardizing order forms and routing systems can also reduce complexity and helps workers understand processes and thus suggest improvements.

Womack and Jones (2005) have developed lean thinking principles for the processes of consumption. This involves streamlining the systems for providing goods and services using six principles:

1. Solve the customer's problem completely by ensuring that all the goods and services work, and work together.
2. Don't waste the customer's time.
3. Provide exactly *what* the customer wants.
4. Provide what's wanted exactly *where* it's wanted.
5. Provide what's wanted where it's wanted exactly *when* it's wanted.
6. Continually aggregate solutions to reduce the customer's time and hassle.

www.wileyopenpage.com

How Much Waste is there in the Service Industry?

Over the weekend a question was posed to me via Twitter (@theleanmanager if you'd like to follow) about the amount of waste (wasted time) in the back office of banks/service/insurance operations. Now I took this to mean the call centres, data processing centres, mail rooms, customer response teams etc.

The guys asking the questions @wisemonkeyash and @channingwalton wanted to know could it be as high as 90%? (Update: we do know that in some legal firms the time to process matters is being improved by 50%, by using lean thinking, indicating that wasted time could be considerable in the professional services sector.)

I decided I should expand upon my 140 character replies, which were based on my experience.

Variation of demand is the first factor to consider i.e. what does the busiest day (for demand, not completed work) look like and what does a quiet day look like and what are the patterns the peaks and troughs for the demand.

What causes this demand, the peaks and troughs? Our experience? it's normally another part of the business which generates and stokes the demand and therefore changes here can reduce the peaks.

This could be letters with incorrect details, mass direct marketing mailing, customers chasing progress etc.

This variation often causes capacity (people) to be 50% more than required to achieve the current results.

The implications here are that you can deliver improvement by changing something outside of the back offices, without changing what many individuals do – making continuous improvement more readily accepted.

Remember that so far we haven't looked at the waste in the activities undertaken in these departments. Now as a lean person we look for the 7 hidden wastes, yes I know others have 8 or even 9 but we stick to the 7.

To give you just one example, have you rung a call centre, in the last 6 months, to be told 'I'm sorry the system is a bit slow today'?

Sometimes that is genuine, the system is slow, it may be that the networking is slow or the server needs upgrading or the PC workstation is old. So say you have 50 agents handling 20 calls an hour? How much time are you wasting because the technology isn't up to speed?

The more common reason for 'I'm sorry the system is a bit slow today', that we see is that staff have two screens in front of them and they may be running 4 different programmes at once. As the programmes can't transfer information directly to one another, the staff take info from one system, send to their own e-mail, cut and paste it into another programme and then have to delete the e-mail.

This is just one example and adding up the rest we often find that 50% of the activity time is wasted.

What does this mean overall?

If we start with 100% and 50% is waste due to Variation demand, this leaves 50%.

Of the remaining 50%, we reckon 50% is wasted time, so we get to the figure of 25% (50% *50%), or 75% of the work can be classified as waste.

Remember this is based on what we have seen, so not as high as the 90% the guys originally asked.

Within an hour I spotted this article 'Aviva shakes up its Customer Service' from the FT, which shows the global serving UK based insurance firm Aviva put the waste figure in call centres as 60%.

It's also worth noting that Aviva thought it was completing work in 5 days, in reality it was taking 39.

How can this happen? Well sometimes companies split activities into discrete chunks and add up the time each chunk takes, assuming this equals the processing time. They forget the hand-offs and delays that each happen between each activity. We've definitely seen office work with activities of an hour take over 10 days to complete in reality.

Okay there is a variation in the figures but should we split hairs on whether waste in offices is 50% as in the professional services firms or 60%–75% for the back offices and call centres, the reality is that the waste appears to be relatively large, though maybe not as large as the 90% that started the question.

Do you have any views on what the waste could be?

Source: http://theleanmanager.wordpress.com/2011/05/12/how-much-waste-is-there-in-the-service-industry/. Reproduced with permission.

Questions

1. Identify sources of waste that occur from the point of when a call centre agent picks up the phone to serve a customer.
2. Discuss why waste in the service industry is apparently so high.

IMPLEMENTING LEAN OPERATIONS

Lean operations has been covered in this chapter both as a philosophy and as a set of techniques.

From the viewpoint of lean as a philosophy of the elimination of waste and continuous improvement it can be seen as applicable to all organizations, small or large, manufacturing or service. At this level the main implementation issues concern the requirement of a problem solving culture of trust and cooperation within the workforce. It is also likely that problem identification and proble-solving activities will be more successful at a higher volume of output, which gives a better chance for learning to occur. Implementing lean as a philosophy that permeates the organization is likely to represent a substantial challenge for the organization but can deliver a competitive advantage.

At the level of lean as a collection of tools and techniques it is more likely to be applicable to medium to high volumes of products that have reached a mature development phase in the market. Just-in-time techniques include the *kanban* production control system. Prerequisites for the implementation of this type of system include aspects such as layout design (for example, cell manufacturing) (Chapter 5), setup time reduction (SUR) (Chapter 13), line balancing (Chapter 4) and total quality management (TQM) techniques (Chapter 17) such as statistical process control (SPC) (Chapter 17). Organizations may choose to select and implement lean techniques which are relevant to their key performance objectives without pursuing the implementation of a lean philosophy.

SUMMARY

- Lean operations can be seen on one level as a philosophy and on another level as a set of tools and techniques.
- The concepts of waste elimination and continuous improvement are the core of the lean philosophy.
- Lean tools and techniques are required to implement lean operations.
- Lean tools and techniques include design for manufacture, value stream mapping, cellular manufacturing, JIT supplier networks, total preventative maintenance, setup reduction and visual control.
- Just-in-time planning and control is based on the *kanban* production control system.
- Heijunka attempts to match the production of each item with demand.
- Lean techniques are applicable to service and administration systems.

CASE STUDY 13.5

It Pays to Cut Out Waste but Not to Trim All the Value Away

When Hoyt Buck started making hunting knives in the early years of the twentieth century, his competitors were other Kansas blacksmiths. One hundred years later, Buck Knives is up against companies from across the world, many of them based in countries where labour, utility and other costs are substantially below those in the US. Most companies in these circumstances send their manufacturing offshore. If you can't beat them, join them. But Hoyt Buck's descendants were reluctant. Instead of exporting jobs to Asia, three years ago they started to import an Asian idea – the 'lean' manufacturing methods pioneered by Toyota.

The story shows, first, that the doctrines of the Toyota production system have spread far beyond the automotive sector. Fifteen years after the publication of The Machine That Changed the World, the book that popularized Toyota's management methods, the war against muda – Japanese for waste – is being fought across swaths of manufacturing

industry and increasingly in services, too. Second, the experience of Buck Knives underlines that lean thinking can be a powerful weapon in the fight to keep manufacturing and other jobs in developed countries.

Lean thinking teaches managers to eradicate anything from the production process that does not add value for customers, including inventory. Instead of stockpiling goods in warehouses and praying that demand forecasts turn out to be accurate – the conventional 'push' model – lean manufacturers aim to produce only in response to firm orders. When an order is placed, raw materials are 'pulled' from the supply chain and down the production line as fast as possible. The result: high speed, no waste, low cost and a happy customer.

Irrespective of whether this ideal is achieved in practice, lean thinkers tend to be sceptical about the supposed benefits of sending jobs to low-wage economies. It is hard to run a low inventory, just-in-time supply chain when you are sourcing components from across the globe. What if the widgets required for tomorrow's production run are delayed by a typhoon or stuck for three days at the border? Besides, there is nothing lean about shipping steel, shoes or electronic components halfway around the world by container ship. Think of all that muda in time, capital and diesel fuel.

Another strand of lean thinking is the notion that frontline workers – whether on the production line or in customer service – are best placed to identify and solve problems. But they can do this only if they are very familiar with the products and can talk directly to the engineers and managers who are likely to be at the root cause of any problem. On this view, sending jobs offshore will result in fewer problems solved and unhappier customers in the long run.

James Womack and Daniel Jones, authors (with Daniel Roos) of The Machine That Changed the World, write in their new book, Lean Solutions, that the best location for service and support jobs is 'near the corporate technical centres that developed the products or near the operations centres of client firms'. Similarly, lean thinkers tend to be sceptical about the value of outsourcing jobs to contractors, even if the workers stay close by. Overheads may be reduced in the short term, but learning opportunities are likely to be lost.

At Buck Knives you can see these ideas in action. The old production line has been redesigned into a series of circular 'cells' that build knives from start to finish. The new layout minimizes the distance travelled by each product (less muda) and encourages communication among employees, allowing them to see the entire manufacturing process. This way of working makes it more likely that production bottlenecks or product defects will be recognized early and dealt

with on the spot, says CJ Buck, chief executive and great-grandson of the founder. There is less need for expensive (and sometimes oppressive) supervision.

In true Toyota style, Buck Knives last month staged a symposium for its suppliers to explore ways of improving cooperation. Running a just-in-time supply chain requires a higher degree of collaboration – and trust – than is usual among manufacturers used to carrying weeks or months of surplus inventory. 'Much of what we are doing today is making the company more like it was when my grandfather was running the business and everything was done on a handshake', says Mr Buck.

To be sure, lean thinking is no panacea. It is hard to learn and even harder to sustain. It has limits. Going lean was not sufficient to get Buck Knives' unit costs down to competitive levels. After more than 50 years in California, where Hoyt Buck moved in 1947, the company last year relocated to Idaho in search of lower overheads. While many of its products still carry a 'Made in USA' stamp, its less expensive models are now made in Taiwan. And as every chief executive knows, a world-class cost structure and commitment to continuous improvement is only table stakes these days. If Buck Knives wants to be around for another decade – let alone another century – it will have to come up with products that are consistently more desirable than the domestic and international competition. Innovation and inspiration must also be on the cutting edge.

Source: Simon London, *Financial Times* (October 12, 2005). Reproduced with permission.

Question

Discuss how lean thinking can lead to the keeping of manufacturing jobs in developed countries.

Harley-Davidson

The Harley Davidson Vision is to 'fulfil dreams inspired by the many roads of the world by providing extraordinary motorcycles and customer experiences. We fuel the passion for freedom in our customers to express their own individuality', there is no doubt that they produce what many see as American Dream product, but the question is how?

The assembly plant in York, the biggest of four manufacturing plants in the US has offered free factory tours since 1973, and whilst many factories struggle tremendously to achieve a factory standard that allows further process improvements, a factory that allows customers, competitors and tourists inside the walls has no choice than to be presentable, logical and cleaned at all times. Lines at the plant have been implemented to bring forth and embed the efficiencies of Lean Synchronisation, they are well designed and there's a lot of modern technology in use, in fact a motorcycle rolls off the assembly lines every 90 seconds, with minimal waste and in flowing movement.

The factory's 5S-program is clear to see, but whilst H-D see 'sort', 'stabilize', 'shine', 'standardize', and 'sustain' as necessary, it can be very difficult within many organisations to sustain, but is at the core of a modern and agile plant that is able to cater for the complexity and variety that customers demand.

True to Lean values, the factory runs a 'Continuous Improvement System', which has been implemented with success the last few years, with visual A3 boards bringing clarity to progress and inclusion. Through daily meeting structures, the lean aspect of involving people is given great opportunity; a practical example of how the employees challenge themselves to reinvent the process, they came up with a much improved way to cover holes in the frames before painting. 'We're all one team here – we include everybody in how to improve our operations'.

Whilst the lean implementation has not gone without its challenges and drawbacks, In February 2011, Keith Wandell, President and CEO said that 'The Company is well on its way to build a world-class, sustainable, lean operating structure'. The plan is to spread the efficient systems through the entire organisation, and in February of 2011 H-D announced that they would move forward with the implementation of a new production system at its Kansas City facility, following a vote by the plant's unionized employees ratifying a new seven-year labour agreement.

When fully implemented, Harley-Davidson expects previously announced company-wide restructuring activities, together with the implementation of the changes at Kansas City, to result in one-time charges of $510 million to $525 million, and annual ongoing savings of $305 million to $325 million. In 2011 on a combined basis, Harley-Davidson expected to incur restructuring charges of $95 million to $105 million. The Company continues to expect to realize savings on a combined basis in 2011 of $210 million to $230 million from restructuring activities initiated since early 2009.

Sources

http://better-operations.com/2012/07/21/lean-in-harley-davidson-launching-the-harley-davidson-operating-system/

PR Newswire, February 2011, Harley-Davidson to Implement New Production System at Kansas City Following Vote Approving Contract http://www.prnewswire.com/news-releases/harley-davidson-to-implement-new-production-system-at-kansas-city-following-vote-approving-contract-117081978.html

http://www.harley-davidson.com/en_GB/Content/Pages/home.html

Source: Written by Briony Boydell and Chris Milner. Reproduced with permission.

Question

The HD factory shows the value and impact of running a lean and efficient operation, The minimization of waste and the involvement of its people is key to their success, but why is it so imperative to sustain a culture of continuous improvement, and what challenges do they face in doing so?

Activity

When you return home today, conduct a 5S exercise on your desk. Once complete, reflect upon your thought and consider the impact such can have within an organizational setting.

Quizzes to test yourself further are available in your interactive e-book at **www.wileyopenpage.com**

Flashcards to test yourself further are available in your interactive e-book at **www.wileyopenpage.com**

EXERCISES

1. Explain the main elements of the lean philosophy.

2. Provide an analysis of the techniques used to implement a lean philosophy in a manufacturing organization.

3. Distinguish between preventative and predictive maintenance.

4. Explain, using an example, how you would use the concepts of lean in a service operations environment.

5. Evaluate the advantages and disadvantages of the JIT approach to production planning.

6. To gain efficiency it is essential to minimize the time it takes to make a car. Compare how this is achieved under traditional and lean operations approaches.

7. Why is the traditional approach to production control termed a 'buffered system'?

8. Discuss how lean operations can enhance flexibility.

www.wileyopenpage.com

FURTHER READING

Drew, J., McCallum, B. and Roggenhofer, S. (2004) *Journey to Lean: Making Operational Change Stick*, Palgrave Macmillan.

Keyte, B. and Locher, D. (2005) *The Complete Lean Enterprise: Value Stream Mapping for Administration and Office Processes*, Productivity Press.

Krafcik, J.F. (1988) Triumph of the lean production system. *Sloan Management Review*, Fall, 41–52.

Parry, S., Barlow, S. and Faulkner, M. (2005) *Sense and Respond: The Journey to Customer Purpose*, Palgrave Macmillan.

Schonberger, R. (2008) *World Class Manufacturing: The Lessons of Simplicity Applied*, Free Press.

Womack, J.P. and Jones, D.T. (2007) *Lean Solutions: How Producers and Consumers Achieve Mutual Value and Create Wealth*, Simon & Schuster.

WEB LINKS

www.lean.org (accessed 8 December 2011). Lean Enterprise Institute. Details workshops and tools for lean implementation.

www.nummi.com (accessed 8 December 2011). New United Motor Manufacturing Inc. Joint venture of General Motors Corporation and Toyota Motor Corporation to introduce the Toyota Production System and a teamwork-based working environment to the United States.

www.shingoprize.com (accessed 8 December 2011). Shingo Prize for Excellence in Manufacturing.

www.toyota.com (accessed 8 December 2011). Toyota UK. News and information regarding Toyota.

REFERENCES

Bicheno, J. (2004) *The New Lean Toolbox: Towards Fast, Flexible Flow*, PICSIE Books, Buckingham.

Frei, F. X. (2006), 'Customer-Introduced variability in service operations'. HBS No. 606-063, Boston: Harvard Business School Publishing.

Hall, R.W. (1989) *Attaining Manufacturing Excellence*, IRWIN.

Krafcik, J. F. (1988) Triumph of the lean production system, *Sloan Management Review*, 30 (1), 41–51.

Ohno, T. (1988) *Toyota Production System: Beyond Large-Scale Production*, Productivity Press.

Schniederjans, M.J. (1993) *Topics in Just-In-Time Management*, Allyn & Bacon.

Shingo, S. (1996) *Quick Changeover for Operators: The SMED System*, Productivity Press.

Womack, J.P. and Jones, D.T. (2005) Lean consumption. *Harvard Business Review*, March, 1–11.

Womack, J.P., Jones, D.T. and Roos, D. (2007) *The Machine that Changed the World*, Free Press.

CHAPTER 14

Enterprise Resource Planning

- **Introduction**
- **Enterprise resource planning (ERP) systems**
- **Customer relationship management (CRM) systems**
- **Resource planning**
- **Materials requirements planning**
- **Manufacturing resource planning (MRP II)**
- **Distribution requirements planning (DRP)**

LEARNING OBJECTIVES

- Understand the concept of enterprise resource planning (ERP)
- Describe the elements in resource planning
- Understand the concept of materials requirements planning (MRP)
- Describe the components of MRP
- Understand the concept of manufacturing resource planning (MRP II)
- Understand the concept of distribution requirements planning (DRP)

ERP AND OPERATIONS STRATEGY

In one sense ERP is an investment in process technology to improve efficiency but it is an investment that can have a major effect on the management of the organization. This is because it requires the organization to follow the process designs defined within the ERP process blueprints.

This change in process design may have a large impact on the operations strategic capability and is particularly relevant to organizations following a resource-based strategy. As a competitive strategy in itself implementing ERP can improve performance but it is unlikely to provide a sustained competitive advantage as other organizations can purchase the same system from the same supplier. However, implementation may be needed to enable the firm to stay competitive with other organizations who have previously installed ERP. It may also be vital in ensuring electronic links are available to other members in the supply chain.

In summary, although the benefits of ERP are many, the risks of adopting ERP should also be considered both in terms the risk inherent in implementing large, costly information technology projects and the risks in terms of compromising the current operations strategy. Issues to consider include the difficulty and expense of implementation due to factors such as high software costs, additional training required, loss of output during implementation and unsuccessful implementation. There is also the risk that working to new ERP defined process designs restricts the ability to meet market requirements and the risk that customizing standard ERP process designs may mean efficiencies are not maximized.

INTRODUCTION

This chapter covers the use of information systems that provide assistance to the operations manager in resource-planning activities. Enterprise resource planning (ERP) systems provide integration of software applications in different functional areas and provide links to external customers and suppliers in the supply chain. The elements of resource planning are then outlined before the use of MRP, manufacturing resource planning (MRP II) and distribution requirements planning (DRP) systems are discussed. Materials requirements planning systems are used to determine the timing and quantity of material requirements. Materials requirements planning aims to ensure that just the right quantity of each item is held at the right time in order to meet the needs of the production schedule taking into account ordering and manufacturing lead times. Manufacturing resource planning (MRP II) systems are a development of MRP and connect the system to other functional areas such as marketing and finance. Distribution requirements planning (DRP) widens the traditional acquisition, handling and production functions of MRP across the supply chain so that another form of dependent demand can be considered between the producer of goods, the regional distribution centre, the local distribution outlets or retailers and the customer.

ENTERPRISE RESOURCE PLANNING (ERP) SYSTEMS

Enterprise resource planning (ERP) systems (often termed enterprise systems) support the business processes of an organization across functional boundaries that exist within that organization. They usually use Internet technology to integrate information within the business and with external stakeholders such as customers, suppliers and partners. The main elements of an enterprise resource planning (ERP)

FIGURE 14.1

SAP ERP.

Source: © Copyright 2013. SAP AG. All rights reserved. Reproduced with permission.

 www.wileyopenpage.com

system are concerned with internal production, distribution and financial processes but may also include elements such as the following:

- **customer relationship management (CRM)** which is concerned with marketing and sales processes (see later section in this chapter).
- **supply chain management (SCM)** which is concerned with the flow of materials, information and customers through the supply chain (Chapter 15).
- **supplier relationship management (SRM)** which is concerned with all activities involved with obtaining items from a supplier, which includes procurement, but also inbound logistics such as transportation, goods-in and warehousing before the item is used (Chapters 12–15).

FIGURE 14.2

An IT Application within an Information Island.

Other elements may include product life cycle management (PLM), financial management and human capital management. Figure 14.1 shows a selection of enterprise software applications available from the SAP software vendor.

Enterprise resource planning systems are normally purchased as an off-the-shelf package which then can be tailored to meet the needs of the organization. Enterprise resource planning is particularly relevant in the integration of supply chains in enabling organizations in the supply chain to access one another's databases. ERP systems may access other members of the supply chain via electronic data interchange (EDI) facilities (Chapter 15) but usually use the Internet as a platform to allow secure access to information by members of the supply chain.

The main reason for implementing an ERP system is that it can replace a number of separate IT applications using incompatible data (sometimes known as 'information islands') in different functional parts of the company (Figure 14.2).

There are two main reasons for the existence of information islands. Firstly, some organizations have grown through the merger of firms, each with its own systems, which were incompatible with those of other firms. The second reason is that in many organizations the selection of software applications became devolved, with the end-users in individual departments making their own purchasing decisions. This often led to separate applications from different vendors in different departments, often with poor data transfer between applications. The goal of ERP is to achieve integration across the organization (Figure 14.3).

This integration of applications across the organization fits with the process view that organizations have used in improvement approaches such as business process management (Chapter 8). Using a process view, the organization is seen as a family of processes (such as order fulfilment), rather than as a set of departments. Enterprise resource planning is seen as a way of implementing a process view in the organization through the use of software.

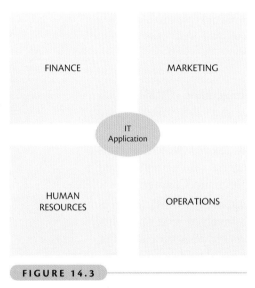

FINANCE

MARKETING

IT
Application

HUMAN
RESOURCES

OPERATIONS

FIGURE 14.3

An IT Application Integrated across the Organization.

Although many successful ERP implementations exist there are potential disadvantages to ERP systems, the most prominent of which is the potential high costs of installing a system which replaces all the previous departmental applications. The cost of an ERP system can be in the millions of euros and so it may not be a feasible option for many small and medium-sized organizations. However, scaled-down versions of ERP software are appearing for small and medium-sized enterprises. The move to an ERP system with a common database can also mean that working practices have to change. This has implications for the cost of training personnel in new ways of working and any loss of performance that may derive from the need to adapt to the ERP system, rather than use applications developed to departmental requirements.

In common with other investment decisions that operations managers have to make in terms of people and equipment, it is important that decisions are based on achieving strategic objectives. It is unlikely that one ERP software supplier will provide all the most current and relevant application software for a particular company. If alternative software is available that may provide a competitive advantage then a decision to forego the advantages of integration may have to be taken. It should also be considered that the main reason for ERP, in terms of achieving integration of systems, can usually be achieved at a price in terms of the time and cost of writing integration software. The major choice facing an organization is whether to renew IT systems in a number of 'big bangs' with the installation of detailed specified major systems or to develop systems that contain a mix of new and old (legacy) systems in a more incremental manner. Either of these choices may make sense and can incorporate the advantages of the other.

Enterprise resource planning systems may allow some customization (without requiring a whole new system) through the use of application programming interfaces (APIs), which allow programmers some access to the ERP software package. Mixed systems can provide compatibility by defining standards at the communications interface level. Thus the internal operation of software can be tailored to local needs but all software must work to a common interface. However, the choice made should be directed by the need to improve strategic performance, in regards to the performance objectives such as lower prices, higher quality, lower lead times that gives the organization a competitive advantage in the marketplace.

CASE STUDY 14.1

ERP: A convincing case must be made before investment

Finance software that captures every transaction a company conducts and automatically routes it to the correct ledger is at the heart of every enterprise resource planning (ERP) system.

Implemented well, these complex software suites – which also include applications for manufacturing, logistics, human resources and customer relationship management – can make a chief financial officer's life easier, by automating otherwise time-consuming manual processes and streamlining financial reporting.

Implemented poorly, however, they can quickly become a CFO's worst nightmare, blowing a hole in the company budget and leaving staff struggling to perform day-to-day duties.

After more than 20 years of ERP implementations, the disaster stories keep coming.

Last year, for example, Ingram Micro, an IT distributor, reported two consecutive quarters of profit shortfalls, which it blamed on problems in its Australian operations implementing an ERP system from SAP, a software group. In the US, ERP software specialists Epicor and Lawson are both facing lawsuits from disgruntled customers over failed projects that they say led to substantial cost overruns.

While there are plenty of success stories too, an annual survey released this month by Panorama Consulting Solutions, an ERP specialist, suggests that some of the blame for failures lies with customers who fail to identify project costs and potential savings – both of which are clear areas of responsibility for the CFO.

Panorama Consulting surveyed 246 companies from 64 countries worldwide over the course of 2011, and found that in 50 per cent of cases, at least 50 per cent of expected benefits from an ERP implementation were not realised.

More than half of ERP projects (56 per cent) went over budget and nearly one in three organisations said they had yet to recoup project costs.

The report suggests that better business cases are needed for ERP investments. 'A business case captures potential costs savings and establishes a baseline,' it says.

'While organisations want to know when they will realise the total cost of a project, a good organisation will capitalise on the ERP system. Not only should a company calculate its break even point, but also its overall return on investment,' it continues.

That view is echoed by Andrew Meade, UK and Ireland lead for finance and enterprise performance at Accenture, a consultancy.

While the CFO's role should include working with the chief information officer on the business case and project costs relating to an ERP implementation, he says, they should also 'set the tone for the rules of the design and build of the ERP system', so the strategy is based on both 'real business needs and business affordability'.

That means that, from the start, CFOs need to take a careful view of the business as a whole – a view that extends beyond their own department.

Employees in the finance function are likely to be among the main users of the system, certainly, but the needs of employees elsewhere also need to be taken into account.

At Selecta Biosciences, a start-up pharmaceutical company that develops vaccines, David Siewers, the CFO, has been able to develop the company's ERP strategy from scratch.

When he chose a cloud-based ERP system from NetSuite, a seller of on-demand business software, he was mindful of the fact that, as Selecta grows, it is likely to require additional modules to the finance applications now in place.

www.wileyopenpage.com

'Finance applications drove this selection, but the ability to add HR software or sales software was a key factor in my choice,' he says.

'From the start, I knew that I didn't want to be replacing the ERP system further down the line.' The cloud computing approach, with its subscription-based model of payment, he says, means Selecta only pays for the applications it uses at any given time.

But what approach should CFOs take, who are working in companies that already have ERP systems in place?

According to a 2011 report from Gartner, an IT market analysis company, these CFOs should take a step back from automatically approving a hefty annual budget for upgrades and improvements.

'Specifically, we recommend that CFOs interrupt the annual default administrative ERP project funding trend, by placing a two-year moratorium on funding fresh ERP-based finance and HR solution additions, upgrades, enhancements and so forth if their organisations have already completed [these] within the past two years,' writes Ken McGee, a Gartner analyst.

That moratorium does not need to be absolute, he adds – but only the most robust appeal should be allowed to override it.

The message is clear: just because an implementation was successful, that does not mean the system should go on making large claims on a budget.

Source: Financial Times (2012). Reproduced with permission.

Question

What are the barriers to the successful implementation of ERP and how can these barriers be overcome?

The evolution of ERP systems implementation

ERP systems have existed since the 1960s and their evolution reflects the changes in information systems since that time. The first ERP used a mainframe architecture consisting of a central computer connected to a number of terminals. These systems were expensive, lacked scalability and were mostly sold by a single supplier, IBM, until the 1980s. Consequently their use was mainly limited to large organizations.

The second stage of ERP development is the use of a client server architecture that distributes the workload of the application across multiple, smaller applications servers. This architecture significantly reduces the costs of purchasing and using an ERP and improves the scalability of the system.

The third stage of ERP development is the use of web-based systems to integrate several client-server applications and create an enterprise application. This increases the flexibility of the ERP at a relatively low cost and the web provides a standard platform for integration of applications across organizations. These systems can be referred to as **web-integrated ERP systems**.

CUSTOMER RELATIONSHIP MANAGEMENT (CRM) SYSTEMS

Customer relationship management covers the whole process by which relationships with customers are built and maintained. Customer relationship management systems are designed to integrate the range of information systems that contain information regarding the customer. These include applications such as customer details and preference databases, sales order processing applications and sales force automation. The idea is to acquire customers, retain customers and increase customer involvement with the organization.

Customer relationship management systems are built around a database and when this database is accessed, by employees and customers, using a web site, the technology is often referred to as eCRM. Common applications that would be integrated in a CRM system include:

- *Customer data collection*. This can include personal details such as age, sex and contact address. Also a record of purchase transactions undertaken in terms of factors such as location, date, time, quantity and price. This information can be used by call-centre staff to improve and tailor their services to individual customers.
- *Customer data analysis*. The captured data allows the categorization and targeting of customers according to criteria set by the firm. This information can be used to improve the effectiveness of marketing campaigns.
- *Sales force automation*. The entire sales cycle from lead generation to close of sale and after-sales service can be facilitated using CRM.

The technology must support all of these applications through whatever communications channel the customer and employee use. Communication channels include face-to-face, mail, phone, email as well as Web-based interaction. As with other technologies the implementation of CRM is a choice between attempting to integrate a number of legacy (existing) systems such as sales order processing or choosing a single-vendor supplier such as for ERP. Single-vendor systems from suppliers such as SAP and Oracle are able to provide better integration and thus potentially better customer service. However, they are relatively expensive to install and one firm is unlikely to supply the best-in-class applications in all aspects of the CRM implementation.

RESOURCE PLANNING

This section outlines the steps in the resource-planning process that is at the core of any ERP system. This is an important activity in operations management as it ensures that appropriate resources are available to undertake the operations function. The elements involved in resource planning are shown in Figure 14.4.

The first step in resource planning is to generate an **aggregate plan** (also called the production plan) which identifies the resources required in the medium term (6–18 months). The **demand profile** consists of the products and services required by the marketing plan, future customer orders and other demand factors such as the manufacture of items for spares. The aggregate plan will specify aspects such as overall production rate, size of the workforce, the amount of subcontracting required to deliver the mix of products or service required to meet the demand profile. The plan will not normally detail the amount of resource necessary for a particular product or service but will provide figures aggregated at the level of product or service families. The plans may be updated on a monthly basis and can incorporate the concepts of lead capacity, lag capacity and the use of inventory to smooth demand (see the capacity timing section in Chapter 5). There are many different aggregate plans that can be formulated to produce a particular output, so each plan should be evaluated in terms of factors such as cost, customer service, operational effectiveness and effect on workforce morale.

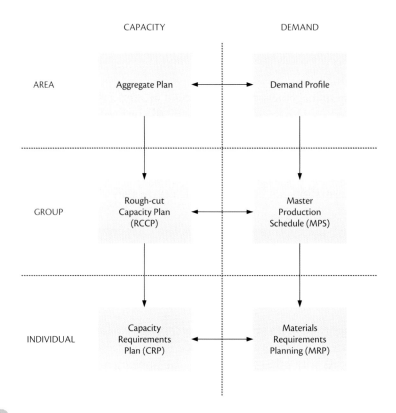

CAPACITY   DEMAND

AREA   Aggregate Plan ←⋯→ Demand Profile

GROUP   Rough-cut
              Capacity Plan ←⋯→ Master
              (RCCP)   Production
                                  Schedule (MPS)

INDIVIDUAL   Capacity
              Requirements ←⋯→ Materials
              Plan (CRP)   Requirements
                                  Planning (MRP)

FIGURE 14.4

Elements in Resource Planning.

The next stage in the planning process is to develop the **master production schedule (MPS)**, which shows how many products or services are planned for each time period, based on the resources authorized in the aggregate plan. Thus the aggregate plan shows the number of products or services to be produced in a time period (say 500 a month) while the master production schedule specifies the actual products or services to be produced (say 200 of service A, 150 of service B and 150 of service C, making 500 in total). The MPS is based on information from the aggregate plan (based on the demand profile) and any other forms of demand that require capacity in the short term (for example, new customer orders). The MPS is then used by the rough-cut capacity planning process to calculate rough estimates of the workload placed by the schedule on key resource constraints. Most operations will have bottleneck resources that constrain the overall production capacity. Checking at this level may save unnecessary detailed planning. If the capacity is not available to meet the MPS, either additional capacity must be secured or the MPS must be adjusted, although this may mean that the marketing plan may not be achieved.

As stated earlier, the aggregate plan takes information from the marketing plan to identify the resources required to deliver the products and services specified. The **rough-cut capacity plan (RCCP)** takes information from the MPS to evaluate the feasibility of the MPS. A third level of checking of capacity is the **capacity requirements plan (CRP)** which takes information from the MRP system (see next section for a discussion of MRP) to calculate workloads for critical work centres or workers. This allows the feasibility of the MRP system and the use of the critical work centres or workers to be evaluated.

MATERIALS REQUIREMENTS PLANNING

Materials requirements planning (MRP) is an information system used to calculate the requirements for component materials needed to produce end items. These components have what is called dependent demand (the management of independent demand items is covered in Chapter 12). A dependent demand item has a demand that is relatively predictable because it is dependent on other factors. For example, a fireplace mantel consists of two legs and one shelf. If daily demand for the mantel, derived from the production schedule, is 50 mantels, then a daily demand of 100 legs and 50 shelves can be predicted. Thus a dependent demand item can be classified as having a demand that can be calculated as the quantity of the item needed to produce a scheduled quantity of an assembly that uses that item. MRP systems manage dependent demand items by calculating the quantity needed and the timing required (taking into account purchasing and manufacturing lead times) of each item. The components of an MRP system that use and process this information are shown in Figure 14.5 and each component of the MRP system is now described.

Master Production Schedule (MPS)

An ideal *master production schedule (MPS)* is one which most efficiently uses the organization's capacity while being able to meet customer due dates. The master schedule provides a plan for the quantity and timing of when orders are required. The MRP system will use this information and, taking into account delivery, production and supply lead times, will indicate when materials are needed to achieve

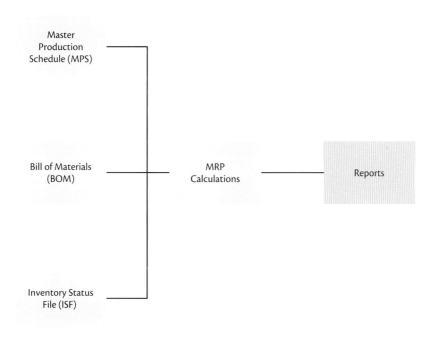

FIGURE 14.5

Components of an MRP System.

the master schedule. The MPS will usually show plans based on time 'buckets' based on, for example, a day or a week. The length of the time bucket will generally be longer (for instance a month) for planning purposes and become shorter closer to the present time for detailed production planning tasks.

The MPS will usually contain a mix of both plans for customer ordered items and plans to produce to forecast sales. The forecast is a best estimate of what future demand will be, which may be derived from past sales and contact with the customer. These forecasts should be replaced by firm orders as the expected order date approaches. If actual orders exceed the forecast then either the order will be delivered to the customer late or extra capacity must be obtained (for example, overtime, subcontracting) to meet the customer delivery date.

The mix of forecast and firm orders that a business can work to depends on the nature of the business. A resource-to-order company (such as a construction firm) will only allocate resources and materials to a firm order. Purchase-to-order organizations will not order materials until a firm order is made but will have labour and equipment permanently available. A make-to-stock business, however, will work mainly to forecast demand. Most operations will actually operate with different P:D ratios (Chapter 10) for different product or service types. The mix between firm orders and forecast demand may also vary over time for a certain business. For example, seasonal effects may increase the number of firm orders taken in certain time periods.

Bill of Materials (BOM)

The **bill of materials (BOM)** identifies all the components required to produce a scheduled quantity of an assembly and the structure of how these components fit together to make that assembly. The BOM can be viewed as a product structure tree, similar to an organization chart (Figure 14.6). In this example the item description is followed by the number of items required in square brackets and the item part number.

The final assembly of the product structure is denoted as level 0, while the structure is 'exploded' to further levels representing subassemblies below this. These subassemblies are then broken down into further levels until the individual order components are reached. Individual order components can either be a single component item or subassemblies purchased from suppliers and thus treated as a single component. The tree structure shown in Figure 14.6 is useful to show the relationships among

FIGURE 14.6

Bill of Materials (BOM) Product Structure.

 www.wileyopenpage.com

TABLE 14.1

Indented Bill of Materials.

Level	Part no.	Quantity	Description
0	2705	1	Kitchen cabinet
1	1018	4	Leg
1	2978	3	Drawer
2	7219	1	Foot
2	3319	1	Top
2	7583	1	Back
2	7723	2	Side
2	3867	1	Base

components but to present the structure in a format suitable for processing by the computerized MRP system an indented BOM is used (Table 14.1).

The MRP system holds information on the number required of any item in the structure and the 'parent' item of which it is a component. Usually the product structure is stored in a series of single-level bills of materials, each of which holds a component part number and a list of the part numbers and quantities of the next lower level. The computer will move through all component BOMs in the product structure to derive a total number of components required for the product. Note the same component may appear in different parts of the product structure if it is used more than once. What is needed is the total number required for each component to make the final assembly. The accuracy of the BOM is obviously vital in generating the correct schedule of parts at the right time.

Inventory Status File (ISF)

The BOM indicates the quantity of components needed from the product structure but this will not be directly translated into demand for components because it is likely that some of the components will be currently held in inventory. The **inventory status file** provides information on the identification and quantity of items in stock. The MRP system will determine if a sufficient quantity of an item is in stock or whether an order must be placed. The inventory status file will also contain the lead time, or time between order and availability, for each component.

As with the BOM, the accuracy of the inventory status file is vital and some organizations use perpetual physical inventory checking (PPI) to ensure that inventory records are accurate. This means a continuous check of inventory records against actual stock, instead of the traditional year end checks for accounting purposes.

Materials Requirements Planning Calculations

The time-phased inventory status record can be used to show the inventory data requirements for each stock item and to follow the calculations necessary by the MRP programme. A simplified status record is shown in Table 14.2.

www.wileyopenpage.com

TABLE 14.2

Time-Phased Inventory Record

Item: subassembly 1	Week					
	0	1	2	3	4	5
Gross requirements		100	0	200	0	30
Scheduled receipts				200		
Projected on hand	100	0	0	0	0	−30

TABLE 14.3

Inventory Status File Showing Net Requirements.

Item: subassembly 1	Week					
	0	1	2	3	4	5
Gross requirements		100	0	200	0	30
Scheduled receipts				200		
Projected on hand	100	0	0	0	0	−30
Net requirements						30
Planned order release				30		

In this case weekly time buckets have been used, which is usual for short-term plans. Longer time buckets may be used for long-term planning purposes. The definition of each row is given below:

- *Gross requirements.* This row simply states the estimated requirements, in this case per week, for the item described. It is assumed that requirements occur during the time bucket (week) so that the scheduled receipts at the beginning of the week will cover them.
- *Scheduled receipts.* This row indicates when the item becomes available for use, from a previously released order. It is assumed that the receipt of the item occurs at the start of the time bucket period.
- *Projected on hand.* Numbers in this row show the number of units to be available at the end of each time bucket based on the balance of requirements and receipts. The formula for projected on hand is:

projected on hand = inventory on hand + scheduled receipts − gross requirements.

To account for a negative projected on hand, the time-phased inventory status record is extended as in Table 14.3.

- *Net requirements.* If the projected on hand is negative it is called a net requirement and means there will not be enough of this component to produce the quantities required to meet the master production schedule. Thus when a negative projected on hand is shown this will increase the net requirements row by a positive amount equal to the negative on hand.

● *Planned order release* (POR). The POR row indicates when an order should be released to ensure that the projected-on-hand figure does not become negative (that there are enough items to satisfy the MPS). The POR time must take into consideration the lead time between placing the order and the component becoming available (in the case of Figure 14.5 the lead time is two weeks). Thus the planned order release is offset by the required time amount to ensure enough items are available to cover net requirements and sometimes to also cover net requirements in future time buckets. It is important that the MRP programme works through all the levels of the assembly before calculating the net requirement for a time bucket as the same item may be needed at different levels of the same assembly or in different assemblies.

WORKED EXAMPLE 14.1

A dentist has scheduled appointments for the surgery over the next four weeks.

	Week			
	1	**2**	**3**	**4**
Appointments scheduled	30	60	55	60

Surgical gloves are ordered 100 pairs at a time and the ordering lead time is two weeks. There are 75 pairs of gloves in inventory at the start of week 1 with another 100 pairs expected to arrive during that week. Use MRP to schedule planned order releases for the gloves.

		Week			
Item: gloves	**0**	**1**	**2**	**3**	**4**
Gross requirements		30	80	75	60
Scheduled receipts		100		100	
Projected on hand	75	145	65	90	30
Net requirements					
Planned order release		100			

Thus there is a need for an order release in week 1 to ensure there is sufficient stock in week 3.

Materials Requirements Planning Reports

A number of reports can be generated by the MRP programme, which include information on the quantity of each item to order in the current and future time period, indication of which due dates cannot be met and showing when they can be met and also changes to quantities of currently ordered items. The system can also show the results of simulation of scenarios for planning purposes. For instance, by entering a customer order to the master schedule the effect of this extra work on overall customer due-date performance can be examined. If capacity restrictions mean that the order cannot be completed by the required due date, a new due date can be suggested.

Implementation of MRP

The use of MRP can reduce inventory by providing information on the actual inventory required for parent items (rather than stocking enough components for estimated parent demand). It can also help to prioritize orders to ensure delivery due dates are met, provide information on resource (labour and equipment) requirements for planning purposes and provide financial information on projected inventory expenditure. It is most useful in complex scheduling situations when the number of levels of subassemblies and components is high.

However, there are a number of limitations of MRP. For instance, when using MRP it is not always possible to assess the feasibility of meeting the due date quoted to a customer. Repeated changes to order due dates will entail new plans generated from the MRP system, which could lead to ever-changing schedules. The need to manufacture in batches negates the advantage of only scheduling inventory when needed. If batches are used extensively the component batch size will be a major factor in manufacturing lead time. If insufficient capacity is available, it is necessary to adjust planned order dates or make available additional resources. The knock-on effect may not be clear until the MRP schedule is regenerated. This may lead to a lengthy process of trying to find a feasible schedule. The MRP system has limited ability to assess the robustness of the schedule to random events (for example, machine breakdown). Changes to the inputs to the MRP system may be so rapid (customer needs change, design changes and so forth) that the planning function of MRP may be extremely limited. Many of the problems of MRP revolve around the problem of estimating capacity at various time frames. The aggregate plan, rough-cut capacity plan and the capacity requirements plan discussed earlier help with this.

MANUFACTURING RESOURCE PLANNING (MRP II)

Manufacturing resource planning (MRP II) extends the idea of MRP to other areas in the firm such as marketing and finance (Wight, 1984). Thus central databases hold information on product structure (the BOM file), which can be updated due to design changes by engineering for example. By incorporating financial elements into item details, inventory cost information can be used by finance departments. At a wider level information provided by the MRP II system from simulations of business plans can be used to estimate plant investment needs and workforce requirements. This information can then be used to coordinate efforts across departments including marketing, finance, engineering and manufacturing.

Although MRP II overcame many of the problems of MRP systems, there are still problems with MRP II implementations. A major problem remains the issue of ensuring the accuracy of information such as inventory records and bills of materials to ensure a usable system. Some MRP II systems are so complex they often require installation by external agencies who may not understand the business needs of the company. Companies were also faced with expensive modifications to systems that did not provide all the functionality required for the business. The MRP systems are based around meeting performance targets in terms of meeting customer due dates. However, conflicting objectives, such as financial targets, may override these, so undermining the planning process defined by the MRP implementation.

DISTRIBUTION REQUIREMENTS PLANNING (DRP)

Traditionally, MRP is associated with managing dependent demand items which form an assembly which has as independent demand (the demand is not dependent on other items). However, if the concept of MRP is widened from the traditional acquisition, handling and production functions across the supply chain to the customer then another form of dependent demand can be considered between the producer of goods, the regional distribution centre, the local distribution outlets or retailers and the customer. **Distribution requirements planning (DRP)** manages these linkages between all these elements on the supply chain beginning with an analysis of demand at each customer service location. These demands are aggregated across distribution centres to form a gross requirement which is fed into the master production schedule. Independent demand items are incorporated into the MRP logic by having a safety stock level below which a replenishment order is triggered. The order amount is determined by a lot sizing calculation. This method is called time-phased order point.

SUMMARY

- ERP provides an integrated solution to resource planning across the supply chain and across business functions such as production, distribution, sales, finance and human resources management.
- Resource planning involves developing an MPS, which is derived from the medium-term aggregate plan of resource requirements and the demand profile. The feasibility of the MPS is checked by the RCCP and the CRP.
- Materials requirements planning (MRP) is a computer software package that provides resource planning facilities. It is used to calculate demand for component materials needed to produce end items.
- Materials requirements planning calculations are based on how many products or services are planned, held in the MPS, the product structures, held in the BOM, and current inventory levels, held in the ISF.
- Manufacturing resource planning extends the concept of MRP to other areas in the organization such as marketing and finance to form an integrated business system.
- Distribution requirements planning extends the concept of MRP across the supply chain to producers and distributors of goods.

The Challenge of Changing Everything at Once

For Kolok, a South African distributor of printer consumables, such as ink cartridges and toner, meeting demand meant making changes. It moved premises, more than doubling warehouse space, added additional shifts and installed new warehouse and enterprise resource planning systems – all at the same time.

In southern Africa – Kolok's main market is South Africa but it also exports to neighbouring countries including Namibia and Botswana – customers expect quick delivery. Kolok, part of the Bidvest group, sells to retailers and directly to larger businesses. Neither set of customers wants to hold large stocks of supplies and many simply cannot afford to. 'The South African market is not like the US or Europe', says Allan Thompson, Kolok's managing director. 'We have persuaded our customers not to tie up their resources in stock, but to use our resources. And corporate customers expect delivery within a couple of hours.'

The weakness of the rand and other southern African currencies against the dollar and euro adds to this pressure, but also puts pressure on margins at both Kolok and its customers. 'Inflation here is 14% and that affects customers' spending ability, even though IT markets are growing at 19%', says Mr Thompson. He adds that currency swings can quickly wipe out any margins. On the day Mr Thompson spoke to Digital Business, the rand fell 6% against the dollar. As a result, much of Kolok's recent investment has been aimed at improving stock control.

Within South Africa, Kolok's Johannesburg warehouse covers a territory that stretches 1200 km north and 1400 km south, to the Cape. The company handles 4500 product lines from a 7000 m² warehouse with 8000 storage locations, some

of which are 12 m high. It also has to manage a mix of long- and short-term products. Some stock turns over 16 times a year but other lines turn just twice a year. The existing infrastructure could not cope. 'In the past, we would take deliveries and it would take four to five days to unload the containers', admits Mr Thompson. 'Once we had put the stock away, we didn't know where it was. We had spreadsheets we were trying to update, which was impossible with the volumes we handle. We now have stock management on a 24-hour basis, instead of a nine hours a day basis, and our "pick and pack" operations run for 16 hours rather than eight. We are getting much better utilization of our assets.'

For the systems update, which took place alongside the relocation of the company's main Johannesburg warehouse, spending on software and IT infrastructure came to $3.5 million. This excluded costs such as training and management time. However, the changeover was as smooth as Kolok had hoped. The scale of the upgrade – bringing warehouse storage locations onstream; updating the warehouse system with software from Manhattan Associates; and installing a new ERP platform in the shape of Microsoft Dynamics AX – put the company under real strain. Some staff, used to the previous DOS-based systems, had never operated a computer with a mouse before.

Integrating the ERP and warehouse systems proved harder than the company, and its suppliers, had expected. Service standards fell and Mr Thompson says these are only now returning to a level he considers acceptable. 'I would not update both the ERP and warehouse management systems at the same time again, but we had no option', he explains. 'For a year, we could not find stock, and we had to find stock to sell it. We had a short period from inception to the go-live date to have all the software tested, so we could not do the ERP today and the warehouse tomorrow. We would have been totally in the dark.'

Integration was further hampered by the difficulty of taking staff away from the job for training. And the security situation and poor public transport in South Africa do not allow staff to stay late for training courses. But the systems have now been integrated, at least for larger customers. 'The big customers are now seeing the benefit, but for me, it's as important to serve the small and mid-sized companies who might grow into large ones', Mr Thompson says.

The results for the business overall have justified the investment. Volumes handled by Kolok are up 27% on February 2007, and capacity in the warehouse operations has doubled. 'We are more efficient, and have more control of our assets, both mechanical equipment and human resources. Now, we can see where the pressure points are and where resources are needed. Previously, we had to go on gut feeling.' An order can now be ready for customer collection or delivery 15 minutes after it reaches the warehouse.

Once the integration problems have been resolved, Mr Thompson expects to realize a full return on investment in the IT side of the project within 18 months, primarily through better visibility of stock levels. 'We need to move stock as quickly as possible', he says. 'If it is a Monday, and we get 14 containers, we want to have none left by Friday.'

Source: Financial Times (2008). Reproduced with permission.

Questions

1. What are the main advantages of the ERP system described in the case study?
2. Can you identify any risks involved with an organization implementing ERP?

Lambton Clothing Co.

Lambton Tailoring was founded in 1999 by Edward Lambert and Matthew Norton, who operate with the key objective of supplying made-to-measure, bespoke and ready to wear garments to the retail & tailoring trade. The business was born out of the UK tailoring factory that was previously a vertically integrated part of the successful Norton & Townsend visiting tailoring business, but after years of tailoring exclusively for N&T the founders identified opportunities (against a background of increasing mass customization) in supplying the retail trade in general.

Lambtons have developed into a small (40 staff) but focused tailoring firm who specialise in bespoke pieces for their clients, offering great flexibility with a truly endless range of fabrics, styles and stitching. The Lambton Clothing Company have been around for 13 years and like so many organizations, prior to their recent success they have been through times of trouble; the success stemmed from the design and implementation of their ERP system.

At the start of Lambton's 'new era' they contacted a bespoke software house to design and construct an ERP system which would fully manage and integrate the processes of the firm; ranging from material acquisition, bespoke measurement, through the delivery and billing of the client.

The system integrates Lambton's with its suppliers to make procurement of materials fast and efficient as well as reducing storage costs as materials can be ordered on an 'as and when basis', and has enabled a number of system efficiencies and cost saving decisions to be made, one of which is a reduction in staff number due to the system automation, and significant reduction in waste, which was previously caused by human error.

The organization has reported that the ERP system has brought a reduction in cost, with an increase in quality and efficiency. The system has increased efficiency to a point that in the last 12 months they have made an average of 450 2-piece suits per week in their made to measure business, operating with a 20 to 22 working day dispatch target. Considering the industry average, and that over 300 pattern and additional lining ranges are on offer, this represents a significant improvement on past performance and in comparison to competitor delivery times.

The system has also resulted in greater speed and flexible on short (up to 100 garments) and medium runs (up to 500 garments) on the ready-to-wear/off-the-rack trade, and have been able to breach new markets such as their made to measure ladies range.

Lambtons now are seen as a 'one-stop shop' for tailoring in structured garments. Their flexible, tried and tested CAD patterns accompanied by their new ERP system have been the foundation of many tens of thousands of individually tailored garments. They have a huge library of cuts and style variations. When combined with a flexible manufacturing approach (use of UK and overseas facilities for both simple and complicated garments) Lambton Tailors supply consistent, high quality garments offering the reseller the optimum chance of satisfying their naturally demanding customer.

Source:

http://www.lambtontailoring.co.uk/.

Source: Written by Briony Boydell and Chris Milner. Reproduced with permission.

Questions

1. How has the implementation of an ERP system helped Lambtons?
2. What factors are required in an operation for ERP to be successful?

Quizzes to test yourself further are available in your interactive e-book at **www.wileyopenpage.com**

Flashcards to test yourself further are available in your interactive e-book at **www.wileyopenpage.com**

  www.wileyopenpage.com

EXERCISES

1. Discuss the advantages and disadvantages of implementing an ERP system.

2. Discuss the use of ERP software to replace software packages used in single areas of the organization, such as operations, marketing and accounting.

3. Identify and explain the role of the main components of an MRP system.

4. A company makes a product with a product code S40. Each S40 consists of two subassemblies A10 and B5. Subassembly A10 consists of part 1765 (two required) and part 1867 (one required). Part 1867 is in turn made from part 8644 (one required) and part 2888 (five required). Subassembly B5 consists of part 2887 (two required) and part 2888 (four required).

   a. Draw a tree diagram showing the product structure of product S40.

   b. Show an indented bill of materials for product S40.

5. A company has the following master schedule for its most popular dining table.

Week					
1	2	3	4	5	6
400	300	450	300	450	400

   Each table has four legs which have a production lead time of two weeks. 3500 legs are available projected on-hand inventory. An order for 2000 legs has already been released and is scheduled to arrive in week 2. The legs may be produced in any quantity. Use MRP to schedule planned order releases.

6. What are the main factors in the successful implementation of a Materials Requirement Planning system?

7. Evaluate the advantages and disadvantages of the MRP approach to production planning.

8. An electrical retailer operates two regional warehouses both of which are supplied from a central distribution centre. Delivery time from the distribution centre to the warehouses is one week. A particular model of dishwasher has a production lead time to the distribution centre of two weeks. It is shipped in standard quantities of fifty units. Use DRP to determine planned order releases for each warehouse and for the distribution centre using the following data.

Warehouse 1

Week	0	1	2	3	4
Gross requirements		30	30	40	20
Scheduled receipts					
Projected on hand	40				

Warehouse 2

Week	0	1	2	3	4
Gross requirements		20	30	30	30
Scheduled receipts					
Projected on hand	40				

WEB EXERCISE

Investigate the functions of a commercial ERP system at www.sap.com/uk/solutions/business-suite/erp/featuresfunctions/index.epx (accessed 15 December 2011).

FURTHER READING

Bocij, P., Greasley, A. and Hickie, S. (2008) *Business Information Systems: Technology, Development and Management*, 4th edn, Pearson Education Ltd.

WEB LINKS

www.bpic.co.uk (accessed 15 December 2011). Portal for resources for MRP and ERP installations.

www.manufacturingtalk.com (accessed 15 December 2011). Portal for resources for manufacturing, including MRP and ERP.

ERP Vendors

www.infor.com/solutions/erp/ (accessed 15 December 2011). Infor ERP Solutions.

http://www.oracle.com/applications/jdedwards-enterprise-one.html (accessed 15 December 2011). Oracle's JD Edwards Enterprise One ERP software.

www.sap.com (accessed 15 December 2011). SAP Business Suite.

REFERENCE

Wight, O. (1984) *Manufacturing Resource Planning: MRP II*, Oliver Wight Ltd.

CHAPTER 15

Supply Chain Management

- **Introduction**
- **Supply chain design**
- **Activities in the supply chain**

LEARNING OBJECTIVES

- Identify the elements of a supply chain management system
- Understand how demand fluctuations can occur in supply chains
- Understand the concepts of the lean and agile supply chain
- Describe the varying degrees of cooperation and integration in the supply chain
- Understand the role of procurement in the supply chain
- Discuss the area of physical distribution management in terms of material handling, warehousing, packaging and transportation.

SUPPLY CHAIN MANAGEMENT AND OPERATIONS STRATEGY

The operations strategy will provide the basis for supply chain decisions covering areas such as supply chain integration and activities including procurement and physical distribution management. Three approaches to supply chain management of Agile, Lean and QRM have been proposed in order to meet priorities set by the operations strategy. Lean supply chains adopt the concept of lean operations and emphasize efficiency, agile supply chains help to implement a strategy based on the ability to respond to market variability and QRM provides a way of implementing agile by a primary focus on the reduction of lean times. Leagility is a combination of the lean and agile approaches which attempts to achieve the advantages of lean (efficiency) and the advantages of agile (effectiveness in responding to market demand). One way of implementing leagile supply chains is the concept of postponement. This involves the use of a decoupling point which holds 'strategic' inventory in modular form until precise customer requirements are known. Companies can use lean methods up to the decoupling point and then agile methods beyond it. This is an attempt to meet the strategic priorities of customers who require both customization and relatively short lead times in products and services.

INTRODUCTION

The **supply chain** consists of the series of activities that moves materials from suppliers, through operations to customers. Each product or service will have its own supply chain, which may involve many organizations in processing, transportation, warehousing and retail. The set of relationships between a firm and its suppliers and customers in the supply chain is termed the supply network (Chapter 5).

A representation of the structure of a supply chain is shown in Figure 15.1. Activities on the input side to the organization are termed 'upstream' or 'supply' side and are divided into tiers of suppliers.

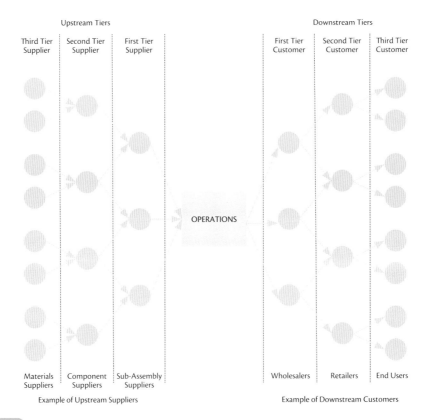

FIGURE 15.1

The Structure of a Supply Chain.

 www.wileyopenpage.com

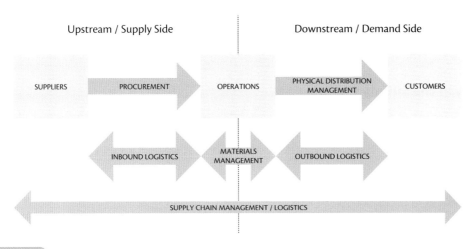

FIGURE 15.2

Terms used to Describe the Management of the Supply Chain.

Upstream suppliers that supply the organization directly are termed 'first tier' and suppliers that supply first tier organizations are termed 'second tier' and so on. Examples of upstream suppliers are component and subassembly suppliers.

Activities on the output side are termed 'downstream' or 'demand' side and are divided into tiers of customers. Examples of **downstream customers** are wholesalers and retailers. There will be a separate supply chain for each product or service that an organization produces and this structure is sometimes referred to as the 'supply network' or 'supply web'.

The terms used in the area of supply chain management are defined in a number of ways and so the most common terms are first defined as they will be used in this text (Figure 15.2). **Supply chain management** and logistics are terms used to refer to the management of the flow of materials through the entire supply chain. Sometimes logistics or business logistics refer to activities in the downstream portion of the chain. **Inbound (or inward) logistics** is used to describe the activity of moving material in from suppliers and **outbound (or outward) logistics** is used to describe the activity of moving materials out to customers. The movement of materials within the organization is termed **materials management** (materials management can also be used to refer to the management of upstream supply chain activities). Materials management activities are specifically addressed in this text in Chapters 12, 13 and 14. In this chapter, supply chain activities are presented around the areas of procurement, which is the operations interface with upstream activities, and physical distribution management, which deals with downstream activities such as warehousing and transportation.

SUPPLY CHAIN DESIGN

This section discusses the strategic issue of how the supply chain should be designed to optimize performance. Other strategic issues regarding supply chain design are facility location and long-term capacity planning, both covered in Chapter 5. One of the key issues in supply chain design is that organizations need to cooperate with one another in order to provide customer satisfaction. One of the reasons for that cooperation is to limit fluctuations in demand which occur in these networks and affect performance. The reasons behind those fluctuations will be discussed, before exploring the various ways in which the supply chain network can be configured to promote cooperation.

Variability in the Supply Chain

There are a number of factors that increase variability in the supply chain. These include a time lag between ordering materials and getting them delivered to the customer. This time lag can be expressed as the 'lead time gap':

$$\text{Lead Time Gap} = \text{Logistics Pipeline} - \text{Customers Order Cycle Time}$$

where

Logistics Pipeline = Time to source materials, convert them into products and move them to the marketplace

Customers Order Cycle Time = How long the customer is prepared to wait for the product

To overcome the lead time gap, the traditional way is to make a forecast of inventory which may lead to over-ordering in advance to ensure sufficient stock is available to meet customer demand. This approach can be costly, for example, losses in the apparel pipeline have been estimated at 25% of retail sales, consisting of forced markdowns 14.6%, stock-outs 4% and the carrying cost of inventory 6.4% (Lowson et al., 1999).

Also the use of order batching (when orders are not placed until they reach a predetermined batch size) can cause a mismatch between demand and the order quantity. Price fluctuations such as price cuts and quantity discounts also lead to more demand variability in the supply chain as companies buy products before they need them. These effects can be amplified across the supply chain by a behaviour known as the Forrester effect or **bullwhip effect** as described by Jay Forrester (1961). The effect occurs when there is a lack of synchronization in supply chain members, when even a slight change in consumer sales will ripple backwards in the form of magnified oscillations in demand upstream. To demonstrate this effect Figure 15.3 shows a spreadsheet of the relationship between four members of a supply chain, the customer, retailer, wholesaler and manufacturer. As can be seen a slight change in customer demand, rising from 100 units to 108 units in week 2, has an ever increasing effect on demand at each stage of the upstream demand. Note also that it takes until week 6 for the supply chain to revert to the stable pattern shown in week 1, despite customer demand reverting to 100 units from week 3 onwards.

The calculations used in the spreadsheet are as follows:

$$\text{demand} = \text{orders made by next tier in supply chain}$$
$$\text{opening stock} = \text{closing stock from previous week}$$
$$\text{closing stock} = \text{demand for that week}$$
$$\text{orders} = \text{demand} + (\text{closing stock} - \text{opening stock}).$$

The bullwhip effect occurs because each tier in the supply chain increases demand by the current amount but also assumes that demand is now at this new level, so increases demand to cover the next week too. Thus each member in the supply chain updates its demand forecast with every inventory review. Thus in week 2 an increase in customer demand of eight units is translated into an order of 16 units from the retailer to the warehouse (eight units to cover this week and eight units to cover next

FIGURE 15.3

Spreadsheet Showing Effect of Varying Sales Demand on Supply Chain.

week's demand), who then orders 32 units from the manufacturer, who then orders 64 units from the supplier and so on. Thus each member in the supply chain is replenishing each level in the supply chain above it, rather than being linked directly to customer demand.

Dealing with Variability in the Supply Chain

A number of steps can be taken to deal with the issue of variability in the supply chain. The traditional way to deal with uncertainty of demand is to improve forecast quality but this is difficult to do in volatile markets, so there is an emphasis on reducing three critical lead times:

1. *Time-to-market* – how long does it take to recognize a market opportunity and bring products/ services to the market?
2. *Time-to-serve* – how long does it take to capture a customer's order and to deliver the product?
3. *Time-to-react* – how long does it take to adjust the output of the business in response to volatile demand?

Another approach to reduce variability is to use smaller batch sizes in order to smooth the demand pattern. Often batch sizes are large because of the relatively high cost of each order. Technologies such as e-procurement and electronic data interchange (EDI) can reduce the cost of placing an order and so help eliminate the need for large batch orders. The use of a stable pricing policy can also help limit demand fluctuations.

In order to limit the bullwhip effect certain actions can be taken. The major aspect that can limit supply chain variability is to share information amongst members of the supply chain. In particular it is useful for members to have access to the product demand to the final seller, so that all members in the chain are aware of the true customer demand. Information technology such as electronic point-of-sale (EPOS) systems can be used by retailers to collect customer demand information at cash registers which can be transmitted to warehouses and suppliers further down the supply chain. If information is available to all parts of the supply chain it will also help to reduce lead times between ordering and delivery by using a system of coordinated or synchronized material movements.

The video 'Wal-Mart India's Raj Jain on Modernizing Supply Chains' is available in your interactive e-book at **www.wileyopenpage.com**

Agile and Lean Supply Chains

Agile operations aim to respond quickly to market demand in order to retain current markets and gain new market share. As a strategy agile operations can be seen to embrace uncertainty in markets and achieve competitive advantage by the flexibility and speed of their response to them. The focus of agility has moved from an individual organization to supply chains in which several companies work together.

Harrison (1999) defines four characteristics of agile supply chains:

1. *Market sensitive.* The supply chain is able to receive real-time demand change information and make a quick response. For example, use point-of-sale data and market research to find current demand. There is a use of Computer-Aided Design (CAD) to quickly design new products.
2. *Virtual.* Virtual supply chains are information based, using IT to share between participants, rather than inventory based. For example, retailers provide customer sales data to their suppliers.
3. *Network based.* Companies in the supply chain have a commitment to agile practices, such as compatible information architecture.
4. *Process aligned.* A focus on the chain of events from a customer's order inquiry to satisfaction of that customer. For example, the use of a web-based platform to connect organizations together with incompatible internal systems.

Agile supply chains should offer the following benefits:

- *Visibility*. Supply chain participants should have full visibility of customer demand, supply sources, inventory levels, promotion plans etc. This visibility should help companies increase the speed of the flow of materials, information and customers through their organization and thus speed up response times.
- *Flexibility*. Key areas are product development, sourcing, manufacturing and logistics flexibility.
- *Speed*. The end-to-end cycle time from manufacture to distribution. The smaller the cycle time the more quickly responses can be implemented.
- *Predictability*. The response of the supply chain to changes should be predictable to all supply chain participants.
- *Scalability*. The ability to respond to demand changes.

Leagility

An alternative model to the agile supply chain is the concept of the lean supply chain. Lean supply chains adopt the concept of lean operations (Chapter 13) across the supply chain. Lean supply chains emphasize efficiency which is achieved by policies such as minimizing inventory across the supply chain and continuous improvement across the supply chain. It has also been proposed that the lean and agile supply chain approaches can be combined using the concept of **leagility**. Christopher and Towill (2001) propose three ways of bringing lean and agile together:

1. *Pareto Rule (80/20 rule)*. 80% of the volume in the supply chain is generated from 20% of the product line so use lean for 20% of predictable high volume product lines to seek economies of scale and make to forecast. Use agile for the 80% of less predictable product lines and aim for quick response and make to order (see Figure 15.4).

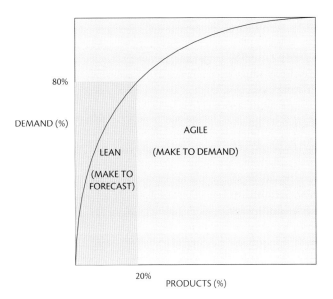

FIGURE 15.4

Combining Lean and Agile Using the Pareto Rule.

STRATEGIC INVENTORY

LEAN

MAKE TO
FORECAST

PUSH-PULL BOUNDARY

AGILE

MAKE TO
DEMAND

FIGURE 15.5

Combining Lean and Agile Using Postponement.

2. *Postponement.* This involves the use of a decoupling point which holds 'strategic' inventory in modular form until precise customer requirements are known. Companies can use lean methods up to the decoupling point and then agile methods beyond it (Figure 15.5). The concept can also be used with an information decoupling point. This represents the furthest point upstream at which 'real' demand information flows (i.e. information not distorted by policies such as reorder points). The point at which strategic inventory is held is also called the push-pull boundary as production is pushed up to the boundary point based on forecast demand and then inventory is pulled from the boundary point based on actual demand. A number of factors are considered when choosing the position in the supply chain that the push-pull boundary should occur. These include the need to position the boundary before proliferation of product or service designs and the need to ensure that the lead time after the boundary is relatively short in order to ensure fast response to customer orders.

3. *Base and Surge.* Base demand can be forecast on the basis of history and so can be met using lean to maximize efficiency. Surge demand is met by more flexible (agile) processes (Figure 15.6). One strategy is to source base demand in low cost countries and meet surge demand in local markets (albeit at higher cost but more effective overall). This strategy is used in the fashion industry by such companies as Zara and Benetton.

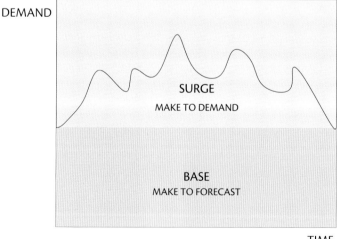

DEMAND

SURGE
MAKE TO DEMAND

BASE
MAKE TO FORECAST

TIME

FIGURE 15.6

Combining Lean and Agile by Separating Base and Surge Demand.

Quick Response Manufacturing (QRM)

An alternative approach to managing supply chains is named Quick Response Manufacturing (QRM). QRM is a company-wide strategy for reducing lead times throughout the enterprise. External lead times are reduced by rapidly designing and manufacturing products to customers' needs and internal lead times are reduced in order to improve quality, lower cost and provide quicker response to the customer.

QRM is based on four core concepts (Suri, 2010):

1. *The power of time.* The reduction of lead time should drive all decisions. Lead time is defined as the typical amount of calendar time from when a customer creates an order, through the critical path until the first piece of that order is delivered to the customer. The approach is that reducing lead time will lead to a quicker response.

2. *Organization structure.* This involves a move from functional departments to flexible cells, from top-down control to team ownership, from specialized and narrowly focused workers to a cross-trained workforce and from efficiency/utilization goals to lead time reduction.

3. *System dynamics.* This looks at how interaction between machines, people and products impact lead times. The approach is to avoid too high utilization of resources as this can increase lead times considerably. Also the aim is to reduce the variability in flow time (arrival time + process time) to reduce lead time and choose a batch size that minimizes lead time.

4. *Enterprise-wide application.* Apply the principle of minimizing lead times across all departments, apply the principle of minimizing lead time to suppliers and apply the principle of QRM to rapid new product development.

Supply Chain Integration

Organizations in a supply chain can have varying degrees of cooperation and integration. In order of increasing ownership, the options are: a market relationship, strategic partnerships and alliances, virtual organization and vertical integration (Figure 15.7).

| MARKET RELATIONSHIP | STRATEGIC PARTNERSHIPS AND ALLIANCES | VIRTUAL ORGANIZATION | VERTICAL INTEGRATION |

DEGREE OF INTEGRATION →

FIGURE 15.7

Supply Chain Relationships by Degree of Integration.

At the level of an individual product or service the amount of integration in the supply chain can be characterized as an analysis of the costs and risks in either making a component in-house or buying it from a supplier, termed a 'make-or-buy decision'. However, this approach does not take into account what may be critical strategic issues involved in deciding what it should do itself and what can be done by others. At a strategic level supply chain integration decisions should be related to the way that the organization competes in the marketplace. For example, if speed of delivery is an order winner then it may be necessary to make certain components in-house to ensure a fast and reliable supply.

One way of looking at supply chain integration decisions is to use the technique of value-chain analysis (Porter and Millar, 1985), which views the decision in terms of which set of activities (for example, design, assembly) should be undertaken, rather than from the viewpoint of products or services. This approach allows consideration of the fact that the outsourcing of one product or service may have cost implications for other products and services, which are produced using the same resources. Thus the impact of economies of scope is taken into account, as well as economies of scale (see Chapter 5 for more information on economies of scale and economies of scope).

However, value-chain analysis aims to configure activities in order to minimize cost, given a firm's competitive strategy, and not specifically define where (inside or outside the firm) activities should occur. It is suggested that the degree of ownership should be directed by the capability or core competences (Chapter 2) that the organization requires to support the current and future strategy. This decision will need to be made within the constraints of the financial resources available to the organization in acquiring supply chain elements and the challenge of the coordination of activities within the supply chain.

The different degrees of integration in the supply chain are now discussed.

Market Relationships

Cooperation can simply mean the act of conducting a transaction between two organizations. Here each purchase is treated as a separate transaction and the **market relationship** between the buyer and seller lasts as long as this transaction takes. There can be some additional arrangements around this relationship such as the use of electronic data interchange (EDI) facilities to share information, combining orders in a single delivery to reduce transportation costs, agreements on packaging standards to improve materials handling and other factors. This approach does have a number of advantages in that it permits flexibility, given that suppliers can be changed or discontinued if demand drops or a supplier introduces a new product. Other advantages include the use of competition between suppliers to improve performance in aspects such as price, delivery and quality. However, there can be disadvantages in this arrangement in that either side can end the relationship at any time. A supplier withdrawal requires the often lengthy task of finding a new supplier. From a supplier perspective the withdrawal of a buyer may cause a sudden drop in demand on the operations facility leading to disruption and idle resources.

Strategic Partnerships and Alliances

When an organization and supplier are trading successfully they can decide to form a **strategic alliance or strategic partnership**. This involves a long-term relationship in which organizations work together and share information regarding aspects such as planning systems and development of products and processes. There may also be agreement on such aspects as product costs and product margins. The idea of a partnership or alliance is to combine the advantages of a marketplace relationship, which encourages flexibility and innovation, with the advantages of vertical integration, which allows close coordination and control of such aspects as quality.

From a supplier viewpoint a long-term strategic partnership may give them the confidence to invest in resources and focus on a product line to serve a particular customer. Lambert et al. (1996) categorize the factors that make a successful partnership as:

- *Drivers* – these are compelling reasons for forming partnerships, such as cost reduction, better customer service or security.
- *Facilitators* – these are supportive corporate factors that encourage partnerships, such as compatibility of operations, similar management styles and common aims.
- *Components* – these are the joint activities and operations used to build and sustain a relationship, such as communication channels, joint planning, shared risk and rewards and investments.

Some factors may mitigate against the formation of a partnership. For instance for low-value items the use of a partnership may not be worthwhile. Also a company may not want to share sensitive information or lose control of a particular product or process.

The Virtual Organization

The form of an organization's relationship within its supply chain is increasingly being affected by developments in e-Business systems. **E-Business** involves electronically mediated information exchanges, both within an organization and between organizations. Evans and Wurster (1997) describe how information can impact the value chain in three ways:

1. *Reach* – a business can share information with more stakeholders or gain a larger audience at a relatively low cost.
2. *Customization* – information can be more readily tailored for sharing with a large number of partners.
3. *Dialogue* – interaction between the parties is two-way rather than the traditional push of information. For example, it is possible for a supplier to anticipate a retailer's product requirements from examining their inventory forecast rather than awaiting a faxed order.

CASE STUDY 15.1

BASF and Aker Kvaerner

BASF and Aker Kvaerner benefit from an innovative alliance for maintaining one of the UK's largest chemical plants. BASF is the world's leading chemical company. It has production facilities in 39 countries and trades in 170 countries. Its strategy at its Seal Sands plant on Teesside in the UK has been to marry technological and commercial innovation through partnering. One of the ways it has done this is through a partnership with the maintenance arm of Aker Kvaerner, a provider of services to the engineering and construction sectors. Throughout the history of the Seal Sands plant the maintenance provision has been managed by BASF but outsourced to a number of different providers. Whilst the company names have changed, many of the employees had worked on the site for more than 20 years. Although the general belief for many years was that the service was world class, in reality an emphasis on cost control was stifling development and long-term improvements. BASF decided to shake things up by looking at partnering. Its first step was to define what it meant by a partnership – 'a long-term, mutually beneficial relationship where resources, knowledge, skills and values are shared with the purpose of enhancing each partner's competitive position'. When BASF settled on Aker Kvaerner to provide the whole maintenance service for the site, the main reason was the approach of its senior management team. BASF saw the team as having the ability to see beyond traditional approaches and to adopt the new ways of working enthusiastically. The core of the agreement is a performance-based contract whereby Aker Kvaerner is paid according to a set of Key Performance Indicators (KPIs). Where Aker Kvaerner achieves or exceeds performance, BASF's productivity and profitability are enhanced. BASF then shares its additional gains with Aker Kvaerner.

Source: The Department of Trade and Industry (www.dti.gov.uk/bestpractice).

Question

What steps did BASF take to encourage a successful strategic partnership?

Thus the implication of e-Business developments is that it becomes easier to outsource more and more supply chain activities to third parties and the boundaries between and within organizations become blurred. This development is known as virtualization and companies that follow this route are known as **virtual organizations**. The objective is that the absence of any rigid boundary or hierarchy within the organization should lead to a more responsive and flexible company with greater market orientation. Kraut et al. (1998) suggest that the features of a virtual organization are:

- Processes transcend the boundaries of a single form and are not controlled by a single organizational hierarchy.
- Production processes are flexible with different parties involved at different times.
- Parties involved in the production of a single product are often geographically dispersed.
- Given this dispersion, coordination is heavily dependent on telecommunications and data networks.

E-Business can also be used to alter the supply chain structure by bypassing some of the tiers using a process known as **disintermediation**. Figure 15.8 shows a traditional demand side supply chain from operations through a wholesaler and retailer to the customer. Disintermediation is shown omitting both the wholesaler and retailer. This process is facilitated by the use of Web-based **e-Commerce** systems, which involve electronically mediated information exchanges between organizations. By omitting these stages in the supply chain, the producer is able to reduce their costs.

Perhaps a more significant phenomenon using e-Commerce systems is the use of **reintermediation** – the creation of new intermediaries between customers and suppliers in the supply chain. Figure 15.9

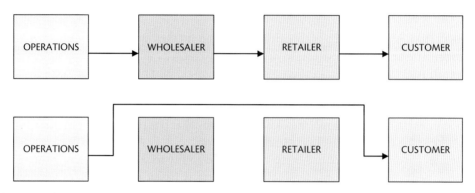

FIGURE 15.8

Disintermediation in the Supply Chain.

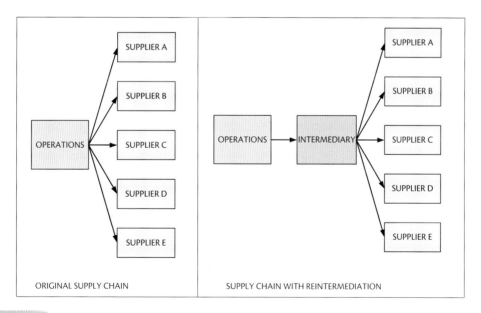

FIGURE 15.9

Reintermediation in the Supply Chain.

demonstrates the change in structure when an intermediary is placed between operations and suppliers in the supply chain. Reintermediation removes the inefficiency of checking all the suppliers by placing an intermediary between purchaser and seller. This intermediary performs the price evaluation stage of fulfilment since its e-procurement or ERP system (Chapter 14) has links updated from the different suppliers. The next section on procurement will cover these systems in more detail.

Vertical Integration

Complete integration is achieved by an organization when it takes ownership of other organizations in the supply chain. The amount of ownership of the supply chain by an organization is termed its level of **vertical integration**. When an organization owns upstream or supply-side elements of the supply chain it is termed 'backward vertical integration'. Ownership of downstream or demand-side elements of the supply chain is termed 'forward vertical integration' (see Figure 15.10). When a company owns elements of a different supply chain, for example, a holding company that has interests in organizations operating in various markets, the term used is 'horizontal integration'.

One potential advantage of vertical integration is the ability to secure a greater control of the competitive environment. Although a market-based economy is based on the idea of competition, many firms will attempt to reduce competition and thus provide an opportunity to increase profits. For example, a manufacturer can use forward integration to buy retailers to limit the availability of competing product ranges. Backward integration, implemented by owning suppliers, can secure supplies of components whose availability and price to competitors can be controlled. Another factor is that technological innovations in one part of the organization are available to other elements in the supply chain. Thus product and process improvements can be disseminated quickly. Also improved communication can help coordinate planning and control systems in the supply chain to improve delivery speed and dependability.

Another reason for vertical integration is to keep distinctive competence or capability in-house and not available to competitors. If an activity is seen as strategically important, or it uses specialized knowledge, or is in an area where the company has superior performance to competitors then it is likely that the company will want to keep that activity as part of its supply chain.

There are, however, a number of disadvantages of vertical integration and perhaps the major reason for outsourcing is the cost incurred in owning major elements of the

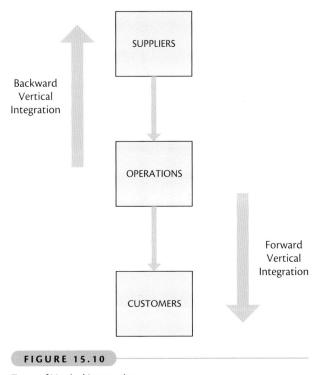

FIGURE 15.10

Types of Vertical Integration.

supply chain. The resources required to own elements of the supply chain are resources that cannot be dedicated to the activities that represent the core tasks of the organization. This suggests that there is a risk, in that trying to do everything will mean that the company is not competitive against companies who are focusing their resources and skills on particular elements of the supply chain. For example, the activity of warehousing may not be a core task for a manufacturer. By outsourcing this function the facilities of a third party are available who can share storage costs amongst a number of companies and invest in up-to-date warehouse technologies in order to increase efficiency. Another factor is the increased flexibility available when using a number of suppliers to meet fluctuations in demand. This means the organization only buys the capacity it needs and does not have idle capacity in-house.

In summary, a number of factors need to be taken into account when deciding the amount of vertical integration that is appropriate for an organization. Firstly, the amount of vertical integration that can feasibly be undertaken will be dependent on the financial resources of the organization. It is unlikely that smaller firms will be able to own large sections of the supply chain, but even large organizations may find this difficult. For example, a car manufacturer may source an engine for a new car from a third party rather than invest millions of euros in developing a new design. Apart from cost, the time taken to acquire supply chain capabilities maybe a barrier. It may also be felt that resources used for vertical integration could be better spent elsewhere (R&D or marketing for example). Finally an organization needs to consider that it is unlikely that it will be able to undertake all the activities in the supply chain well and it may leave certain aspects to specialist suppliers.

Even if the organization has the capability to undertake further activities in the supply chain it may not make sense to take ownership of them. The virtual organization concept using e-Business systems described earlier may allow efficient coordination of supply chain activities without the need to own them. Disadvantages of nonownership of supply chain elements include the potential high cost of switching partners, loss of intellectual property, which may provide the competitive advantage of the firm and the termination of partnerships if the strategic interests of the supply chain partners diverge.

ACTIVITIES IN THE SUPPLY CHAIN

In this section supply chain activities are presented around the areas of procurement, which is the operations interface with upstream activities, and physical distribution management, which deals with downstream activities such as warehousing and transportation.

Procurement

The role of **procurement** is to acquire all the materials needed by an organization in the form of purchases, rentals, contracts and other acquisition methods. The procurement process also includes activities such as selecting suppliers, approving orders and receiving goods from suppliers. The term 'purchasing' usually refers to the actual act of buying the raw materials, parts, equipment and all the other goods and services used in operations systems. However, the procurement process is often located in what is called the purchasing department.

Procurement is an important aspect of the operations function as the cost of materials can represent a substantial amount of the total cost of a product or service. There has recently been an enhanced

The supplier will then produce the goods or service and deliver them to the relevant department and provide an invoice form requesting payment. When the organization is satisfied the goods or services and the invoice details are satisfactory a payment will be issued to the supplier.

Choosing Suppliers

Before choosing a supplier, the organization must decide whether it is feasible and desirable to produce the good or service in-house. Buyers in purchasing departments, with assistance from operations, will regularly perform a make-or-buy analysis to determine the source of supply. Often goods can be sourced internally at a lower cost, with higher quality or faster delivery than from a supplier. On the other hand suppliers who focus on delivering a good or service can specialize their expertise and resources and thus provide better performance. Strategic issues may also need to be considered when contemplating the outsourcing of supplies. For instance internal skills required to offer a distinctive competence may be lost if certain activities are outsourced. It may also mean that distinctive competencies can be offered to competitors by the supplier.

If a decision is made to use an external supplier, the next decision relates to the choice of that supplier. Criteria for choosing suppliers for quotation and approval include the following:

- *Price* – as stated in the introduction, the cost of goods and services from suppliers is forming an increasingly large percentage of the cost of goods and services that are delivered to customers. Thus minimizing the price of purchased goods and services can provide a significant cost advantage to the organization.
- *Quality* – to be considered as a supplier, it is expected that a company will provide an assured level of quality of product or service. This is because poor quality goods and services can have a significant disruptive effect on the performance of the operations function. For example, resources may have to be deployed checking for quality before products can be used, poor quality products that get into the production system may be processed at expense before faults are found and poor quality goods and services that reach the customer will lead to returns and loss of goodwill.
- *Delivery* – in terms of delivery, suppliers who can deliver on time, every time, in other words show reliability, are required. The ability to deliver with a short lead time and respond quickly once an order has been placed can also be an important aspect of performance.

The process of locating a supplier will depend on the nature of the good or service and its importance to the organization. If there are few suppliers capable of providing the service then they will most likely be well known to the organization. If there are a number of potential suppliers and the goods are important to the organization then a relatively lengthy process of searching for suppliers and the evaluation of quotations may take place.

Most organizations have a list of approved suppliers that they have used in the past, or that are otherwise known to be reliable. However, it is important to monitor suppliers in order to ensure that they continue to provide a satisfactory service. A system of supplier rating, or vendor rating is used to undertake this. One form of vendor rating is a checklist, which provides feedback to the supplier on their performance and suggestions for improvement. Another approach is to identify the important performance criteria required of the supplier, for example, delivery reliability, product quality and price. The supplier can then be rated on each of these performance measures against historical performance and competitor performance.

TABLE 15.1

Advantages of Single Sourcing and Multisourcing.

Advantages of single sourcing	Advantages of multisourcing
Stronger relationship between parties, leading to greater commitment to success.	Reduces risk of loss of supply from single supplier.
Opportunities for savings due to economies of scale with larger order quantities.	Can be used to reduce price by encouraging competition between suppliers.
Facilitates better communication and reduces administration overhead.	Provides more flexibility in meeting changes in demand.
Easier to maintain confidential terms of business.	A range of suppliers can give access to a wider knowledge about goods and services.

When choosing suppliers, a decision is made whether to source each good or service from an individual supplier, termed 'single sourcing', or whether to use a number of suppliers, termed 'multisourcing'. Although the trend toward alliances and partnerships between firms leads towards single sourcing, there are certain advantages to the multisourcing approach (Table 15.1).

CASE STUDY 15.2

Supplier Evaluation at EADS

On 8 March 2004, John Summers, head of the supply management strategy at EADS, a company based in Europe, got the assignment from the Procurement Directors Board (PDB) to make suggestions for improving the company's supplier evaluation system. The proposal was to be presented at the PDB meeting the following month.

EADS and the Aerospace Industry

EADS was one of the largest players in the aerospace industry. There were only a few other companies in the market and therefore the competition was characterized by oligopolistic structures.

EADS had a sales volume of approximately €30 billion while its biggest competitor sold aeroplanes and other products for the aerospace industry worth around €40 billion, followed by some other competitors with sales volumes of €10 billion to €20 billion. Due to its strong sales position in North America and Europe, but some weaknesses in Asia and South America, EADS was looking for new ways to improve its competitive position on the last-named continents.

EADS's main customers were airlines from all over the world, which were using their increasing purchasing power to get price reductions and flexible contracts.

Since EADS and its competitors had a degree of value added of only 25%–35%, the suppliers were an important source of competitive advantage and a potential leverage for cost reductions, revenue enhancements and risk reduction.

The Supply Situation in the Aerospace Industry

Due to long development cycles and extremely long product lives in the aerospace industry, the supplier situation in this industry was determined by some special requirements. The suppliers had to be able to guarantee the durability and quality of their products in a high-tech environment and under extreme conditions. EADS and its suppliers had to fulfil the needs of its global customers on the one hand and very demanding requirements from official bodies such as the Federal Aviation Administration (FAA) of the United States of America on the other hand. Therefore, every supplier for critical parts had to go through a tough and costly quality audit process and had to prove regularly that his products met the certification requirements.

Due to the outstanding product complexity, EADS and its competitors could not handle all requirements and necessary activities of aeroplane manufacturing on their own. Interdependent relationships occurred between EADS and its most important suppliers in terms of innovation and efficiency management. As a consequence, EADS had to buy most of its crucial manufacturing parts from single-source suppliers.

The Supply Organization of EADS

The final decision-making body for all supply management issues of EADS was the Procurement Directors Board. The PDB consisted of the procurement directors of the eight business units of EADS. On the second level, the corporate supply organization was divided into PDB subgroups that were responsible for different tasks such as the management of the specific lead-buyers within the organization, the e-procurement processes or the supply management strategy for which John Summers was responsible. On the third level, there were the different sourcing organizations of EADS's business units with about 1800 buyers.

The Supply Strategy of EADS

The supply vision of EADS was to achieve competitive advantage by winning, integrating and developing the world's best suppliers. Therefore, EADS had a supply strategy that aimed at getting the best suppliers possible in order to fulfil the following objectives:

- Procurement marketing: the supply activities of EADS needed to support its sales department because selling aeroplanes to certain countries required that the aeroplanes were produced in line with local content requirements.
- Risk and opportunity management: suppliers had to share the risks and opportunities of the aerospace industry with EADS.

The Supplier Evaluation System of EADS

When John Summer and his team analysed the supplier evaluation system at EADS they found five common criteria for evaluation:

- commercial performance (product cost, delivery cost, quality cost, etc.)
- logistics performance (reliability, delivery precision, etc.)
- customer support (geographical distribution of plants and service stations, etc.)
- quality performance (quality level, quality reliability, etc.)
- technical performance (product design and development, process development, etc.).

EADS had implemented a system that measured the different evaluation ratings for each supplier on the basis of the delivered commodities on business unit and corporate levels (see Figure 15.12). The supplier value was determined on the aggregated performance and future contracts were given to high scoring suppliers. However, the rating measures sometimes bore little relationship to the supply strategy requirements.

The Supplier Structure of EADS

In 2003, EADS had approximately 24 000 suppliers in total. However, it bought almost 65% of

FIGURE 15.12

The Supplier Evaluation System at Eads.

its supply volume from only about 250 suppliers. It sourced more than two-thirds of the products and services in Europe and only a fourth in North America. The supply volumes in Asia or South America were almost negligible. Therefore, the supply volume of EADS was even more unequally distributed than its sales volume.

John's Suggestions for Improvement

John knew that the current supplier evaluation system had worked smoothly for more than four years and was well implemented. However, he was not sure whether EADS was really measuring all important dimensions of the supplier value in order to achieve new competitive advantages in the relevant markets.

This case was written by Roger Moser, Supply Management Institute SMI™, European Business School. It was prepare solely to provide material for class discussion and does not intend to illustrate either effective or ineffective handling of a managerial situation. The author may have disguised certain names and other identifying information to protect confidential data.

Source: Roger Moser, Supply Management Institute SMI™, ebs European Business School. Reproduced with permission.

Question

Identify the weaknesses in the EADS supplier evaluation system and suggest improvements to the system.

Procurement Information Systems

There are a number of steps in the procurement process, which has implications in terms of time, cost and reliability. One problem is the time lapse between a department requesting a good or service and receiving it. This is due to the time it takes to undertake all the steps involved, including supplier selection and the exchange of documentation. The cost involved in employing personnel to undertake these tasks can be particularly onerous for companies who procure many low-cost goods and services. In this situation the purchasing costs are likely to be a relatively high proportion of total costs. Another issue is the reliability of a process in which personnel have to coordinate activities of a number of suppliers and complete and track a large amount of documentation. In order to improve the procurement process an electronic purchasing system was developed called electronic data interchange (EDI).

Electronic Data Interchange (EDI)

Electronic data interchange can be defined as the exchange, using digital media, of structured business information, particularly for sales transactions such as purchase orders and invoices between buyers and sellers. A complementary technology is electronic funds transfer (EFT), which allows the automated digital transmission of money between organizations and banks. Electronic data interchange has traditionally been carried out over specialist computer networks, but recently Internet EDI systems, which can lower costs by using the public Internet network, have been used. Electronic

---

CASE STUDY 15.3

Chance & Hunt

Chance & Hunt has employed technology right across its business – including EDI – which has allowed an extensive degree of supply chain integration. The company, which markets and distributes chemicals, wanted to improve its telemetry system for managing its clients' inventories – with the aim of offering a better service and cutting costs. The idea was that automatic exchange of business information with clients could bring dramatic efficiency savings and help cement long-term relationships. The company's solution was to invest in the infrastructure to provide remote network access, online credit card purchasing – an industry first – and an integrated, EDI ordering system that checks stock and links to the warehouse. The system constantly monitors client inventories checking stock levels against optimum levels. Should stocks fall below this level, the system delivers alerts to the client budget holders and relevant sales staff, before channelling orders back to Chance & Hunt's internal systems.

Source: The Department of Trade and Industry (www.dti.gov.uk/bestpractice).

Question

What business benefits do you think would be gained from the use of EDI described in the case study?

---

www.wileyopenpage.com

data interchange can improve the procurement process by reducing the time information is in transit, reducing data entry errors and reducing costs such as staff time. Many EDI systems have adopted the use of **extensible markup language (XML)** which allows documents to be easily transferred between computer systems and applications software. An XML document created using one application can be used with other programs without the need to convert it or process it in any other way. XML lends itself to applications that include e-Commerce and e-procurement. The use of XML in e-procurement systems is likely to replace many EDI-based applications over the coming years.

E-Procurement

E-procurement refers to the electronic integration and management of all procurement activities including purchase request, authorization, ordering, delivery and payment between purchaser and supplier. E-procurement can achieve significant savings and other benefits, which directly impact the customer.

- Faster purchase cycle times leading to a need for less material in inventory.
- Less staff time spent in searching and ordering products and reconciling deliveries with invoices.
- Savings also occur through automated validation of pre-approved spending budgets for individuals or departments, leading to fewer people processing each order, and in less time.
- A reduction in the cost of physical materials such as specially printed order forms and invoices.
- Enables greater flexibility in ordering goods from different suppliers according to best value.

E-procurement also tends to change the role of buyers in the purchasing department. By removing administrative tasks such as placing orders and reconciling deliveries and invoices with purchase orders, buyers can spend more time on value-adding activities. Such activities may include more time spent with key suppliers to improve product delivery and costs or analysis and control of purchasing behaviour.

E-procurement can be classified in terms of business and consumer models of Internet access. Business-to-consumer (B2C) transactions are between an organization and consumers, whilst business-to-business (B2B) is used to describe transactions between an organization and other organizations. Although the use of the Internet by consumers for purchases has received most media attention, the majority of commerce over the Internet is actually between businesses, using the B2B model and most e-procurement is undertaken in this way.

A risk of implementing an e-procurement system, typical of many e-Business implementations, is the difficulty in integrating information systems. Figure 15.13 shows how different types of information system cover different parts of the procurement cycle. The different types of systems are described below.

- *Stock control system* – this relates mainly to production-related procurement; the system highlights when reordering is required when the number in stock falls below reorder thresholds.
- *CD- or Web-based catalogue* – paper catalogues have been replaced by electronic forms that make it quicker to find suppliers.
- *Email or database-based workflow systems* – integrate the entry of the order by the originator, approval by manager and placement by buyer. The order is routed from one person to the next and will wait in their inbox for actioning. Such systems may be extended to accounting systems.

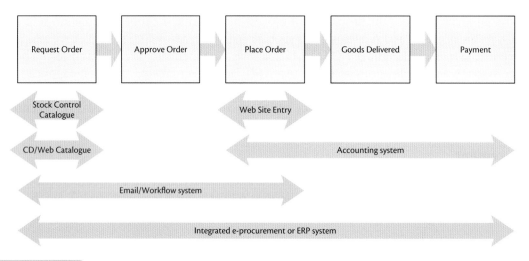

FIGURE 15.13

Use of Different Information Systems for Procurement.

- *Order-entry on web site* – the buyer often has the opportunity to order directly on the supplier web site, but this will involve rekeying and there is no integration with systems for requisitioning or accounting.
- *Accounting systems* – networked accounting systems enable staff in the buying department to enter an order which can then be used by accounting staff to make payment when the invoice arrives.
- *Integrated e-procurement or ERP systems* – these aim to integrate all the facilities above and will also include integration with suppliers' systems.

Apart from the use of the appropriate technology the introduction of an information system should address change in terms of its implications for people and processes. The introduction of e-procurement will require people to change the way that they work in order to secure the benefits of the information system. It may also require changes to current supplier-customer relationships and both of these issues can lead to resistance and dissatisfaction. There is also a need to avoid replacing poor manual procurement processes with poor automated procurement processes. This may mean the use of a process-centred design effort, using techniques such as process mapping, as part of the e-procurement implementation. Another point to consider is that no matter how efficient the electronic e-procurement systems are, the success of the procurement process will still depend on the efficiency, derived from their operations capability, with which the suppliers in the supply chain can deliver the physical goods or services requested.

Perhaps the major barrier to the use of e-procurement is in the difficulty of linking systems with suppliers whose systems may be incompatible or nonexistent. It may be that small firms may find themselves increasingly excluded by buyers due to their lack of investment in the required information technology infrastructure. For organizations that are attempting to provide an integrated e-procurement or ERP implementation one of the main issues is gaining access to the price catalogues of suppliers. One approach is to house electronic catalogues from different suppliers inside the company and use a firewall for security. These catalogues can be updated by either an occasional link beyond the firewall or the delivery of a CD version from the supplier. An alternative approach is to 'punch out' through the firewall to access the catalogue either on a supplier's site or intermediary site such as a B2B marketplace. A B2B marketplace provides a web site that connects buyers and sellers to enable trading in a private and secure environment.

Physical Distribution Management

Physical distribution management, sometimes called business logistics, refers to the movement of materials from the operation to the customer. Four main areas of physical distribution management are materials handling, warehousing, packaging and transportation.

Materials Handling

Materials handling relates to the movement of materials, either within warehouses or between storage area and transportation links. The aim of materials handling is to move materials as efficiently as possible. The type of materials handling systems available can be categorized as manual, mechanized and automated. A manual handling system uses people to move material. This provides a flexible system, but is only feasible when materials are movable using people with little assistance. An example is a supermarket where trolleys are used to assist with movement, but the presence of customers and the nature of the items make the use of mechanization or automation not feasible. Mechanized warehouses use equipment such as forklift trucks, cranes and conveyor systems to provide a more efficient handling system, which can also handle items too heavy for people. Automated warehouses use technology such as automated guided vehicles (AGVs) and loading/unloading machines to process high volumes of material efficiently. More information on process technologies is provided in Chapter 6.

Warehousing

When producing a tangible item it is possible to provide a buffer between supply and demand by holding a stock of the item – **warehousing**. Many organizations have a specific location to hold this stock, termed a 'warehouse' or 'distribution centre'. Most warehouses are used to hold a stock of incoming raw materials used in production or hold finished goods ready for distribution to customers. Warehouses are also used to store work-in-progress items or spares for equipment.

Because of the need to process goods and services through the supply chain as quickly as possible to serve customer demand, warehouses are not simply seen as long-term storage areas for goods, but provide a useful staging post for activities such as sorting, consolidating and packing goods for distribution along the supply chain. Consolidation occurs by merging products from multiple suppliers over time, for transportation in a single load to the operations site. Finished goods sourced from a number of suppliers may also be grouped together for delivery to a customer in order to reduce the number of communication and transportation links between suppliers and customers. The opposite of consolidation is break-bulk where a supplier sends all the demand for a particular geographical area to a local warehouse. The warehouse then processes the goods and delivers the separate orders to the customers.

One of the major issues in warehouse management is the level of decentralization and thus the number and size of the warehouses required in inventory distribution. Decentralized facilities offer a service closer to the customer and thus should provide a better service level in terms of knowledge of customer needs and speed of service. Centralization, however, offers the potential for less handling of goods between service points, less control costs and less overall inventory levels due to lower overall

- Supply chain integration can range, in order of increasing integration, from a market relationship to a strategic partnership, to a virtual organization and to vertical integration. A market relationship permits flexibility but can be ended by either organization at any time. A strategic partnership or alliance involves a long-term relationship in which the organizations work together and share information. A virtual organization is where information technology is used to allow outsourcing of supply chain activities and the boundaries between and within organizations become blurred. Vertical integration is when an organization takes ownership of other organizations in the supply chain.
- The role of procurement is to acquire all the materials needed by an organization in the form of purchases, rentals, contracts and other acquisition methods.
- Physical distribution management refers to the movement of materials from the operation to the customers. It covers the areas of materials handling, warehousing, packaging and transportation.

CASE STUDY 15.4

Amazon – A Virtual Supply Chain

Amazon is proving to be the online master retailer, serving consumers worldwide through its websites, offering a wide range of consumer goods, well presented for customer viewing convenience and then delivered to the door of the consumer.

Customers are 'served' through an online storefront with distribution and fulfilment provided both by Amazon, as well as third-party logistics companies.

Amazon originated as a book supplier, able to take on the main high street stores by offering a much wider range of titles held in large distribution centres and warehouses. They have successfully expanded to provide a significant range of consumer products, far beyond the original book seller model.

Amazon stock and distribute their own products, the Kindle being a notable success, these are distributed from regional centres by Amazon approved carriers. These goods arrive in Amazon packaging and will fall under all Amazon delivery conditions. Yet additionally and for a significant proportion of their business, Amazon also connects suppliers of non-Amazon produced goods with the existing Amazon customer base. They run a business of linking the manufacturers with their market, without the need for the traditional bricks and mortar option of the high street.

In doing so, Amazon can provide leading branded goods through their website and are not restricted in what they can offer. If a consumer wants a product Amazon and their partners can probably provide it. These sellers can use Amazon's vast distribution network or products can be shipped direct to the customer. In fact, retailers who use Amazon's third-party marketplace now account for 35% to 40% of all units that Amazon sells per year. Amazon takes a healthy commission off each sale it makes – making third-party sales a higher-margin venture than its core retail business – without having the risk of developing those products or holding the inventory.

This system relies upon a strong and established supply chain policy. Amazon is able to make a promise for delivery with confidence that this will be fulfilled by a selected supplier. Each

 www.wileyopenpage.com

individual supplier will benefit from the extensive 'shop window' that Amazon has to offer to its vast customer base, yet in turn, must be able to deliver on Amazon's commitment. The customer, whilst acknowledging their product may not come specifically from Amazon itself, will hold Amazon responsible for any failure in the system.

Fulfilment is key to the success of this model, and is not always simple. Amazon experienced a number of delivery problems with the logistics provider, Yodel, and faced a backlash from angry customers, complaining of missing, damaged and late goods. Amazon is one of the largest online retailers to use Yodel, but customer complaints about the delivery service threatened their reputation.

Sources

http://business.time.com/2012/07/16/will-amazon-take-over-the-world/#ixzz29xJhgEvU

guardian.co.uk, Amazon deluged with complaints over Yodel's poor delivery service

www.amazon.co.uk

Source: Written by Briony Boydell and Chris Milner. Reproduced with permission.

Questions

1. What could be the impact of the problems with the Yodel delivery group?
2. Amazon adopts a virtual supply chain strategy. What other organizations work on the same lines?

Quizzes to test yourself further are available in your interactive e-book at **www.wileyopenpage.com**

Flashcards to test yourself further are available in your interactive e-book at **www.wileyopenpage.com**

EXERCISES

1. Describe the elements of a supply chain.
2. Explain the term 'bullwhip effect'. How can it be overcome?
3. Compare and contrast lean and agile supply chain approaches.
4. Evaluate the main supply chain relationships in terms of their degree of integration.
5. Discuss the increasing importance of procurement.
6. What are the key factors in choosing suppliers?
7. What is the impact of e-Commerce on procurement activities?
8. Discuss the relative merits of the centralization and decentralization of warehouse facilities.

INTRODUCTION

Projects are unique, one-time operations designed to accomplish a specific set of objectives in a limited time frame. More information of project characteristics is covered in Chapter 3 on process types. Historically projects are associated with either large construction type activities or the introduction of new products and processes. Under the mass production era (until the 1980s) product/process life cycles were relatively long and aimed at mass markets so project development costs and time accounted for only a small proportion of product cost. However in recent years the ability to manage projects has become more important for operations managers. Increased global competition has led to the use of customized products serving niche markets. This expansion of product lines has led to the need for more project management of product and process development projects. Product life cycles have shortened, leading to the need to pay back project costs over less time meaning the project management process must use fewer resources and minimize cost. Information-intensive products are generally costly to produce but cheap to reproduce (e.g. software, pharmaceuticals) so their cost structures are dominated by developing products and processes rather than the variable costs of production and distribution. Projects may consist of many activities and must therefore be carefully planned and coordinated if a project is to meet cost and time targets. However, not all aspects of implementation can be controlled or planned but the chance of success can be increased by anticipating potential problems and by applying corrective strategies. Network analysis can be used to assist the project planning and control activities.

PROJECT MANAGEMENT IN THE ORGANIZATION

Not all project problems are at the execution stage, but may relate to the process of identifying possible projects and making an appropriate selection of projects to execute. Problems include taking on too many projects for the resources available and not aligning individual projects with the organization's strategy. The aim should be to pick the best portfolio of projects, not necessarily the best individual projects as their objectives and use of resources may conflict. Care should be taken against spreading the most skilled staff across too many projects (no more than two or three projects at the same time according to Wheelwright and Clark (1992)) as they may spend too much time updating themselves on each project's progress rather than utilizing their specialist skills. Project completion times are often unrealistic due to not taking into account capacity availability (usually people's time) and the number of other projects ongoing at any one time. Also projects have different characteristics that require different approaches. Projects may range from small enhancements of current processes to major changes in process design or development of products for new markets. Responsibility for facing these challenges is assigned to the project manager, sometimes known as a team leader or project coordinator. Included in the functions of the project manager are providing clearly defined goals to project participants and ensuring that adequately skilled and experienced human resources are employed on the project.

Throughout the project it is necessary to manage the three performance objectives of project management of time, cost and quality (Figure 16.1). The job of project managers is difficult since they are under pressure to meet quality performance measures within the constraints of a fixed timescale and fixed budget. Often it is necessary to make a compromise between project outcomes and the time and resources available. For example, if a customer wants a particular new product feature, then the cost and duration will increase or other features will have to be omitted. For some projects the importance of particular objectives will be overriding, for example, the London 2012 Olympic facilities had a fixed completion date and high quality facilities had been promised and so costs rose to ensure that these objectives were met (see Case Study 16.1).

FIGURE 16.1

The Project Management Performance Objectives of Quality, Cost and Time.

CASE STUDY 16.1

Project Management: Lessons can be learned from successful delivery

The team behind Britain's most high profile infrastructure project in recent times says there was no 'magic ingredient' in its successful delivery, but having £9.3bn available is likely to have helped.

The construction of the Olympic park in east London was widely hailed as a success long before the first athlete set foot in it last month.

While the fate of a few key venues is still unclear, there is a strong consensus on the park's delivery. 'On time and under budget' is the most common appraisal batted around by politicians and Olympic organisers – though the latter description is not entirely accurate.

The success of the build has prompted some soul-searching about lessons that can be applied to future developments, partly to avoid repeats of projects that went wrong, such as Wembley Stadium.

'In reputation terms [the Olympic project] was an opportunity, clearly,' says Sir John Armitt, the man in charge of the body that built the park.

He says that the UK's reputation for major construction and infrastructure developments has always been high, but admits that Wembley 'didn't go so well'.

The fact that the world was watching and judging as the Olympic park was erected on top of former industrial wasteland added more pressure to get it right. 'The Olympic project is the most high profile project that you could imagine,' he says.

Sir John says successful programme management starts from the client, in this case the Olympic Delivery Authority, which he led. He says the ODA knew what it valued, balancing cost and quality, and made that clear to its suppliers.

'If you talk to the suppliers on the Olympics what they will say is that the ODA was an intelligent client, and a consistent client in contractual terms,' says Sir John. Consistency, he says, reinforced to suppliers what was expected of them.

The ODA oversaw the procurement of more than £6bn worth of contracts to deliver the Olympic park, and arguably its most important contract was with its delivery partner – CLM, a consortium that includes CH2M Hill.

But the creation and structure of the ODA itself was also key to the success of the project.

'One of the weakest points of London's bid originally was the sense that the UK, and London in particular, had such a range of agencies and bodies that would need to be corralled together to make anything happen,' says Tim Jones, a partner at Freshfields law firm who was heavily involved in the negotiations that spawned the ODA.

The ODA served as a 'single governmental interface' with planning authority, he says, removing the need for time-consuming negotiations with various local bodies.

It also assumed power for some aspects of Olympic transport and security. 'The ODA was where all those functions were really brought together,' says Mr Jones. Having a delivery partner enabled the relatively small ODA to function efficiently, he adds.

That sentiment is echoed in an ODA report on the project, which says having a delivery partner gave it 'flexibility and agility' and their partnership underpinned its success.

But not everything went to plan. Sir John says the impact of the financial crisis on delivering the athletes' village was the 'biggest challenge' the ODA faced during the construction period.

Both the village and the media centre had to be bailed out by the government.

'You couldn't get a sensible financial package out of the banks, so the decision was made to use contingency money to fund [the village] and then sell the asset as soon as we could after . . . to recover the money,' says Sir John.

Some £557m was recouped last year, when a Qatari-backed consortium bought half of the homes in the village and several plots of land in the Olympic park. Triathlon Homes had already paid £268m for 1,379 units, which are earmarked for affordable housing.

The contingency money that was drawn on for the village was available only because the Olympics budget was revised to £9.3bn in 2007, from an original estimate of £2.4bn. The ODA spent £6.8bn delivering the Olympic park.

The immovable deadline also drove the project. The opening ceremony was always going to happen on July 27, and frequent missions from the International Olympic Committee served as a potent reminder.

Cross-party support was another unique factor from which the build benefited. 'You don't always get that [support],' admits Sir John.

It is unclear whether local authorities would be willing to yield some elements of power again, under different circumstances.

Mr Jones is hopeful but unsure. 'They only agreed to do it that time because it was the Olympics and they all wanted this to happen,' he says. 'Maybe it is rather optimistic to suspect that you would get such support for another project, that people would actually surrender their power.'

Source: Financial Times (2012). Reproduced with permission.

Question

Discuss the delivery of the Olympic Park in terms of time, cost and quality performance objectives.

Because of the unique nature of projects and the potentially high number of interrelated tasks involved an effective way is needed to communicate project plans and progress across the project team. There are three main ways of structuring the organization of a project named project structure, functional structure and matrix structure. The reasons for choosing a particular structure are outlined below.

The Project Structure

This consists of an organization that not only follows a team approach to projects but has an organizational structure based on teams formed specifically for projects. The approach delivers a high focus on completing project objectives but can involve duplication of resources across teams, an inhibition of diffusion of learning across teams, a lack of hierarchical career structure and less continuity of employment. Many professional service firms such as management consultancies use this approach.

The Functional Structure

Here a project is given to the most appropriate functional department. Thus the organizational structure remains in the standard hierarchical form. The approach ensures there is limited disruption to the normal organizational activities but can lead to a lack of focus on project objectives. A lack of coordination can result, especially if outside help is required. There can be a failure to meet customer needs if other departmental activities are taking priority over project work.

The Matrix Structure

Here several project teams are overlaid on a functional structure in an effort to provide a balance between functional and project needs. There are three different forms of matrix structure:

- *Functional matrix.* Here the project manager reports to functional heads to coordinate staff across departments.
- *Balanced matrix.* Here the project manager manages the project jointly with functional heads.
- *Project matrix.* Here functional staff join a project team for a fixed period of time.

 The video 'NASA Project Management Challenge' is available in your interactive e-book at **www.wileyopenpage.com**

PROJECT MANAGEMENT ACTIVITIES

Projects require a clear definition and boundary to determine what should be included and what should be outside the scope of the project. Scoping the project is very important when outsourcing as disputes can occur if the project does not have a clear definition. Definition may be made by detailed evaluation at the start of the project or evolved through a process of interaction with the customer during development. Once the project definition phase is complete the project management process includes the following main elements of estimate, plan and control.

Project Estimating

At the start of the project a broad plan is drawn up assuming unlimited resources. Once **project estimates** have been made of the resources required to undertake these activities it is then possible to compare overall project requirements with available resources. If highly specialized resources are required then the project completion date may have to be set to ensure these resources are not overloaded. This is a **resource-constrained project**. Alternatively there may be a need to complete a project in a specific time frame (for example, due date specified by customer). In this case alternative resources may have to be used (for example, subcontractors) to ensure timely project completion. This is a **time-constrained project**.

The next step is to generate estimates for the time and resources required to undertake each task defined in the project. This information can then be used to plan what resources are required and what activities should be undertaken over the life cycle of the project. Statistical methods should be used when the project is large (and therefore complex) or novel. This allows the project team to replace a single estimate of duration with a range within which they are confident the real duration will lie. This is particularly useful for the early stage of the project when uncertainty is greatest. The accuracy of the estimates can also be improved as their use changes from project evaluation purposes to approval and day-to-day project control. The project evaluation and review technique (PERT) approach described later in this chapter allows optimistic, pessimistic and most likely times to be specified for each task from which a probabilistic estimate of project completion time can be computed. When estimating the amount of time a task will take for human activity it is important to distinguish between two different types of time that need to be estimated. **Effort time** is the total amount of work that needs to occur to complete a task. The **elapsed time** indicates how long in time (such as calendar days) the task will take (duration). Estimating starts by considering the amount of effort time that needs to be put in to complete each task. Effort time is then converted into elapsed time, which indicates how long the task will take through real-time measures such as months or days. Effort time does not usually equal elapsed time, since if a task has more than one worker the elapsed time will be less than the effort time. Conversely, if workers on a task are also working on other projects, then they will not be available all the time and the elapsed time will be longer than the effort time. An additional factor is that different workers may have different speeds. A productive worker will need less elapsed time than an inexperienced worker. These constraints on elapsed time can be formalized in a simple equation:

$$Elapsed\ time = Effort\ times \times \frac{100}{Availability\ \%} \times \frac{100}{Work\ rate\ \%}$$

The equation indicates that if the availability or work rate of a worker is less than 100 per cent, the elapsed time will increase proportionally, since availability and work rate are the denominators on the right-hand side of the equation. The equation will need to be applied for each worker, who may have different availabilities and work rates.

Once the activities have been identified and their resource requirements estimated it is necessary to define their relationship to one another. There are some activities that can only begin when other activities have been completed. This is termed a 'serial relationship'. Other activities may be totally independent and thus they have a parallel relationship. These relationships are shown graphically in Figure 16.2 and Figure 16.3.

For a reasonable sized project there may be a range of alternative plans that may meet the project objectives. Project management software can be used to assist in choosing the most feasible schedule by recalculating resource requirements and timings for each operation.

FIGURE 16.2

Serial Relationship of Activities.

Project Planning

The purpose of the **project planning** stage is to ensure that the project objectives of cost, time and quality are met. It does this by estimating both the level and timing of resources needed over the project duration. These steps

www.wileyopenpage.com

may need to be undertaken repeatedly in a complex project due to uncertainties and to accommodate changes as the project progresses. The planning process does not eradicate the need for the experience of the project manager in anticipating problems or the need for skill in dealing with unforeseen and novel incidences during project execution. However, the use of plans that can be executed sensibly will greatly improve the performance of the project.

The project management method uses a systems approach to deal with a complex task in that the components of the project are broken down repeatedly into smaller tasks until a manageable

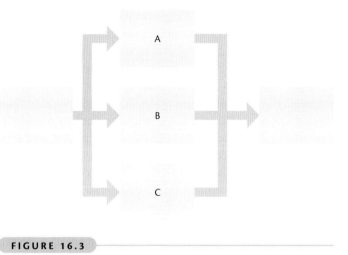

FIGURE 16.3

Parallel Relationship of Activities.

chunk is defined. Each task is given its own cost, time and quality objectives. It is then essential that responsibility is assigned to achieving these objectives for each particular task. This procedure should produce a work breakdown structure (WBS), which shows the hierarchical relationship between the project tasks (Figure 16.4). A typical WBS will have at the top level the project and at the bottom level the individual work package. A work package is an individual work element that can be accurately defined, budgeted, scheduled and controlled. Between the top and bottom levels various categories can be defined. These categories are usually organized in a product-oriented fashion but may be task oriented for service operations such as design or management.

Project Control

Project control involves the monitoring of the project objectives of cost, time and quality as the project progresses. It is important to monitor and assess performance as the project progresses in order that the project does not deviate from plans to a large extent. Milestones or time events are defined during the project when performance against objectives can be measured. The amount of control will depend

FIGURE 16.4

Work Breakdown Structure (WBS) for Building a Shed.

on the size of the project. Larger projects will require development of control activities from the project leader to team leaders. Computer project-management packages can be used to automate the collection of project progress data and production of progress reports.

The type of project structure required will depend on the size of the team undertaking the project. Projects with up to six team members can simply report directly to a project leader at appropriate intervals during project execution. For larger projects requiring up to 20 team members it is usual to implement an additional tier of management in the form of team leaders. The team leader could be responsible for either a phase of the development or a type of work. For any structure it is important that the project leader ensures consistency across development phases or development areas as appropriate. For projects with more than 20 members it is likely that additional management layers will be needed in order to ensure that no one person is involved with too much supervision.

The two main methods of reporting the progress of a project are by written reports and verbally at meetings of the project team. It is important that a formal statement of progress is made in written form, preferably in a standard report format, to ensure that everyone is aware of the current project situation. This is particularly important when changes to specifications are made during the project. In order to facilitate two-way communication between team members and team management, regular meetings should be arranged by the project manager. These meetings can increase the commitment of team members by allowing discussion of points of interest and dissemination of information on how each team's effort is contributing to the overall progression of the project.

NETWORK ANALYSIS

Network analysis refers to the use of network-based techniques for the analysis and management of projects. This section describes two network analysis techniques of the critical path method (CPM) and PERT. The CPM method described here was developed by DuPont during the 1950s to manage plant construction. The PERT approach was developed by the US Navy during the development of the Polaris Submarine Launched Ballistic Missile System during the same decade (Sapolsky, 1972). The main difference between the approaches is the ability of PERT to take into consideration uncertainty in activity durations.

In order to undertake network analysis it is necessary to break the project down into a number of identifiable activities or tasks. This enables individuals to be assigned responsibility to particular tasks that have a well-defined start and finish time. Performance objectives of time, cost and quality can be associated with each activity. The next stage is to retrieve information concerning the duration of the tasks involved in the project. This can be collated from a number of sources, such as documentation, observation and interviewing. The accuracy of the project plan will depend on the accuracy of these estimates. The next step is to identify any relationships between tasks in the project. For instance a particular task may not be able to begin until another task has finished. Thus the task waiting to begin depends on the former task. Other tasks may not have a dependent relationship and can thus occur simultaneously.

Critical Path Method (CPM)

Critical path diagrams are used extensively to show the activities undertaken during a project and the dependencies between these activities. Thus it is easy to see that activity C for example can only take place when activity A and activity B have completed. There are two methods of constructing critical path diagrams, activity on arrow (AOA), where the arrows represent the activities, and activity on node (AON), where the nodes represent the activities. The issues involved in which one to use will be discussed later. The following description on critical path analysis will use the AON method. For the activity-on-node notation each activity task is represented by a node with the format in Figure 16.5.

Early Start	Duration	Early Finish
	Task Name	
Late Start	Slack	Late Finish

FIGURE 16.5

Activity on Node Notation.

Thus a completed network will consist of a number of nodes connected by lines, one for each task, between a start and end node. An example of a completed network is shown in Figure 16.6.

Once the network diagram has been constructed it is possible to follow a sequence of activities, called a path, through the network from start to end. The length of time it takes to follow the path is the sum of all the durations of activities on that path. The path with the longest duration gives the project completion time. This is called the critical path because any change in duration in any activities on this path will cause the whole project duration to either become shorter or longer. The following four steps show how to identify the critical path.

1. Calculate the earliest start/finish times (forward pass). From the duration of each task and the dependency relationship between the tasks it is possible to estimate the earliest start and finish time for each task as follows. You move left to right along the network, forward through time.

   a. Assume the start (first) task begins at time = 0.

   b. Calculate the earliest finish time where: earliest finish = earliest start + duration.

   c. Calculate the earliest start time of the next task where: earliest start = earliest finish of task immediately before. If there is more than one task immediately before, take the task with the latest finish time to calculate the earliest start time for the current task.

   d. Repeat steps (b) and (c) for all tasks.

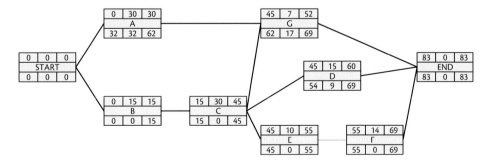

FIGURE 16.6

Activity on Node Network Diagram.

2. Calculate the latest start/finish times (backward pass). It is now possible to estimate the latest start and finish time for each task as follows. You move right to left along the network, backward through time.

   a. Assume the end (last) task end time is the earliest finish time (unless the project end time is given).

   b. Calculate the latest start time where: latest start = latest finish − duration.

   c. Calculate the latest finish time of the previous task where: latest finish = latest start of task immediately after. If there is more than one task immediately after take the task with the earliest start time to calculate the latest finish time for the current task.

   d. Repeat steps (b) and (c) for all tasks.

3. Calculate the slack/float times. The slack or float value is the difference between the earliest start and latest start (or earliest finish and latest finish) times for each task. To calculate the slack time

   a. Slack = latest start – earliest start OR slack = latest finish – earliest finish.

   b. Repeat step (a) for all tasks.

4. Identify the critical path.

Any tasks with a slack time of 0 must obviously be undertaken on schedule at the earliest start time. The critical path is the pathway connecting all the nodes with a zero slack time. There must be at least one critical path through the network but there can be more than one. The significance of the critical path is that if any node on the path finishes later than the earliest finish time, the overall network time will increase by the same amount, putting the project behind schedule. Thus any planning and control activities should focus on ensuring tasks on the critical path remain within schedule.

WORKED EXAMPLE 16.1

Critical Path Method

A particular project comprises the following activities:

Activity	Duration (days)	Immediate predecessor(s)
A	30	
B	15	–
C	30	B
D	15	C
E	10	C
F	14	E
G	7	A, C
H	14	D, F, G

(a) Draw an AON diagram for this project.

(b) Calculate the earliest start, earliest finish, latest start, latest finish and slack times for each activity.

(c) Identify the critical path.

 www.wileyopenpage.com

Solution

(a) The AON diagram is constructed by using the predecessor information contained in the table to connect the nodes as appropriate. For instance activity G has two predecessors, A and C, so both these nodes must point to the start of activity G.

(b) The earliest start/finish times are calculated by a forward pass (left to right) through the network. For instance activity A earliest start = 0, duration = 15, therefore earliest end = 15 − 0 = 15. Activity G, earliest start = 45 (= earliest finish of activities immediately before; A = 30, C = 45).

The latest start/finish times are calculated by a backward pass (right to left) through the network. For instance activity H latest end = 83, duration = 14, therefore latest start = 83 − 14 = 69. Activity C, latest end = 45 (= latest start of task immediately after; G = 62, D = 54, E = 45).

The slack time is the difference between the earliest and latest start times for each activity. For instance slack for G = 17 (= latest start − earliest start = 62 − 45 = 17).

(c) The critical path is the path or paths through the network with all nodes having a zero slack time. In this case there is one critical path; B, C, E, F, H.

The Activity-On-Arrow Method

The format for the activity-on-arrow method will now be described. The symbol used in this method is shown in Figure 16.7. Rather than considering the earliest and latest start and finish times of the activities directly, this method uses the earliest and latest event times as below:

- Earliest event time. This is determined by the earliest time at which any subsequent activity can start.
- Latest event time. This is determined by the latest time at which any subsequent activity can start.
- Thus for a single activity the format would be as shown in Figure 16.8.

FIGURE 16.7

Activity-on-Arrow Notation.

Conversely costs below budget may be an indication of a project running late. The performance measures used to do this are called the **earned value** or budgeted cost of work performed (BCWP) and show, for any day in the project, how much work has actually been done in terms of budgeted costs. This measure can be compared with the budgeted cost of work scheduled (BCWS) to find the schedule variance (SV) (SV = BCWP − BCWS) and the actual cost of work performed (ACWP) to find the cost variance (CV) (CV = BCWP − ACWP).

Project Crashing

Within any project there will be a number of time-cost trade-offs to consider. Most projects will have tasks that can be completed with an injection of additional resources, such as equipment or people. Reasons to reduce project completion time include:

- reduce high indirect costs associated with equipment.
- reduce new product development time to market
- avoid penalties for late completion
- gain incentives for early completion
- release resources for other projects.

The use of additional resources to reduce project completion time is termed **project crashing**. The idea is to reduce overall indirect project costs by increasing direct costs on a particular task. One of the most obvious ways of decreasing task duration is to allocate additional labour to a task. This can be either an additional team member or through overtime working. The following information is required to enable a decision to be made on the potential benefits of crashing a task:

- the normal task duration
- the crash task duration
- The cost of crashing the task to the crash task duration per unit time.

A task is chosen for crashing by observing which task can be reduced for the required time for the lowest cost. As stated before, the overall project completion time is the sum of the task durations on the critical path. Thus it is always necessary to crash a task which is on the critical path. As the duration of tasks on the critical path is reduced, however, other paths in the network will also become critical. If this happens it will require the crashing process to be undertaken on all the paths that are critical at any one time.

WORKED EXAMPLE 16.2

Project Crashing

Software Ltd has established a project team to undertake some important market research work. It is possible to reduce the expected or 'normal' times for certain activities in units of one week (but not in fractions of a week) but at an extra cost. The relevant information is given below.

www.wileyopenpage.com

		Normal		Crash	
Activity	Predecessor	(weeks) Duration	Cost of weeks (£)	Duration (weeks)	Extra cost per week saved (£)
A		5	4000	3	2000
B	–	4	3000	4	–
C	A	2	6000	1	15000
D	C	4	1000	4	–
E	B	5	4000	3	3000
F	B	5	7000	1	7000
G	B, C	4	4000	2	20000
H	F	3	5000	2	10000

In addition to the costs shown there is a cost of retainer fees and administration overheads of £10 000 for each week that the project lasts.

(a) What is the normal expected duration of the project, and its total cost? What is the critical path?

(b) What would be the cost of completing the project using the normal durations?

(c) What would be the duration of the project if costs are to be minimized?

Solution

(a) Construct the AON diagram by using the predecessor information in the table. From the diagram the duration of the project is 12 weeks. The critical path is B, F, H.

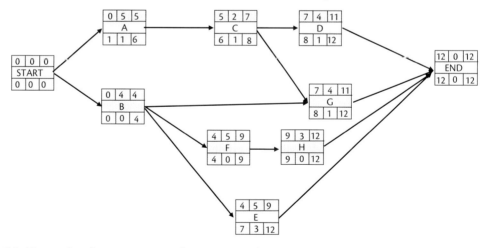

(b) The total project cost = cost of activities + other costs = £34 000 + 12 × £10 000 = £154 000.

(c) The minimum cost solution can be found by looking at the normal time solution.

Ignore B and D because they cannot be reduced.

Ignore C, G and H because it is too expensive to reduce these activities.

This leaves A, E and F.

Fast Homes – Courtesy of Prefabrication

On a muddy building site in the flat Cambridgeshire countryside in the UK, a crane swings a prefabricated concrete slab over a half-finished house and a team of workers slots it in to form part of the ground floor ceiling. A three-storey house built using prefabricated methods employed by Bovis Homes in the new village of Cambourne can be weathertight within ten days compared with the five-and-a-half weeks required by conventional techniques. This allows electricians and plumbers to get to work sooner and means the house can be completed in less than half the 22 weeks normally needed, says David Lowther, Bovis's research and development director.

Bovis and a handful of other housebuilders see prefabrication as the way forward while the government is keen for the building industry to modernize its production techniques. But despite years of trials and the use of timber-frame construction methods in Scotland, Scandinavia and the US, prefabrication remains controversial. The home-buying public associates it with postwar austerity and with the draughty, condensation-prone, system-built high-rises of the 1960s and 1970s. The verdict in the City is that prefabrication is a useful way of speeding up production and improving the housebuilders' return on capital. But the industry has yet to show that faster build times justify the higher costs and prefabrication is not a reason for giving a company a higher rating.

Malcolm Harris, Bovis chief executive, believes factory-finished components – a term he prefers to prefabrication – is essential to overcome skill shortages among trades such as bricklayers and to boost quality. Units made in advance in a factory can be built to much tighter tolerances than are possible on a muddy, windy building site. This results in fewer complaints. After trials Bovis is using its modern techniques at Cambourne, a development that will grow to 3300 homes over the next 10 years. Houses are being built with inner walls made of 'aircrete' blocks that are stuck together with glue. The blocks, made from relatively light aerated concrete, are the size of about 10 bricks, allowing walls to be built more quickly. Unlike traditional mortar, the glue can be used in freezing conditions, which means construction can continue throughout the winter. The selling points of concrete over timber are that it feels more solid and is fire-proof, rot-proof and provides better insulation.

Once the walls and floors are up, the roof trusses can be fixed and covered with waterproof felt, allowing work on installing the electrics, plumbing and internal finishes to be carried out. Bovis's plan is to build complete roof units on the ground – where work can go ahead faster and more safely than on the top of a house – and lift them into place. If the tiling industry can develop lightweight roof tiles, Bovis's aim is to fix the tiles as well before lifting the roof into position. With the roof in place, factory-made one-piece dormer windows are lifted by crane into position. Underneath, completed door and window units are fitted in the gaps left in the walls.

Once the inner wall is up and work is going on inside, the bricklayer can be brought in to build a brick outer 'skin' so the house looks just like its traditional counterparts. 'The beauty of this method is that it removes the bricklayer from the critical path of building the house', says Mr Harris.

Bovis is not alone in shifting to prefabrication although it buys the components rather than making them itself. Two other large housebuilders,

Westbury and Wilson Connolly, have in-house operations making timber-frame units. But while Westbury is increasing production, Wilson Connolly is cutting back because it has not achieved savings. The problem with prefabrication is that it is more expensive than traditional methods – although costs should come down as more experience is gained and volumes increase. Faster build times mean a higher return on capital invested but, for companies with manufacturing arms, moving to factory production requires the housebuilders to forecast demand in a notoriously cyclical market, analysts warn.

Source: Financial Times (2001). Reproduced with permission.

Question

Discuss the strategies used in this case to reduce the project completion time of new homes.

CASE STUDY 16.3

The Orbit Tower

Whether you see the ArcelorMittal Orbit as an ambitious work of art, an Olympic landmark or as a waste of resources, it was a project that although behind the scenes had artistic and economic struggles, has become a chaotic, confusing, yet inspiring mark on the London skyline, standing at 114.5m high and constructed between November 2010, and April 2012.

Construction took 18 months and required 560 metres of tubular red steel to form the sculpture's lattice superstructure. 60 per cent of the 2 000 tonnes of steel used in the sculpture being drawn from recycled sources and has 455 steps and has been designed to enable the guests to experience the feeling that they are orbiting around the structure as they descend it. The design incorporates the five Olympic rings and offers visitors panoramic views of the Olympic Stadium, Olympic Park and the whole of London.

As well as being a central part of the Olympic Park, the project scope included the objective to accommodate around 5 000 visitors a day and to attract around one million people during its first year of operation, to have the capacity to accommodate between 400–600 visitors per hour, and include full wheelchair access. Planning approval had to be granted by Newham Council and the ODA.

ArcelorMittal committed funding of £19.6 million of the £22.7 million cost of the Orbit, with the outstanding £3.1 million provided by the London Development Agency. It has been estimated that the resulting visitor attraction will generate up to £10 million of revenue per annum, charging visitors £15 per ticket, and create up to 50 new jobs following the 2012 Olympic and Paralympic Games.

ArcelorMittal is the world's leading steel company with operations in more than 60 countries, employs about 260 000 people worldwide and in 2009, had revenues of $65.1 billion and crude steel production of 73.2 million tonnes, representing approximately 8 per cent of world steel output.

The search for a permanent artwork on the Olympic Park was instigated by the Mayor of London's Office, which invited more than 30 international artists to submit their ideas for a sculpture. The Mayor of London and the Olympics Minister Tessa Jowell agreed the commission in partnership with Mr Mittal (Chairman and CEO of ArcelorMittal) after bringing together a panel from the art and design world to advise on a long list of proposals.

The highly complex project had little choice to be completed on time and budget, had numerous stakeholders, and involved a number of influential coalition and supply members and construction partners.

Ushida Findlay Architects' role as the delivery architects has been to work with the joint vision of the Artist and Turner Prize Winner Anish Kapoor who thanked the project team for making the Orbit possible and for their work on what is technically a very challenging project, and the engineer and co-creator, world leading structural designer Cecil Balmond from engineering firm Arup, who wanted to deliver a lasting legacy to the city.

ArcelorMittal handed over the Orbit to the London Legacy Development Corporation so that Balfour Beatty Workplace could complete the fit-out. The Mayor of London, Boris Johnson, brought forth that the Tower is a symbol of prosperity and growth of which long after the Games are over, will sustain as a stunning spectacle in east London that will be recognized around the world.

Sources

www.arcelormittal.com

http://www.london2012.com/spectators/venues/olympic-park/orbit/

http://www.e-architect.co.uk/london/olympic_park_landmark.htm

http://www.bbc.co.uk/programmes/b01k2jf4

Source: Written by Briony Boydell and Chris Milner. Reproduced with permission.

Questions

1. What characteristics and traits should an effective project manager have?

2. Do you think the London Olympics was a success from a project management perspective? Conduct external research in order to bring forth your answer.

 Quizzes to test yourself further are available in your interactive e-book at **www.wileyopenpage.com**

 Flashcards to test yourself further are available in your interactive e-book at **www.wileyopenpage.com**

EXERCISES

1. Discuss the project management activities of estimate, plan and control.

2. What assumptions does the network analysis method make?

3. A company has identified the following activities that will make up a project.

 www.wileyopenpage.com

Activity	Duration (hours)	Immediate predecessor(s)
A	1	–
B	1	A
C	3	B
D	2	B
E	2	D
F	1	E
H	2	F, G
I	1	H
J	1	I
K	1	I
L	1	J, K

a. Draw an AON diagram for this project.

b. Calculate the earliest start, earliest finish, latest start, latest finish and slack times for each activity.

c. Identify the critical path.

4. A company has identified the following activities and resource requirements for the following project:

Activity	Duration (hours)	Immediate predecessor	Members required (days)
A	3		4
B	4	–	3
C	9	–	4
D	4	A, B	7
E	5	B	8
F	6	D, C	9
G	6	E, C	5
H	10	F, G	2

a. Draw an AON diagram for this project.

b. Calculate the earliest start, earliest finish, latest start, latest finish and slack times for each activity.

c. Identify the critical path.

d. Draw a Gantt chart of the project indicating the slack times for each activity.

e. Draw a capacity loading graph based on the Gantt chart.

5. The following describes the introduction of a new product to be manufactured by a firm. The product has been developed and market tested by the R&D centre, but the manufacturing processes required to produce the product have yet to be developed. The process engineering group has been assigned the responsibility of the design project and have been given a target of 60 days to arrive at an overall process design. Although 60 days seemed very short to the process engineers at first, after some discussion it was concluded that they could probably pull it off because the product and its processes were so similar to the present processing technologies in use at their

plant. These activities, their precedence relationships and their durations were estimated by the engineers as follows:

Activity	Description	Precedence	Duration
A	Initial product design study	–	12
B	Preliminary product redesign for production	A	10
C	Preliminary facility redesign for product	A	15
D	Preliminary process technologies study	A	9
E	Facility modification for product redesign	B	6
F	Intermediate facility redesign	C, E	12
G	Intermediate product redesign	B	14
H	Specific process machinery design	B, D	21
I	Final facility, product and process design	F, G, H	10

a. Draw an AON diagram for this project.

b. Calculate the earliest start, earliest finish, latest start, latest finish and slack times for each activity.

c. Identify the critical path.

6. The HairCare company manufactures a range of hair-care products, including a range of hair styling gels. A competitor has recently introduced a new hair gel, which in the last six months has taken a significant share of the market, with adverse effects on HairCare's sales. The management at HairCare has decided that a competitive product must be introduced as quickly as possible and has asked Walter Dobie, the management accountant, to draw up a plan for developing and marketing the new product. As the first step in planning the project, Walter has identified the following major tasks, which will be involved in the new product launch. He has also estimated how long each task will take and what other tasks must precede each one.

Activity	Description	Precedence	Estimated duration (weeks)
A	Design new product	–	8
B	Design packaging	–	4
C	Organize production facilities	A	4
D	Obtain production materials	A	2
E	Manufacture trial batch	C, D	3
F	Obtain packaging	B	2
G	Decide on test market area	–	1
H	Package trial batch	E, F	2
I	Distribute product in test area	H, G	3
J	Conduct test market	I	4
K	Assess test market	J	3
L	Plan national launch	K	4

a. Draw an AON diagram for this project and determine how long it will be before the new product can be launched.

b. Calculate the slack time available for all the activities.

c. The time taken to complete tasks A, B, D, K and L is somewhat uncertain and so the following optimistic and pessimistic estimates have also been made to supplement the most likely figure given above. The additional estimates are:

Activity	Optimistic time (weeks)	Pessimistic time (weeks)
A	5	13
B	2	6
D	1	4
K	2	6
L	2	8

What now is the expected time until the product can be launched and what is the probability of this time exceeding 35 weeks? (You should assume that the overall project duration follows a normal distribution.)

7. A computer system has recently been installed in the accounts department of a manufacturing company. The activities involved in introducing the system are listed below together with their normal durations and costs. It would be possible to shorten the overall project duration by crashing certain activities at extra cost, so the relevant details are also included. In addition there will be a weekly charge of £2500 to cover overheads.

| Activity | Predecessor | Normal | | Crash | |
		Duration (weeks)	Cost	Duration (weeks)	Cost
A		3	3000	2	4000
B	–	6	6000	–	–
C	A	4	8000	1	11000
D	B	2	1500	–	–
E	A	8	4000	5	5000
F	B	4	3000	2	5000
G	C, D	2	2000	–	–
H	F	3	3000	1	6000

The crash time represents the shortest time in which the activity can be completed given the use of more costly methods of completion. Assume that it is possible to reduce the normal time to the crash time in steps of one week and that the extra cost will be proportional to the time saved.

a. Using the normal durations and costs construct an activity network for the introduction of the new computer system. Determine the critical path and associated cost.

b. Activities E and F have to be supervised by the chief accountant who will not be available for the first seven weeks of the project period. Both activities, however, can be supervised simultaneously. Determine whether or not this will affect the completion date and, if so, state how it will be affected.

c. Assuming that the chief accountant will be available whenever required and that all resources necessary to implement the crashing procedures will also be available, determine the minimum cost of undertaking the project.

8. Explain the following terms associated with project management.

   a. Critical path
   b. Slack time
   c. Crashing
   d. PERT.

FURTHER READING

Cadle, J. and Yeates, D. (2008) *Project Management for Information Systems*, 5th edn, Pearson Education.
Hughes, B. and Cotterell, M. (2009) *Software Project Management*, 5th edn, McGraw-Hill.
Lock, D. (2008) *Project Management*, 9th edn, Gower.
Maylor, H. (2010) *Project Management*, 4th edn, FT Prentice Hall.

WEB LINKS

https://www.comp.glam.ac.uk/staff/dwfarthi/projman.htm (accessed 6 June 2012). Dave W. Farthing's Software Project Management web link page – contains many links to project management resources.

www.pmi.org (accessed 6 June 2012). Project Management Institute. Contains information regarding news and events in the area of project management.

http://www.oracle.com/us/products/applications/primavera/overview/index.html (accessed 6 June 2012). Oracle's Primavera Enterprise Project Portfolio Management software.

www.projectmanagement.com (accessed 6 June 2012). Contains many articles regarding project management.

REFERENCES

Nicholas, J.M. and Steyn, H. (2011) *Project Management for Business, Engineering, and Technology: Principles and Practice*, 4th edn, Elsevier Butterworth-Heinemann.
Sapolsky, H.M. (1972) *The Polaris System Development: Bureaucratic and Programmatic Success in Government*, Harvard University Press, pp. 118–19.
Wheelwright, S. and Clark, K. (1992) *Revolutionizing Product Development*, The Free Press.

CHAPTER 17

Quality

- **Introduction**
- **Defining quality**
- **Measuring quality**
- **Improving quality**
- **Methodologies for quality improvement**
- **Six Sigma quality**
- **Statistical process control (SPC)**
- **Acceptance sampling**

LEARNING OBJECTIVES

- Explore the definition of quality
- Understand operational, financial and customer-based measures of quality
- Understand techniques for quality improvement from operational, financial and customer perspectives
- Understand the philosophy of total quality management (TQM)
- Describe the concept of Six Sigma improvement
- Understand the objectives of the ISO 9000 quality standard
- Understand the use of statistical process control and acceptance sampling

QUALITY AND OPERATIONS STRATEGY

Quality is one of the 5 operations performance objectives and so has an important role in operations strategy. TQM is most concerned with the performance objective of quality and implementing infrastructural elements (systems, policies and practices) to ensure high quality. Chapter 2 explains that the improvement priority given to a performance objective is dependent on market position according to the Hill methodology. Thus the importance of quality in strategic terms will be dependent on customer and competitor requirements. However, according to the sandcone theory (Chapter 2) quality is the most important of the five generic performance objectives. Under this theory a generic 'best' sequence of improvement should start with the performance objective of quality as this is a precondition for all lasting improvement. The shape of the sandcone indicates the relative effort that should be made to improve each performance objective with quality receiving most of the effort and cost the least.

INTRODUCTION

Quality is one of the five performance objectives and having a high quality product or service often represents an essential element when being considered by the customer.

Quality is a particular challenge for service organizations in that both the tangible and intangible aspects of the service (for example, the food and the service at a restaurant) must meet quality standards in order to earn repeat customers. The quality of the intangible aspect of the service may be difficult to measure and often depends on an unpredictable interaction between the service provider and customer.

Quality is a concept that can be viewed from a variety of perspectives and so the chapter begins by discussing various ways in which the concept of quality has been defined for products and services. The task of measuring quality is then discussed using operational, financial and customer quality measures. The chapter then considers techniques relevant to the pursuit of quality improvement from these three perspectives.

Various methodologies are then discussed for quality improvement. Total quality management (TQM) is a philosophy and approach that aims to ensure that high quality is a primary concern throughout the organization. The realization that a high level of quality can deliver competitive advantage is reflected in the widening use of Six Sigma initiatives.

Finally two operational-oriented quality improvement techniques are covered in detail. Statistical process control is a particularly important technique in ensuring that the process of delivering the product/service is performing satisfactorily and acceptance sampling is relevant to organizations when the cost of inspection is high relative to the cost of a defect being identified.

DEFINING QUALITY

Quality can actually mean quite different things to different people. This section starts by looking at different perspectives of what we mean by quality. Most definitions of quality will recognize the role of the customer in judging the quality of a product or service, so we will then look at the dimensions that customers may use in judging the quality of products and services.

 www.wileyopenpage.com

What Does Quality Mean?

Garvin (1988) provides a model that presents five different perspectives on a definition of quality:

- *Transcendent*. This views quality as excellence or the best available. An Aston Martin sports car or a seven-star hotel would wish to be seen in this way. This view implies that customers will be able to recognize excellence when they see it.
- *Product based*. This views quality as a precise and measurable variable that is made up of a number of characteristics. This implies quality can be measured as a number of attributes making up a product or service. Thus, the quality of a car could be measured by its acceleration, top speed, engine size, etc. The assessment of product variables may vary considerably amongst individuals.
- *User based*. This views quality as the level of satisfaction held by an individual customer. This implies that quality is a subjective concept and will vary with the needs of individual customers. This means a car with a large range of options for engine sizes and accessories that can be customized to an individual customer's needs. Quality using this perception is defined as how well the product performs its intended function according to the customer.
- *Operations based*. This views quality as conformance to internally developed specifications in service operations or manufacturing. This implies that quality will be defined in terms of productivity targets. Thus a car produced consistently over time with no defective components and matching the design specification would be considered of high quality.
- *Value based*. This views quality in terms of best price for a given purpose. This implies quality is viewed from a customer perspective in terms of 'value for money'. Thus a Ford Fiesta could be seen to be a better quality product than a BMW if it can meet customers' needs for a lower price. Thus a quality product is seen to be as useful as competing products but cheaper or offering greater satisfaction than products sold at a comparable price.

These five perspectives demonstrate that there is no single 'correct' view of how to define quality and all of these perspectives may be relevant but have their limitations if taken in isolation. For example, the product-based and operations-based views may fail to take into account customer views. A product-based approach may have an over focus on internal design attributes and an operations-based approach may have an over focus on conformance to the design specification. On the other hand the transcendent, user-based and value-based approaches may find it difficult to operationalize the many individual customer expectations into viable products and services. A transcendent approach relies on the subjective judgement of individual potential customers as to what is the 'best'. The user-based approach may lead to unprofitable offerings in an attempt to please as many customers as possible. A value-based approach has the difficulty of determining how customers might trade off aspects of quality with cost considerations.

Slack, Chambers and Johnston (2010) attempt to reconcile these different views with the following definition of quality: *quality is consistent conformance to customers' expectations*.

Consistent implies that conformance to specification is not an *ad hoc* event but the product or service delivery process has been designed so that the product or service meets the specification using a set of measurable characteristics (product-based view). *Conformance* implies there that is a need to meet a clear specification (operations-based view). *Customers' expectations* implies that the customer receives a product or service with attributes that they can reasonably expect (user based) at a reasonable cost (value based).

Finally the perspectives are also useful in relating responsibility for quality to areas within the organization. For example, the marketing department would have a large responsibility for quality defined in the customer-oriented perspectives of transcendent-based, product-based and user-based. Operations would be largely responsible for the conformance to specification viewpoint of the operations-based perspective of quality. The design function would be largely responsible for achieving a value-based perspective through low cost product and process design.

How Do Customers Define Product Quality?

Whatever the perspectives of quality taken in the previous section it is clear that an important aspect when considering quality is understanding and meeting customer requirements. However, since different customers will have different product needs and requirements it follows that they will have different quality expectations. In an attempt to understand the criteria that customers use to judge quality, Garvin (1984) breaks the concept of quality down into eight dimensions or elements:

- performance
- features
- reliability
- conformance
- durability
- serviceability
- aesthetics
- other perceptions.

Each of these dimensions is self-contained and distinct and each provides an independent basis for ranking products. For example, in some markets customers will equate quality with superior performance, while in others they base their ratings on reliability. This view of quality implies there is no one way to superior quality; different organizations may choose to focus on different aspects of quality and they may all be successful; but an understanding of customer needs is important in determining a quality strategy.

How Do Customers Define Service Quality?

For services, the assessment of quality is made during the service delivery process. The nature of services in terms of their intangibility, the fact that they often involve customer contact and the customized nature of professional services means that defining quality is difficult. One approach to the definition of quality in services is given by Parasuraman, Zeithaml and Berry (1985) in terms of five principal dimensions that customers use to judge service quality:

- *Reliability*. This relates to the ability to perform a service dependably and accurately. Customers expect reliable service – that is, a service that is delivered on time, in the same manner and without errors every time.
- *Responsiveness*. This relates to the willingness to help customers and to provide prompt service. Customers in particular dislike waiting for a service especially if there is no apparent reason for the

wait. A quick recovery if a service failure occurs is also important in achieving a favourable customer experience.

- *Assurance*. This relates to the abilities of employees delivering the service to the customer. They should demonstrate competence, respect for the customer and be able to effectively communicate with the customer.
- *Empathy*. This also concerns the abilities of employees and relates to the provision of a caring, individualized service requiring approachability, sensitivity and to demonstrate an effort to understand the customer's needs.
- *Tangibles*. This relates to the physical aspects of the service delivery environment such as the condition of the physical surroundings. Clean and tidy physical surroundings provide the customer with evidence of the care and attention to detail shown by the service provider.

The concept is that customers use these five dimensions to form their judgement of service quality, which are based on a comparison between expectations and perceptions of that service quality. These measurements are gathered from customers using the survey research instrument SERVQUAL described in the 'Measuring quality' section of this chapter. The difference between the expected and perceived service level is termed the 'service quality gap' and can be used to identify areas for improvement in service quality. The service quality gap model is also considered in more detail in the improving quality section of this chapter.

MEASURING QUALITY

In order to control quality it needs to be measured. However, we have just seen different perspectives on how to define quality so it follows there will be different approaches to its measurement. Three main categories of measures are operational, financial and customer based.

Operational Quality Measures

These measures cover operational performance indicators that are not financial or customer-based measures. Operational quality measures include scrap rates which measure the proportion of parts and materials that have been damaged by movement or manufacture and are not possible to be reused after rework. Another operational performance measure is defect rates for parts and materials that fail to meet design specifications. Performance indicators can also include service operational quality measures such as the on-time delivery performance of suppliers. Tools for improving operational quality measures include statistical process quality and quality acceptance sampling discussed later in this chapter.

Financial Quality Measures

Quality gurus such as Juran and Crosby argue that the costs of poor quality and thus the benefits of improvements in quality should be identified. Quality costs are defined as any expenditures in excess of those that would have occurred had the product been manufactured or the service been delivered right first time. These quality costs can be categorized as either the cost of achieving good quality – the cost of quality assurance – or the cost of poor quality products – the cost of not conforming to specifications.

The Cost of Achieving Good Quality

The costs of maintaining an effective quality management programme can be categorized into **prevention costs** and **appraisal costs**. Prevention costs reflect the quality philosophy of 'doing it right the first time' and include those costs incurred in trying to prevent problems occurring in the first place. Examples of prevention costs include:

- the cost of designing products with quality control characteristics
- the cost of designing processes which conform to quality specifications
- the cost of the implementation of staff training programmes.

Appraisal costs are the costs associated with controlling quality through the use of measuring and testing products and processes to ensure conformance to quality specifications. Examples of appraisal costs include:

- the cost of testing and inspecting products
- the costs of maintaining testing equipment
- the time spent in gathering data for testing
- the time spent adjusting equipment to maintain quality.

Tools for improving financial quality measures include the zero defects approach discussed later in this chapter.

The Cost of Poor Quality

This can be seen as the difference between what it actually costs to provide a good or service and what it would cost if there was no poor quality or failures. This can account for 70 to 90% of total quality costs and can be categorized into internal failure costs and external failure costs. Internal failure costs occur before the good is delivered to the customer. Examples of internal failure costs include:

- the scrap cost of poor quality parts that must be discarded
- the rework cost of fixing defective products
- the downtime cost of machine time lost due to fixing equipment or replacing defective product.

External failure costs occur after the customer has received the product and primarily relate to customer service. Examples of external failure costs include:

- the cost of responding to customer complaints
- the cost of handling and replacing poor-quality products
- the litigation cost resulting from product liability
- the lost sales incurred because of customer goodwill affecting future business.

The Quality-Cost Trade-Off

The classical economic trade-off between costs shows that when the cost of achieving good quality (prevention and appraisal costs) increases, the cost of poor quality (internal and external failure costs) declines. This relationship is shown graphically in Figure 17.1.

FIGURE 17.1

The Traditional Quality-Cost Trade-Off.

Adding the two costs together produces the total cost curve. The optimal quality level is thus at the point when quality costs are minimized. This implies that prevention costs should be increased until this point is reached.

However, many Japanese organizations did not accept assumptions behind the traditional model and aimed for a zero-defect performance instead. The two views on the costs of quality can be seen by comparing the 'Traditional' (Figure 17.1) and 'Zero Defect' (Figure 17.2) cost-of-quality graphs. According to the traditional view the costs of prevention rise substantially as the zero-defect level is approached. This is based on the assumption that the last errors are the hardest to find and correct. The zero-defect approach assumes that it costs no more to remove the last error than the first. It may take longer to determine what the source of the last error is but the steps to correct it are likely to be simple. While there is debate about the shape of the cost-quality curves and about whether zero defects is really the lowest cost way to make a product, it is beyond doubt that the new approach to quality performance is beneficial.

Customer Quality Measures

Earlier in this chapter the role of the customer in the definition of quality was outlined. Customer quality measures move beyond operational and financial measures and incorporate the customer perspective. Parasuraman, Zeithaml and Berry (1988) have developed a survey research instrument called **SERVQUAL** that is based on the premise that customers can measure a firm's service quality by comparing their perception of its service with their own expectations. SERVQUAL measures the five dimensions that customers use to judge service quality (outlined in the 'defining quality' section earlier in this

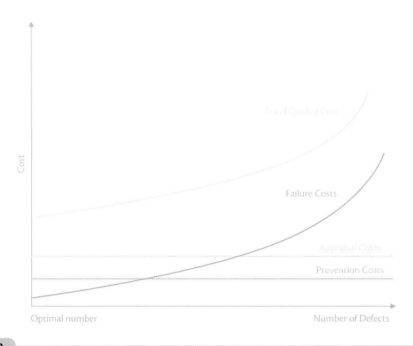

FIGURE 17.2

The Zero Defects Quality-Cost Trade-Off.

chapter) of reliability, responsiveness, assurance, empathy and tangibles. The survey has an initial section that records customer expectations of a service followed by a second section to record a customer's perceptions for a particular service firm offering this service. SERVQUAL can be used either to track service quality over a period of time by repeatedly administering the survey or by conducting a multi-site survey to identify poor-performing units.

IMPROVING QUALITY

In this section the techniques for quality improvement are categorized as for the quality measures in the previous section into operational, financial and customer-oriented techniques.

Operational-Oriented Quality Improvement

The operational-oriented quality improvement methods of statistical process control (SPC) and acceptance sampling are covered at the end of this chapter. Other methods of ensuring quality at the design stage such as failure mode and effect analysis (FMEA) and Taguchi's quality loss function (QLF) are covered in Chapter 7.

Financially Oriented Quality Improvement

This section will cover the financially oriented quality improvement approach of the **cost of quality (COQ)**. The identification and measurements of the costs of quality began in the 1950s as an extension

www.wileyopenpage.com

to the standard financial reporting used by organizations to control and improve organizational performance. When an attempt to measure costs was undertaken it was found that the costs of quality were much larger than previously thought, were incurred across the organization (not just in manufacturing) and most of these costs were avoidable. The measurement of these costs in financial terms alerted senior management to their significance and enabled responsibility for their reduction to be assigned.

As a first step in identifying quality costs they can be organized into the categories defined in the 'Financial quality measures' section earlier in this chapter. These categories are prevention costs, appraisal costs, internal failure costs and external failure costs. Costs can be further analysed by location in terms of product line, process or department. Once the type and location of the quality costs has been determined then techniques such as Pareto analysis (Chapter 7) can be used to identify the small number of causes of the majority of costs, which will provide the greatest return on corrective action taken.

It is usual that organizations find that the highest quality costs are found in the external failure category followed by internal failure, appraisal and then prevention. The aim should be to reverse this order and eliminate external and internal failure costs as much as possible. This will mean investing in appraisal activities to identify failure costs and then when failure costs decrease the amount of appraisal can be reduced and the emphasis can shift to prevention activities.

Other financially oriented approaches to quality improvement include the need to ensure that quality is designed into the product to eliminate costly problems later at the manufacturing stage. Techniques such as value engineering (Chapter 7) can be used to do this.

Customer-Oriented Quality Improvement

This section will cover the customer-oriented quality improvement technique of the **quality gap approach**. This model uses customer-based information from the SERVQUAL survey instrument (see 'Measuring quality' section) and attempts to identify the nature and the location of quality problem areas. The approach was developed by Parasuraman, Zeithaml and Berry (1985) to devise a way of improving quality by identifying the gap between what customers expect from a service and what they perceive they are actually getting. The difference between the two is termed the 'quality gap' and the size of this gap determines customer dissatisfaction. Although the concept was originally devised for service operations it can be used to assess quality failures in manufactured products. There are five possible quality gaps in the model (Figure 17.3).

The gaps are described in turn:

- *Gap 1: operation's concept of product or service – customer's expectations of product or service*. This is when the operation's concept of the product or service does not meet customer expectations. For example, a customer may expect

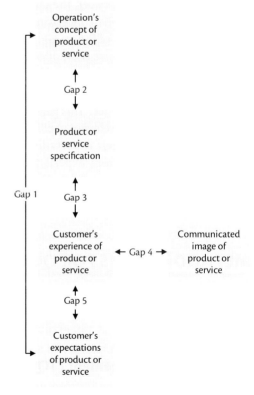

FIGURE 17.3

The Quality Gaps Model.
Source: Adapted from Parasuraman, A.; Zeithaml, V.A.; Berry, L.L. (1985) A conceptual model of service quality and its implications for future research, Journal of Marketing, vol. 49, no. 4, pp. 41–50

- *Improve* – eliminate the root causes of nonrandom variation to achieve improvements in predictability, dispersion and centring. If no special causes can be found the improvement effort may need to focus on the design of the product or process.
- *Control* – verify and embed the change through the use of techniques such as control charts. Share experiences to transfer knowledge between process improvement teams.

Implementing Six Sigma

The DMAIC methodology is one aspect of a framework for implementation of the Six Sigma concept. Other aspects of this framework include top management commitment, stakeholder involvement and training and measurement. Top management commitment is required in order to implement Six Sigma in all parts of the organization. Six Sigma requires the involvement of stakeholders such as employees, suppliers and customers. Employees are required to be trained and implement the concept and suppliers must deliver high-quality inputs to the organization. The whole rationale behind Six Sigma is to understand and meet the needs of customers, so their involvement is also vital. Training is important in order to implement the statistical tools necessary for Six Sigma and is based on various levels of expertise. These levels are often denoted by the terms White Belts, Green Belts, Black Belts, Master Black Belts and Champions in order of increasing training duration and level. In terms of measurement Six Sigma focuses on the measure of variation and uses the metric of defects per million opportunities (dpmo). As stated earlier the goal is to reduce variation to within Six Sigma control limits, corresponding to a rate of 3.4 defective parts per million (PPM).

To summarize, the Six Sigma approach emphasizes a measurable improvement in revenues through increasing effectiveness and efficiency. It uses the DMAIC methodology to ensure process improvement efforts are based on factual data. It uses customer focused improvements to ensure change increases revenue and uses training to ensure the appropriate tools are used for specific improvement projects.

CASE STUDY 17.2

Adventures in Six Sigma: How the Problem-solving Technique Helped Xerox

Like many other US companies, Xerox was introduced to Six Sigma through its interactions with General Electric. The financial services to biotechnology conglomerate adopted the metrics-mad process improvement technique in the mid-1990s. Thanks to its size and influence, it has served as an effective missionary. Anne Mulcahy's conversion came as she was negotiating the outsourcing of Xerox's troubled billing and collections operation to GE Capital. She recalls: 'I remember sitting there and watching the discipline with which [the GE team] defined the problem, scoped the

problem and attacked it from a Six Sigma perspective. I remember feeling for the first time that the problem would be fixed.'

The precise definition of Six Sigma quality is an error rate of 3.4 per million. More important than the exact number, however, is an approach to problem solving that emphasizes small teams, measurement and economic return. Quality improvement techniques were by no means new to Xerox. In the 1980s, it was one of the first US companies to adopt Total Quality Management (TQM) as it fought to turn back the tide of Japanese competition. As an

www.wileyopenpage.com

up-and-coming manager, Ms Mulcahy experienced TQM first hand. 'The financial metrics were not as precise with TQM,' she recalls. 'Six Sigma is very rigid and very disciplined by comparison. Every project is managed with economic profit metrics. There is none of the squishy stuff.' The 'squishy stuff' is the emphasis in TQM on consensus building that, while part of an earnest desire to replicate the best of Japanese management, did not always play well at US companies.

Ms Mulcahy is also at pains to point out that Xerox practises Lean Six Sigma, a variation that asks managers to think not only how processes can be improved but also how waste can be reduced: 'Lean is an important nuance. The learning process begins with taking out waste, working out where value gets added and where it does not. For big companies, this is very important.' While companies generally adopt Six Sigma to improve efficiency, converts insist that there are other benefits. The introduction of a company-wide approach to project management is reckoned to break down barriers between departments, and make it easier to work with suppliers and customers. Ms Mulcahy says: 'The reality of our business is that in order to compete you have to find ways to deliver 8, 9, 10% productivity improvements every single year. You only get there if you have a systemic approach.'

Source: Financial Times (2005). Reproduced with permission.

Question

Discuss the advantages of Six Sigma outlined in the case study.

The ISO 9000 Quality Standard

ISO 9000 provides a quality standard between suppliers and a customer developed by the International Organization for Standardization (www.iso.ch). Having a predefined quality standard reduces the complexity of managing a number of different quality standards when a customer has many suppliers. Many countries have adopted ISO 9000 and so it is particularly useful in standardizing the relationship between customers and suppliers on a global basis. The ISO 9000 model contains eight quality management principles on which to base a quality management system (QMS):

1. Customer focus
2. Leadership
3. Involvement of people
4. Process approach
5. Systems approach to management
6. Continual improvement
7. Factual approach to decision making
8. Mutually beneficial supplier relationships.

The most recent ISO 9000 series of standards for quality management systems comprises the following:

- *ISO 9000:2000* – fundamentals and vocabulary of quality management systems.
- *ISO 9001:2000* – requirements of quality management systems.
- *ISO 9004:2000* – detailed guidelines for performance improvement in quality management systems.

The standard is general enough to apply to almost any good or service but it is the specific organization or facility that is registered or certified to the standard. A facility must document its procedures for every element in the standard to achieve certification. These procedures are then audited by a third party periodically. The system thus ensures that the organization is following a documented, and thus consistent, procedure, which makes errors easier to find and correct.

Quality Awards

Programmes which provide national and international standards for quality are the European Quality Award (EQA), the EFQM Excellence Model®, the Baldrige Award and the Deming Prize. The EQA was launched in 1992 by members of the European Foundation for Quality Management (EFQM) and is a yearly competition in which companies are scored in various categories such as leadership, processes and key performance results. The EFQM has also developed an Excellence Model®, which allows a company to compare the way it runs its business to best practice. A checklist is provided covering the areas of leadership, policy and strategy, people, partnerships and resources, processes, customer results, people results, society results and key performance results. The Baldrige Award was established in the USA in 1987 and seeks to recognize and encourage quality improvements. It measures performance in the seven areas of leadership, strategic planning, customer and market focus, measurement, analysis and knowledge management, human resource focus, process management and business results. The Deming Prize was established in 1951 in Japan and is awarded annually to companies that have distinguished quality management programmes.

STATISTICAL PROCESS CONTROL (SPC)

Statistical process control is an operational-oriented technique for quality improvement. It involves taking a sample that checks the quality of an item that is engaged in a process. Thus SPC should be seen as a quality check for process rather than product design. Statistical process control works by identifying the nature of variations in a process, which are classified as being caused by 'chance' causes or 'assignable' causes.

Chance Causes of Variation

All processes will have some inherent variability due to factors such as ambient temperature, wear of moving parts or slight variations in the composition of the material that is being processed. The technique of SPC involves calculating the limits of these chance-cause variations for a stable system, so any problems with the process can be identified quickly. The limits of the **chance causes of variations** are called control limits and are shown on a control chart, which also shows sample data of the measured characteristic over time. There are control limits above and below the target value for the measurement, termed the upper control limit (UCL) and lower control limit (LCL) respectively. An example control chart is shown in Figure 17.5.

The behaviour of the process can thus be observed by studying the control chart. If the sample data plotted on the chart shows a random pattern within the upper and lower control limits then the process is 'in-control'. However, if a sample falls outside the control limits or the plot shows a nonrandom pattern then the process is 'out-of-control'.

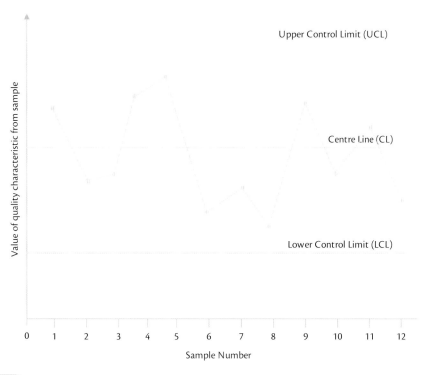

FIGURE 17.5

Statistical Process Control Chart.

Assignable Causes of Variation

If an 'out-of-control' process is discovered, then it is assumed to have been caused by an assignable cause of variation. This is a variation in the process that is not due to random variation but can be attributed to some change in the process, which needs to be investigated and rectified. However, in some instances the process could actually be working properly and the results could have been caused by Upper Control Limit (UCL):

- *Type I error* – an error is indicated from the sample output when none actually occurs. The probability of a type I error is termed α.
- *Type II error* – an error is occurring but has not been indicated by the sample output. The probability of a type II error is termed β.

Thus type I errors may lead to some costly investigation and rectification work, which is unnecessary. They may even lead to an unnecessary recall of 'faulty' products. Type II errors will lead to defective products as a result of an out-of-control process going unnoticed. Customer compensation and loss of sales may result if defective products reach the marketplace. The sampling methodology should ensure that the probability of type I and type II errors should be kept as low as reasonably possible.

Control Charts for Variable Data

Control charts for variable data display samples of a measurement that can take a value from a range of possible values. Values will fall in or out of a range around a specified target value. Examples of variable data could be a customer transaction time in a bank or the width of an assembly component. Two control charts are used in measuring variable data. The $\overline{X}$ chart shows the distance of sample values from the target value (central tendency) and the R chart shows the variability of sample values (dispersion).

$\overline{X}$ Chart

The $\overline{X}$ (X-bar) chart consists of a series of tests on a sample of data to check that the mean value of the process aligns with the target value. The sample size tends to be small, four or five. The $\overline{X}$ chart uses the central limit theorem, which states that the sample means will be normally distributed if the process distribution is also normal. Otherwise if the process does not follow a normal distribution the distribution of the sample means will be normally distributed if the sample size is sufficiently large. Thus to construct control limits for an $\overline{X}$ chart the following calculations can be used:

$$\text{UCL} = \mu + z \times \sigma_x$$
$$\text{LCL} = \mu - z \times \sigma_x$$

where

  μ = process average
  $\sigma_x = \sigma/\sqrt{n}$
  σ = process standard deviation
  n = sample size
  z = 3 (for a three-sigma chart).

When the process mean, μ, is not known, the average of the sample means, $\overline{\overline{X}}$, can be used instead and substituted in the previous equation.

A z value of 3 corresponds to a normal probability of 99.74%. Sometimes the z value is 2, giving a probability of 95%, thus giving more narrow control limits. A smaller value of z increases the risk that the process sample will fall outside the control limits due to normal random variations. Conversely a large value of z means that nonrandom changes may not be discovered. Traditionally control charts use z = 3, called three-sigma (3σ) or three standard deviation limits.

Using $\overline{X}$ with R Charts

Usually the $\overline{X}$ and R charts are used together and in this case the sample range is used as a measure of process variability. Thus the control limits can be calculated as follows:

$$\text{CV} = \overline{\overline{X}}$$
$$\text{UCL} = \overline{\overline{X}} + A_2 \times \overline{R}$$
$$\text{LCL} = \overline{\overline{X}} - A_2 \times \overline{R}$$

where
  $\overline{\overline{X}}$ = average of sample means
  $\overline{R}$ = average sample range.
  values of A_2 vary with the sample size and are shown in Table 17.1.

TABLE 17.1

Factors for Determining Control Limits for $(\overline{X})$ and R Charts.

Sample size n	Factor for $(\overline{X})$ chart A_2	Factor for R chart D_3	Factor for R chart D_4
2	1.88	0	3.27
3	1.02	0	2.57
4	0.73	0	2.28
5	0.58	0	2.11
6	0.48	0	2.00
7	0.42	0.08	1.92
8	0.37	0.14	1.86
9	0.34	0.18	1.82
10	0.31	0.22	1.78
11	0.29	0.26	1.74
12	0.27	0.28	1.72
13	0.25	0.31	1.69
14	0.24	0.33	1.67
15	0.22	0.35	1.65
16	0.21	0.36	1.64
17	0.20	0.38	1.62
18	0.19	0.39	1.61
19	0.19	0.40	1.60
20	0.18	0.41	1.59
21	0.17	0.43	1.58
22	0.17	0.43	1.57
23	0.16	0.44	1.56
24	0.16	0.45	1.55
25	0.15	0.46	1.54

R Chart

Control limits for range limits are found using the following calculations:

$$CV = \overline{R}$$
$$UCL = D_4\overline{R}$$
$$LCL = D_3\overline{R}$$
$$R = \text{average sample range}$$

values of D_3 and D_4 vary with the sample size and can be found in Table 17.1. It is usual to plot both an $\overline{X}$ and a separate R chart for a process to provide perspectives on both movements in the process mean and movements in process dispersion respectively.

WORKED EXAMPLE 17.1

Control Charts for Variable Data

As part of its process control activities a bakery wishes to monitor the weight of dough portions being measured out prior to baking. Below are given the weight of thirteen samples each of five portions. Plot these data onto the appropriate charts and comment on the stability or otherwise of the process.

Sample/weight (grams)												
1	2	3	4	5	6	7	8	9	10	11	12	13
375	375	375	373	375	378	375	379	378	374	378	374	379
378	374	375	376	379	373	373	374	378	376	376	379	380
376	376	378	377	376	376	377	376	375	373	380	379	379
378	379	377	376	378	375	376	376	377	376	379	376	377
377	376	376	375	376	378	377	379	378	377	377	379	379

Solution

The first step is to calculate the mean ($\overline{X}$) and range (R) for each sample. 4

Sample	1	2	3	4	5	6	7	8	9	10	11	12	13
$\overline{X}$	376.8	376	376.2	375.4	376.8	376	375.6	376.8	377.2	375.2	378	377.4	378.8
R	3	5	3	4	4	5	4	5	3	4	4	5	3

Then calculate the mean of the means:

$$\overline{\overline{X}} = 376.6 \text{ and } \overline{R} = 4$$

For the means chart:

Sample size is 5 therefore A_2 is 0.58 (lookup value in Table 17.1).

$$LCL = 376.6 - 0.58 \times 4 = 374.28$$
$$CV = 376.6$$
$$UCL = 376.6 + 0.58 \times 4 = 378.92$$

For the ranges chart:

Sample size is 5 therefore $D_3 = 0$ and $D_4 = 2.11$ (lookup values in Table 17.1).

$$LCL = 4 \times 0 = 0$$
$$CV = 4$$
$$UCL = 4 \times 2.11 = 8.44$$

From the means chart it can be seen that the machine is overfilling.

Control Charts for Attribute Data

Attribute control charts measure discrete values such as if a component is defective or not. Thus there are no values, as in a variable control chart, from which a mean and range can be calculated. The data will simply provide a count of how many items conform to a specification and how many do not. Two control charts will be described for attribute data. The p-chart shows the proportion of defectives in a sample; the c-chart shows the number of defectives in a sample.

p-chart

The p-chart is used when it is possible to distinguish between defectives and non-defectives for each sample item, and thus calculate the number of defectives as a percentage of the whole (i.e. the proportion).

A p-chart takes samples from a process over time and the proportion of defective items is calculated to see if it falls within the control limits on the chart. Assuming a significant sample size and a three-sigma chart, the calculations can be based on a normal distribution to calculate the control limits as follows:

$$CV = p$$
$$LCL = p - 3\sqrt{\left(\frac{p(1-p)}{n}\right)}$$
$$UCL = p + 3\sqrt{\left(\frac{p(1-p)}{n}\right)}$$

where
p = population proportion defective (process mean)
n = sample size.

When the process mean, p, is not known the proportion defective, $\bar{p}$, can be calculated from the samples and substituted in the previous equation.

WORKED EXAMPLE 17.2

Control Charts for Attribute Data

The following table gives the results of daily inspections of 500 units of a standard-design electronic device produced during the month of June 1998.

Date in June	3	4	5	6	7	10	11	12	13	14
Rejects	10	14	18	10	14	21	17	12	15	16
Date in June	17	18	19	20	21	24	25	26	27	28
Rejects	16	25	26	12	14	17	15	9	10	14

(a) Estimate the total proportion of rejects during this month.

(b) Establish a single set of control limits for the daily fraction of rejects based on these figures and plot a control chart, showing the daily results.

(c) Comment on the stability of the manufacturing process. What appears to have happened to cause the sudden change between 19 and 20 June?

(d) Based on the records of this month, what would you recommend as the central value, p, to use for the following month's control chart for fraction rejects?

Solution

(a) The number of inspections in June 1998 is 500 units per day for 20 days, totalling 10 000 units. During this month a total of 305 units are rejected. Hence the proportion rejected, p, is:

$$p = \frac{305}{1000}$$
$$= 0.0305 \ (3.05\%)$$

(b) The control limits are as follows:

$$p = 0.0305$$
$$n = 500$$
$$UCL = 0.0305 + 0.02306 = 0.0536$$
$$CV = 0.0305$$
$$LCL = 0.0305 - 0.02306 = 0.0074$$

The proportion of rejects over the 20 working days of June 1998 is as follows:

Date	3	4	5	6	7	10	11	12	13	14
Proportion Defective	0.02	0.028	0.036	0.02	0.028	0.042	0.034	0.024	0.030	0.032
Date	17	18	19	20	21	24	25	26	27	28
Proportion Defective	0.032	0.050	0.052	0.024	0.028	0.034	0.030	0.018	0.020	0.028

(c) The manufacturing process appears to be under control for the first half of June, and again over the last few days of the month. However, it seems clear that the process was interrupted between 19 and 20 June. It seems likely that the process controller decided that the process had gone out of control during 18 and 19 June, with two consecutive observations so close to the upper control limit. This fault was rectified so that the later results were an improvement.

(d) When recommending a central value for the following month it would seem sensible to only use those days in June when the process was stable. Hence the results of 18 and 19 June would be ignored. The recommended value for p for the following month is:

$$p = \frac{305 - (25 + 26)}{10\,000 - 1000} = \frac{254}{9000} = 0.0282$$

Alternatively we might use the results of just the last seven days of June (the days after adjustment) to form the basis of the recommendation. This gives:

$$p = 91/3500 = 0.026$$

c-Chart

A c-chart counts the actual number of defects when the proportion cannot be calculated. For example, if the quality of paint on a car body panel is being inspected, the number of blemishes (defects) can be counted but the proportion cannot be calculated because the total number is not known. The Poisson distribution is theoretically used to represent the probability of a defect from an extremely large population, but the normal distribution is used as a substitute for the c-chart. Assuming a three-sigma chart the control limits can be calculated as follows:

$$CV = c$$
$$UCL = c + 3 \times \sqrt{c}$$
$$LCL = c - 3 \times \sqrt{c}$$

where
   c = mean number of defects per sample.

When the process mean, c, is not known the sample mean, $\bar{c}$, can be estimated by dividing the number of defects by the number of samples and substituting in the previous equation.

Investigating Control Chart Patterns

Apart from the plots on the control charts that lie outside the control limits, it is still possible that the process may be out of control due to nonrandom behaviour within the control limits. If the behaviour is random then the plots should follow no discernible pattern and occur either side of the centre line. There are several guidelines for identifying nonrandom behaviour. Several of these guidelines are shown in Figure 17.6.

Run Patterns

It is possible to use a z pattern test or run test to determine the probability of certain plot patterns occurring. The general form of the calculation for the z test is as follows:

$$z_{TEST} = \frac{\text{observed runs} - \text{expected runs}}{\sigma}$$

where
   σ = standard deviation.

From this the following calculation is derived for a run of sample values that consistently go up or down within the control limits:

$$z_{U/D} = \frac{r - [(2N - 1)/3]}{\sqrt{(16N - 29)/90}}$$

where
   r = observed number of runs
   N = sample size.

For a run of sample values which are above or below the centre line, the calculation is as follows:

$$z_{A/B} = \frac{r - [(N/2) + 1]}{\sqrt{(N - 1)/4}}$$

where
   r = observed number of runs
   N = sample size.

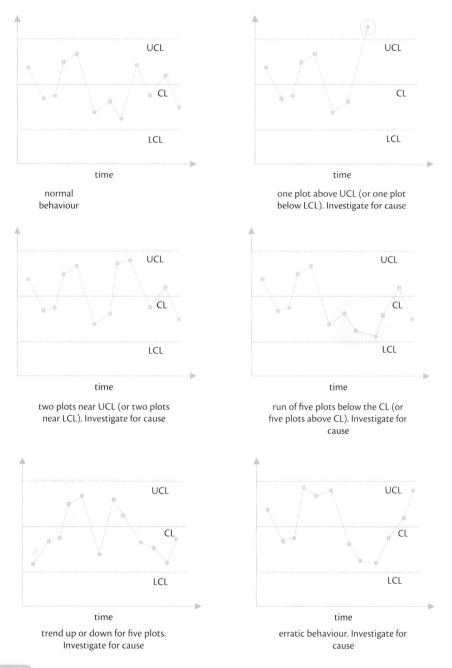

FIGURE 17.6

Control Chart Patterns.

The z test values are compared to a z value for a particular level of variability. Thus at a 95% probability level the z value will be $+/- 1.96$. This means if the $Z_{A/B}$ or $Z_{U/D}$ is not within $+/- 1.96$ then there is a 95% chance that the variability is not due to random variation.

Control Chart Patterns

A company wants to perform run tests to see if there is a pattern of nonrandomness exhibited within the control limits. It wants to use a test statistic consistent with a 95% probability that the nonrandom patterns exist. The following run pattern has been identified:

Sample	Above/below	Up/down
1	B	-
2	A	U
3	B	D
4	A	U
5	B	D
6	B	D
7	A	U
8	B	D
9	A	U
10	B	D

Solution

$r = 9, N = 10$

$$Z_{A/B} = \frac{9 - ((10/2) + 1)}{\sqrt{((10 - 1)/4)}} = 2.00$$

$r = 8, N = 10$

$$Z_{U/D} = \frac{8 - ((20 - 1)/3)}{\sqrt{((160 - 29)/90)}} = 1.38$$

At a 95% probability $z = +/- 1.96$. The above/below test is slightly over this limit at $+2.00$, indicating that there may be some nonrandom pattern in the samples and the process should be checked.

Determining the Sample Size for Variable and Attribute Control Charts

It is important to note that the required sample size for each plot for a variable or attribute control chart is quite different. For $\overline{X}$ and R charts, sample sizes are usually four or five and can be as low as two. This is because even two observations should provide a reasonable measure of the sample range and sample average. For p-charts and c-charts sample size is usually in the hundreds to achieve a useful quality measure. For example, a defective proportion of 5% would require five defective items from 100. In practice sample size is also kept to a minimum to save operator time in observation. This will also permit more observation points to be implemented, which will assist in finding the cause of any quality problem. Also observations of output from a mix of machines may make it difficult to identify which machine is the source of the error.

www.wileyopenpage.com

Tolerances, Control Limits and Process Capability

It is important to distinguish between the above terms, referring to the variability of process output. They can be defined as follows:

- *Tolerance* – a specified range of values (for example, from customer needs) in which individual units of output must fall in order to be acceptable.
- *Control limits* – statistical limits on how sample statistics (such as mean or range) can vary due to randomness alone.
- *Process capability* – the inherent variability in a process.

The relationship between control limits and process capability can be expressed in the following formula:

$$\text{Control Limits} = \text{Process Mean} +/- \frac{z \times \text{Process Capability}}{\sqrt{n}}$$

where

z = number of standard deviations from the mean

n = sample size.

Thus it can be seen that control limits are based on the variability of samples of process output whose variability is a function of the process capability. Tolerances, however, are product/service specifications and are not specified in terms of the process by which the product/service is generated. Thus a process that is performing statistically 'in control' may not necessarily be conforming to the external tolerance specifications imposed. Therefore it is essential to ensure that the process is capable of meeting the required specifications and then ensure that it can meet this tolerance consistently over time using process control. Conversely, if the natural variation of the process exceeds the designed tolerances of the product, the process cannot produce the product according to specifications as the process variations which occur naturally, at random, are greater than the designed variation. To avoid this situation it is important that process capability studies are undertaken during the product/service design stage.

ACCEPTANCE SAMPLING

Acceptance sampling, like SPC, is an operational-oriented quality improvement technique. It involves taking a random sample from a larger batch or lot of material to be inspected. The quality of the sample is assumed to reflect the overall quality of the lot. If the sample has an unacceptable amount of defects the whole lot will be rejected. The point at which the defect level becomes unacceptable is based on an agreement between the customer and supplier of the goods. Because acceptance sampling is based on the traditional approach which assumes that a number of defects will be produced by a process, it is usually associated with the receiving inspection process from external suppliers.

Although the acceptable defect rate may be quoted as a percentage the comments on Six Sigma quality levels in the SPC section also apply here. Thus many organizations that take a TQM approach would expect defect levels measured in the parts per million (PPM). Indeed, if suppliers have successfully achieved a TQM philosophy and are in a stable partnership with the supplier the receiving inspection process may be eliminated.

Acceptance sampling is, however, still relevant to organizations that have not yet achieved TQM quality levels and has also traditionally been used when the cost of inspection (for example, destructive testing or sampling food) is high relative to the cost of the defect being identified. As in SPC when the product is inspected to see if it conforms to a specification the measurement can be variable or in the form of an attribute.

The sampling design includes the following aspects.

- the operating characteristic curve
- producer's and consumer's risk
- average outgoing quality.

The Operating Characteristic Curve

We are only using a sample to estimate the actual number of defects in the lot, so this may lead to errors in accepting or rejecting a lot due to sampling error. For example, if there is a target of 2% fraction defectives in a lot, a particular sample may contain a higher percentage than this even though the whole lot may not. Therefore the lot will be incorrectly rejected.

The operating characteristic (OC) curve indicates how effective the sampling plan is in discriminating between good and bad lots by showing the probability of accepting a lot for different quality levels for a given sample size and acceptance level. The shape and location of the OC curve is determined by the sample size (n) and the acceptance level (c) for the sampling plan. A selection of OC curves for different values of n and c is shown in Figure 17.7. Note when the sample size is the same as the lot size the curve is a vertical line indicating 100% inspection with no risk.

Producer's and Consumer's Risk

As discerned for the OC curve sampling error may mean either that a good lot is rejected (type I sample error) or that a bad lot is accepted (type II sample error). The acceptable quality level (AQL) is the maximum percentage (fraction defective) that is considered acceptable. The probability of rejecting a lot that has an acceptable quality level is termed the producer's risk and is related to $\propto$, the probability of a type I error. Due to sampling error there may be a sample taken that does not accurately reflect the quality level of the lot and thus a lot that does not meet the AQL is passed on to the customer. The upper limit of defective items which the customer will accept is termed the lot tolerance percent defective (LTPD). The probability of accepting a lot in which the quality level (fraction defective) exceeds the LTPD is termed the consumer's risk and relates to β, the probability of a type II error.

Usually the customer will prefer the quality of lots to be as good or better than the AQL but is willing to accept some lots with quality levels no worse than the LTPD. A common scenario is to have a producer's risk (α) at 5% and consumer's risk (β) at 10%. This means the customer expects to reject lots that are good or better than the AQL about 5% of the time and to accept lots that exceed the LTPD about 10% of the time.

A sampling plan is devised from these measures by using the OC curve. The α and AQL measures specify a point on the probability of acceptance axis and the β and LTPD measures define a point on the proportion defective axis. However, a trial-and-error process is required to determine the sample size (n) and acceptance number (c) to achieve these performance measures. This involves determining

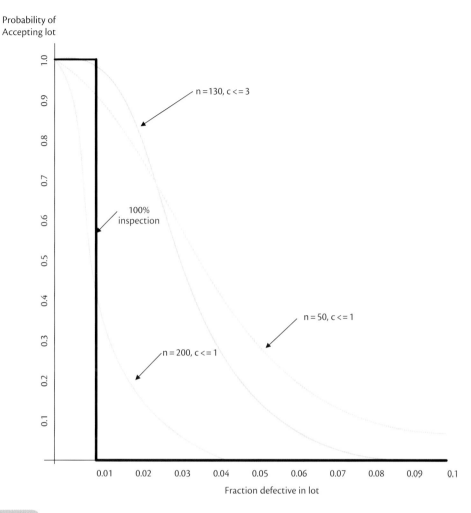

OC Curves for Different Sample Size (n) and Acceptance Number (c).

the probabilities of accepting a lot for various lot percentage defective values. A typical OC curve is shown in Figure 17.8.

From Figure 17.8, it can be seen in this case that if a lot has 3% defective items, for example, the probability of accepting a lot is 0.95. If management defines the AQL at 3%, then the probability that the lot will be rejected (α) is 1 minus the probability of accepting a lot ($1 - 0.95 = 0.05$). If management is willing to accept lots with a percentage defective up to 15% (LTPD), this corresponds to a probability (β) of 0.10 that the lot will be accepted.

To avoid the time-consuming task of using a trial-and-error method to construct OC curves, standardized tables, called the Dodge-Romig Inspection tables, can be used based on a given set of risks. Computer software is also available, which will develop sampling plans based on values for AQL, LTPD, α and β.

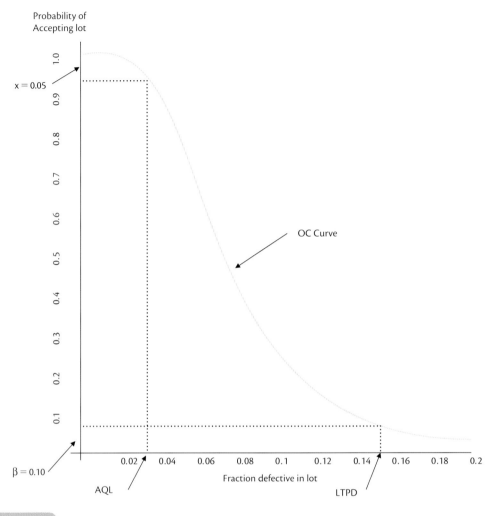

FIGURE 17.8

An Operating Characteristic Curve.

Average Outgoing Quality (AOQ)

Even though the probability of accepting a lot containing defects may be very small, all lots, whether they are accepted or not, will pass on some defects to the customer. The expected number of these defective items is measured by the AOQ. Assuming that defective items rejected are replaced the defective items that are passed on to the customer are contained in the lots that are accepted. Thus

$$AOQ = pP_a\left(\frac{(N - n)}{N}\right)$$

where

p = percentage defectives (horizontal axis in OC chart)
P_a = possibility of accepting a lot (vertical axis in OC chart)

www.wileyopenpage.com

N = lot size
n = sample size.

Values for AOQ against fraction defectives are shown in Figure 17.9.

From Figure 17.9 it can be seen that the AOQ rises to a point from the origin and then falls back again. The peak is termed the average outgoing quality limit (AOQL) and represents when the sampling plan does its worst job of upgrading quality, i.e. below this there are few defects accepted, above this there are more defects, but they are rejected and replaced. Each sampling plan will have a different AOQ curve and the AOQL can be used to select a suitable sampling plan.

Sampling Plans

The method of sampling or sampling plan can take a number of forms including the following.

Single-Sampling Plan

For a single sample attribute plan the method consists of selecting a sample at random from a larger lot and determining if the goods are defective or not (a discrete decision).

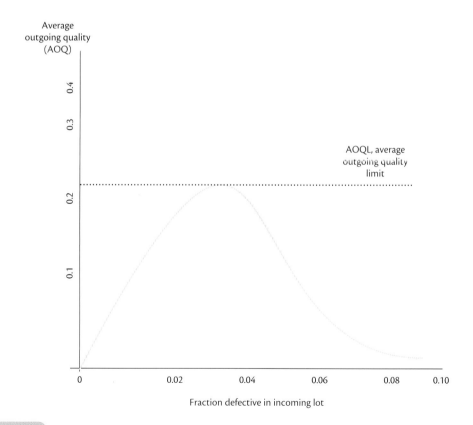

FIGURE 17.9

Average Outgoing Quality versus Fraction Defectives.

Double-Sampling Plan

In a double-sampling plan a smaller sample is taken than in a single-sampling plan. If the quality is very good or very bad the lot is accepted or rejected as before. If the result is inconclusive then a second sample is taken and the lot is rejected or accepted on the combined results of the two samples. The technique should allow an overall saving of inspection costs by the use of a smaller sample, which will usually provide a definite result.

Multiple-Sampling Plan

Here an initial sample (which can be as small as one unit) is taken. If the number of defectives is above or below a specified limit the lot is rejected or accepted as appropriate. If the number of defectives is between these limits, a second sample is taken and the total number of defects is compared to an increased set of upper and lower limits. The process repeats until the lot is accepted or rejected. Multiple-sampling plans are particularly appropriate when inspection costs are relatively high. For example, for destructive testing, when the cost of testing the whole sample would be prohibitive.

Variable-Sampling Plan

A variable-sampling plan takes samples from a measure that can take a range of values, as opposed to an attribute plan, which is a discrete value. Variable-sampling plans are constructed in a similar way to attribute plans but instead of the binomial and Poisson distribution, a normal distribution is assumed (especially for a sample size greater than 30). This means the trial and error approach to develop the plan is not needed, but standardized variable tables are available to develop plans for various AQL values.

SUMMARY

- The concept of quality can be viewed from different perspectives.
- Measurements of quality can be categorized as operational (for example, scrap rates), financial (for example, quality costs) and customer based (for example, measures from SERVQUAL).
- Techniques for quality improvement can be categorized as operational (for example, SPC), financial (for example, cost of quality) and customer based (for example, quality gaps). Total quality management is a philosophy that aims to ensure high quality is a primary concern for the organization.
- Deming proposes a TQM implementation plan that emphasizes continuous improvement to achieve conformance to specification. Crosby proposes a TQM implementation plan that emphasizes changing people's perception of the cost of quality.
- Six Sigma is a company-wide initiative to reduce costs through process efficiency and increase revenues through process effectiveness.
- ISO 9000 provides a quality standard between suppliers and customers.

- Statistical process control is a sampling technique that checks the quality of an item that is engaged in a process.
- Acceptance sampling consists of taking a random sample from a larger batch or lot of material to be inspected.

CASE STUDY 17.3

A Disciple of Japanese Quality Management

Order and efficiency are hallmarks of the TVS motorbike factory near Bangalore in southern India. To direct foot traffic, arrows are painted on the shiny shop floor of India's third-largest motorcycle maker. Large banners with exhortations such as 'Let Us Achieve Zero Defects' and 'Quality is a Way of Life' hang across the bright facility where nearly 2000 vehicles are built each day on neat assembly lines. Tea breaks are 9:15 to 9:22 and 14:15 to 14:22, according to a memo on the wall. Japan's veneration for order has been fully transplanted to this TVS factory in the city of Hosur. Venu Srinivasan, the mild-mannered 55-year-old managing director and chairman of TVS, has indoctrinated the company with the Japanese management strategy of total quality management (TQM). TVS's turnaround has hinged on principles of attention to process, consistency, transparency and employee involvement.

Total quality management was launched at TVS in 1989 and is credited with reviving the ailing company. Since then, TVS and sister companies in the $2.2 billion TVS Group have won the prestigious Japan Quality Medal and the Deming Prize, a quality award from Japan. TVS rolled out 923 000 motorbikes last fiscal year in India with sales growing 19% to reach about $900 million. It recently opened a factory in Indonesia and aims to globalize its business over the next few years. The scenario before and after TQM reflects how far TVS has come in nearly two decades. Productivity, quality and sales have improved dramatically. Previously, the rate of 're-work' – parts plagued by faults – was 15%. That figure has fallen to 100 parts per million. The factory used to make four deliveries a month to customers compared with two daily now.

It was no easy task to overhaul the family-owned company that was founded in 1911 by Mr Srinivasan's grandfather, TV Sundaram Iyengar. For three decades after 1960, India closed its markets to global competition. Imports were restricted and licences were required to start businesses, creating little incentive to improve or strive for quality. After earning a degree in engineering from Madras University in today's Chennai, Mr Srinivasan went to the US for graduate studies, like many scions of India's business families. In 1979 he earned a master's in science and management at Purdue University in Indiana – the degree became known as an MBA in 2001 – where he received a 'strong dose' of industrial engineering.

He visited factories of US automakers such as General Motors but was unimpressed. 'US factories did not have that exactness,' he recalls. A trip to Japan in 1981 and visits to the Suzuki and Honda factories proved pivotal. 'Even the bullet train aligned exactly on the platform. People were highly motivated and committed.' He was inspired by 'a country that could create this kind of excellence' and sought to restore the high quality for which TVS was known in the 1940s when it ran a highly efficient bus network and General Motors dealership.

Mr Srinivasan began reading books about TQM and 'desperately tried to get hold of Japanese professors, but India was not on the radar' in the early 1980s. The mission to restructure TVS grew more urgent in the 1980s when profits slipped although sales grew. 'That triggered the need for change. I knew that if we continued like that we wouldn't be in business.' Mr Srinivasan introduced TQM to the company in 1989 and implemented and improved it over the next nine years. Experts from Japan still visit the company.

TVS's adaptation of TQM rests on five pillars. They include policy deployment; involving every person at the company; *kaizen,* or continuous improvement; standardization of processes; and new product development. Seated at a long boardroom table at the TVS office, Mr Srinivasan takes a pen and draws a series of boxes to illustrate the 'silos' that hobbled the company before. There were six layers of management. With little cooperation or communication between divisions, 'most meetings were full of fault-finding and finger pointing'. Under the new regime, silos were broken down. For instance, different teams collaborated on design of new motorcycles so staff from R&D worked jointly with production and assembly. As a result, innovation has been boosted. TVS rolled out its first 20 models in 21 years but it has produced 10 new products in the past three years alone. This year TVS expects to roll out six new models.

On the factory floor, inefficiencies were identified and weeded out. TVS used to keep ten weeks of inventory at its factory compared with two weeks now. The assembly line suffered frequent delays. 'We couldn't predict what we could supply to customers', says Mr Srinivasan. 'It used to be a real mess.' Mr Srinivasan recalls that previously the factory floor was haphazardly organized. 'One man operated one machine with another man doing inspections. Relative to today it would be dirty.' Today employees are trained to operate different machines, allowing for a leaner workforce. In traditionally hierarchical India, Mr Srinivasan shocked employees by picking up cigarette butts from the factory floor in keeping with one of the pillars of involving every employee.

He started tracking all the company's statistics and breaking them down, line by line. Figures were conveyed to employees through charts displayed in the factory. 'Everybody could see the actual graph. Before, people would fudge', says Mr Srinivasan. 'But every hour productivity is displayed. We created a feedback loop.' Changing an entrenched mindset was a difficult task. 'It requires a high degree of understanding between employees and management', says C. Narasimhan, formerly president of Sundaram-Clayton, the auto-components firm and sister company of TVS. But employees were encouraged to offer suggestions for improvement. 'Some employees give 200 suggestions a year', says Mr Narasimhan. 'Awards are given for the best suggestion.' Roles of each employee are now clarified and targets clearly assigned. Results are displayed for everyone to see in order 'to hold the gains'. Changing his own role at TVS was also a challenge for Mr Srinivasan, whose position as family trustee shifted as the company's president became more empowered. 'For me to move back and change my role took a lot of change myself', admits Mr Srinivasan. 'You've got to look at yourself in the mirror honestly. But you have to make the change to get other people to make the changes you expect of them.'

Source: Financial Times (2008). Reproduced with permission.

Question

How do the principles of TQM relate to the management of the TVS motorbike factory?

Yell

With some 3400 employees, Yell is an international directories business operating in the classified advertising market. Its vision is to be the best business information bridge between buyers and sellers, regardless of channel, time or location in the markets in which they operate. The company aims to put buyers in touch with sellers through an integrated portfolio of simple to use advertising solutions – including printed (Yellow Pages), on-line (Yell.com) phone products and services.

Yell started introducing quality management in the late 1980s by adopting a TQM approach, and this approach became integrated into the way Yell manages its business. The company has used tools such as the EFQM Excellence Model®, Six Sigma, ISO 9001:2000, ISO 14001:1996, OHSAS 18001:1999 and Investors in People (IiP) to review and refine its overall management approach. A critical enabler of activities has been Yell's commitment to effective leadership, involvement and communication. Its focus is now on becoming the best in everything the company does.

Yell sets the scope and direction for its system of management through its vision and business purpose. It also defines the way this will be achieved through strong and clear values. Together these provide the framework for all their activities. Yell brings this alive for people, through a structured approach that focuses on both the process and the people:

- alignment of goals and objectives through a systematic planning process
- integration of policies and processes through a key process framework
- enablement of activity through effective leadership, involvement and communication.

Senior managers generate the policy and strategy through an annual planning process. They work closely with members of the strategic planning team to ensure alignment with vision, purpose and strategic goals. All managers and their people are involved in the effective deployment of strategy by agreeing business initiatives and departmental plans and budgets. This is a highly interactive process with managers using a scorecard approach to help them to align objectives with strategy.

Policy and strategy are delivered through a key process framework, which provides the top-level architecture for their process management system. It consists of a value chain of customer facing processes supported by five internal management processes. 'Providing Strategic Direction' is the first part of the Key Process Framework.

Strategy is communicated via face-to-face presentations to managers, and they then communicate to their team. This is supported by an 'objectives' intranet site where people can trace their progress. In addition, the theme for objectives is revised each year, to provide renewed focus – in the 'You make us unique' objectives brochure every employee's name was featured in the design. Other themes have included 'Breaking Boundaries', 'Superbrand-Superfuture' and 'Accelerating Performance'

Against the backdrop of regulatory conditions and the changing economy between 2001 and 2004, Yell has achieved consistent annual UK revenue growth of approximately 5%. This is matched in its growth in customer base by approximately 5% and by continuous improvement in processes and customer services. The company has achieved positive trends, sustained high performance and good comparisons with other organizations, for example errors in over 1 million individually produced adverts have been reduced by several per cent over the past 10 years to just 0.1%.

Yell UK is considered to be a benchmark in its approach to engaging with its people. For example, the objectives communication process is supported by a communication approach called 'Storytellers', which is highly interactive and encourages all employees to think strategically about their contribution to Yell. The company also runs an 'Uncles Programme', where senior managers meet with geographically dispersed teams and talk about business strategy and individual concerns. Senior managers go outside their own function and it keeps them in touch with front line issues as well as enabling them to explain strategic decisions.

Yell is very proud of its record on communicating individual responsibilities, and carries out a census survey amongst its employees once a year. The most recent survey achieved a 94% response rate. Since 1998 they have averaged over 97% for people saying that they clearly understand what is expected of them.

In 1999 Yell won the European Quality Award, and in 2004 became the first company to win the award for a second time. Yell also received two Special Prizes for 'Leadership' and 'People Development and Management.'

One of the challenges the company has faced was the proliferation of Areas for Improvement (AFIs). When Yell began its quality journey, and following any of its many assessments, it highlighted a daunting number of AFIs. This led to the introduction of a prioritizing approach, with improvement activities that are followed through until completed – with the focus clearly on actions and outcomes. Achievements are always recognized and this is communicated throughout the organization.

The company has also been very careful not to establish a 'flavour of the month'. The focus of the approach was placed upon improvement and not introducing 'another' initiative. This was also achieved by integrating tools such as the EFQM Excellence Model®, ISO 9001 and IiP into the overall management system.

Source: The Department of Trade and Industry (www.dti.gov.uk/bestpractice).

Question

What is Yell trying to achieve with its use of quality management standards and techniques?

CASE STUDY 17.5

Mouse Bread

Britain's largest food producer was fined nearly £17 000 by Oxford Crown Court, for manufacturing a loaf of bread that was found to contain a dead mouse inside. The mouse was found by Stephen Forse, whilst making lunch for his children and their visiting friends.

Mr Force initially thought the darkened corner of the bread to be unmixed dough, but on closer inspection, discovered it was covered in fur. Some of the bread at the top of the loaf had already been eaten the previous day; however the mouse was detected before the lower half, containing the mouse had been handled.

Mr Force contacted the local council, who sent environmental health officers to visit the family's home and inspect the bread. They confirmed the contamination was indeed a rodent and noted that it was missing its tail. This was not found in any of the breads packaging or remaining contents, leaving it unclear as to whether this had been eaten or fallen off before the loaf was packed.

The loaf of bread was sliced – and it appeared that the body of the mouse too had been sliced in line with the cuts of the loaf, implying that the contamination possibly occurred during the manufacturing process.

Premier Foods, who manufactured the bread, produce and deliver a significant proportion of British groceries, with the majority of their production in branded sales. In 2011, 99% of UK households bought at least one of their products, with each home spending an average of £70 per year on Premier goods.

The company pleaded guilty to:

- Failing to ensure all stages of food production were protected against contamination and
- Failing to maintain a robust pest management system at its British Bakeries site in Mitcham, London.

A spokesman for Premier Foods said: 'We apologise profusely for the distress caused as a result of this isolated incident. As soon as this complaint was made we stopped all bakery production at that site and appointed an independent specialist contractor to conduct a thorough investigation. They confirmed this to be an isolated incident, affecting a single product. There was no evidence of mice within the bakery and no history of any similar issues.'

The spokesman added that the council had agreed 'the bakery was a well-managed site and that Premier Foods took its obligations for health and hygiene seriously'.

Sources

http://www.oxfordmail.co.uk/news/8416917 .Shock_at_dead_mouse_in_loaf/

http://www.bbc.co.uk/news/uk-england-oxfordshire-11419498

http://www.telegraph.co.uk/news/newstopics/ howaboutthat/8029591/Mouse-found-baked-into-loaf-of-bread.html

www.premierfoods.co.uk/.

Source: Written by Briony Boydell and Chris Milner. Reproduced with permission.

Questions

1. What could be the consequences of poor quality bread loaves? How serious is this situation?
2. How could implementing total quality management help an organization like Premier foods?

Quizzes to test yourself further are available in your interactive e-book at **www.wileyopenpage.com**

Flashcards to test yourself further are available in your interactive e-book at **www.wileyopenpage.com**

EXERCISES

1. How do customers define product and service quality?

2. Contrast the traditional quality/cost trade-off with the zero defects quality/cost trade-off.

3. How can the quality gap approach be used to improve quality?

4. What is the purpose of TQM?

5. Explain the relationship between Six Sigma and process management.

6. Use the Web to compare the Baldrige Award and the European Quality Award.

7. The following table gives the number of defectives in successive samples of 100 final assemblies removed at random from that day's production.

Day	Number of defectives	Day	Number of defectives
1	6	11	11
2	8	12	8
3	7	13	13
4	10	14	14
5	11	15	15
6	5	16	12
7	13	17	7
8	9	18	34
9	9	19	29
10	10	20	8

a. Estimate the total proportion of rejects.

b. Establish a single set of control limits for the daily fraction of rejects based on these figures and plot a control chart, showing the daily results.

c. Comment on the stability of the manufacturing process.

8. The following table gives the means and ranges, from a sample size of 10, for the diameter of a machined part.

Mean	Range R	Mean	Range R	Mean	Range R
0.52	0.03	0.5	0.11	0.57	0.10
0.53	0.10	0.53	0.08	0.52	0.07
0.57	0.09	0.52	0.05	0.52	0.12
0.49	0.08	0.48	0.09	0.51	0.11
0.48	0.12	0.54	0.03	0.49	0.09

Use the data to set up a control chart for means and for ranges.

 www.wileyopenpage.com

9. A machine produces components to a specified average length of 9.03 cm. Every hour a random sample of five components is selected from the process and their lengths measured. After 10 hours the data given below have been collected.

Sample number	Measurements (cm)				
1	9.00	9.10	9.00	9.05	8.95
2	9.10	9.10	9.00	9.05	9.05
3	9.00	9.05	9.00	9.05	9.00
4	9.00	9.00	8.95	9.00	9.05
5	9.00	9.10	9.05	9.05	9.00
6	9.00	9.10	9.10	9.05	9.00
7	9.00	9.10	9.05	9.15	9.05
8	9.00	9.10	9.10	9.00	9.05
9	9.00	9.00	8.95	9.00	9.00
10	9.00	9.05	9.00	9.10	8.95

Use the data to set up a control chart for means and for ranges.

10. Explain the concepts of producer's risk and consumer's risk in acceptance sampling.

WEB EXERCISE

Write a description of the EFQM excellence model using information from the EFQM web site at www.efqm.org (accessed 1 June 2012).

FURTHER READING

Besterfield, D.H. (2012) *Quality Improvement*, 9th edn, Prentice Hall.
Dale, B.G. (2008) *Managing Quality*, 5th edn, Wiley Blackwell Publishers Inc.
Rummler, G.A. (2007) Serious Performance Consulting: According to Rummler, Jossey Bass.
Taguchi, G., Chowdhury, S. and Wu, Y. (2005) *Taguchi's Quality Engineering Handbook*, John Wiley & Sons, Inc.
Wheeler, D.J. (2000) *Understanding Variation: The Key to Managing Chaos*, 2nd edn, SPC Press Inc.

WEB LINKS

www.asq.org (accessed 1 June 2012). American Society for Quality. Publications and courses in the area of quality management.
www.baldrige.nist.gov (accessed 1 June 2012). National Institute of Standards and Technology. Details of the Baldrige Award.

www.efqm.org (accessed 1 June 2012). European Foundation for Quality Management. Details of the European Quality Award.

www.iso.ch (accessed 1 June 2012). International Organization for Standardization (ISO). Site providing details on ISO 9000 and other standards.

www.qfdi.org (accessed 1 June 2012). QFD Institute. Contains newsletters and forums in the area of QFD.

www.quality.co.uk (accessed 1 June 2012). Quality Network. Resources on benchmarking, ISO 9000 and environmental management.

www.qualitydigest.com (accessed 1 June 2012). Quality Digest. Access to magazine, news and tips on quality management.

www.quality-foundation.co.uk (accessed 1 June 2012). British Quality Foundation. A not for profit organization that promotes business excellence to the private, public and voluntary sectors.

www.ukas.com (accessed 1 June 2012). UK Accreditation Service. Accredits the certification bodies which oversee the implementation of quality management systems based on ISO 9001:2000.

REFERENCES

Crosby, P.B. (1996) *Quality is Still Free: Making Quality Certain in Uncertain Times*, McGraw-Hill.

Deming, W.E. (1985) *Transformation of Western-style management. Interfaces*, 15(3), 6–11.

Feigenbaum, A.V. (2007) *Total Quality Control*, 4th edn, McGraw-Hill.

Garvin, D.A. (1984) What does quality really mean. *Sloan Management Review*, 26(1), 25–43.

Garvin, D.A. (1988) *Managing Quality*, Free Press.

Juran, J.M. (2010) *Juran's Quality Handbook*, 6th edn, McGraw-Hill.

Oakland, J.S. (2003) *TQM: Text with Cases*, 3rd edn, Butterworth Heinemann.

Parasuraman, A., Zeithaml, V.A. and Berry, L.L. (1985) A conceptual model of service quality and its implications for future research. *Journal of Marketing*, 49(4), 41–50.

Parasuraman, A., Zeithaml, V.A. and Berry, L.L. (1988) SERVQUAL: a multiple item scale for measuring consumer perceptions of service quality. *Journal of Retailing*, 64(1), 12–40.

Shewhart, W. (1980) *Economic Control of Quality of Manufactured Product*, ASQC/Quality Press.

Slack, N., Chambers, S. and Johnston, R. (2010) *Operations Management*, 6th edition, Prentice Hall.

Performance Measurement and Improvement

LEARNING OBJECTIVES

- Understand the use of performance measures
- Describe the use of performance measuring methods such as activity-based costing, the balanced scorecard and the SCOR model
- Understand how areas for improvement are identified using performance targets
- Describe the use of benchmarking to define performance targets
- Understand methods for improving performance such as business process management, business process re-engineering and continuous improvement.

PERFORMANCE MEASUREMENT AND IMPROVEMENT AND OPERATIONS STRATEGY

In order to assess the success of an operations strategy it is necessary to measure the performance of operations from the perspective of stakeholders in the organization such as the employees, managers, owners, customers and suppliers. In this chapter the 'How do we measure performance'

section provides approaches to measuring performance from a financial perspective (activity-based costing), from a stakeholder perspective (the balanced scorecard) and from a supply chain perspective (the SCOR model). Once a performance measurement system is implemented we then need to identify where performance needs to be improved. This information may come from comparing performance to historical data and deriving sales or financial targets or by comparing performance in relation to competitors using a benchmarking approach. In relation to operations strategy the Hill methodology covered in Chapter 2 uses the concepts of order winning and qualifying factors to help identify what aspects of operations performance, as expressed by the five performance objectives, need improving. Finally, we need to decide an approach to making the improvements in performance identified as necessary and three frameworks are considered of business process management, business process re-engineering and continuous improvement.

INTRODUCTION

This chapter covers the topic of performance measurement and improvement. Before improvement can take place we need to identify suitable measures of performance. Traditional measures of performance such as productivity and efficiency are covered and then measures associated with operations' five performance objectives are discussed. The measure of cost is explored further and the use of activity-based costing is covered. The need to incorporate measures from a number of perspectives and link strategic measures to operational targets is discussed in the context of the balanced scorecard measurement system.

The next step, once measures of performance have been identified, is to compare each performance measure against a performance standard in order to identify areas for improvement. This standard can be internal to the organization, such as a comparison against previous performance or against targets for future performance. External targets include comparison to competitor performance, best practice or 'best-in-class' performance or market requirements. Internal targets are often based on comparing past financial and sales performance with targets for future performance. This section also covers the use of benchmarking and the methods covered in Chapter 2 for identifying performance objectives that require improvement.

Once priorities for improvement have been identified then an improvement programme can be implemented. In this chapter the improvement approaches of business process management (BPM), business process re-engineering (BPR) and continuous improvement (CI) are discussed.

HOW DO WE MEASURE PERFORMANCE?

Performance measurement involves both choosing the measures that will be used to identify where improvements should take place and also determining if improvement has taken place after change has been implemented. This section looks at a variety of performance measures that are used in operations management.

Traditionally performance measures in operations have focused on indicators such as **productivity,** which divides the value of the output by the value of the input resources consumed:

$$productivity = \frac{output}{input}$$

Productivity is used at both the organizational and national level as a comparative measure of performance. From the equation it can be seen that productivity can be increased by either increasing output without a proportionate increase in input or decreasing input without a proportionate decrease in output. Productivity can be a valid tool for the operations manager and provides an indication of the level of utilization of resources. However, it can be difficult to find appropriate input and output parameters for the calculation and the measure also fails to consider performance from a wider viewpoint encompassing customer and other stakeholder needs.

Other performance measures include **efficiency**:

$$efficiency = \frac{actual\ output}{effective\ capacity}$$

In Chapter 11 efficiency is defined as a measure of the use of capacity remaining after the loss of output due to planned factors such as maintenance and training. In other words efficiency relates to the use of a resource in terms of availability. However, a high level of efficiency does not necessarily imply that resources are being used effectively in improving overall performance. **Effectiveness** can be defined as the extent to which the output of a process meets the requirements of its customers. This is more difficult to measure quantitatively than productivity or efficiency. In service operations effectiveness is often measured by surveys of customer satisfaction. As was discussed in Chapter 17, however, customer satisfaction will be dependent on the perceptions and expectations of individual customers. Other indicators of effectiveness could be sales volume and sales margin figures for products and services.

Chapter 2 (strategy) considers that the focus of improvement should be directed towards appropriate areas of the operation where any increase in performance will help the organization meet its strategic goals. In this text the **five performance objectives** of quality, speed, dependability, flexibility and cost are used to measure operations performance in relation to its strategy. It also shows that strategies that rely on immediate cost cutting (achieving **economy** by lowering the costs of inputs into the operations transformation process) should be replaced by strategies that aim to improve performance on the other performance objectives which will then lead to a reduction in cost. Measures for each of the performance objectives are shown in Table 18.1.

Activity Based Costing (ABC)

Cost is traditionally calculated by estimating in terms of staff, facilities and material the resources that are required for the input and transformation processes in an operation. However, the way these costs are allocated to products and services is often arbitrary. For example, the actual costs of producing a product in a factory where hundreds of other products are also being made is dependent on an accurate allocation of direct costs (staff, equipment and material costs directly connected to the product)

TABLE 18.1

Performance Measures for the Performance Objectives.

Performance objectives	Measures
Quality	Operational, financial and customer measures (see Chapter 17).
Dependability	Percentage of customers that receive the product or service when promised.
Speed	Time delay between request and receiving product or service.
Flexibility	The amount of change (range) or speed of change (response) in product/service, mix, volume or delivery (see Chapter 2).
Cost	Staff, facilities and material costs for product or service. Cost of activities undertaken to produce product or service (see activity-based costing in Chapter 18).

and indirect costs (for example, overheads such as factory space, energy, administration and central staffing costs). The aim of performance measurement is to identify where cost is being incurred within an operation so improvement efforts can be focused in the correct areas. As an alternative to the usual overhead-based costing methods **activity-based costing** provides a way of allocating costs to manufacturing and service activities in order that a company can determine how much it costs to make a certain product or deliver a service. In ABC there are three main drivers of cost: the cost driver, the resource driver and the activity driver.

- The cost driver relates to the amount of resources needed to perform an activity and can be reduced by, for example, redesigning the process.
- The resource driver relates to the type of resources needed for an activity and can be reduced, for example, by using different personnel, information technology or equipment.
- The activity driver relates to the number of times the process occurs and can be reduced, for example, by training to improve the reliability of a process.

Turney (1996) outlines an ABC model, which has two main views (Figure 18.1): The cost assignment view of ABC allocates costs to activities by identifying resource drivers, which determine the cost of resources, and activity drivers, which determine the use of these resources. The process view of ABC provides information about the effort needed for the activity termed 'the cost driver' and provides performance measures of the outcome of the activities. The cost assignment view can be used to reduce the activity cost by either reconfiguring the resources needed for an activity (resource driver) or reducing the amount of resource required (activity driver). The process view provides a link between the inputs needed to perform an activity (cost driver) and the outputs required by the internal or external customer of that activity (performance measure). Thus an investigation of a combination of resource drivers, activity drivers and cost drivers for an activity can improve process performance by identifying why cost has been incurred. Case Study 18.1 shows the advantages of being able to identify where cost is being incurred.

www.wileyopenpage.com

Cost Assignment View

Process View

Resources

Resource Cost
Assignment ← Resource Drivers

Cost Drivers → Activities → Performance
Measures

Activity Cost
Assignment ← Activity Drivers

Cost Objects

FIGURE 18.1

The Two Perspectives of Activity-Based Costing.

CASE STUDY 18.1

Activity-Based Costing at a Police Service

A study was undertaken of the costs involved in operating a custody suite at a police service in the UK. The custody suite is involved in the processing of arrested persons and their subsequent release, interview or detention. Like most service operations the custody operation is characterized by having a large part of its resources in the form of labour. Unfortunately this often leads to a situation of management of resources by inputs (budgets). Thus the amount of resources (for example, people and capital) deployed is based on historical budgets with a large proportion classified as overhead and fixed with an annual addition for inflation. Departments are then managed by tracking variances in expenditure from budgeted amounts. In this case an ABC approach was taken in order to identify where cost was being incurred, as a first step to improving performance.

In terms of cost drivers, a major source of cost was found to be the time taken to undertake the paper-based booking-in process, which occurs for all arrested persons. In order to reduce the amount of resource needed for this the booking-in process was redesigned using BPR and a proposal for computerization put in place.

The resource drivers in this case relate primarily to the pay rates of personnel involved in the arrest process. A civilianization programme, which involves using trained civilians for activities formerly undertaken by police personnel, was proposed.

In this case the activity driver relates to the timing and frequency of arrests. The activity driver depends on environmental factors such as the crime rate and government policy on crime as well as factors under the control of the police. It was found, however, that a high proportion of arrests were for minor theft offences involving children, which could possibly be processed using alternative methods.

Question

What are the benefits of the ABC analysis of the custody suite?

The Balanced Scorecard

Another approach to performance measurement has been the use of the **balanced scorecard** developed by Kaplan and Norton (1996). The balanced scorecard approach is an attempt to incorporate the interests of a broader range of stakeholders through performance measures across four perspectives of financial, customer, business process and learning and growth (Figure 18.2).

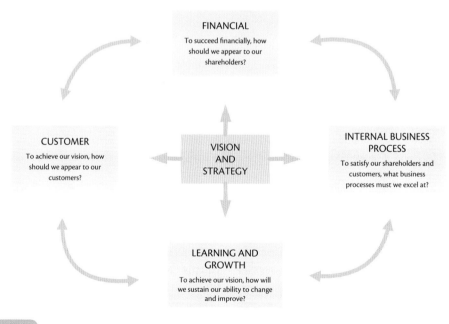

FIGURE 18.2

The Balanced Scorecard.
Source: Adapted from Kaplan, R.S.; Norton, D.P. (2006) Alignment: How to Apply the Balanced Scorecard to Corporate Strategy, Harvard Business School Press. Reproduced with permission.

 www.wileyopenpage.com

The idea of the scorecard is to provide managers with a multiple perspective of the goals that need to be met for organizational success. Although designed for performance measurement at a strategic level its relevance to operations is that it provides a direction for the organization that will impact on and be impacted by operations (see the Hill methodology for operations strategy in Chapter 2). The balanced scorecard also provides a way of translating strategy into action. It does this by translating performance measures at a strategic level into operational performance measures. Case Study 18.4 shows how strategic targets on absence at a UK Police Service were translated into measures at an operational level.

The SCOR Model

The supply chain operations reference (SCOR) model provides a framework for measuring and evaluating the performance of supply chain processes. Measurements are made of five key processes that are undertaken along the supply chain by all participating organizations. These processes are defined as plan, source, make, deliver and return.

- *Plan* – involves managing the customer-supplier links in the supply chain to ensure that the supply chain strategy aligns requirements with the resources available.
- *Source* – means managing procurement activities and ensuring suppliers are selected, deliveries scheduled and inventories managed.
- *Make* – involves managing the transformation process that adds value to products and services
- *Deliver* – means managing order fulfilment and transporting goods to the customer
- *Return* – involves managing customer returns and other post-delivery customer support.

The SCOR model incorporates benchmarking activities to indicate where performance should be improved and a SCOR roadmap to provide a framework for implementation, i.e. how performance should be improved.

WHERE SHOULD WE IMPROVE PERFORMANCE?

In order to identify where performance improvement should take place it is necessary to compare the performance measure against a **performance standard.** This standard can be internal to the organization such as comparing against previous performance or against targets for future performance. Internal targets are often based on a comparison between past financial and sales performance and targets for future performance. The advantage of these measures is that they are widely used and comparable across organizations and use data that are readily available. However, they may be of limited value in identifying why performance is above or below a target value. External targets include comparison to competitor performance, best practice or 'best-in-class' performance or market requirements. External performance targets have the advantage of providing a comparison of performance against competitors operating in similar competitive markets. This approach is often termed 'benchmarking' and is described later in this chapter.

In terms of the measures associated with the five operations performance objectives, Chapter 2 identifies two models that can be used to identify where performance should be improved.

The Hill model (Hill, A. and Hill T., 2012) is based on market requirements. The concepts of 'order winning' and 'qualifying factors' are used to distinguish between those factors that directly contribute to winning business and those that are necessary to qualify for the customer's consideration between a range of products/services. The importance of this is that while it may be necessary to raise performance on some factors to a certain level in order to be considered by the customer, a further rise in the level of performance may not achieve an increase in competitiveness. Instead competitiveness may then depend on raising the level of performance of different 'order-winning' factors.

The second model of Slack (1991) uses a combination of market and competitive factors and two dimensions – importance and performance – to help operations managers prioritize performance objectives. The relative importance of a competitive factor is assessed in terms of its importance to internal or external customers using a nine-point scale of degrees of order winning, qualifying and less important customer viewed competitive factors. The next step ranks the relative *performance* of a competitive factor against competitor achievement. A nine-point performance scale (rating from consistently better than the nearest competitor to consistently worse than most competitors) is used for each performance objective. The next step is to plot each importance rating and performance rating in an importance-performance matrix. This indicates what customers find important in achieved performance when compared with competitor performance.

More details are given on the Hill and Slack models in Chapter 2.

Benchmarking

Benchmarking can be defined as the continual measurement of an organization's products and processes against a company recognized as a leader in that industry. The analysis of competitor products is an older technique, which forms part of the product design process (Chapter 7). **Benchmarking** was initially restricted to the comparison of direct competitors in the manufacturing sector. Now it is practised in the service sector (for example, banks), in all functional areas (such as marketing) and in comparison with a wide variety of competitors from which lessons can be learnt (not just the best in class). Because of the widespread use of the technique and the requests by many organizations to visit the same high performance firms, much benchmarking data is held in databases for general use. A number of models for implementing a benchmarking programme have been developed. The main activities involved in benchmarking are summarized below:

- *Planning*. Understand your own processes, identify key processes and form benchmarking teams.
- *Analysis*. Conduct research on possible competitors and formulate questions to elicit the required information. Establish a relationship with a partner organization and collect and share information.
- *Implementation*. Implement and monitor improvements suggested by analysis.

It is important that the relevant processes in the organization are benchmarked before comparison with a competitor. Processes are benchmarked in terms of metrics (numeric measurements) and procedures (process flows). For example, a payment process could be measured by the time taken from receiving the request to delivery of the payment. The technique would also measure the type and amount of personnel involved in each step of the process. One problem with some benchmarking programmes has been the focus on developing metrics and the lack of energy put into implementing changes suggested by the benchmarking process. Other problems are the difficulty in obtaining competitor information and the fact that if the process is simply used to emulate a competitor, competitive advantage may be short-lived as the competitor makes further improvements.

HOW DO WE IMPROVE PERFORMANCE?

Three performance improvement approaches are covered here of Business Process Management (BPM), Business Process Re-engineering (BPR) and Continuous Improvement (CI).

Business Process Management (BPM)

Business process management is the term used to refer to the analysis and improvement of business processes. A process is a set of activities designed to produce a desired output from a specified input. The process orientation matches the idea of the main objectives of the operations function as the management of the transformation process of inputs (resources) into outputs (goods and services) covered in Chapter 1. Although BPM is usually used in the broad sense it is also used more narrowly to refer to software technologies for automating the management of specific processes. In its widest sense, however, BPM brings together aspects such as:

- process mapping techniques such as process mapping and service blueprinting (Chapter 8);
- simulation modelling techniques such as business process simulation (Chapter 8);
- implementation of information technologies such as workflow systems (Chapter 6);
- improvement approaches such as business process re-engineering (BPR) (Chapter 18);
- assessment models such as ISO9000 (Chapter 17).

The video 'Business Process Management (BPM): Improve business processes' from Interfacing Technologies Corp is available in your interactive e-book at **www.wileyopenpage.com**

Business process management has been developed by authors such as Rummler and Brache (1995) who provide a method of undertaking the technique using organizational analysis and process analysis and design. Business process management is concerned with the following:

- linking corporate strategy and business processes;
- providing measurement of process performance at a strategic level;
- design and management of the processes that deliver the organization's goods and services;
- implementation of process change, both manually by employees and by the use of IT systems.

For implementation of processes that are performed by employees, consideration is made of such factors as job descriptions, motivation systems, supervision, training and evaluation of performance. A Six Sigma approach (Chapter 17) may be used in this area. For the implementation of processes automated by IT systems consideration is made of such factors as software development and maintenance. Use is made of software tools such as workflow (Chapter 6), business process simulation (Chapter 8) and packaged enterprise applications such as ERP (Chapter 14).

There is evidence that the full potential of business process management is not being realized. Fingar (2006) states that most BPM projects are tactical and about streamlining individual functions within a company. BPM's full potential offers a strategic capability through process innovation at the three levels of process design discussed earlier. The reason this has not occurred may be due to the fact, as Fingar (2006) notes, that the scope and complexity of process design increases as companies progress from the individual process level (termed point-solution BPM) to the organizational level (enterprise BPM) to the supply chain level (value-chain BPM). Another feature of BPM projects is that they have been most successful in relation to the design of information systems such as workflow systems, but there are few examples of process design incorporating human interactions, for example, of work teams working across organizations. This suggests the need for more understanding of human-driven processes, which requires knowledge of how people actually work and how these work processes change over time.

Business Process Re-engineering

In the early-to-mid 1990s, organization-wide transformational change was advocated under the label of BPR. It was popularized through the pronouncements of Hammer and Champy (1993) and Davenport (1993). The essence of BPR is the assertion that business processes, organizational structures, team structures and employee responsibilities can be fundamentally altered to improve business performance. Hammer and Champy (1993) defined BPR as 'the fundamental rethinking and radical redesign of business processes to achieve dramatic improvements in critical, contemporary measures of performance, such as cost, quality, service, and speed'.

The key words from this definition that encapsulate the BPR concept are:

- *Fundamental rethinking* – re-engineering usually refers to the changing of significant business processes such as customer service, sales order processing or manufacturing.
- *Radical redesign* – re-engineering is not involved with minor, incremental change or automation of existing ways of working. It involves a complete rethinking about the way business processes operate.
- *Dramatic improvements* – the aim of BPR is to achieve improvements measured in tens or hundreds of per cent. With automation of existing processes only single-figure improvements may be possible.
- *Critical contemporary measures of performance* – this point refers to the importance of measuring how well the processes operate in terms of the four important measures of cost, quality, service and speed.

Willcocks and Smith (1995) characterize the typical changes that arise in an organization with process innovation as:

- work units changing from functional departments to process teams;
- jobs change from simple tasks to multidimensional work;

- people's roles change from controlled to empowered;
- focus of performance changes from activities to results;
- values change from protective to productive.

Many re-engineering projects were launched in the 1990s and failed due to their ambitious scale and the problems of managing large information systems projects. Furthermore, BPR was also often linked to downsizing in many organizations, leading to an outflow of staff and knowledge from businesses. As a result BPR as a concept has fallen out of favour and more caution is advocated in attempting to achieve change.

Less radical approaches to organizational transformation are referred to as **business process improvement (BPI)** or by Davenport (1993) as 'business process innovation'. Taking the example of supply chain management, an organization would have to decide on the scope of change. For instance, do all supply chain activities need to be revised simultaneously or can certain activities such as procurement or outbound logistics be targeted initially? Modern thinking would suggest that the latter approach is preferable. A five-step approach to the introduction of BPR has been suggested by Davenport (1993).

1. *Identifying processes for innovation.* The organization should select a process or processes that are critical to the organization and so provide a potentially large increase in performance in return for the re-engineering effort. The scope and number of process redesign projects must be compatible with the organization's ability and experience to undertake them.

2. *Identifying change levers.* The three main enablers or levers of change are information technology (IT), information and organizational/human resource. Davenport provides categories in which IT can provide process innovation (Table 18.2).

   Much information is not manipulated by IT resources in the organization but may still be a powerful lever in making process innovation possible. Examples include the visible display

TABLE 18.2

Categories in which IT can provide Process Innovation.

Category of IT	Process innovation
Automational	For example, robotics in manufacturing, workflow in services.
Informational	The ability of IT to provide additional information about a process that can be used for improvement (see Zuboff, 1988).
Sequential	Transform process execution (such as concurrent engineering).
Tracking	Knowing the status of components (such as mail delivery systems).
Analytical	Providing additional information for decision making.
Geographical	Using worldwide communications system (for example, linked CAD).
Integrative	Case management approach – needs database of information from around the organization.
Intellectual	Database of company knowledge of processes.
Disintermediating	Connects buyers and sellers without intermediaries.

of information on the shop floor in lean production organizations and the market information used by executives in making strategic decisions.

The need to align the organizational culture with technological change is discussed in Chapter 9 on Job Design. For example, many process innovations will lead to increased worker empowerment which may require an adjustment in organizational culture to ensure successful implementation. The successful use of teams is also essential in implementing cross-functional processes.

3. *Developing process vision.* It is essential that the process innovation effort is consistent with the organization's strategy. A process vision consists of measurable objectives and provides the link between strategy and action. A shared vision is essential to ensure true innovation, rather than standard improvement efforts such as simplification and rationalization. A vision allows conventional wisdom about how processes are undertaken to be questioned. Key activities in developing a process vision include assessing existing business strategy for process direction, consulting with process customers, benchmarking process performance targets and developing process performance objectives and attributes.

4. *Understanding existing processes.* This step is necessary to enable those involved in the innovation activities to develop a common understanding of the existing processes, understand complexities, avoid duplicating current problems and provide a benchmark against which improvement can be measured. Traditional process-oriented approaches such as flow charting can be used for this task but do not contain the elements necessary for the implementation of radical change.

5. *Designing and prototyping the new processes.* The design of new processes requires a team with a mix of members who can deliver creative and innovative process solutions and ensure that they are implemented. Key activities in the design and prototype phase are the brainstorming of design activities, assessing the feasibility of these alternatives, prototyping the new process design, developing a migration strategy and implementation of the new organizational structure and systems. Simulation modelling can be a valuable tool in assessing new process design (Chapter 8).

Continuous Improvement

Continuous improvement programmes are associated with incremental changes within the organization whose cumulative effect is to deliver an increased rate of performance improvement. Continuous improvement is associated with the JIT and lean philosophy, where it is referred to as *Kaizen*, a Japanese term, meaning a way of getting to the ideals of JIT by a continuous stream of improvements over time (see Chapter 13).

Continuous improvement is also associated with the concept of the **learning organization**, which aims to create an environment which builds knowledge within the organization and can use that to improve performance. The need for organizational learning has been identified as a consequence of the need for organizations to continually produce innovations in order to maintain a competitive edge. The ability to generate a continuous stream of ideas for improvement and implement them is seen as a sustainable competitive advantage for organizations. To consider how an organization learns is really to consider how learning of individuals within that organization takes place and how the results of that learning are integrated into the practices, procedures and processes of the organization. The transfer of knowledge from individual to organizational system means that the knowledge becomes independent of the individual and is possessed by the organization and is replicable by individuals within that organization. The concept of **knowledge management** overlaps that of organizational learning but may be distinguished from it by a greater focus on the management of knowledge as a strategic asset and an emphasis on encouraging the sharing of knowledge.

The video 'Continuous Improvement - Sterne, Eisenberg, & Wilson' is available in your interactive e-book at **www.wileyopenpage.com**

Continuous improvement requires creating the right environment in which the importance of the approach is recognized and rewarded. This means ensuring the involvement of all the members of the organization and ensuring that these members have the problem-solving skills necessary to achieve worthwhile improvements. The issues of environment, involvement and problem-solving skills will now be explored in relation to continuous improvement implementation.

Environment

In order to create the right environment in which improvement can take place it is important to have a set of procedures for the improvement process, which formalizes actions so that progress can be monitored and measured. A procedure for an improvement study could follow the steps of the Plan-Do-Check-Act (PDCA) cycle (Figure 18.3) as follows:

1. What changes are needed in order to gain continual improvement?
2. Analyse appropriate data. Carry out suggested changes to the process.
3. Evaluate the results of the changes to the process.
4. Make the changes permanent, or try another step (go to step 1).

The PDCA was developed for improving production processes and separates the process creation and execution phases ('plan' and 'do') from the process checking and improvement ('check' and 'act') phases. Thus a continuous feedback loop is created between process operation and process improvement. Russell and Taylor (2010) adapt the ten principles given in Hirano (1989) into the following principles for implementing a continuous improvement effort:

1. *Create a mind-set for improvement.* Do not accept that the present way of doing things is necessarily the best.
2. *Try and try again.* Don't seek immediate perfection but move to your goal by small improvements, checking for mistakes as you progress.
3. *THINK.* Get to the real cause of the problem – ask why? Five times.
4. *Work in teams.* Use the ideas from a number of people to brainstorm new ways.
5. *Recognize that improvement knows no limits.* Get in the habit of always looking for better ways of doing things.

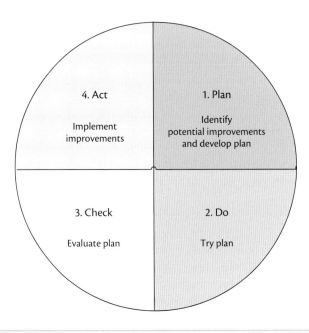

FIGURE 18.3

The Plan-Do-Check-Act (PDCA) Cycle.

Involvement

The idea behind continuous improvement is to use the skills and knowledge of all of the workforce in a sustained attempt to improve every aspect of how the organization operates. It is useful to disseminate information around the organization regarding progress on various performance measures in order to emphasize the importance of the improvement effort. This can be done using meetings, newsletters and boards displaying charts. The most common objectives used are the QCDSM measures of Quality, Cost, Delivery, Safety and Morale.

Suggestion schemes offer the person closest to the work activity the opportunity to suggest improvements to the process. Suggestions by employees are evaluated and if they are assessed as providing a significant saving then a cash award may be paid to the employee. The award could be a fixed amount for all suggestions or a percentage of net savings over a specific time period. Suggestion schemes are most likely to be successful when employees are given training in aspects such as data collection and the scheme is promoted, rather than the size of any award payments.

Process improvement teams or quality circles are using the different skills and experiences of a group of people in order to solve problems and thus provide a basis for continual improvement. In order to do this the team should be aware of the tools available for measuring and thus improving performance such as statistical process control (SPC) (Chapter 17). Expertise outside the group can also be used to contribute to group effectiveness. A quality circle is a small group of people (6–12) who meet voluntarily on a regular basis. Process improvement teams are usually made up of experienced problem solvers from departments affected by the process and are appointed by management. The use of a group can be particularly effective at working through a cause-and-effect diagram (Chapter 7) to find the root cause of a particular problem.

 www.wileyopenpage.com

Problem Solving Skills

Information technology has had a particular impact on the level of problem solving and thus decision making skills required in the organization. The decision-making activity is often classified in order that different decision processes and methods can be adopted for the common features of decisions within these choices. Decision types can be classified into strategic, tactical and operational relating to top, middle and supervisory management levels. The main variables across these levels being the time-span over which decisions are taken and the amount of money involved in the choice of option. However, these classifications fail to recognize the changes that are taking place with the introduction of information systems (see Case Study 18.2).

CASE STUDY 18.2

In the Age of the Smart Machine

Shoshana Zuboff in her book *In the Age of the Smart Machine* (Zuboff, 1988) describes the changes that took place within continuous process factories in the United States which changed to computer controlled systems. The extra information produced by these systems required a different kind of conceptual grasp by the person concerned in order to recognize patterns and understand the consequences of actions on the overall process. This represents a major change from just the monitoring of information on a computer screen. In other words these more sophisticated computer applications, rather than simply replacing repetitive and mechanical tasks, often serve as a sophisticated decision support tool that is most valuable in the hands of a sophisticated user with broad responsibilities. This implies that the link between information and management level may become increasingly inappropriate as the job scope and responsibility of many people within the organization increases with the advent of information systems.

Question

What are the implications of the findings in the case study for operations managers?

CASE STUDY 18.3

Managers Disrupt Learning with their 'Great Ideas'

It is all too easy for businesses to underestimate how much learning is taking place via the informal networks that become established in large organizations – networks that are often invisible to managers. These networks, says Peter Senge, a senior lecturer at the MIT Sloan School of Management, are delicate and can end up being destroyed when senior managers try to introduce new systems. 'A lot of learning is going on in organizations but management is screwing it up with their great ideas on how to do things more efficiently or their great ideas for reorganizing', he warns. 'In any healthy organization, there's a lot of learning going on. But 90% of it is informal and is going on well below the radar screen of the management structure', says Professor Senge. 'So you need to help managers become more aware.' He says that it is important to question assumptions when seeking to raise skill levels in the workplace or to introduce new technology: the rigid hierarchical structure found in many organizations needs to be turned on its head.

Professor Senge, who is founding chair of the Society for Organizational Learning and author of *The Fifth Discipline: The Art and Practice of the Learning Organization*, believes the learning process begins by taking a fresh look at the way the organization operates – and this applies to the implementation of IT systems. 'There's a very understandable life cycle you go through, when you first start using IT, to do what you've always done', he says. 'Someone thinks there's an efficiency gain or the potential for cost reduction or maybe you could do something more reliably – but you rarely think about doing something that you have never done before.' Part of the problem, he says, is that there is usually a disproportionate amount of power at the top of the organization. 'That almost always means a bunch of people with 25 to 30 years' experience', he says. 'That can make them impervious to seeing the significance of developments that a 25-year-old might see.' Companies also suffer because of the persistent belief that learning goes on only in a classroom. Often, however, when employees have been given the formal training on a new system, as much is learnt back at their desk where they can lean over and ask a colleague the best way to carry out a particular function they need at that particular moment. There will always be people within an organization who are better than others at learning how to use IT systems and explaining it to others. Professor Senge believes these people can and should play a big part in IT training. What training specialists provide, he says, is usually often delivered out of context of the workplace. 'No one ever learnt anything in a final sense in a classroom. It's all contextual – it's not the tool. It's how you use the tool in a particular setting with particular people and under particular pressures.'

What Professor Senge is advocating is a grassroots approach to learning. Rather than spreading technical knowledge from above through leaders that have decided what people need to know, he suggests starting at the other end, where some people may be more adept than others at learning and operating IT systems. 'Sample both ends of the spectrum', he says. 'Start by looking at the really good stuff that is working today – and then what's keeping that from spreading.' At higher levels of an organization, this dissemination is just as crucial. After all, for senior managers to be able to make strategic decisions about IT, they need to have an understanding of the systems being used throughout the organization. However, there is often resistance by these people to taking a training course they might see as below them. 'That's a big problem – the executives want the 30-minute summary and want everyone else to spend days on it', says Professor Senge. He suggests starting at the 'shallow end of the pool' by seeking out managers who are more motivated than others and focusing initial attention on them. Most important when introducing any new system, he says: 'Go to the most sophisticated users to first get it working well and then figure out how to help other people get it working well – don't just hand it over to the training department.'

Source: Financial Times (2006). Reproduced with permission.

Question

Discuss how the learning of individuals can be integrated into the practices, procedures and processes of the organization.

The Relationship between BPM, BPR and CI Approaches

Continuous improvement programmes are associated with incremental changes within the organization whose cumulative effect is to deliver an increased rate of performance improvement. The important point about continuous improvement is that it can deliver improvements that are difficult to copy by competitors. For instance, a culture that recognizes and delivers quality and reliability is a long-term project that may not show immediate financial benefit. In order to catch up or overtake competitors it has been realized that continuous improvements may not be enough, but step changes in performance are required. These are associated with innovations in areas such as product design or process design. The BPR technique has been widely cited as an approach that locates suitable areas for change and delivers improvements to them.

These two approaches share orientation to process as the unit of improvement, orientation to strategy execution rather than strategy itself, belief in the importance of measurement and analysis and focus on external criteria (for example, benchmarking) as the basis for judging improvement. When BPR and CI coexist within an organization they should be perceived as being related aspects of an overall performance improvement initiative. Figure 18.4 shows how the two approaches could be combined in an improvement initiative to outperform an organization using only one of the approaches.

In the 1990s many organizations attempted major or breakthrough change by attempting to implement radical process redesigns under the banner of BPR. It was found that many of these efforts failed but the use of a process perspective was seen as useful and so companies are now more likely to try process improvement to enable more limited changes. The concept of business process management (BPM) covered earlier is used to refer to the various methods and technologies that are used to enable a process oriented change using both incremental and breakthrough approaches.

FIGURE 18.4

Combining BPR and CI initiatives.

SUMMARY

- Performance measurement involves choosing both the measures that will be used to identify where improvements should take place and also to determine if improvement has taken place after change has been implemented.
- Activity-based costing assists in determining how much it costs to make a certain product or deliver a service.
- The balanced scorecard incorporates performance measures for improvement across the perspectives of financial, customer, business process and innovation and learning.
- The SCOR model provides a framework for measuring and improving processes in a supply chain.
- In order to identify where performance improvement should take place it is necessary to compare the performance measure against a performance standard.
- Benchmarking can be defined as the continuous measurement of an organization's products and processes against a company recognized as a leader in that industry.
- Business Process Management (BPM) is a collection of tools and techniques used to analyse and improve the performance of business processes.
- Business process re-engineering calls for an analysis of a business from a process rather than functional perspective and then the re-engineering of these processes to optimize performance.
- Implementation of continuous improvement requires attention to the organizational environment, involvement of organizational members and development of problem solving skills.

 The Simulation 'Custody of Prisoner - Business Process Simulation' is available in your interactive e-book at **www.wileyopenpage.com**

CASE STUDY 18.4

Process Improvement at a UK Police Service

The nature of the Police Service as a service industry means that a central task is the management and deployment of human resources. As part of a re-engineering study covering all aspects of police duties an investigation of the human resources division and its information technology infrastructure was undertaken. One particular area selected for redesign was the sickness and absence process located in the HR division. This is of particular interest as the issue of illicit absenteeism from work in the UK Police Service has attracted publicity. It has been estimated that it was costing Police Services in England and Wales £250 million a year, losing an average of 11 working days per officer annually (Sheehan, 2000).

The following steps were undertaken in the process improvement exercise.

1. Derive the critical success factors.
2. Process mapping.
3. Identify processes for improvement.

 www.wileyopenpage.com

4. Process redesign.
5. Measure performance.

Step 1: Derive the Critical Success Factors

Critical success factors (CSF) can provide a guide to determine 'what needs doing well' in order to implement a strategy and fulfil the organizational vision. The critical success factors can be placed within the four perspectives of the balanced scorecard, which provides a balanced set of performance indicators to reflect the views of the wide range of stakeholder groups involved. A balanced scorecard can be constructed at the organizational or departmental level at which a focused strategy can be adopted. The critical success factors for the HR organization were based on the strategic plan developed by the Police Service at a divisional level. The objectives were then passed to the heads of the various departments within the HR division (for example, head of personnel or head of training) for discussion. The CSFs are shown in Table 18.3.

TABLE 18.3

The CSFs for the Balanced Scorecard Perspectives.

Perspective	Critical success factor
Innovation and learning	Increase individual performance This CSF needs positive improvement and measures to improve individual performance. For example, health and welfare of staff, rewards/penalties, attract quality applicants, retain staff, staff relations, development and training of staff.
Business process	Increase effectiveness of strategic management. This CSF will provide accurate management information on which to base strategic development and policies and decisions. For example, improve service to public, develop policies, support and advise on organizational change, empowerment.
	Improve staff communications This CSF will ensure that staff are better informed of and are aware of new legislation, policies and procedures, where to obtain relevant management information and expert advice and set up procedures to enforce policies particularly those mandated by legislation or otherwise.
Stakeholder/customer	Meet legislative requirements Failure to meet this CSF will result in penalties including financial penalties and dismissal.
	Increase effectiveness of service in its delivery to external customers This CSF will require HR to provide accurate management information to the service on which the service can base both strategic and tactical responses to the needs of external customers and agencies.
	Increase effectiveness in delivery to internal customers This CSF will require HR to provide accurate management information and professional advice to heads of departments and line managers (all levels) on which heads of departments and line managers can base both strategic and tactical responses to the needs of their own staff and other internal customers.
Financial	Improve value for money (of HR to the organization) This CSF will require HR management to develop strategic and tactical plans and policies to guide service strategic development in HR aspects and make the most effective use of resources and systems to provide a high quality service.

Step 2: Process Mapping

In order to identify activities within the sickness and absence process the technique of process mapping was used. Process mapping involves a study of how activities link together to form a process. The technique involves interviewing personnel and observation of the relevant process which provides information which is used to draw a process map. The analysis shows the interrelationships between activities and identifies the elements and roles involved in process execution (more details on process mapping are given in Chapter 8).

Step 3: Identify Processes for Improvement

Once the process mapping has been completed it is necessary to prioritize the process elements, which will be allocated resources for improvement. The following example presents a measurement system developed in conjunction with the service. The system consists of a two-dimensional marking guide based on the impact of the process on the critical success factors determined in the balanced scorecard review and an assessment of the scope for innovation (the amount of improvement possible) to the current process design. Processes which are strategically important and offer the largest scope for improvement are prioritized under this model. The marking guide marks each process on a scale of 0 to 5 against 2 measures:

IMPACT – the extent to which the achievement of the CSF depends on the process.

INNOVATION – the extent of the change required to the process in order to meet the CSF.

The marking guides for each measure are shown in Table 18.4 and Table 18.5.

TABLE 18.4

IMPACT (External Perspective) Marking Guide.

Mark	IMPACT (External Perspective) Marking Guide
0	This individual process has minimal or no effect on the individual CSF
1	This individual process is dependent on another process, in to order for it to have an effect on this CSF
2	This individual process has a marked influence on this CSF
3	The individual process has substantial impact on whether another process can maximize its beneficial effects on this CSF
4	The individual process has substantial influence on this CSF
5	The individual process is a critical part of being able to achieve the individual CSF

TABLE 18.5

INNOVATION (Internal Perspective) Marking Guide.

Mark	INNOVATION (Internal Perspective) Marking Guide
0	This process cannot be improved for this CSF
1	This process achieves its objective but could be improved even further
2	This process achieves its objective but could be improved by review of both automation and process improvement
3	This process does not effectively achieve all its objectives and could be improved by review of both automation and process improvement
4	The process exists and functions but needs substantial alteration to meet its objectives
5	The process either does not exist or only partially exists and fails to meet any objectives

 www.wileyopenpage.com

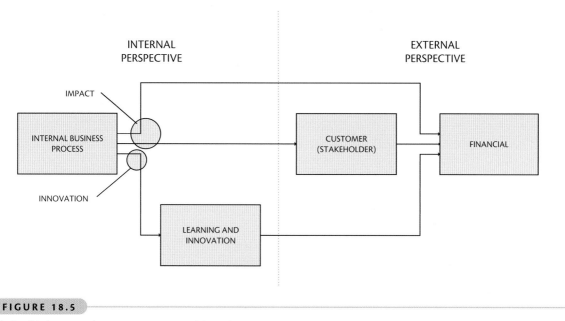

FIGURE 18.5

Relationship between the Scoring Systems and the Balanced Scorecard Perspectives.

In terms of the balanced scorecard the IMPACT measure relates to the achievement of the CSF from the stakeholder and financial (external) perspectives of the balanced scorecard. The INNOVATION measure relates to the amount of change required from the learning and business process (internal) perspectives (Figure 18.5).

Each process element is scored (0–5) against each CSF for the impact and innovation measures. The score for each measure is multiplied to provide a composite score (0–25) for each CSF. An overall composite score for each process is calculated by adding the composite score for each CSF. A spreadsheet sort by composite score identifies a priority list of processes for improvement.

Step 4: Process Redesign

Once suitable processes have been identified for improvement, the next stage was to redesign these processes to improve their performance. Peppard and Rowland (1995) provide a number of areas of potential redesign under the headings of Eliminate, Simplify, Integrate and Automate (ESIA) (see Chapter 8 for more details on ESIA).

In the case of the 'sickness and absence' process, this involved integration of the present 30 separate process maps into a single process. Some duplication of activities was found, primarily due to functions included with the sickness process being based both at Headquarters and Divisional level. The redesign improved performance both internally and externally. Internally process efficiency was increased with an estimated saving per sickness/absence event of between 45 minutes to 60 minutes of staff time, representing a significant resource saving which can be re-deployed to improve performance. External process effectiveness has been increased by increasing the speed of follow-up checks to absent officers and new innovations such as requiring earlier checks by the police doctor.

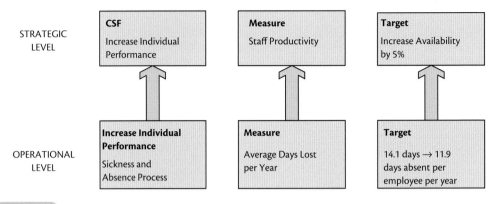

FIGURE 18.6

Deriving Operational Measures from Strategic Objectives.

Step 5: Measure Performance

In this case, in order that progress is maintained towards strategic objectives, it was considered important to relate performance of the process at an operational level to strategic targets. The 'sickness and absence' process is related to the CSF identified in the balanced scorecard initiative of increasing individual performance. At a strategic level, the measure of staff productivity was chosen with a target to increase availability of police officers by 5%. In order to meet this strategic target, measures and targets are needed at an operational level. These are derived both from the strategic measure and an understanding of the relevant business process. The measure chosen for the sickness and absence process was 'average days lost per year'. The target for this measure is 11.9 days lost per year per employee for sickness and absence. This benchmark was derived from the national average performance. The current performance was at 14.1 days lost per year per employee (Figure 18.6).

Slack and Lewis (2011) state that the strategic management of any operation cannot be separated from how resources and processes are managed at a detailed and day-to-day level. The case study presents one way of ensuring the correct processes are identified and redesigned at an operational level in such a way as to support the organization's strategic aims. In addition a performance measurement system is used to attempt to ensure that the changes implemented do actually achieve the desired effect over time.

Source: Adapted from Greasley (2004). Reproduced by permission of Emerald Group Publishing Ltd.

Questions

1. Discuss the choice of performance measures, how areas of improvement are identified and the method of improvement chosen in the case study.

2. How were the strategic targets linked to operational change in the case study?

GOSH and F1

The interactions between Great Ormond Street Hospital (GOSH) and Formula 1 motor racing teams is a form of collaborative benchmarking, whilst the use of such across dissimilar organisations may be very demanding, it has been shown to be extremely effective. GOSH wished to bring about improvement to its processes for handover of care in infant surgical procedures, and approached 'best in class' F1 teams to ask if they would be willing to share knowledge of their precision systems for supporting drivers.

The impetus for this exercise came from two doctors who were watching Formula 1 motor racing on TV while relaxing after lengthy surgeries at GOSH. Realising that F1 pit stops involved processes conceptually identical to those involved in changeover during infant surgery, they began to pay particular attention to them. GOSH treat approximately 500 paediatric cardiac cases every year. Co-ordination and quality of knowledge sharing in the handover of infants from the intensive care team to the theatre team before and after complex heart surgery has been found to be crucial to the success of the procedure, since patient's particular condition is unique. It became evident to the surgeons that there was a common interest in reducing error and improving quality between the two very different contexts. They believed that precision in procedures achieved by a Formula 1 pit team could hold valuable lessons for improvements in handovers during operations. The pit stop in Formula 1 motor racing was seen as a model example of how a multi professional team collaborates to perform a complex task effectively, under huge time pressure, with minimal error. The aim of the benchmarking study was to observe and reflect upon this expertise and combine it with existing knowledge to develop simple, reliable, easily trainable handover protocols to improve safety and quality of patient care in the short but critical period after complex infant heart surgery.

GOSH surgical staff visited and observed the pit crew handover during a race, becoming increasingly interested in the way the team addressed possible failure 'What could go wrong?' 'What are we going to do if it does go wrong?' and 'How important is it if it does go wrong?' Benchmarking against the Ferrari team pushed the hospital to anticipate problems rather than waiting to deal with them as they arose. Observing Ferrari caused the hospital to view its own practice from a completely different perspective. Ferrari staff did not tell them what needed to be changed, or how. The hospital staff reflected upon their observations of good practice among pit crews, aviator trainers and others and adapted the lessons learned to fit their own situation.

The GOSH doctors noted the value in process mapping, process description, and trying to work out what individual tasks should be. Under the new handover process they devised, the anaesthetist was given overall responsibility for coordinating the team, acting in a way which was analogous to the pit crew 'lollypop man', and a dance choreographer was brought in to help the team position their movements so that they would not impede one another while carrying out their particular roles.

Adequate time and money allows motor racing to have rehearsal after rehearsal. In healthcare, where resources are scarce and teams are dealing with living people, a process was required that was simple, easy to learn, and did not depend upon a lot of rehearsal. Through the benchmarking process, GOSH doctors noted not only how fast, but also how quiet and disciplined the pit crew was, and designed new processes for the surgical teams intended to emulate this atmosphere of calm professionalism. Development of a new handover protocol reflected this influence very strongly, emphasizing such factors as teamwork, effective leadership, rhythm, standardised processes, anticipation, and communication. Once in place, the protocol was polished further through reflection upon other contexts such as the work of aviator trainers. It was simple to understand and could be established within 15–30 min at staff induction. Results showed that the new handover procedure broke the link between technical and informational errors. Before the new protocol, approximately 30% of patient errors occurred in both equipment and information; afterward, only 10% of the patient errors occurred in both areas. While the new system was not perfect, GOSH identified significant improvement and adopted a policy of seeking further, continuous improvement in procedures.

The development of a simple, easily trainable handover process using expertise from other high-risk industries reduced errors and improved information transfer with no penalty in handover duration and reliable training overhead. GOSH believe this work may be extrapolated to handovers in other areas of medicine, and would encourage further attempts to evaluate this protocol systematically and to combine expertise from other industries with that of health care.

Sources

Bednar, P.M., Welch, C. and Milner, C. (2011): 'Knowledge Management: an Open Systems Approach,' Proceedings of 8th Conference of the Italian Chapter of the Association for Information Systems, LUISS Guido Carli – Roma, Italy, October 7th–8th, 2011.

Catchpole, K., De Leval, M., McEwan, A., Pigott, N., Elliott, M., McQuilan, A., MacDonauld, C., Goldman, A. (2007). Patient Handover from Surgery to Intensive Care: Using Formula 1 and Aviation Models to Improve Safety and Quality. *Paediatric Anaesthesia* 17(5) 470–478.

Sower, V., Duffy, J.A. and Kohers, G. (2008). Ferrari's Formula One Handovers and Handovers from Surgery to Intensive Care. Chapter 10 in *Benchmarking for Hospitals: achieving best-in-class performance without having to reinvent the wheel.* ASQ Press

Source: Written by Briony Boydell and Chris Milner. Reproduced with permission.

Question

Measuring an operation's current performance and recognizing an opportunity or need to improve is critical to the success of an operation or process; what are the strengths and challenges faced with the different types of benchmarking?

Quizzes to test yourself further are available in your interactive e-book at **www.wileyopenpage.com**

Flashcards to test yourself further are available in your interactive e-book at **www.wileyopenpage.com**

EXERCISES

1. Distinguish between the terms efficiency, effectiveness and economy.

2. Why is activity-based costing a useful tool for the operations manager?

3. Identify the need for using a balanced scorecard rather than measuring performance using a measure such as productivity.

4. Discuss the role of benchmarking.

5. Discuss the main issues involved in the implementation of a continuous improvement effort.

6. Discuss the factors behind the integration of the BPR and CI improvement approaches.

7. Compare and contrast the BPR and CI improvement approaches.

WEB EXERCISE

Using the company profiles at http://www.apqc.org/portal/apqc/site/?path=/research/profiles/index.htm1 (accessed 1 June 2012) provide a summary of the features of a successful benchmarking effort.

FURTHER READING

Greasley, A. (2000) A simulation analysis of arrest costs. *Journal of the Operational Research Society*, 51, 162–7.

Harmon, P. (2007) *Business Process Change: A Guide for Business Managers and BPM and Six Sigma Professionals*, 2nd edn, Morgan Kaufman.

Harrison-Broninski, K. (2005) *Human Interactions: The Heart and Soul of Business Process Management*, Meghan-Kiffer Press.

Kaplan, R.S. and Norton, D.P. (2006) *Alignment: Using the Balanced Scorecard to Create Corporate Synergies*, Harvard Business School Press.

Schurter, T. (2010) *The Insiders' Guide to BPM: 7 steps to process mastery*, Meghan Kiffer.

Shingo, S. (2008) *Kaizen and the Art of Creative Thinking*, Norman Bodek.

Smith, H. and Fingar, P. (2003) *Business Process Management: The Third Wave*, Meghan-Kiffer Press.

Swensen, K.D., Palmer, N. and Kemsley, S. (2011) *Social BPM: Work, Planning and Collaboration under the Impact of Social Technology*, Createspace.

Zuboff, S. and Maxmin, J. (2004) *The Support Economy*, Penguin Books Ltd.

WEB LINKS

www.apqc.org (accessed 1 June 2012). American Productivity and Quality Center. This site provides information on such topics as benchmarking and performance measurement.

www.kaizen.com (accessed 1 June 2012). Kaizen Institute. Contains tips for implementing continuous improvement.

www.prosci.com (accessed 1 June 2012). BPR Online Learning Centre. Contains tutorials and many articles on BPR.

www.supply-chain.org (accessed 1 June 2012). Supply Chain Council. Provides details of the SCOR model.

REFERENCES

Davenport, T.H. (1993) *Process Innovation: Re-engineering Work through Information Technology*, Harvard Business School Press.

Fingar, P. (2006) *Extreme Competition: Innovation and the Great Twenty-First Century Business Reformation*, Meghan-Kiffer Press.

Greasley, A. (2004) Process improvement within a HR division at a UK police force. *International Journal of Operations and Production Management*, 24 (2/3), 230–40.

Hammer, M. and Champy, J. (1993) *Re-engineering the Corporation: A Manifesto for Business Revolution*, Harper Business.

Hill, A. and Hill T. (2012) *Operations Management*, 3rd edn, Palgrave Macmillan.

Hirano, H. (1989) *JIT Factory Revolution: A Pictorial Guide to Factory Design of the Future*, Productivity Press.

Kaplan, R.S. and Norton, D.P. (1996) *The Balanced Scorecard: Translating Strategy into Action*, Harvard Business School Press.

Peppard, J. and Rowland, P. (1995) *The Essence of Business Process Re-engineering*, Prentice Hall.

Rummler, G.A. and Brache, A.P. (1995) *Improving Performance: How to Manage the White Space on the Organization Chart*, Jossey Bass Wiley.

Russell, R.S. and Taylor, B.W. (2010) *Operations Management: Creating Value along the Supply Chain*, 7th edn, John Wiley & Sons, Inc.

Senge, P.M. (2006) *The Fifth Discipline: The Art and Practice of the Learning Organization*, 2nd edn, Century Business.

Sheehan, M. (2000) Police chiefs crack down on shirkers. *Sunday Times,* 27 February, p. 9.

Slack, N. (1991) *Manufacturing Advantage: Achieving Competitive Manufacturing Operations*, Mercury.

Slack, N. and Lewis, M. (2011) *Operations Strategy*, 3rd edn, Pearson Education Ltd.

Turney, P.B.B. (1996) *Activity-based Costing: The Performance Breakthrough*, Kogan Page.

Willcocks, L. and Smith, G. (1995) IT enabled business process re-engineering: organizational and human resource dimension. *Strategic Information Systems,* 4 (3), 279–301.

Zuboff, S. (1988) *In the Age of the Smart Machine: The Future of Work and Power*, Heinemann.

A

ABC classification system This system sorts inventory items into groups depending on the amount of annual expenditure or some other factor.

Acceptance sampling This consists of taking a random sample from a larger batch or lot of material to be inspected. The quality of the sample is assumed to reflect the overall quality of the lot.

Active customer-technology interaction A type of interaction where the customer controls the interaction between themselves and the technology.

Activity-based costing Provides a way of allocating costs to manufacturing and service activities in order that a company can determine how much it costs to make a certain product or deliver a service.

Actual capacity The capacity remaining after loss of output due to both planned factors and unplanned factors. Unplanned factors include equipment breakdown and absenteeism.

Aggregate plan This will specify aspects such as overall production rate, size of the workforce, the amount of subcontracting required to deliver the mix of products or service required to meet the demand profile.

Anthropometric data Information concerning factors related to the physical attributes of a human being.

Appraisal costs These are the costs associated with controlling quality through the use of measuring and testing products and processes to ensure conformance to quality specifications.

Assignable cause of variation These are variations in the process which are not due to random variation but can be attributed to some change in the process, which needs to be investigated and rectified.

Attribute control charts These measure discrete values such as if a component is defective or not. Thus there are no values, as in a variable control chart, from which a mean and range can be calculated. The data will simply provide a count of how many items conform to a specification and how many do not.

Automated material handling systems (AMH) These are designed to improve efficiency in the movement, storage and retrieval of materials.

Autonomation Autonomation or 'automation with a human touch' (Ohno, 1988) is an approach that enables a worker to stop a process if an abnormal situation has been detected.

Autonomous work groups These are groups of people who are able to decide on their own methods of working and should be responsible for handling problems as they arise. They will typically be responsible for the whole delivery of a product or service.

B

Balanced scorecard A measurement system that incorporates performance measures across the four perspectives of financial, stakeholder, business process and innovation and learning.

Balancing capacity This is the equalizing of the capacity of a number of sequential processes.

Balking When customers do not join a queue because they perceive it as too long.

Batch processes Batch processes cover a relatively wide range of volume and variety combinations. Products are grouped into batches whose size can range from two to hundreds.

Benchmarking Comparing a product or service against what is considered the best in that market segment and then making recommendations on how the product or service can be improved to meet that standard.

Bill of materials (BOM) This identifies all the components required to produce a scheduled quantity of an assembly and the structure of how these components fit together to make that assembly.

Bullwhip effect This effect occurs when there is a lack of synchronization in supply chain members. Even a slight change in consumer sales will ripple backwards in the form of magnified oscillations in demand upstream.

Business level strategy Strategy at the organizational or SBU level in large companies. The strategy is concerned with the products and services that should be offered in the market defined at the corporate level.

Business process improvement Optimizing existing processes typically coupled with enhancements in information technology.

Business process management This is the term used to refer to the analysis and improvement of business processes.

Business process outsourcing (BPO) The outsourcing of processes.

Business process simulation The use of computer software, in the context of a process-based change, that allows the operation of a business to be simulated.

Business-to-business (B2B) Web-based commercial transactions between an organization and other organizations.

Business-to-consumer (B2C) Web-based commercial transactions between an organization and consumers.

Buy-side e-Commerce E-commerce transactions between a purchasing organization and its suppliers.

C

Capacity cushion The amount of excess capacity in an operations facility. It can be calculated as the percentage of capacity that is not used on average.

Capacity loading graph Indicates the type and level of capacity required at a point in time.

Capacity requirements plan (CRP) This takes information from the MRP system to calculate workloads for critical work centres or workers.

Cause-and-effect diagrams A technique for identifying the causes of quality problems.

Cell layout Cells are created from placing together resources that service a subset of the total range of products or services.

Cellular manufacturing When equipment is placed in a cell layout which is a close grouping of different types of equipment, each of which performs a different operation.

Centre of gravity method This can be used to determine the location of a distribution centre by minimizing distribution costs. The relative coordinates of the distribution points are placed on a map and the location of the distribution point should be at the centre of gravity of the coordinates.

Chance causes of variation The inherent variability in processes due to factors such as ambient temperature, wear of moving parts or slight variations in the composition of the material that is being processed.

Chase demand A strategy that seeks to match output to the demand pattern over time. Capacity is altered by such policies as changing the amount of part-time staff, changing the amount of staff availability through overtime working, changing equipment levels and subcontracting.

Competitive factors A range of factors such as price, quality and delivery speed, derived from the marketing strategy, on which the product or service wins orders.

Computer-aided design A CAD system allows the designer to create drawings on a computer screen to assist in the visual design of a product or service.

Computer-aided engineering (CAE) This takes the drawings in a CAD and subjects the designs to simulated tests.

Computer-aided manufacturing (CAM) This extends the use of CAD by transmitting the design held in the CAD system electronically to computer controlled machine tools.

Computer-aided process planning (CAPP) This transmits a process plan of how parts will be manufactured to a machine tool. It can also sequence parts through a number of process steps.

Computer-integrated manufacture This is the automation of the product and process design, planning and control and manufacture of the product.

Computer numerically controlled machines (CNC) These are machine tools that can be controlled by computer.

Consumer services Services aimed at the final consumer. These have risen in line with people's increasing disposable income in developed countries.

Continuous improvement Continuous improvement concerns incremental changes within the organization whose cumulative effect is to deliver an increased rate of performance improvement.

Continuous innovation Modifying existing products for improved performance.

Continuous processes A continuous process operates continually to produce a very high volume of a standard product. The products produced by a continuous operation are usually a continuous flow, such as oil and gas, rather than discrete items.

Control charts for variable data Control charts for variable data display samples of a measurement that can take a value from a range of possible values. Values will fall in or out of a range around a specified target value.

Corporate level strategy Provides long-range guidance on the direction of the whole organization.

Cost Cost is considered to be the finance required to obtain the inputs and manage the transformation process that produces finished goods and services.

Cost of quality A concept that is intended to highlight and define the cost of quality and enable quality improvement efforts.

Critical path This is used to show the activities undertaken during a project, the dependencies between these activities and the project duration.

Cumulative representation A running total or cumulative count of inventory, which should always meet or exceed cumulative demand. It is used to ensure no stock-outs occur when using a level capacity plan.

Customer relationship management (CRM) This is concerned with marketing and sales processes.

Customer relationship management systems These systems are designed to integrate the range of information systems that contain information regarding the customer.

Cycle time The cycle time is the time taken to produce or deliver one unit of output.

D

Degree of customer contact The degree of customer contact relates to the amount of interaction between the service provider and customer during the service delivery process.

Demand management This capacity planning strategy attempts to adjust demand to meet available capacity. This can be achieved by strategies such as varying price of goods and services, advertising and using appointment systems.

Demand profile This consists of the products and services required by the marketing plan, future customer orders and other demand factors such as the manufacture of items for spares.

Demand-side influences When the location decision is considered in terms of factors that vary in such a way as to influence customer service as location varies.

Demander-located services These require movement of the service provider to the location of the customer.

Dependability Dependability refers to consistently meeting a promised delivery time for a product or service to a customer.

Design capacity The capacity of an operation that represents the theoretical output of a process as it was designed.

Design for manufacture A concept which views product design as the first step in the manufacture of that product.

Design of experiments These aim to identify factors that affect a product's performance by providing a way of testing a number of design options under various operating and environmental conditions.

Diseconomies of scale When a facility is expanded and the average cost of producing each unit rises.

Disintermediation Using e-Business to alter the supply chain structure by bypassing some of the tiers.

Disruptive innovation A new design that cannot in the short term match the performance most customers expect from the current product/service but because technology can progress faster than market requirements will eventually achieve market acceptable performance and then may dominate the market.

Distribution requirements planning (DRP) This manages linkages between elements of the supply chain beginning with an analysis of demand at each customer service location.

DMAIC methodology This emphasizes the use of statistical tools to gather data at each of the five stages of define, measure, analyse, improve and control.

Downstream customers Customers of the organization such as wholesalers and retailers.

E

Earned value Also termed the budgeted cost of work performed (BCWP), shows, for any day in the project, how much work has actually been done in terms of budgeted costs.

E-Business This involves electronically mediated information exchanges, both within an organization and between organizations.

E-Commerce This involves electronically mediated information exchanges between organizations.

E-procurement This refers to the electronic integration and management of all procurement activities including purchase request, authorization, ordering, delivery and payment between purchaser and supplier.

Economic analysis This consists of developing estimates of production and delivery costs and comparing them with estimates of demand.

Economic order quantity (EOQ) model This model calculates the fixed inventory order volume required while seeking to minimize the sum of the annual costs of holding inventory and the annual costs of ordering inventory.

Economies of scale When a facility is expanded, fixed costs remain the same, and the average cost of producing each unit falls.

Economies of scope Economies of scope are created by the ability to deliver more variety of output from one facility than using separate facilities.

Economy Lowering the cost of inputs into the operations transformation process.

Effective capacity The capacity remaining after loss of output due to planned factors such as maintenance and training.

Effectiveness The extent to which the outputs of a process meet the requirements of its customers.

Efficiency This gives the proportion of time a process is in use compared to its effective capacity.

Effort and elapsed time Effort time is the total amount of work that needs to occur to complete a task. The elapsed time indicates how long in time (such as calendar days) the task will take (duration).

Electronic commerce All electronically mediated information exchanges between an organization and its external stakeholders.

Electronic data interchange (EDI) This can be defined as the exchange, using digital media, of structured business information, particularly for sales transactions such as purchase orders and invoices between buyers and sellers.

Empowerment Empowerment is characterized by an organization in which employees are given more autonomy, discretion and responsibility in decision making.

Enterprise resource planning (ERP) These systems provide a single solution concerned with internal distribution and financial processes.

Ergonomics The collection of information about human characteristics and behaviour to understand the effect of design, methods and environment.

Expediting The short-term rescheduling of orders in order to ensure targets are met.

Experience curves These provide an organization with the ability to predict the improvement in productivity that can occur as experience is gained in a market segment.

Extensible markup language (XML) A data description language that allows documents to store any kind of information.

Extranet An intranet with restricted access which is extended to suppliers, collaborators or customers.

F

Facility location The geographical location of capacity supplied by the organization.

Failure mode and effect analysis This is a systematic approach to identifying the cause and effect of product failures. The idea of FMEA is to anticipate failures and deal with them at the design stage.

Finished goods inventory Inventory ready for dispatch to the customer.

Five performance objectives These are used to measure operations performance in relation to its strategy.

Fixed order inventory model This can be used to calculate the amount to order given a fixed interval between ordering.

Fixed order period inventory systems In a fixed order period inventory system varying quantities are ordered at fixed time intervals.

Fixed order quantity inventory systems In these systems the order quantity is the same each time the order is placed but the time between orders varies according to the rate of use of the inventory item.

Fixed-position layout This is used when the product or service cannot be moved and so the transforming process must take place at the location of product creation or service delivery.

Flexibility Flexibility is the ability of the organization to change what it does quickly. In terms of products or services this can relate to introducing new designs, changing the mix, changing the overall volume and changing the delivery timing.

Flexible manufacturing cell (FMC) These are systems that integrate individual items of automation to form an automated manufacturing system.

Flexible manufacturing systems (FMS) These extend the facilities of an FMC by incorporating automatic parts loading and unloading facilities and an automated guided vehicle system for parts movement.

Focus Focus aligns particular market demands with individual facilities to reduce the level of complexity generated when attempting to service a number of different market segments from an individual organization.

Form design This refers to the product aesthetics such as look, feel and sound if applicable.

Functional analysis A technique for mapping service processes that starts by defining a high-level description of the service and then successively breaking down that description into a number of functions.

Functional design This ensures that the design meets the performance characteristics that are specified in the product concept.

Functional layout This is a layout in which resources (such as equipment and people) which have similar processes or functions are grouped together.

Functional level strategy Where the functions of the business (such as operations, marketing, finance) make long-range plans that support the competitive advantage being pursued by the business-level strategy.

G

Gantt chart These provide a view of which tasks are being undertaken over time. This allows monitoring of project progress against planned progress and so provides a valuable tool for project control.

Global organization Firms that follow a business strategy where activities are coordinated on a worldwide basis.

Group technology The process of grouping products for manufacture or services for delivery.

H

Heijunka (Levelled Scheduling) A system that paces work in order to smooth the flow of materials and components throughout the day.

Heterogeneity Heterogeneity refers to the interaction of the customer, service provider and surroundings causing variability in the performance of the service.

I

Inbound logistics This is used to describe the activity of moving material in from suppliers.

Infrastructual decisions These describe the systems, policies and practices that determine how the operations' structural elements are managed.

Input/output control Input/output control attempts to control the size of the queues at processes in order that queue times are more consistent and predictable.

Intranet The use of the Internet to share company information and software applications. The intranet is only accessible to company employees.

Inventory status file This provides information on the identification and quantity of items in stock.

ISO 9000 A group of quality management standards laid down by the International Organization for Standardization.

J

JIT supplier networks A formation of close long-term relationships with a small number of suppliers.

Job characteristics model Links job characteristics with the desired psychological state of the individual and the outcomes in terms of motivation and job performance.

Job enlargement This involves the horizontal integration of tasks to expand the range of tasks involved in a particular job.

Job enrichment This involves the vertical integration of tasks and the integration of responsibility and decision making.

Job rotation A form of job enlargement that involves a worker changing job roles with another worker on a periodic basis.

Jobbing processes Jobbing processes are used to make a one-off, or low-volume, product to a customer specification. The product moves to the location of transforming resources such as equipment.

K

Kanban production system To implement a pull system a *kanban* is used to pass information such as the part identification, quantity per container that the part is transported in and the preceding and next work station.

Knowledge management Knowledge management involves collecting knowledge and converting it into a form that allows it to be shared across the organization.

L

Lag capacity To only add capacity when extra demand is present that would use the additional resources.

Layout type A category which describes the arrangement of facilities in a service or manufacturing operation.

Lead capacity To obtain extra capacity above forecast demand to ensure capacity is sufficient if demand increases above forecast.

Leagility The combination of the lean and agile approaches which attempts to achieve the advantages of lean (efficiency) and the advantages of agile (effectiveness in responding to market demand).

Lean operations An integration of a philosophy and techniques designed to improve performance.

Learning curves Provide an organization with the ability to predict the improvement in productivity that can occur as experience is gained of a process.

Learning organization This aims to create an environment which builds knowledge within the organization and can be use to improve performance.

Level capacity This capacity planning strategy sets processing capacity at a uniform level throughout the planning period regardless of fluctuations in forecast demand. This means production is set at a fixed rate, usually to meet average demand and inventory is used to absorb variations in demand. For a service organization output cannot be stored as inventory so a level capacity plan involves running at a uniformly high level of capacity.

Line balancing This is used to ensure that the output of each production stage in a line layout is equal and maximum efficiency is attained.

Loading Loading involves determining the available capacity for each stage in a process and allocating a work task to that stage.

Locational cost-volume analysis This will indicate when a particular location is superior for a particular volume level by analysing the mix of fixed and variable costs.

Long-term capacity plan This covers the question of how much long-term capacity should be supplied by the organization. This decision needs to be made within a long-term plan that provides a fit with the operations strategy of the organization.

M

M-business The integration of Internet and wireless communications technology.

Maintainability considers the cost of servicing the product or service when it is in use.

Make-to-order A planning policy that acquires the raw material which is used to construct the product on the receipt of a customer order.

Make-to-stock A planning policy that produces to a forecast of demand for the product.

Manufacturing resource planning (MRP II) This extends the idea of MRP to other areas in the firm such as marketing and finance.

Market analysis This consists of evaluating the design concept with potential customers through interviews, focus groups and other data-collection methods.

Market relationship Here each purchase is treated as a separate transaction and the relationship between the buyer and seller lasts as long as this transaction takes.

Market-based approach to operations strategy Operations strategy is based on decisions regarding the markets and the customers within those markets that the organization intends to target.

Market-based operations strategy In a market-based approach to operations strategy the organization makes a decision regarding the markets and the customers within those markets that it intends to target.

Mass Customization Attempts to combine high-variety and high-volume output in order to provide the customer with customized products at a relatively low price.

Mass processes A mass or line process produces products of high volume and low variety. The process of production will essentially be the same for all the products and so it is cost-effective to use specialized labour and equipment.

Mass services Mass service processes operate with a low variety and high volume. There will be little customization of the service to individual customer needs and limited contact between the customer and people providing the service.

Master production schedule (MPS) This shows how many products or services are planned for each time period, based on the resources authorized in the aggregate plan.

Match capacity To obtain capacity to match forecasted demand.

Materials handling This relates to the movement of materials, either within warehouses or between storage areas and transportation links.

Materials management The movement of materials within the organization.

Materials requirements planning This is an information system used to calculate the requirements for component materials needed to produce end items.

Method study Dividing and analysing a job in order to reduce waste, time and effort.

Mixed model scheduling This attempts to spread the production of several different products evenly throughout each day by continually alternating between product types.

Motion study The study of the individual human motions that are used in a job task with the purpose of trying to ensure that the job does not include any unnecessary motion or movement by the worker.

N

Network analysis This refers to the use of network-based techniques for the analysis and management of projects.

O

Offshoring The transfer of activities to another country.

Operations control This is concerned with ensuring that the current behaviour of the operations system conforms with the required behaviour.

Operations management Operations management is about the management of the processes that produce or deliver goods and services.

Operations planning This is concerned with taking actions, such as ensuring resources are in place, in anticipation of future events.

Optimized production technology This is an operations control system that is based on the identification of bottlenecks within the production process.

Outbound logistics This is used to describe the activity of moving materials out to customers.

Outsourcing When goods and services are obtained outside the organization.

P

Pareto analysis A technique used to organize information and quality problems and help focus problem solving effort on the most important aspects.

Passive customer-technology interaction A type of interaction where the technology controls the interaction between the customer and the technology.

P:D ratio Compares the demand time D (from customer request to receipt of goods/services) to the total throughput time P of the purchase, make and delivery stages.

Performance objectives These allow the organization to measure its operations' performance in achieving its strategic goals. The performance objectives are quality, speed, dependability, flexibility and cost.

Performance standard A target value for a performance measure.

Peripatetic services Involve both customer and provider moving to the location of the service encounter.

Perishability Perishability refers to the fact that because a service is not a physical thing that can be stored, but is a process, it must be consumed when it is produced or it will perish.

PERT This network analysis approach attempts to take into account the fact that most task durations are not fixed by using a statistical distribution to describe the variability inherent in the tasks.

Physical distribution management This refers to the movement of materials from the operation to the customer.

Pokayoke A simple device that prevents defects from being made by taking action when an abnormality has been identified.

Predetermined motion time system (PMTS) This provides generic times for standard micromotions such as reach, move and release, which are common to many jobs.

Prevention costs These reflect the quality philosophy of 'doing it right the first time' and include those costs incurred in trying to prevent problems occurring in the first place.

Private or single-user warehouse A warehouse owned or leased by the organization for its own use.

Process chart This is a charting device that is often used to analyse the steps of a job or how a set of jobs fit together into the overall flow of a process.

Process improvement teams To use the different skills and experiences of a group of people in order to solve problems and thus provide a basis for continual improvement.

Process mapping The use of a flow chart to document the process incorporating process activities and decision points.

Process technology Process technology is used to help transform the three main categories of transformed resources which are materials, customers and information.

Procurement The role of procurement is to acquire all the materials needed by an organization.

Producer services Services that are used in the production and delivery of goods and services and constitute firms providing services to other businesses.

Product layout A layout with the resources required for a product or service arranged around the needs of that product or service.

Production design This involves ensuring that the design takes into consideration the ease and cost of manufacture of a product.

Production flow analysis (PFA) This is a group technology technique that can be used to identify families of parts with similar processing requirements.

Productivity This divides the value of the output by the value of the input resources consumed.

Professional service Professional services are characterized by high levels of customization, in that each service delivery will be tailored to meet individual customer needs. Professional services are characterized by high levels of customer contact and a relatively high proportion of staff service shop processes.

Project control This involves the monitoring of the project objectives of cost, time and quality as the project progresses.

Project cost graphs These provide an indication of the amount of cost incurred over the life of a project.

Project crashing The use of additional resources to reduce project completion time.

Project estimates Estimating the type and amount of resources required to undertake a project.

Project network simulation This can be used to develop estimates of a project's completion time without the assumptions that all paths of a project are independent and the same tasks are not on more than one path.

Project planning Project planning is to ensure that the project objectives of cost, time and quality are met. It does this by estimating both the level and timing of resources needed over the project duration.

Project processes A project process is used to make a one-off product to a customer specification. A feature of a project process is that the location of the product is stationary.

Provider-located services Require the movement of the user to the location of the service provider.

Psychology of queues A series of propositions that can be used by service organizations to instigate policies to influence customer satisfaction with waiting times.

Public or multiuser warehouse A warehouse run as an independent business.

Q

Qualitative forecasting methods Qualitative forecasting methods take a subjective approach and are based on estimates and opinions. They include market surveys, the Delphi method and expert judgement.

Quality Quality covers both the product or service itself and the processes that produce the product or service.

Quality assurance An approach to prevention rather than correction and the use of statistical tools to ensure the quality of processes.

Quality Functional Deployment (QFD) A structured process that translates the voice of the customer (what the customer needs) into technical design requirements (how these needs are met).

Quality gap approach This approach aims to improve quality by identifying the gap between what customers expect from a service and what they perceive they are actually getting. The difference between the two is termed the quality gap and the size of this gap determines customer dissatisfaction.

Quality inspection This involves detection of a quality problem by a quality inspector leading to either rejection or repair of the product.

Quality loss function A simple cost estimate that shows how customer preferences are oriented towards consistently meeting quality expectations and that a customer's dissatisfaction (quality loss) increases geometrically as the actual value deviates from the target value.

Quantitative forecasting methods These use a mathematical expression or model to show the relationship between demand and some independent variable or variables. The methods include time series and causal forecasting models.

Queuing theory Waiting time in queues is caused by fluctuations in arrival rates and variability in service times. Queuing theory can be used to explore the trade-off between the amount of capacity and the level of demand.

R

Radical innovation Generating new products or services that significantly change customer behaviours.

Radio frequency identification (RFID) A system that consists of a tag that can be attached to an item. The tag contains a microchip, which contains information about the item.

Raw materials inventory Inventory received from suppliers.

Reintermediation The creation of new intermediaries between customers and suppliers in the supply chain.

Reliability This measures the probability that a product or service will perform its intended function for a specified period of time under normal conditions of use.

Reneging When customers wait in a queue for a time and then become impatient and leave before service.

Reorder point model The reorder point model identifies the time to order when the stock level drops to a predetermined amount.

Resource-based operations strategy In a resource-based approach to operations strategy an assessment of the operation's tangible and intangible resources and processes leads to a view of the operation's capability.

Resource-based view of operations strategy Operations strategy is based on an assessment of the operation's resources and processes.

Resource-constrained project If highly specialized resources are required then the project completion date may have to be set to ensure these resources are not overloaded.

Resource-to-order When it is not necessary to activate a planning system and acquire resources until a delivery date for an order is received.

Reverse engineering A systematic approach to dismantling and inspecting a competitor's product to look for aspects of design that could be incorporated into the organization's own product.

Robot A programmable machine that can undertake tasks that may be dangerous, dirty or dull for people to carry out.

Robust design The process of designing in the ability of the product to perform under a variety of conditions and so reducing the chance of product failure.

Rough-cut capacity plan (RCCP) This takes information from the MPS to evaluate the feasibility of the MPS.

S

Sandcone theory This maintains that there is an ideal sequence in which operational capabilities should be developed of quality, dependability, speed, flexibility and finally achieving excellence in cost.

Scheduling Scheduling is the allocation of a start and finish time to each order while taking into account the loading and sequencing policies employed.

Self-directed work teams Teams in which workers are empowered to take many of the decisions concerning their work.

Sell-side e-Commerce E-commerce transactions between a supplier organization and its customers.

 www.wileyopenpage.com

Separated services Do not require either the user or provider to physically come together to enable the service to take place.

Sequencing Sequencing is the sequential assignment of tasks or jobs to individual processes.

Service blueprint A charting device for processes, which documents the interaction between the customer and the service provider.

Service concept The overall set of expected benefits provided by the service design that the customer is buying.

Service package The combination of goods and services with information that comprise a service.

Service shop processes Operate with a medium amount of variety and volume. There will be therefore a mix of staff and equipment used to deliver the service, supplying the service in relation to customers.

Servitization Involves companies moving from being manufacturers with 'add-on' services to service companies whose output includes manufactured products.

SERVQUAL A survey research instrument that is based on the premise that customers can measure a firm's service quality by comparing their perception of its service with their own expectations.

Setup reduction The reduction of setup time (the time taken to adjust a machine to work on a different component).

Simultaneity Simultaneity relates to the characteristic that services are produced and consumed at the same time.

Simultaneous development When contributors to the stages of the design effort provide their expertise together throughout the design process as a team.

Six Sigma A company-wide initiative to reduce costs through process efficiency and increase revenues through process effectiveness.

Sociotechnical systems A job design approach that suggests that the social and technical subsystems within the organization should be designed in parallel to achieve an overall optimum system.

Speed Speed is the time delay between a customer request for a product or service and then receiving that product or service.

Stakeholders Anyone with an interest in the activities of an organization, such as employees, customers and government.

Statistical process control This is a sampling technique that checks the quality of an item engaged in a process.

Strategic alliances or partnerships These involve long-term relationships in which organizations work together and share

information regarding aspects such as planning systems and development of products and processes.

Structural decisions These concern aspects of the organization's physical resources such as service delivery systems and capacity provision.

Subcontractor and supplier networks Long-term contractual arrangements made with suppliers to supply goods and services.

Suggestion schemes These offer the person closest to the work activity the opportunity to suggest improvements to the process.

Supplier relationship management (SRM) This is concerned with all activities involved with obtaining items from a supplier including procurement, transportation and warehousing.

Supply chain This consists of the series of activities that moves materials from suppliers, through operations to customers.

Supply chain management (SCM) This is concerned with the management of the flow of materials, information and customers through the supply chain.

Supply-side influences When the location decision is considered in terms of factors that vary in such a way as to influence cost as location varies.

Supported customer-technology interaction A type of interaction in which a human server acts as an intermediary between the customer and the technology.

T

Tangibility If goods are tangible, they are physical things that you can touch. A service is intangible and can be seen as a process that is activated on demand.

Target-oriented quality An approach that strives through the process of continuous improvement to keep as close as possible to the target specification.

Technical analysis This consists of determining whether the technical capability to manufacture the product or deliver the service exists.

The learning organization A learning organization is an organization that facilitates the learning of individuals within that organization.

The SCOR model A framework for measuring and evaluating the performance of supply chain processes.

The supply network The configuration of the organization's relationship with its suppliers and the choice about what activities the organization should undertake internally and what should be subcontracted to other agencies.

Time-constrained project If there is a need to complete a project in a specific time frame alternative resources may have to be utilized to ensure timely project completion.

Time study The use of statistical techniques to arrive at a standard time for performing one cycle of a repetitive job.

Total preventative maintenance This anticipates equipment failures through a programme of routine maintenance that will not only help to reduce breakdowns but also to reduce downtime and lengthen the life of the equipment.

Total quality control An approach that emphasizes a commitment of effort on the part of management and employees throughout an organization to improving quality.

Total quality management A philosophy and approach which aims to ensure that high quality, as defined by the customer, is a primary concern throughout the organization and all parts of the organization work towards this goal.

Trade-offs A trade-off relationship means that to excel in one objective means poor performance in one or more other objectives.

U

Upstream suppliers Suppliers that supply the organization with goods or services.

Utilization This is the proportion of time a process is in actual use compared with its design capacity.

V

Value chain The value chain is the set of processes used to create value for a customer.

Value engineering This aims to eliminate unnecessary features and functions that do not contribute to the value or performance of the product.

Value Stream Mapping (VSM) Value stream mapping (VSM) is a flowcharting technique that is used to improve process flows by visually identifying and mapping each step in the process in order to identify non-value added or wasteful activities.

Vendor Managed Inventory (VMI) A system in which a supplier maintains an inventory level required by the customer facilitated by access to the customer's inventory data.

Vertical integration The amount of ownership of the supply chain by an organization.

Virtual organization An organization in which e-Business is used to outsource more and more supply chain activities to third parties so that the boundaries between and within organizations become blurred.

Visual control This is about maintaining an orderly workplace in which tools are easily available and unusual occurrences are easily noticeable.

W

Warehousing The use of locations to hold a stock of incoming raw materials used in production or hold finished goods ready for distribution to customers. Warehousing is also used to store work-in-progress items or spares for equipment.

Web-integrated ERP systems ERP systems which use the web to provide a platform for ERP application development and provide a standardized architecture for communication of ERP-based information across organizations.

Weighted scoring The procedure consists of determining a list of factors that are relevant to the location decision. Each factor is then given a weighting that indicates its relative importance compared to the other factors. Each location is then scored on each factor and this score is multiplied by the factor value. The alternative with the highest score is then chosen.

Work-in-progress inventory Inventory at some point within the operations process.

Work measurement This determines the length of time it will take to undertake a particular task.

Work sampling A method for determining the proportion of time a worker or machine spends on various activities and as such can be very useful in job redesign and estimating levels of worker output.

Work study Measures the performance of jobs and consists of two elements, method study and work measurement.

Workforce schedule The workforce schedule determines the daily workload for each member of staff.

Y

Yield management This is the use of demand management strategies aimed at maximizing customer revenue in service organizations. It is particularly appropriate when the organization is operating with relatively fixed capacity and it is possible to segment the market into different types of customers.

Note: Page numbers in *italics* denote illustrations

www.wileyopenpage.com